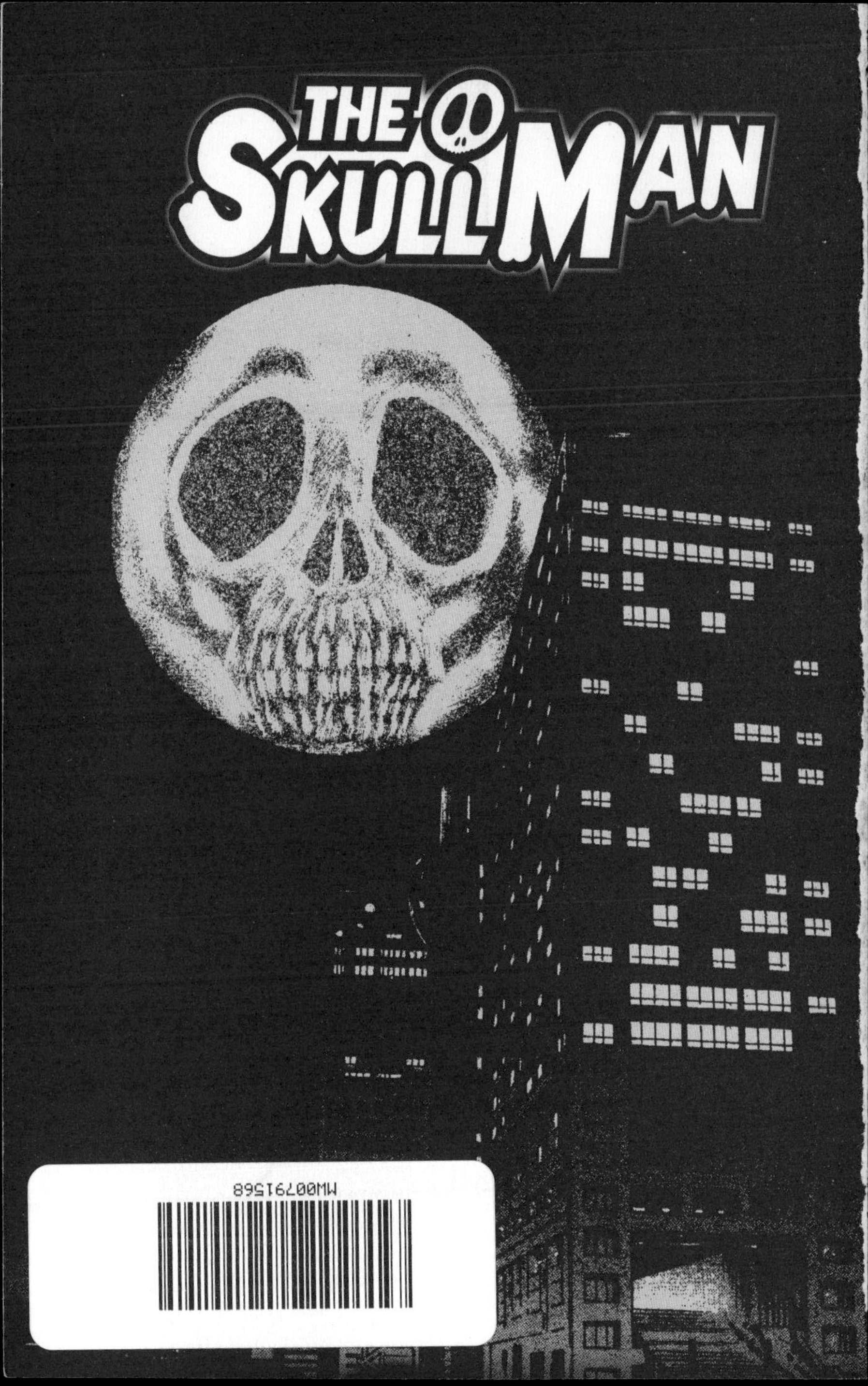
THE SKULL MAN

Other 100% Authentic Manga Available from TOKYOPOP®:

COWBOY BEBOP 1 (of 3)
All-new adventures of interstellar bounty hunting, based on the hit anime seen on Cartoon Network.

MARMALADE BOY 1 (of 8)
A tangled teen romance for the new millennium.

REAL BOUT HIGH SCHOOL 1 (of 4+)
At Daimon High, teachers don't break up fights...they grade them.

MARS 1 (of 15)
Biker Rei and artist Kira are as different as night and day, but fate binds them in this angst-filled romance.

GTO 1 (of 23+)
Biker gang member Onizuka is going back to school...as a teacher!

CHOBITS 1 (of 3+)
In the future, boys will be boys and girls will be...robots? The newest hit series from CLAMP!

DRAGON KNIGHTS 1 (of 17)
Part dragon, part knight, ALL glam. The most inept knights on the block are out to kick some demon butt.

PLANET LADDER 1 (of 4+)
Kaguya knew she was different, but she never imagined she was an orphaned princess from another planet.

Coming soon from TOKYOPOP®:

INITIAL D 1 (of 23+)
Delivery boy Takumi has a gift for driving, but can he compete in the high-stakes world of street racing?

SHAOLIN SISTERS 1 (of 5)
The epic martial-arts/fantasy sequel to Juline, by the creator of Vampire Princess Miyu.

PARADISE KISS 1 (of 3+)
High fashion and deep passion collide in this hot new shojo series!

KARE KANO: He Says, She Says 1 (of 12+)
What happens, when the smartest girl in school gets competition from the cutest guy?

KODOCHA: Sana's Stage 1 (of 10)
There's a rumble in the jungle gym when child star Sana Kurata and bully Akito Hayama collide.

ANGELIC LAYER 1(of 5)
In the future, the most popular game is Angelic Layer, where hand-raised robots battle for supremacy.

LOVE HINA 1 (of 14)
Can Keitaro handle living in a dorm with five cute girls...and still make it through school?

Vol.2

Written and Illustrated by
Kazuhiko Shimamoto

Created by
Shotaro Ishinomori

Los Angeles - Tokyo

English Adaptation – Fred Patten
Translator – Ray Yoshimoto
Retouch Artists – Ryan Caraan and Roselyn Santos
Production Specialist – Santiago Hernandez, Jr.
Graphic Designer – Akemi Imafuku
Editor – Robert Coyner
Associate Editors – Paul Morrissey and Trisha Kunimoto

Senior Editor – Jake Forbes
Production Manager – Fred Lui
Art Director – Matt Alford
VP of Production – Ron Klamert
Publisher – Stuart Levy

Email: editor@TOKYOPOP.com
Come visit us at www.TOKYOPOP.com

A  book

The Skull Man Vol. 2 by Kazuhiko Shimamoto & Shotaro Ishinomori
TOKYOPOP® is a registered trademark
of Mixx Entertainment, Inc.

ISBN: 1-931514-66-6
First TOKYOPOP® Printing: June 2002

10 9 8 7 6 5 4 3 2 1

Manufactured in Canada

The Skull Man
Vol.2

After a quarter-century of dormancy, Shotaro Ishinomori's archetypal anti-hero has been resurrected, so to speak, in the imagination of mangaka Kazuhiko Shimamoto (who collaborated with Ishinomori shortly before the manga legend's death in 1998 to develop this series of The Skull Man). The Spider Man and Maria have tracked The Skull Man back to his ossuarious lair in the ruins of an abandoned church, where the eponymous crime-fighter and his trusted companion Garo lie in wait. And in a climactic battle, The Skull Man unleashes powers beyond his imagination, causing the church to erupt in a violent conflagration. In the aftermath, the police arrive to investigate, as does an alacritous field journalist who is passionately driven to get to the bottom of the mysterious and elusive Skull Man.

THE SKULL MAN

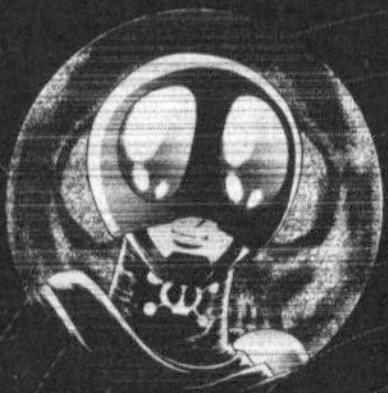

TATSUO

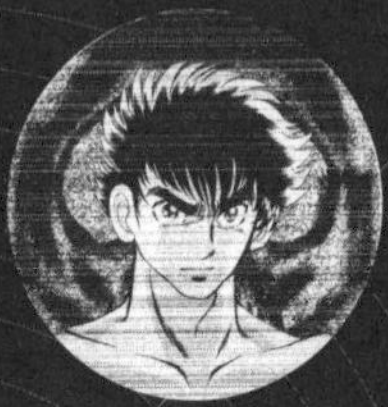

A DARK ANTI-HERO WHOSE QUEST FOR ANSWERS TO HIS PAST CONSUMES HIS PRESENT.

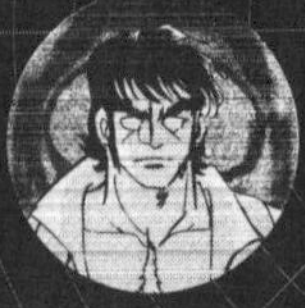

GARO

HE SKULL MAN'S FRIEND AND CONFIDANT. TOGETHER THEY SEARCH FOR THE ORIGINS OF THEIR MUTANT POWERS.

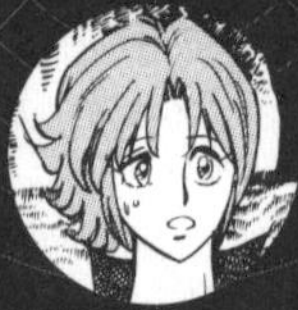

SATSUKI KATSURUGAWA

A REPORTER THAT LABORS TO UNCOVER THE SKULL MAN MYSTERY, BUT SHOULD SHE JOIN FORCES WITH THE POLICE?

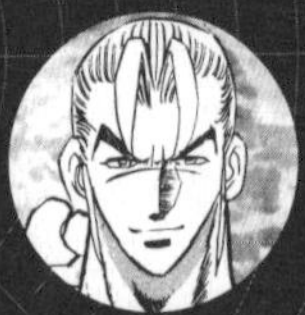

GORO AYASE

TATSUO'S HIGH SCHOOL COMPANION WHOSE AFFILIATIONS WITH A FACELESS ORGANIZATION BRING HIM IN OPPOSITION TO HIS OLD FRIEND.

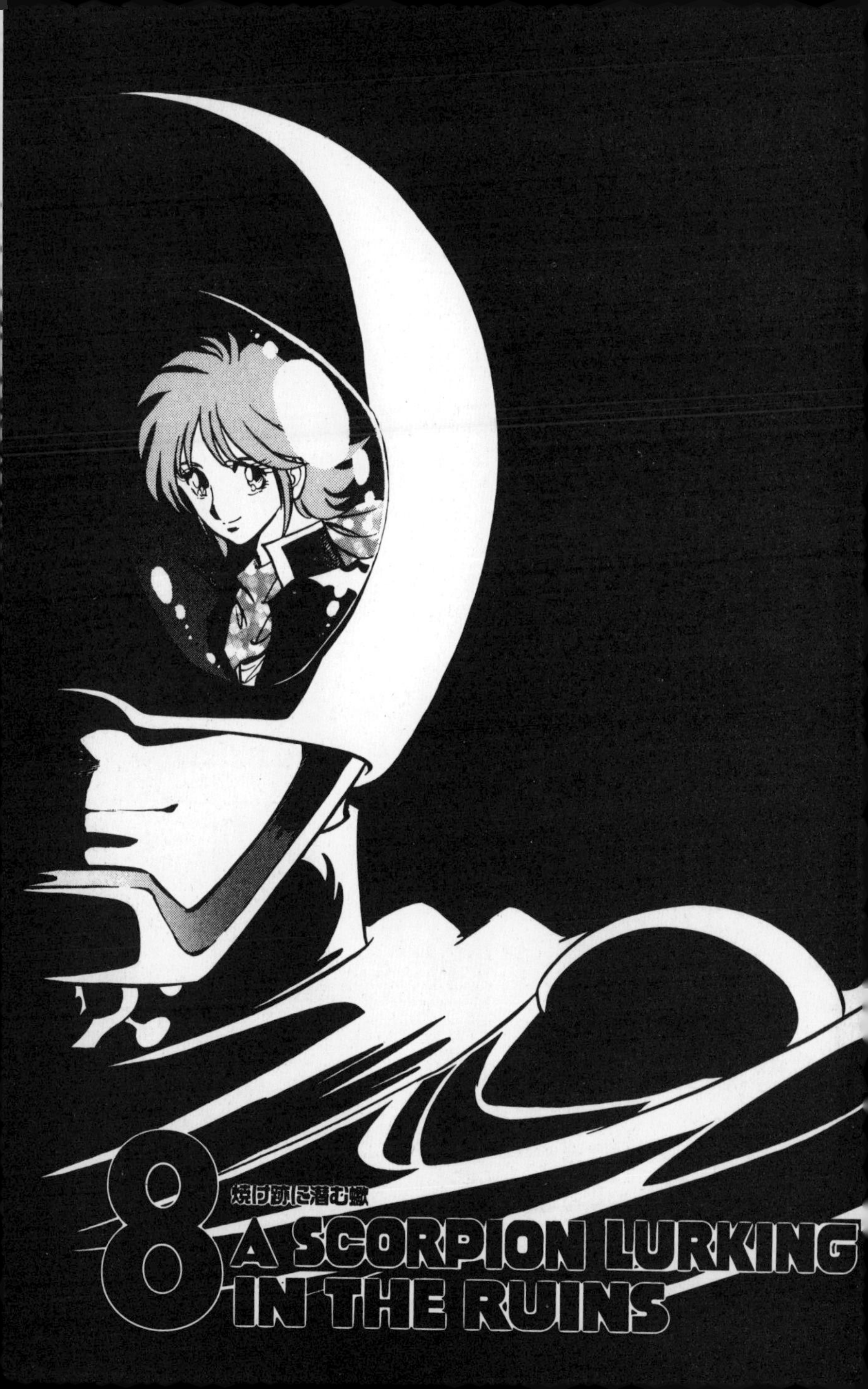

8 焼け跡に潜む蠍
A SCORPION LURKING IN THE RUINS

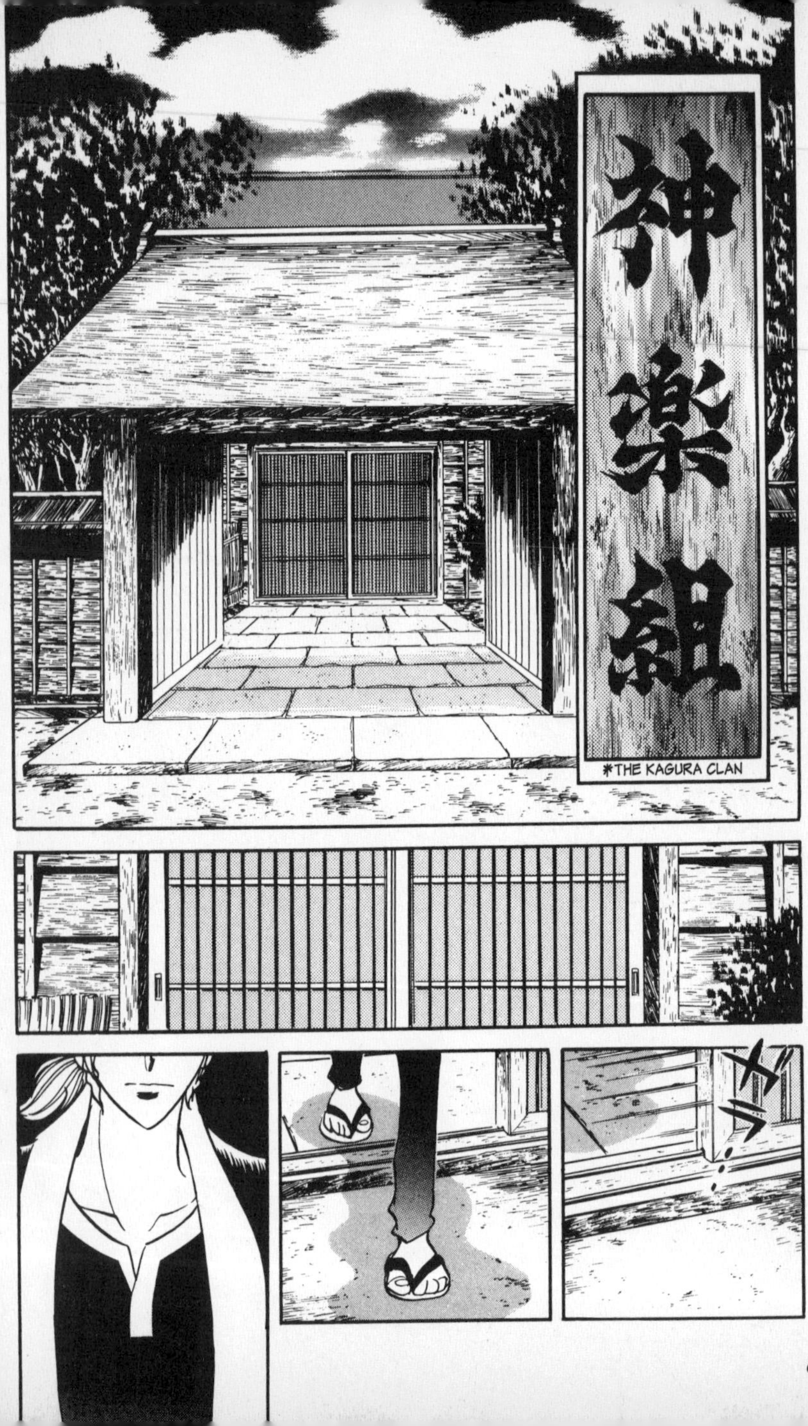
神楽組
*THE KAGURA CLAN

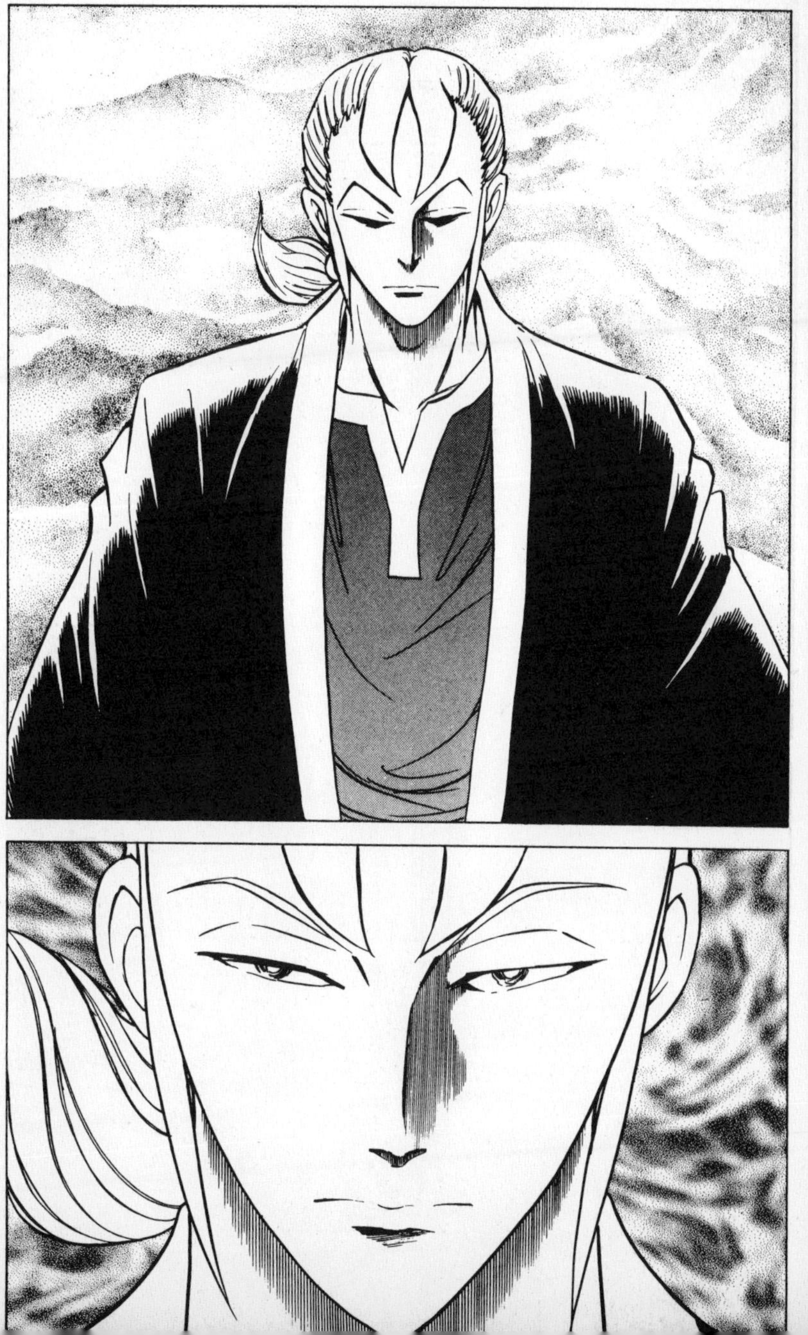

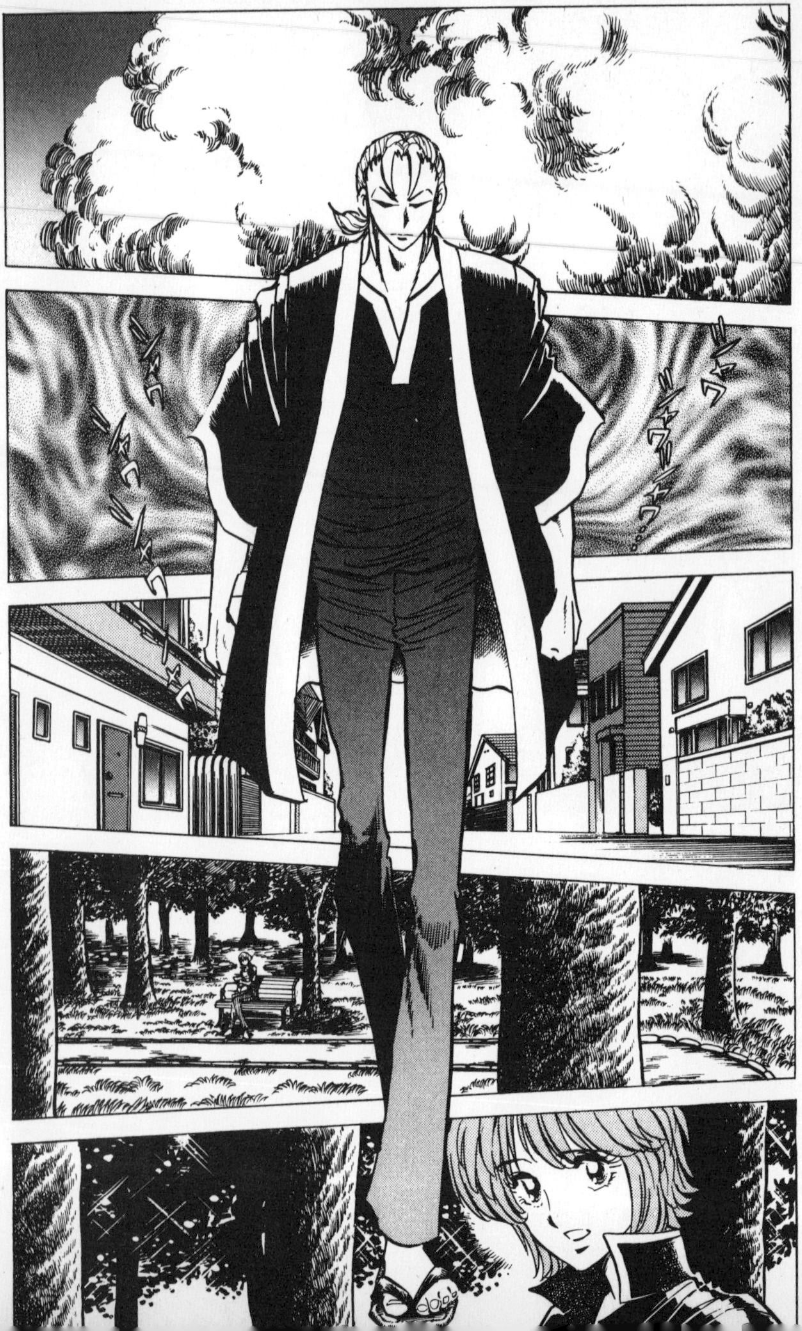

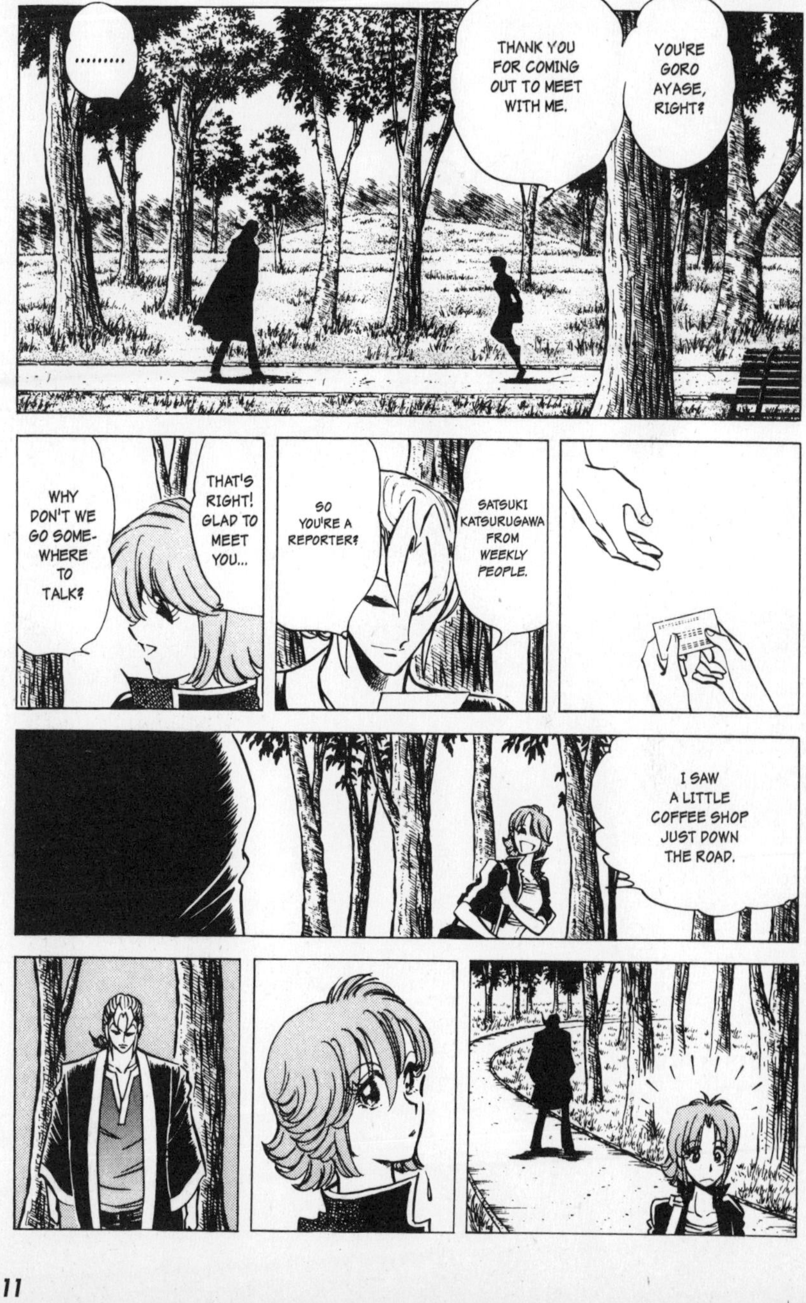
YOU'RE GORO AYASE, RIGHT?
THANK YOU FOR COMING OUT TO MEET WITH ME.
....
SATSUKI KATSURUGAWA FROM WEEKLY PEOPLE.
SO YOU'RE A REPORTER?
THAT'S RIGHT! GLAD TO MEET YOU...
WHY DON'T WE GO SOME-WHERE TO TALK?
I SAW A LITTLE COFFEE SHOP JUST DOWN THE ROAD.

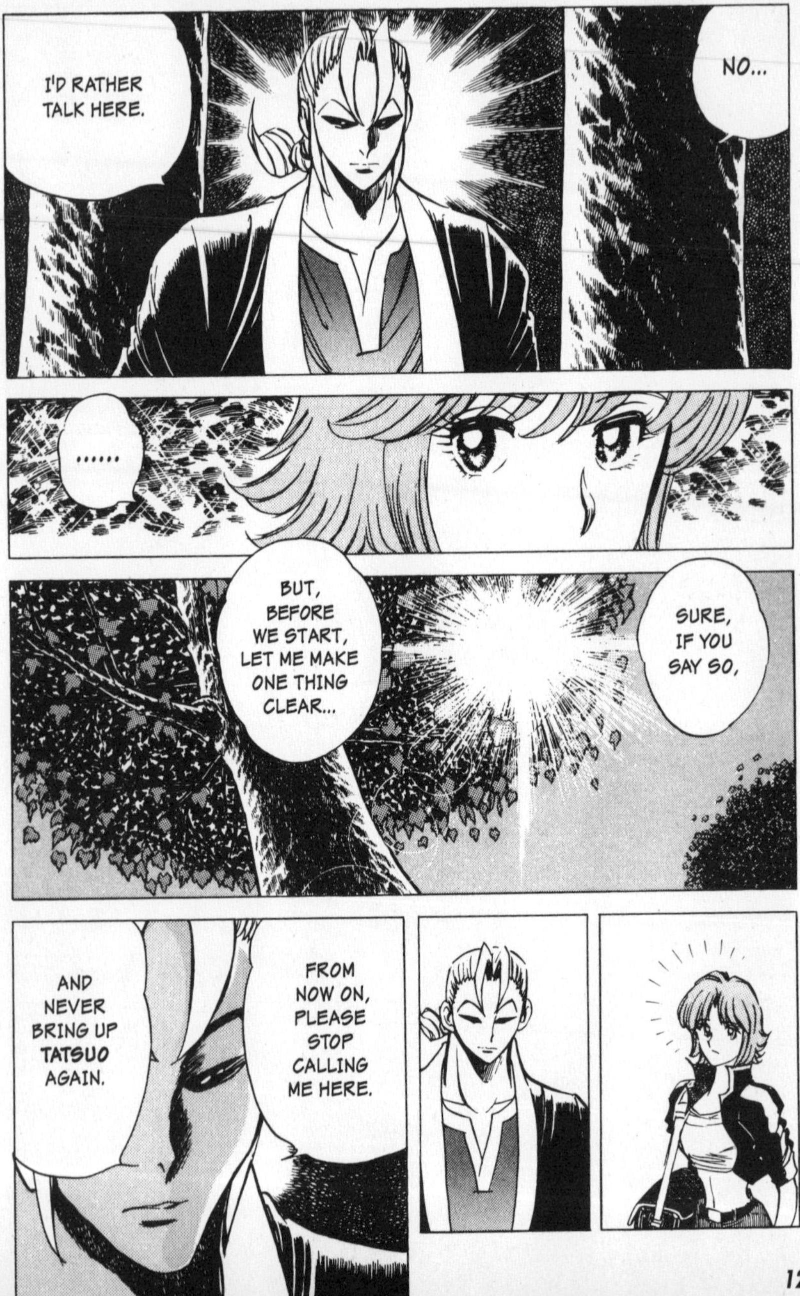
NO...
I'D RATHER TALK HERE.
......
SURE, IF YOU SAY SO,
BUT, BEFORE WE START, LET ME MAKE ONE THING CLEAR...
FROM NOW ON, PLEASE STOP CALLING ME HERE.
AND NEVER BRING UP TATSUO AGAIN.

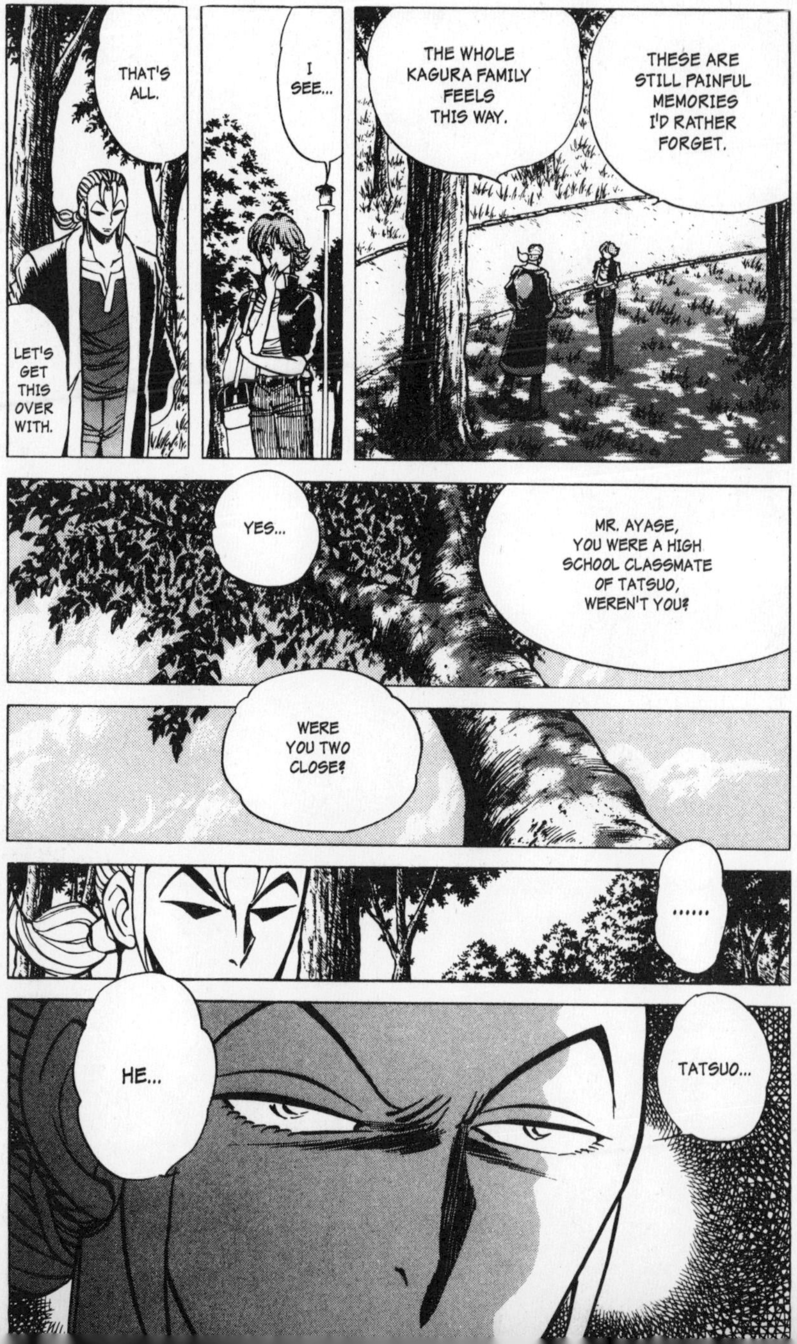
THESE ARE STILL PAINFUL MEMORIES I'D RATHER FORGET.
THE WHOLE KAGURA FAMILY FEELS THIS WAY.
I SEE...
THAT'S ALL.
LET'S GET THIS OVER WITH.
MR. AYASE, YOU WERE A HIGH SCHOOL CLASSMATE OF TATSUO, WEREN'T YOU?
YES...
WERE YOU TWO CLOSE?
......
TATSUO...
HE...

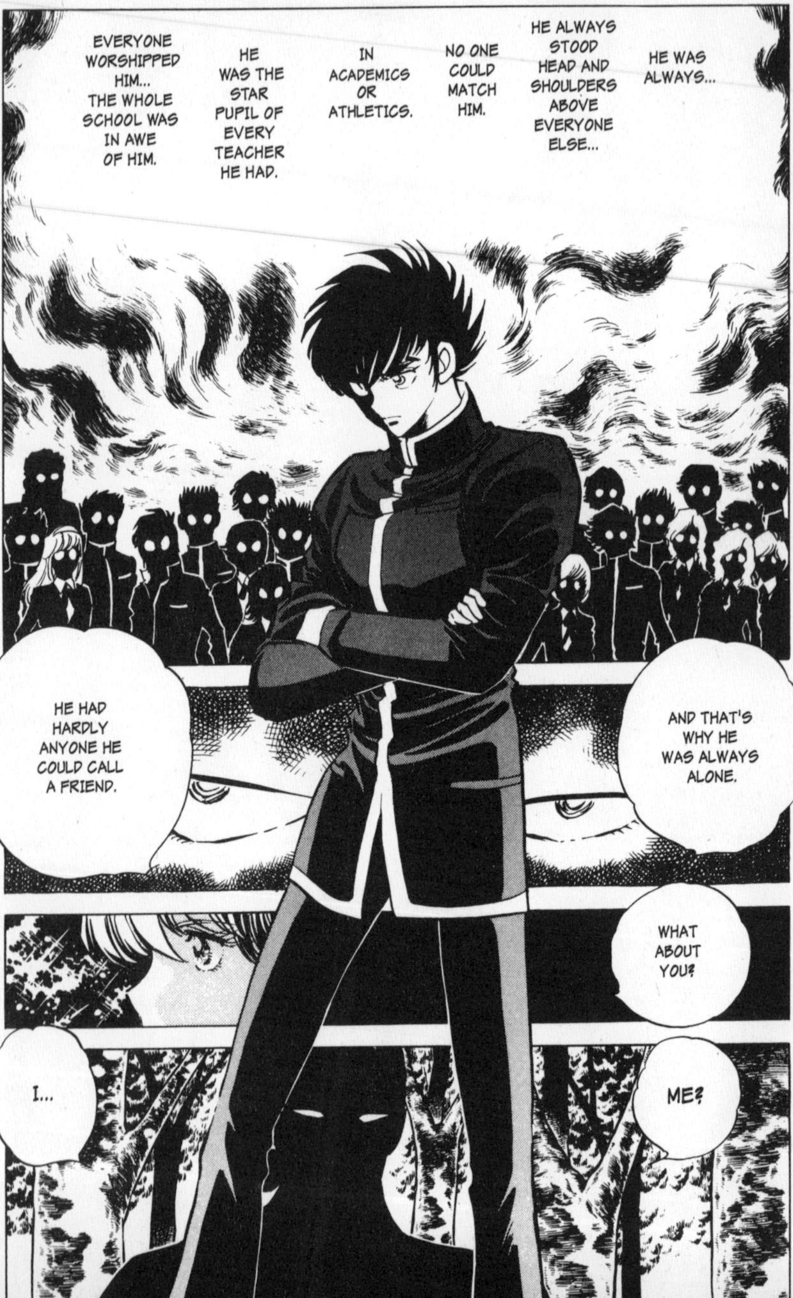
HE WAS ALWAYS...
HE ALWAYS STOOD HEAD AND SHOULDERS ABOVE EVERYONE ELSE...
NO ONE COULD MATCH HIM.
IN ACADEMICS OR ATHLETICS.
HE WAS THE STAR PUPIL OF EVERY TEACHER HE HAD.
EVERYONE WORSHIPPED HIM... THE WHOLE SCHOOL WAS IN AWE OF HIM.
AND THAT'S WHY HE WAS ALWAYS ALONE.
HE HAD HARDLY ANYONE HE COULD CALL A FRIEND.
WHAT ABOUT YOU?
ME?
I...

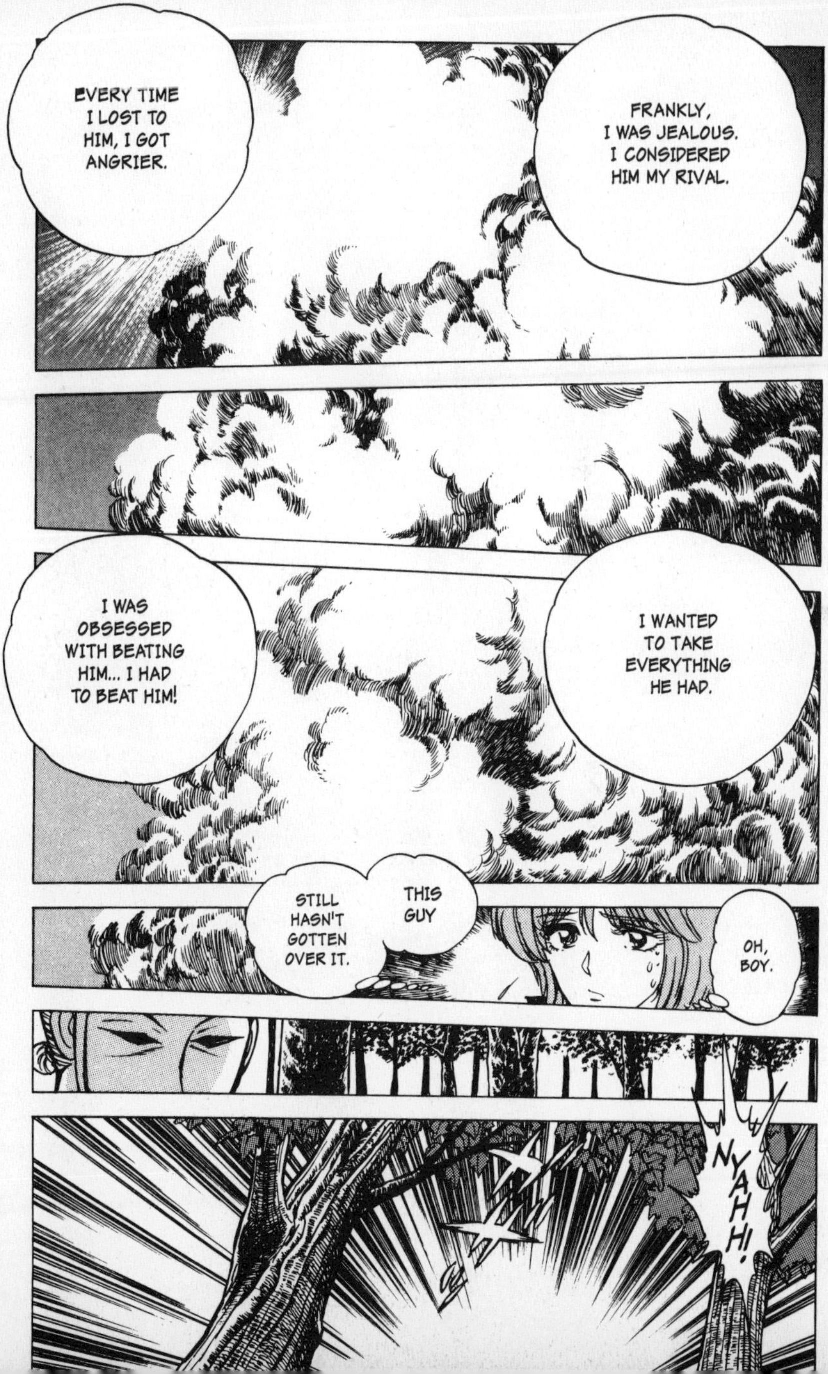
FRANKLY, I WAS JEALOUS. I CONSIDERED HIM MY RIVAL.
EVERY TIME I LOST TO HIM, I GOT ANGRIER.
I WANTED TO TAKE EVERYTHING HE HAD.
I WAS OBSESSED WITH BEATING HIM... I HAD TO BEAT HIM!
OH, BOY.
THIS GUY STILL HASN'T GOTTEN OVER IT.
NYAHH!

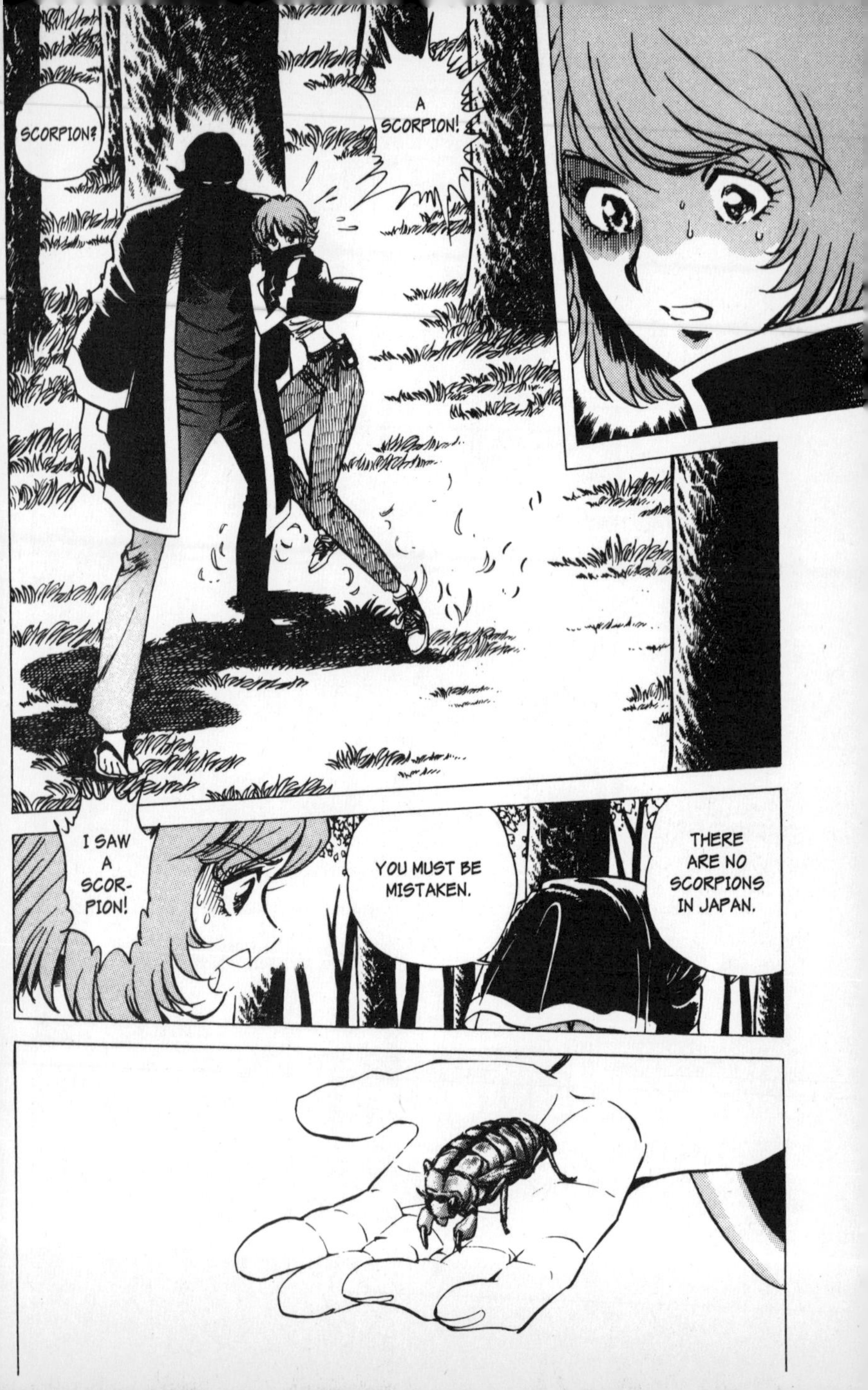
A SCORPION!
SCORPION?
THERE ARE NO SCORPIONS IN JAPAN.
YOU MUST BE MISTAKEN.
I SAW A SCOR-PION!

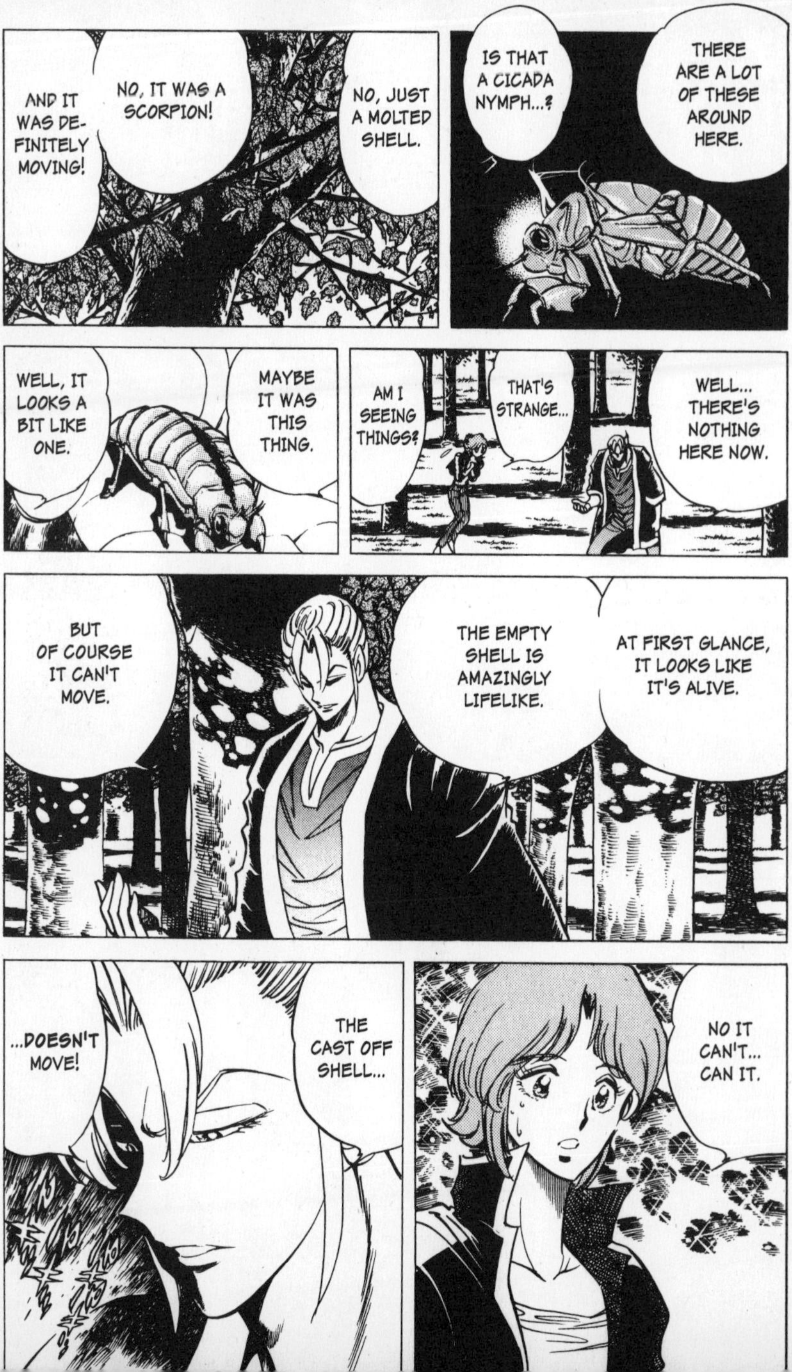
THERE ARE A LOT OF THESE AROUND HERE.
IS THAT A CICADA NYMPH...?
NO, JUST A MOLTED SHELL.
NO, IT WAS A SCORPION!
AND IT WAS DE-FINITELY MOVING!
WELL... THERE'S NOTHING HERE NOW.
THAT'S STRANGE...
AM I SEEING THINGS?
MAYBE IT WAS THIS THING.
WELL, IT LOOKS A BIT LIKE ONE.
AT FIRST GLANCE, IT LOOKS LIKE IT'S ALIVE.
THE EMPTY SHELL IS AMAZINGLY LIFELIKE.
BUT OF COURSE IT CAN'T MOVE.
NO IT CAN'T... CAN IT.
THE CAST OFF SHELL...
...DOESN'T MOVE!

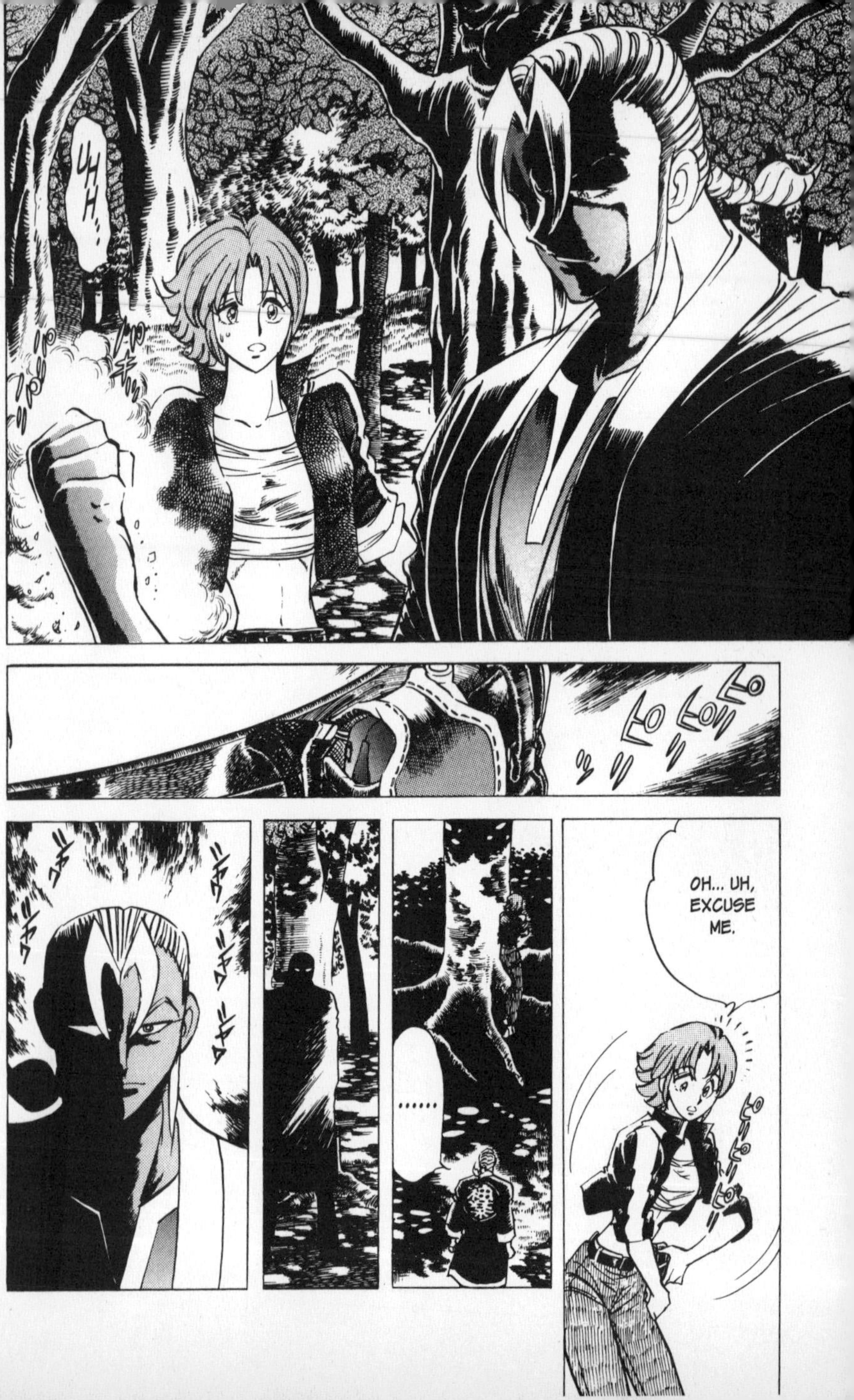
UHH...
OH... UH, EXCUSE ME.
......

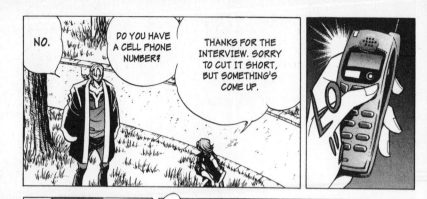

THANKS FOR THE INTERVIEW. SORRY TO CUT IT SHORT, BUT SOMETHING'S COME UP.
DO YOU HAVE A CELL PHONE NUMBER?
NO.
WHAT? HOW CAN YOU NOT HAVE ONE THESE DAYS? WELL...
THEN CAN YOU CALL ME?
Since you don't want me calling you.
......
YOU CAN CATCH ME TOMORROW AFTERNOON.
I'LL BE WAIT-ING...

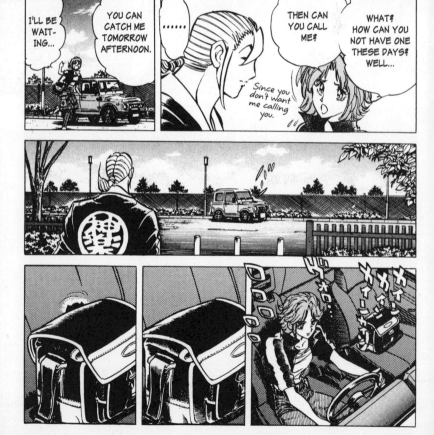

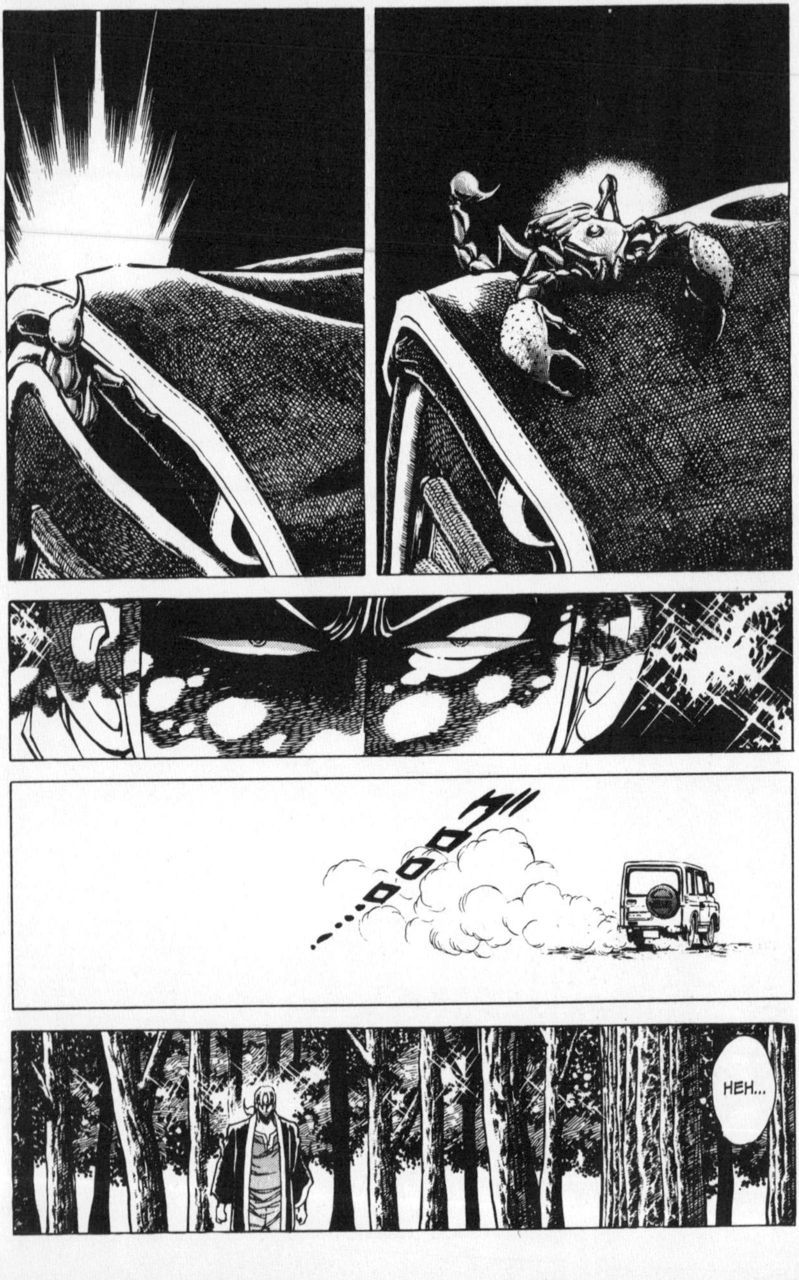
DDDD...
HEH...

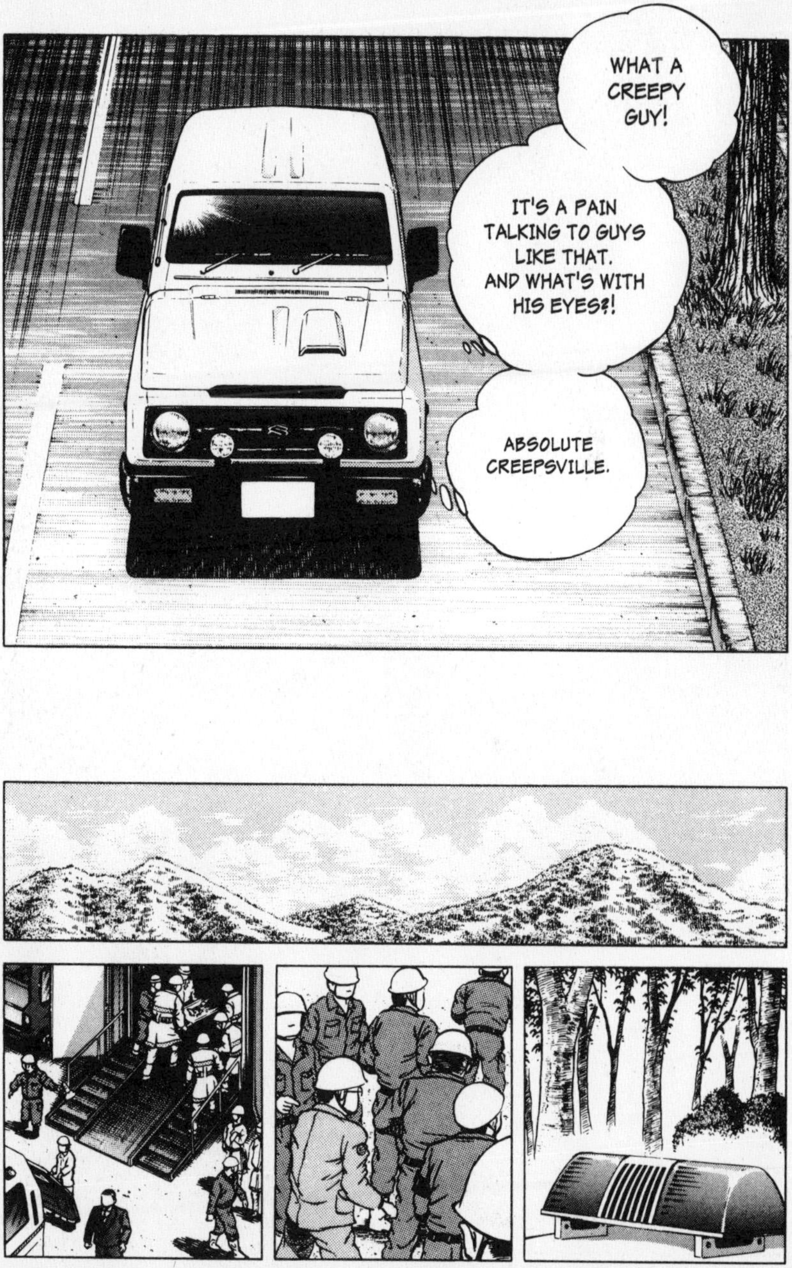
WHAT A CREEPY GUY!
IT'S A PAIN TALKING TO GUYS LIKE THAT. AND WHAT'S WITH HIS EYES?!
ABSOLUTE CREEPSVILLE.

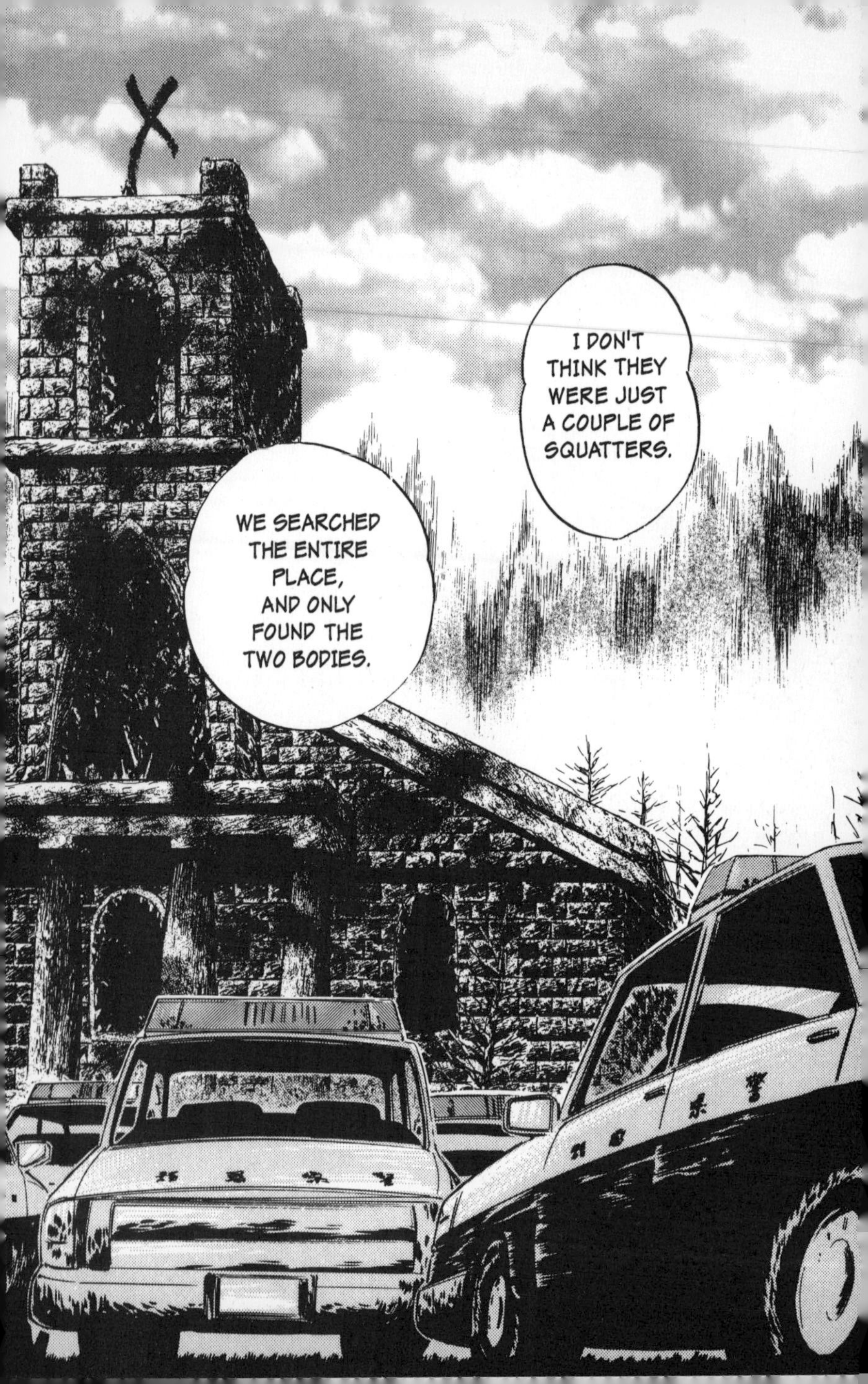
I DON'T THINK THEY WERE JUST A COUPLE OF SQUATTERS.
WE SEARCHED THE ENTIRE PLACE, AND ONLY FOUND THE TWO BODIES.

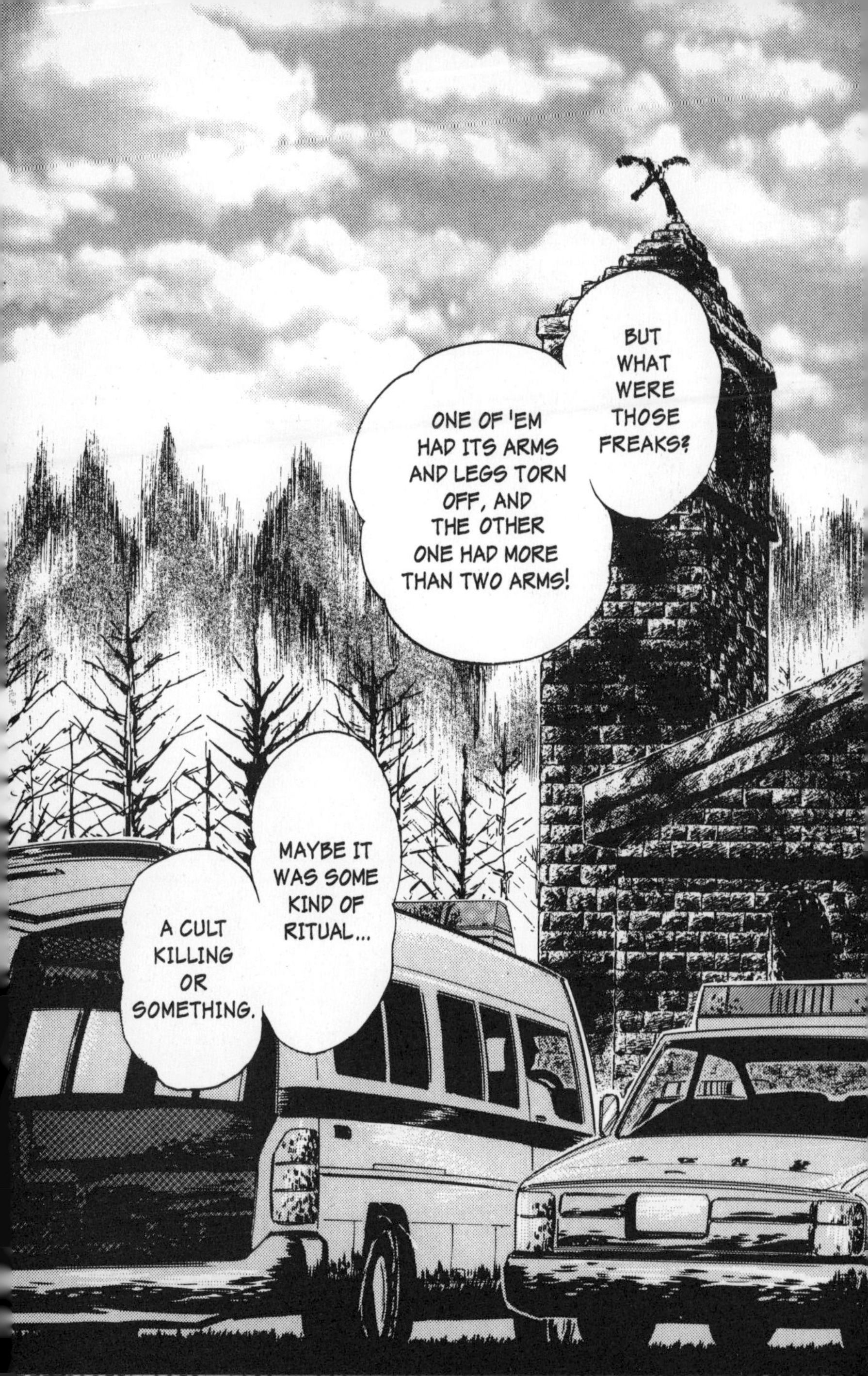
BUT WHAT WERE THOSE FREAKS?
ONE OF 'EM HAD ITS ARMS AND LEGS TORN OFF, AND THE OTHER ONE HAD MORE THAN TWO ARMS!
MAYBE IT WAS SOME KIND OF RITUAL...
A CULT KILLING OR SOMETHING.

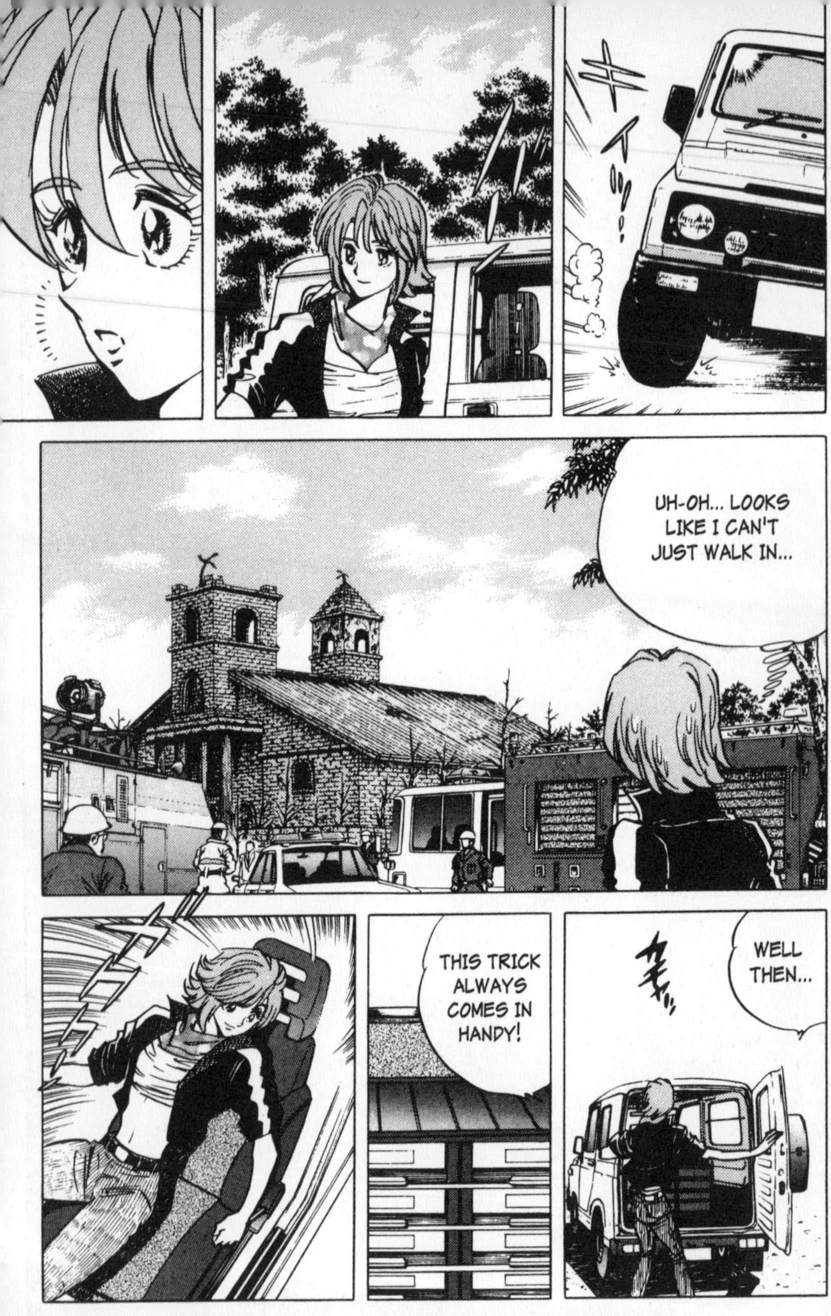
UH-OH... LOOKS LIKE I CAN'T JUST WALK IN...
WELL THEN...
THIS TRICK ALWAYS COMES IN HANDY!

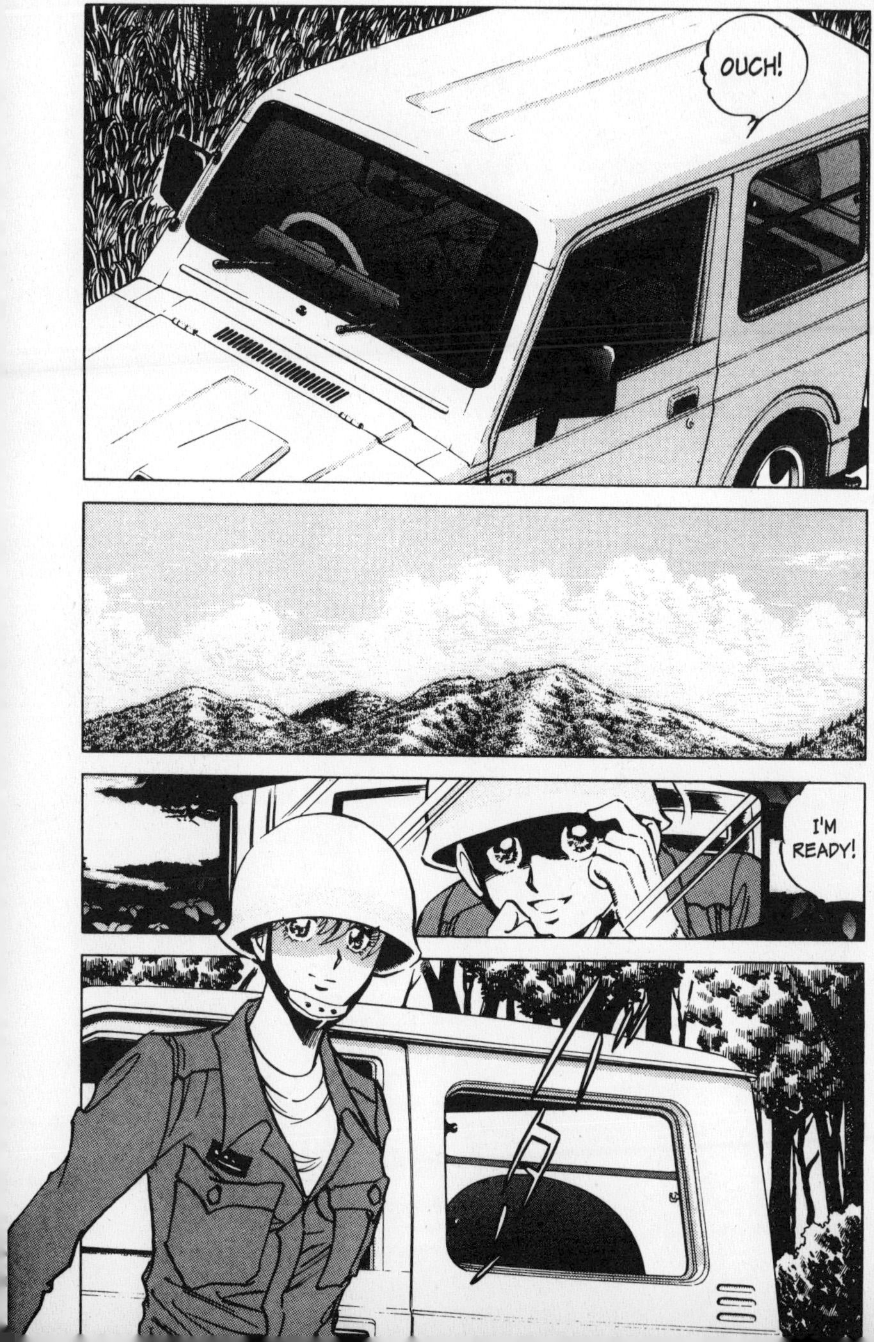
OUCH!
I'M READY!

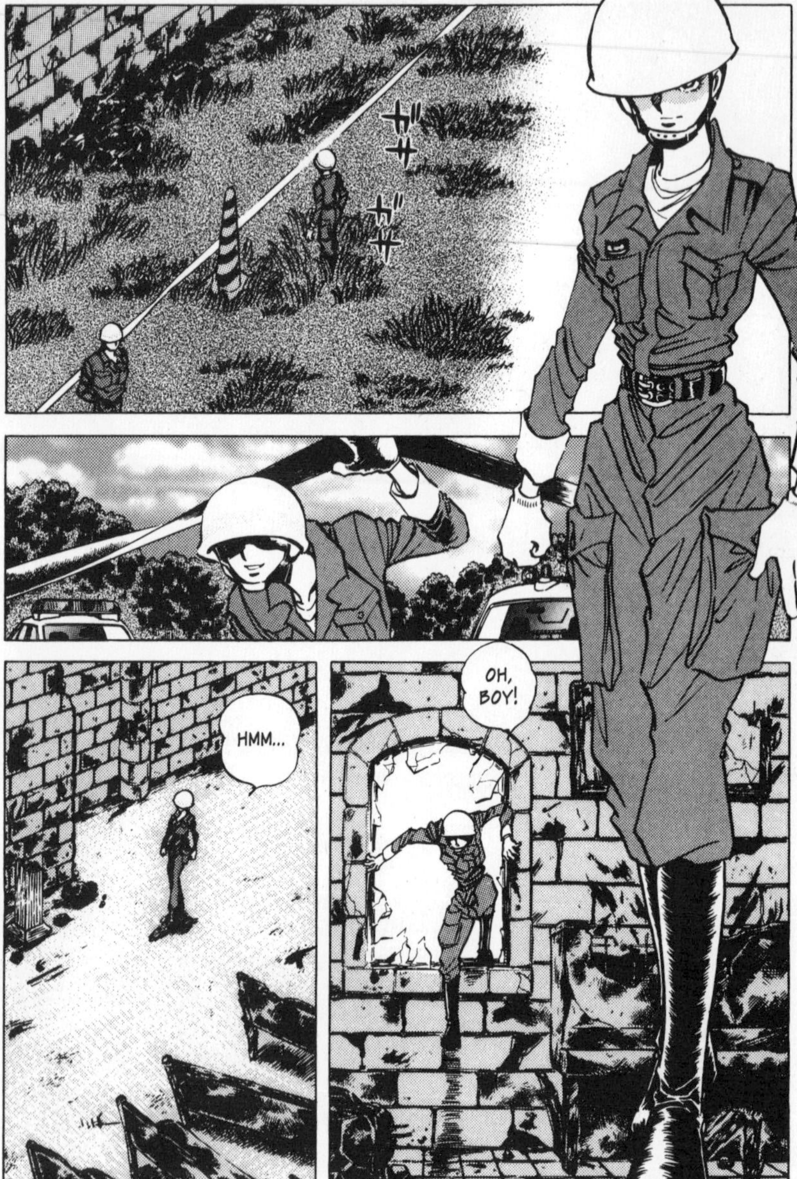
ザザ
ザザ
OH, BOY!
HMM...

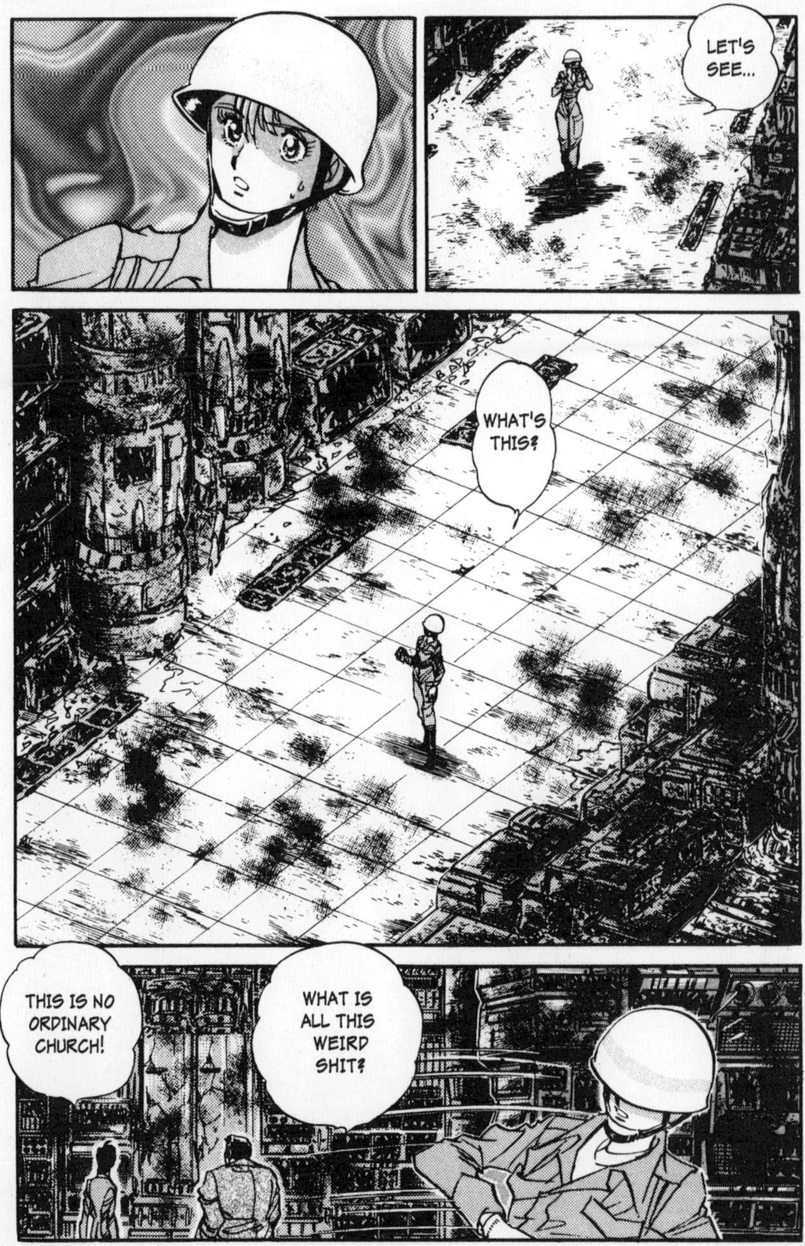
LET'S SEE...
WHAT'S THIS?
WHAT IS ALL THIS WEIRD SHIT?
THIS IS NO ORDINARY CHURCH!

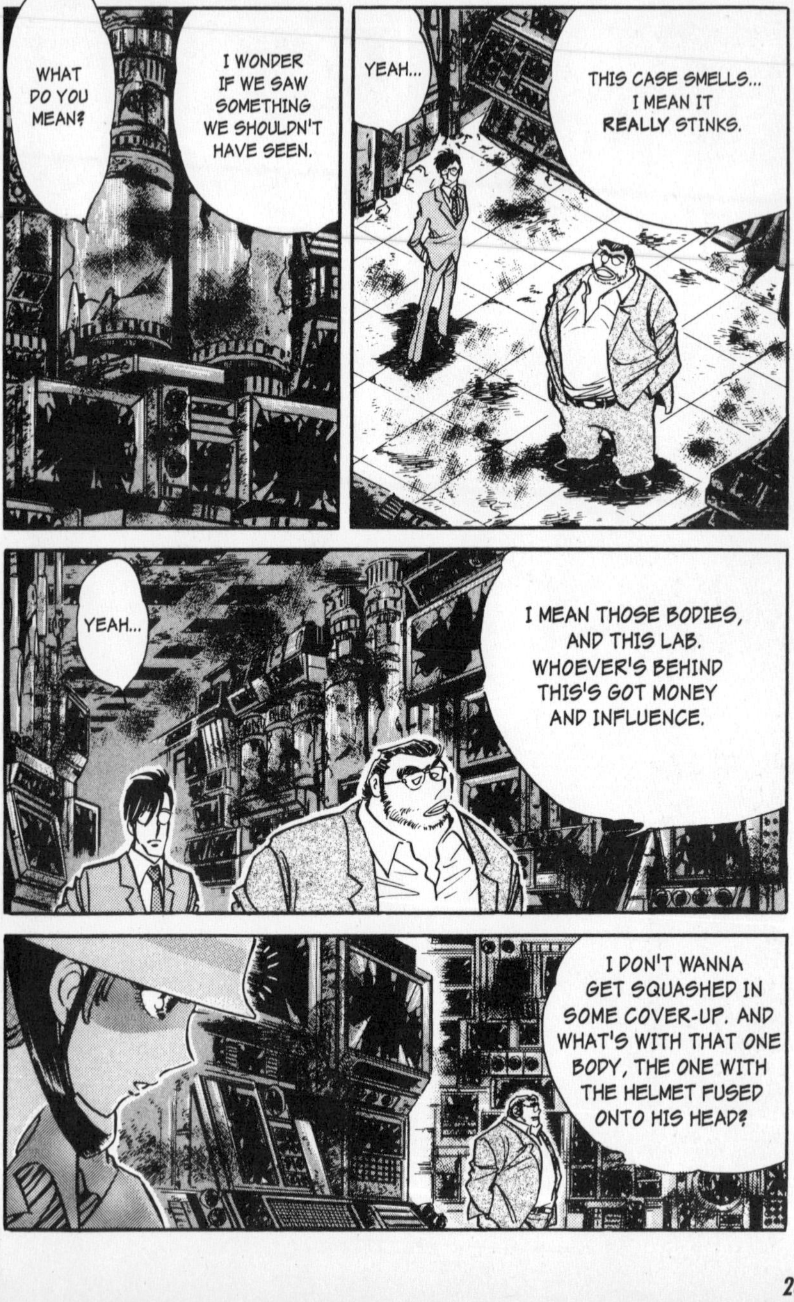
THIS CASE SMELLS... I MEAN IT REALLY STINKS.
YEAH...
I WONDER IF WE SAW SOMETHING WE SHOULDN'T HAVE SEEN.
WHAT DO YOU MEAN?
I MEAN THOSE BODIES, AND THIS LAB. WHOEVER'S BEHIND THIS'S GOT MONEY AND INFLUENCE.
YEAH...
I DON'T WANNA GET SQUASHED IN SOME COVER-UP. AND WHAT'S WITH THAT ONE BODY, THE ONE WITH THE HELMET FUSED ONTO HIS HEAD?

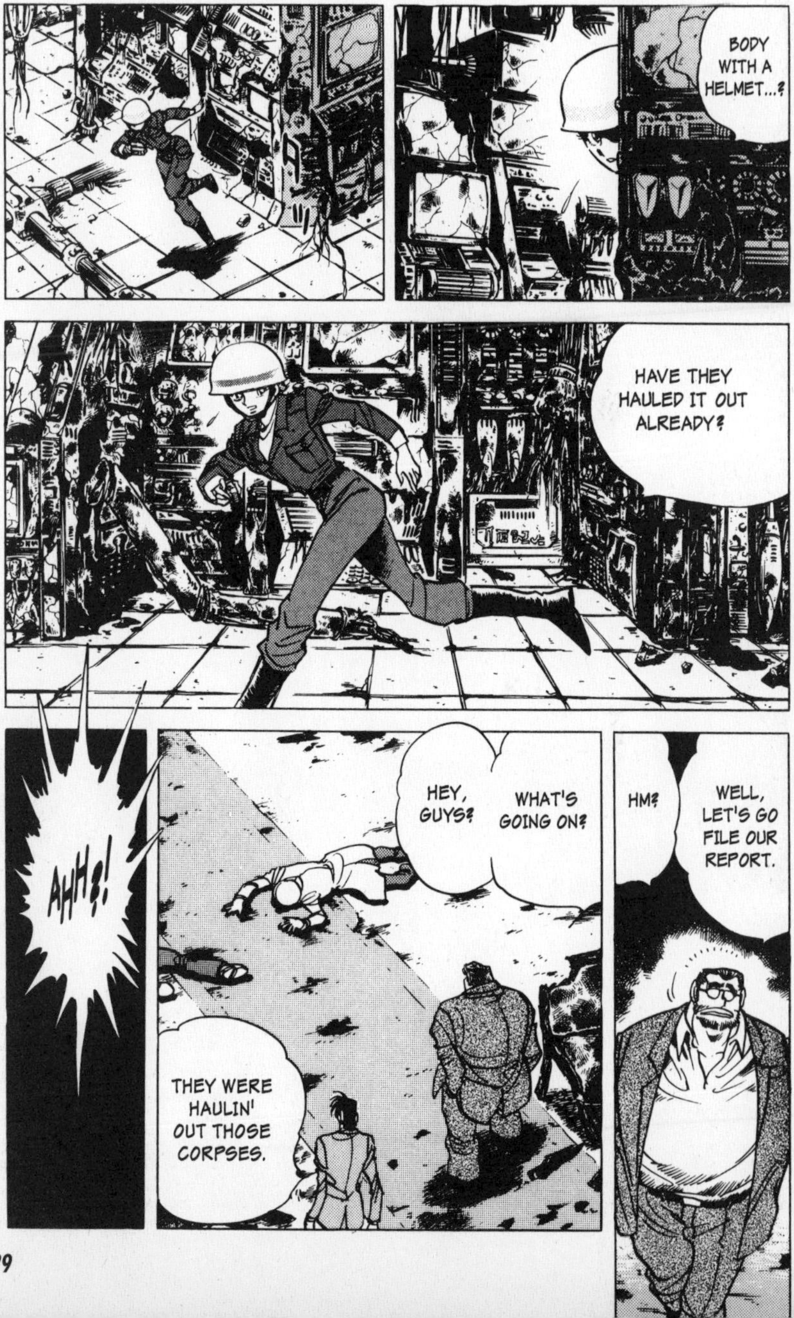
BODY WITH A HELMET...?
HAVE THEY HAULED IT OUT ALREADY?
WELL, LET'S GO FILE OUR REPORT.
HM?
WHAT'S GOING ON?
HEY, GUYS?
THEY WERE HAULIN' OUT THOSE CORPSES.
AHH?!

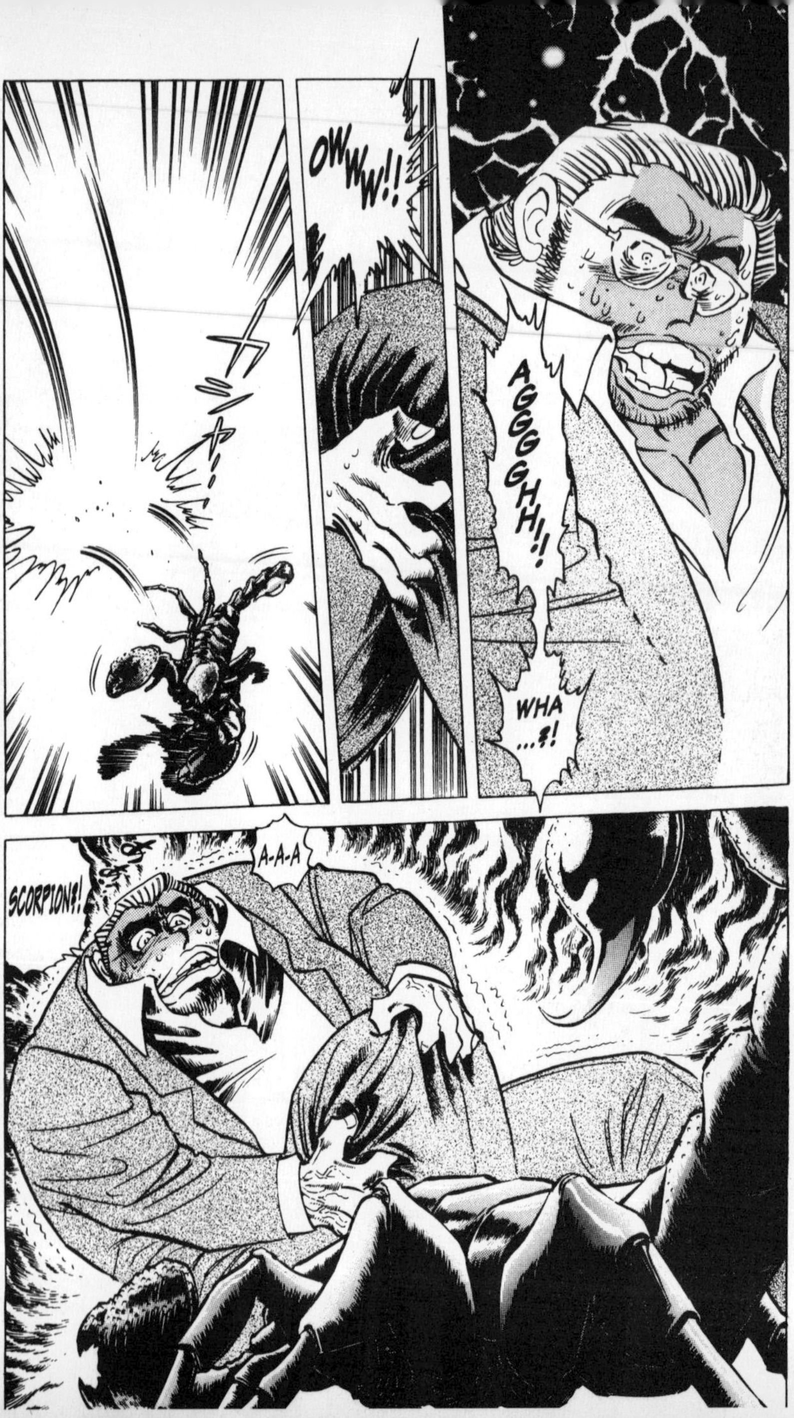
AGGGGHH!!
WHA ...?!
OWWW!!
A-A-A
SCORPION?!

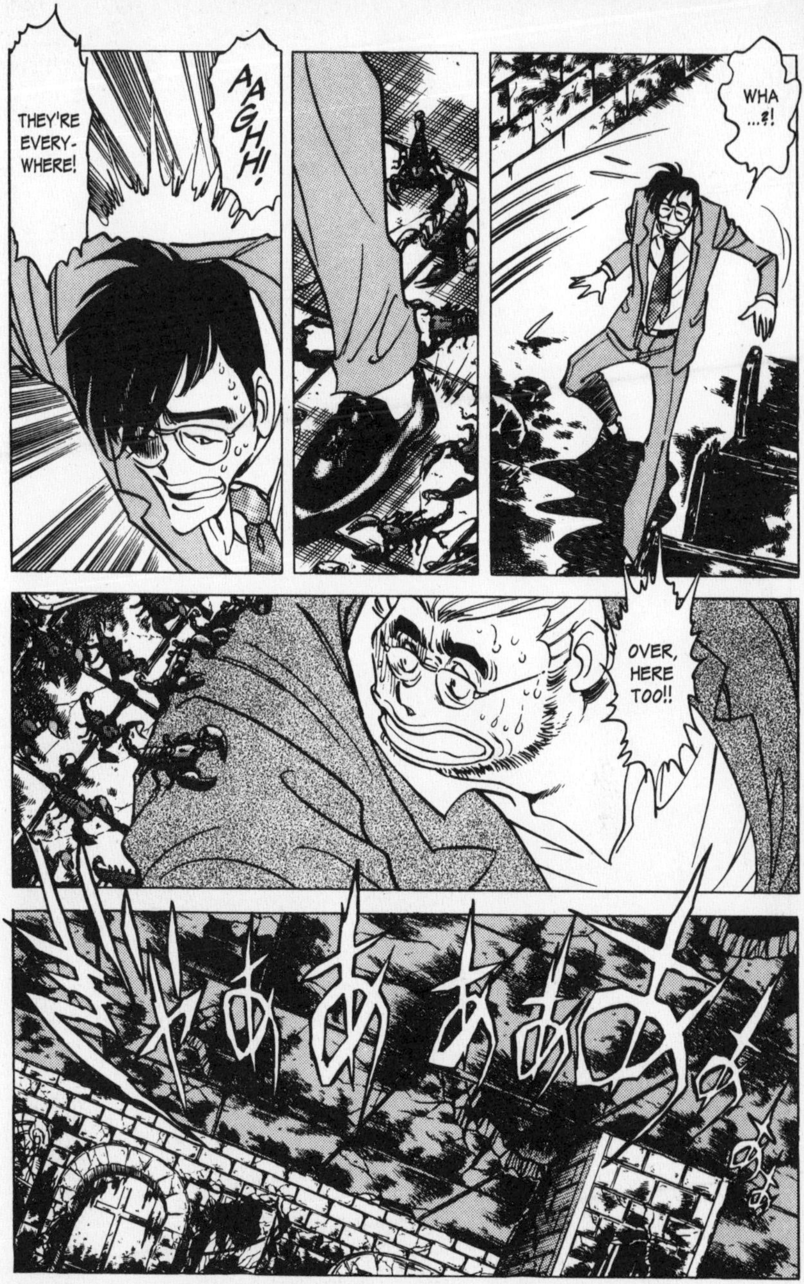
WHA ...?!
AAGHH!
THEY'RE EVERY-WHERE!
OVER, HERE TOO!!

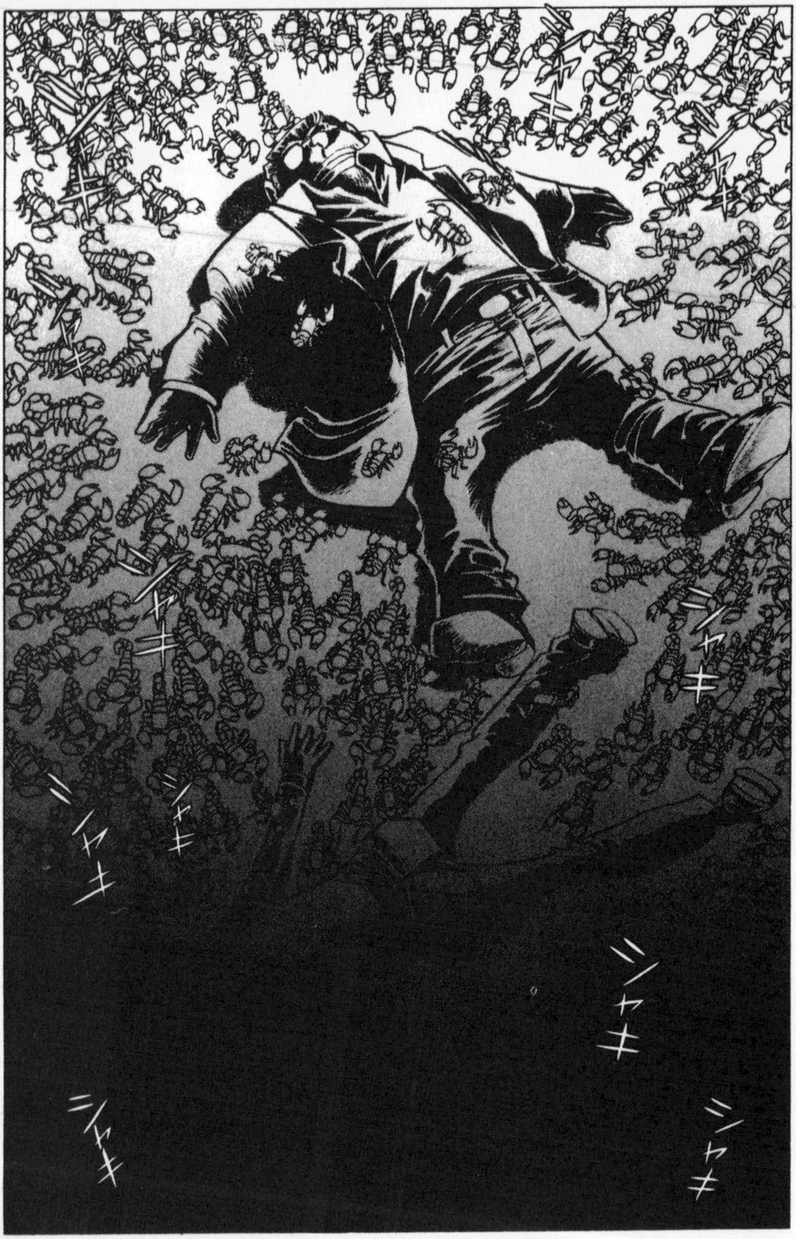
シャキ
シャキ
シャキ
シャキ
シャキ
シャキ
シャキ

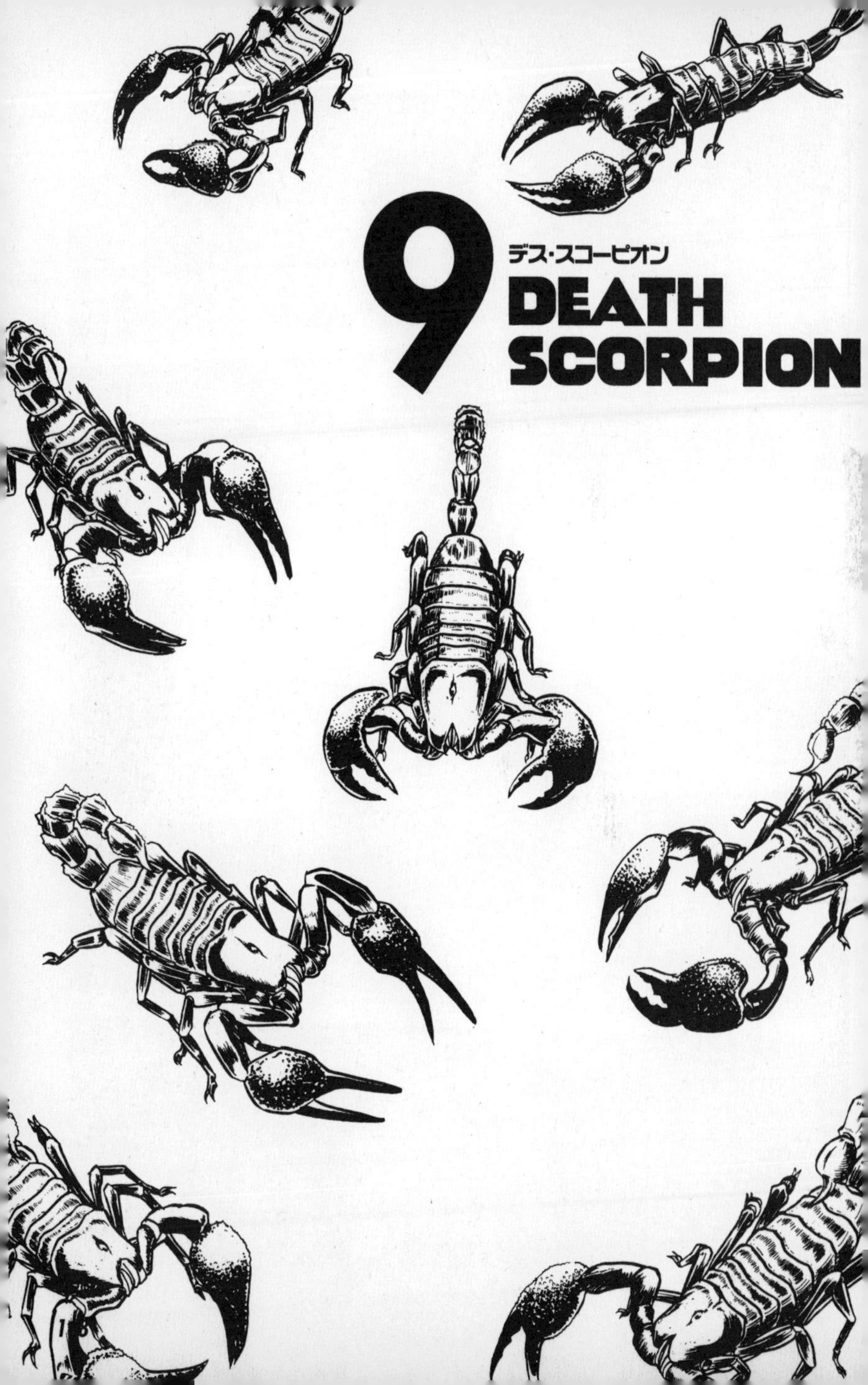

9 デス・スコーピオン DEATH SCORPION

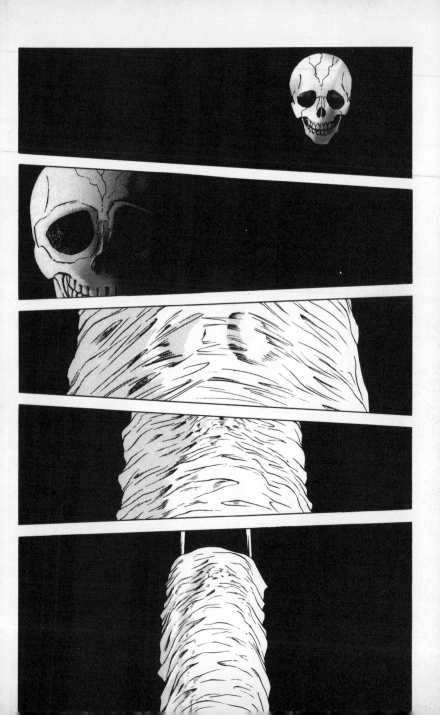

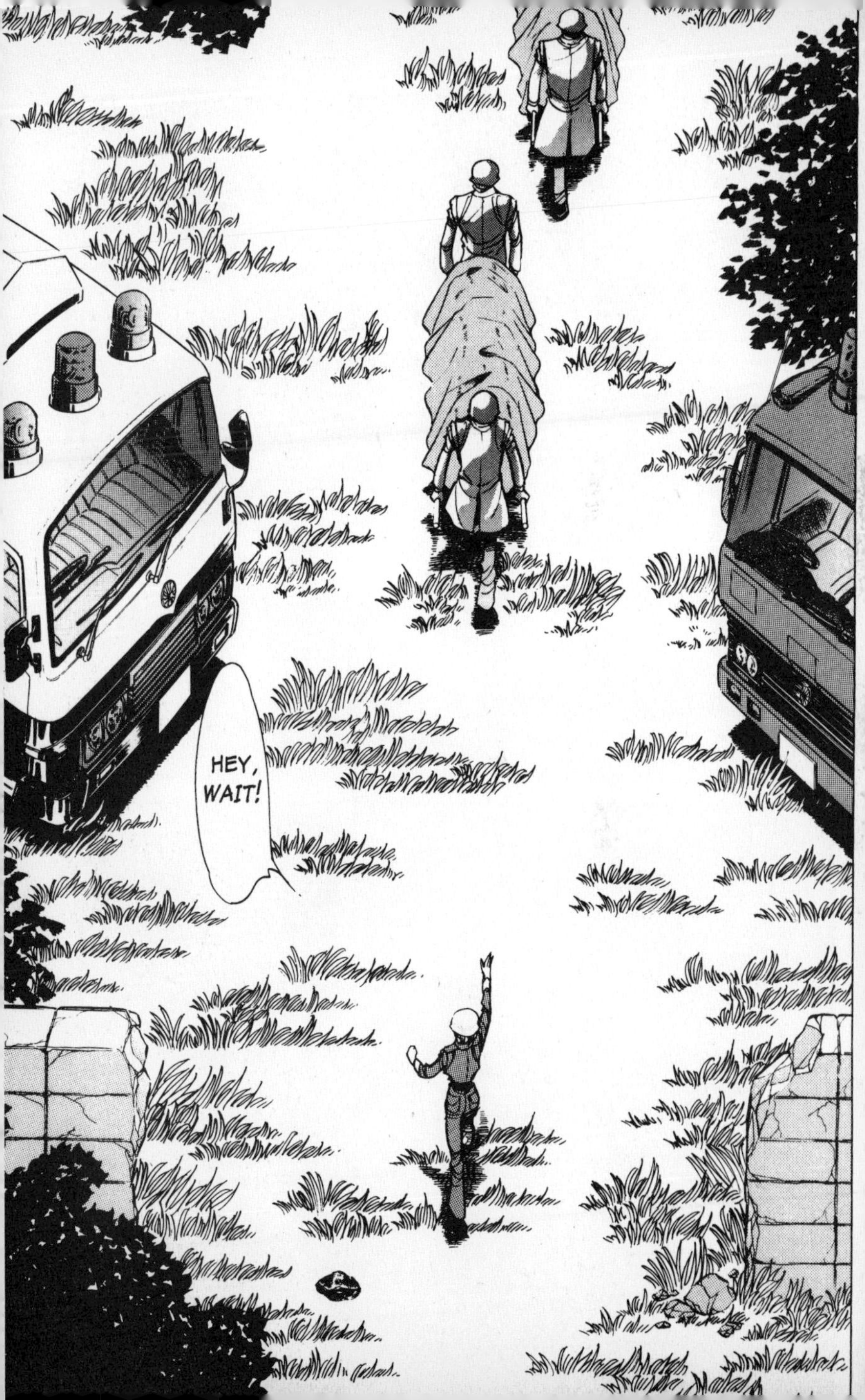
HEY, WAIT!

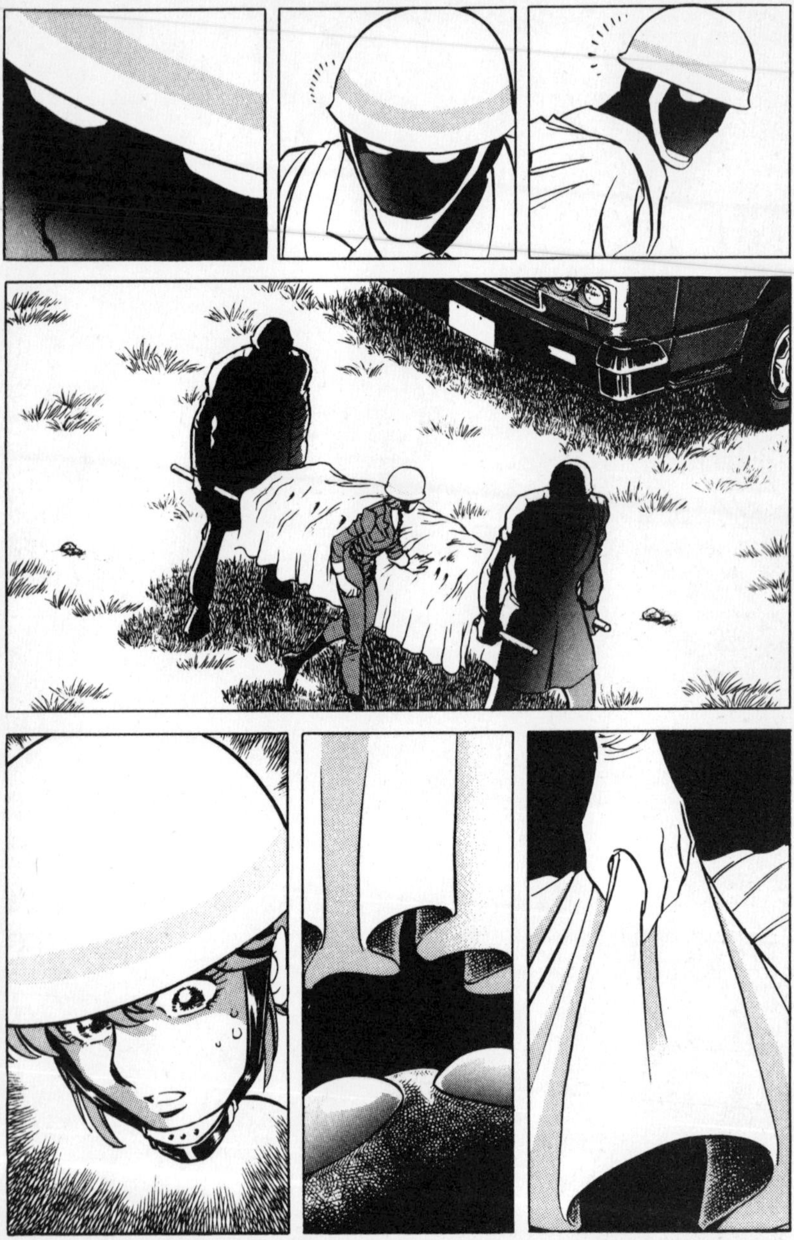

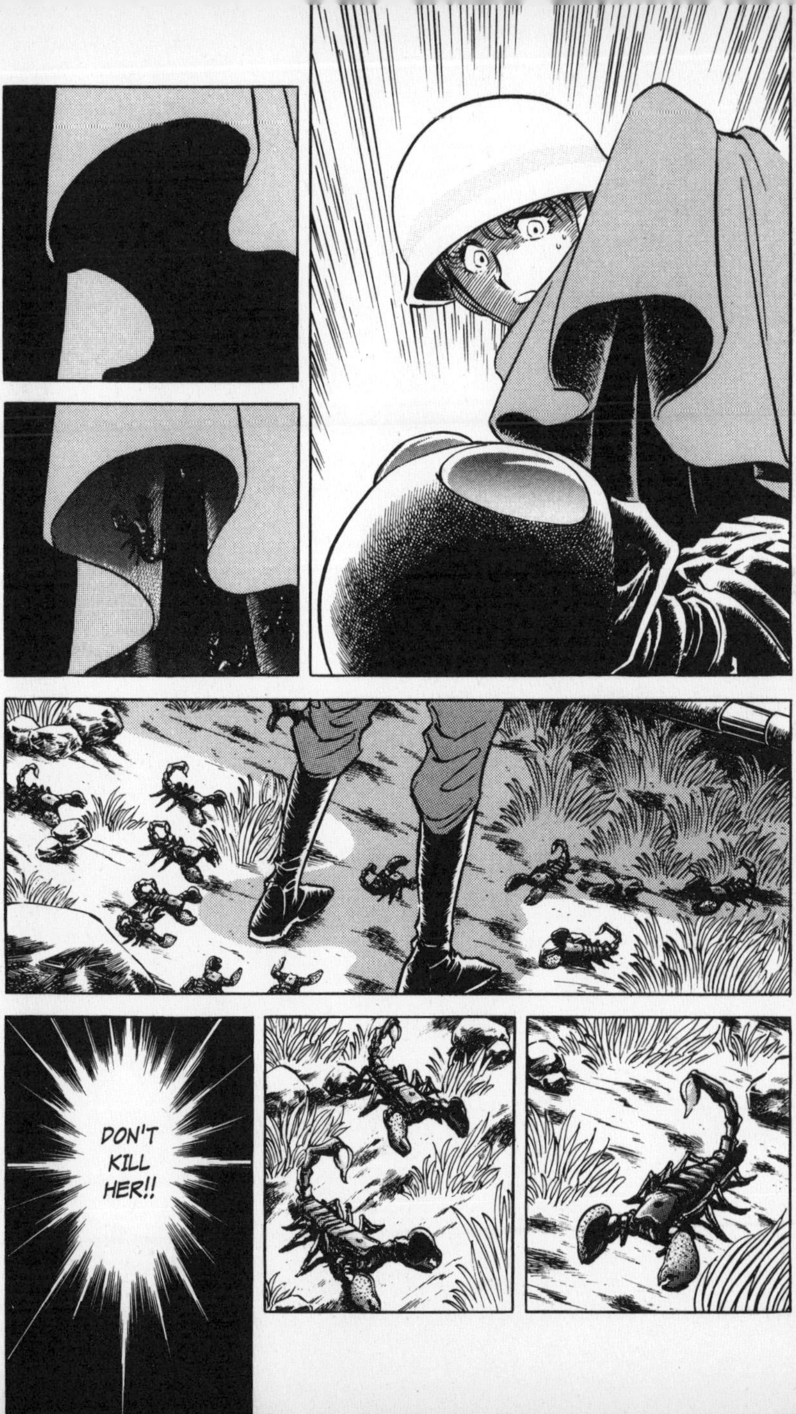
DON'T
KILL
HER!!

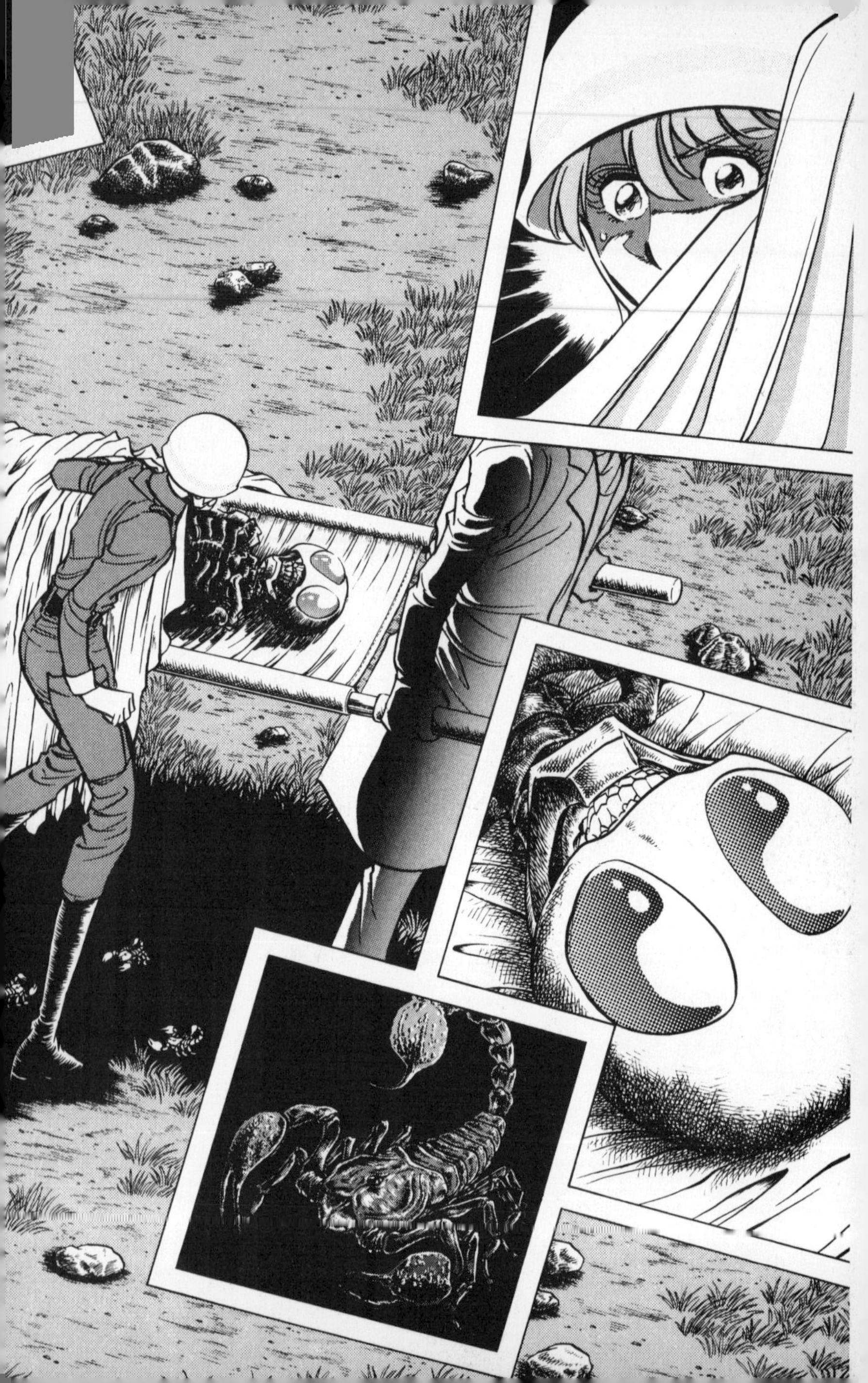

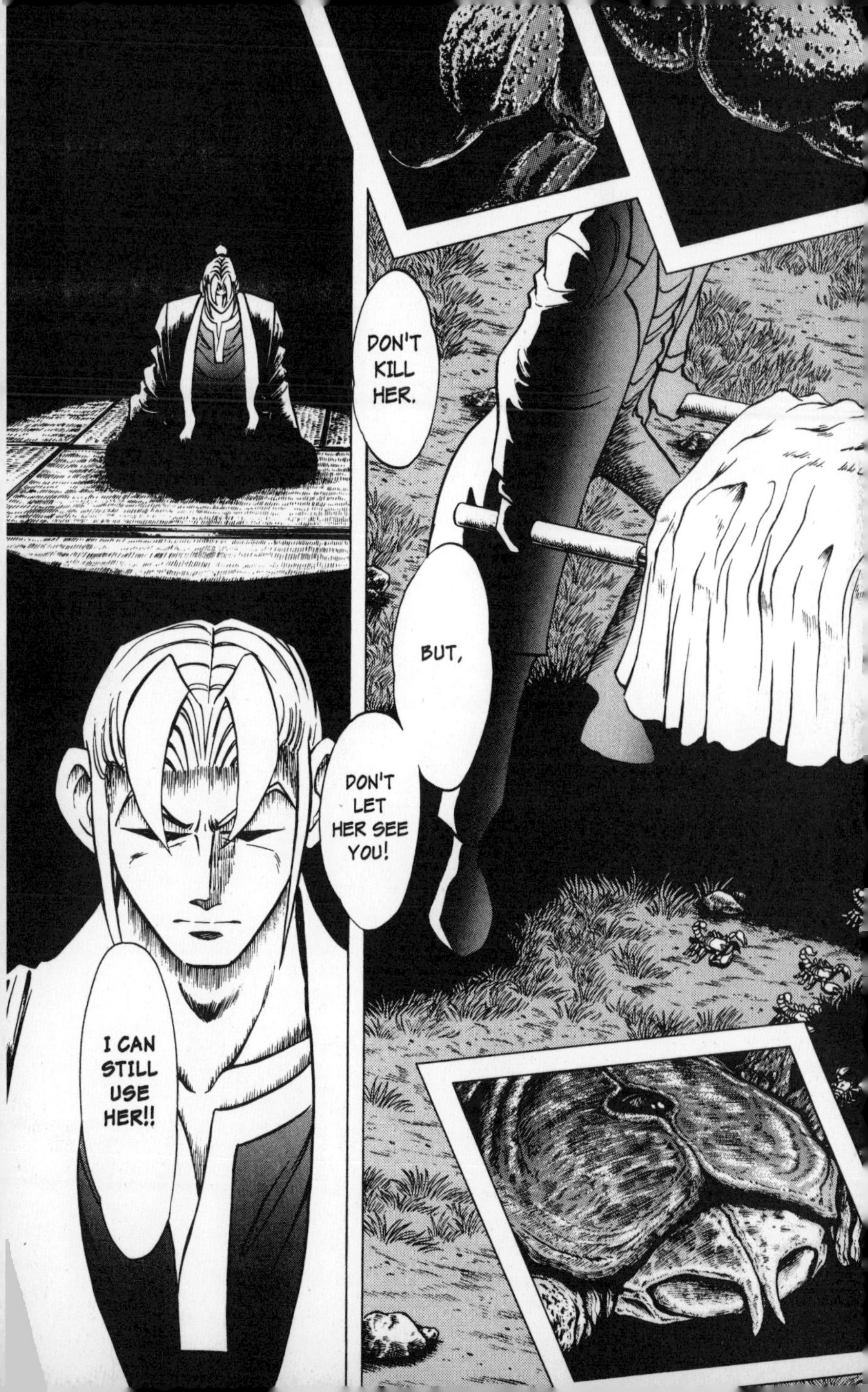
DON'T KILL HER.
BUT,
DON'T LET HER SEE YOU!
I CAN STILL USE HER!!

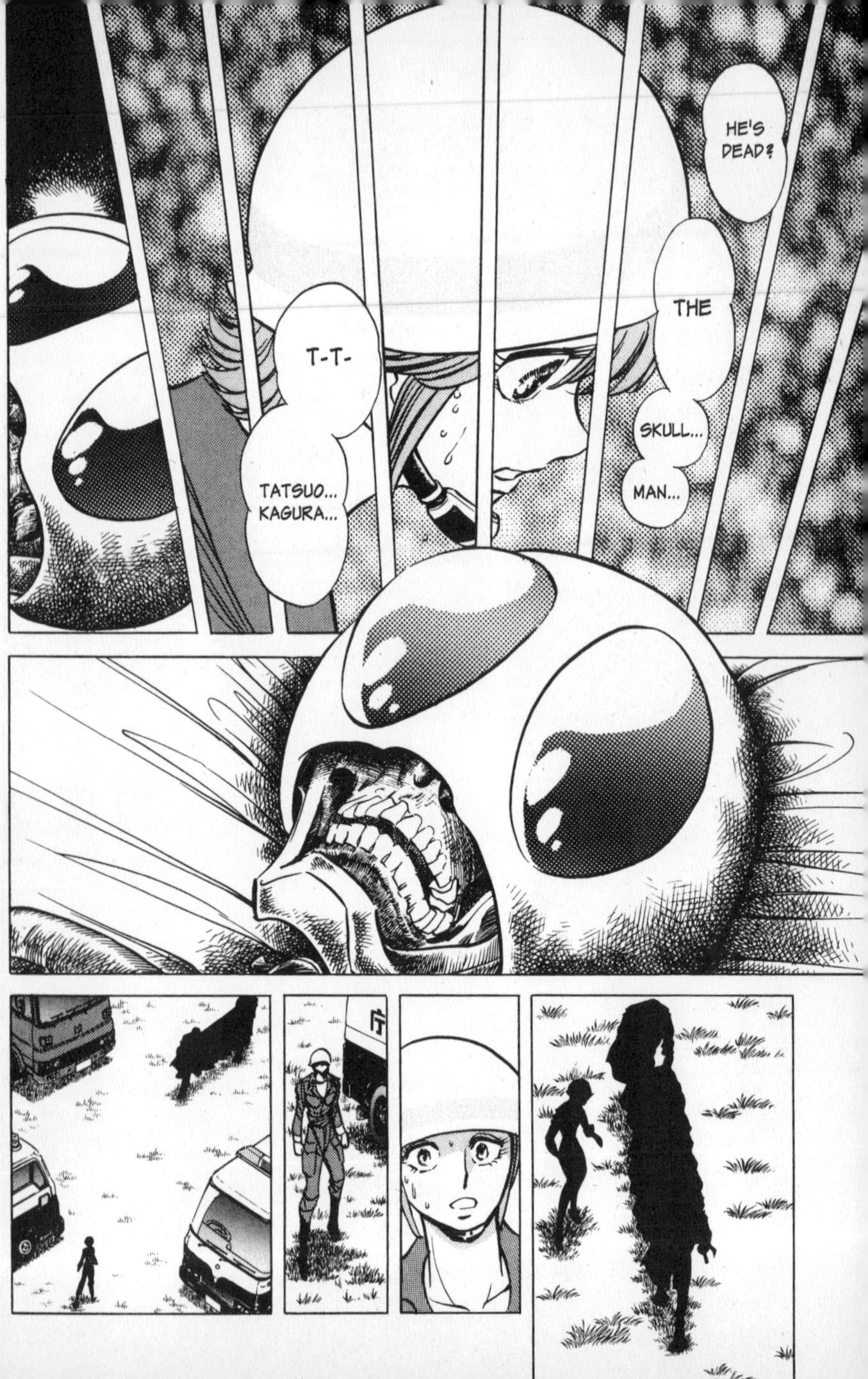
HE'S DEAD?
THE SKULL... MAN...
T-T- TATSUO... KAGURA...

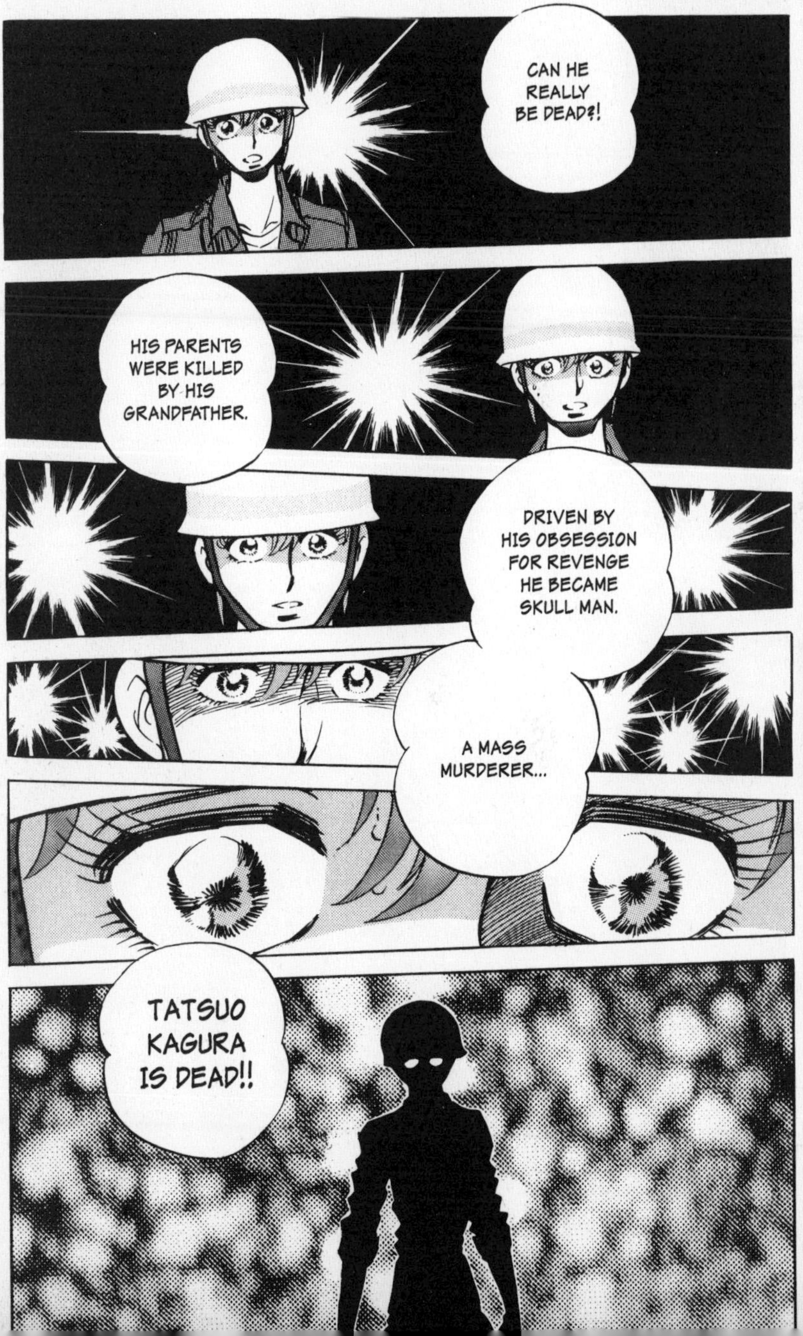
CAN HE REALLY BE DEAD?!
HIS PARENTS WERE KILLED BY HIS GRANDFATHER.
DRIVEN BY HIS OBSESSION FOR REVENGE HE BECAME SKULL MAN.
A MASS MURDERER...
TATSUO KAGURA IS DEAD!!

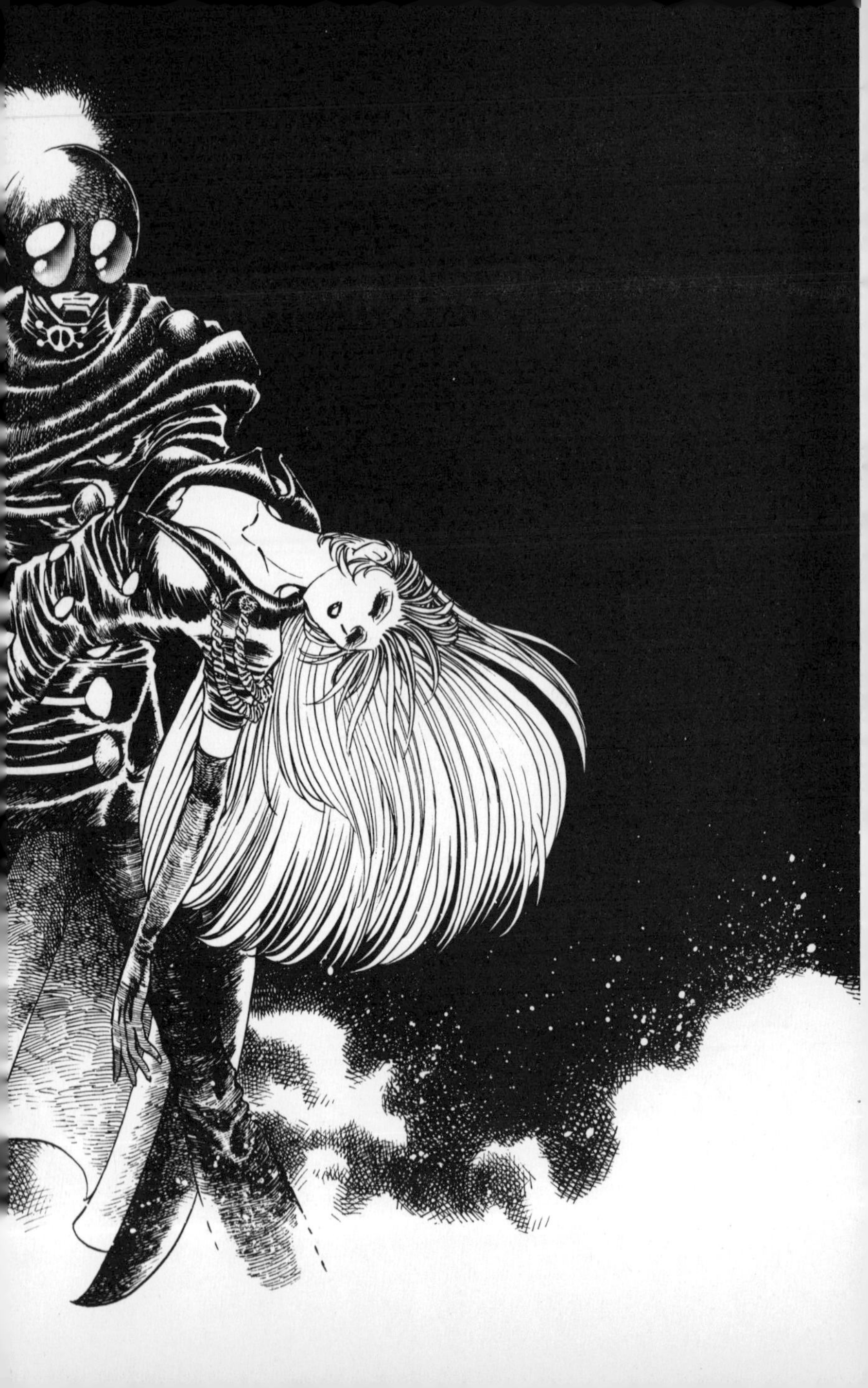

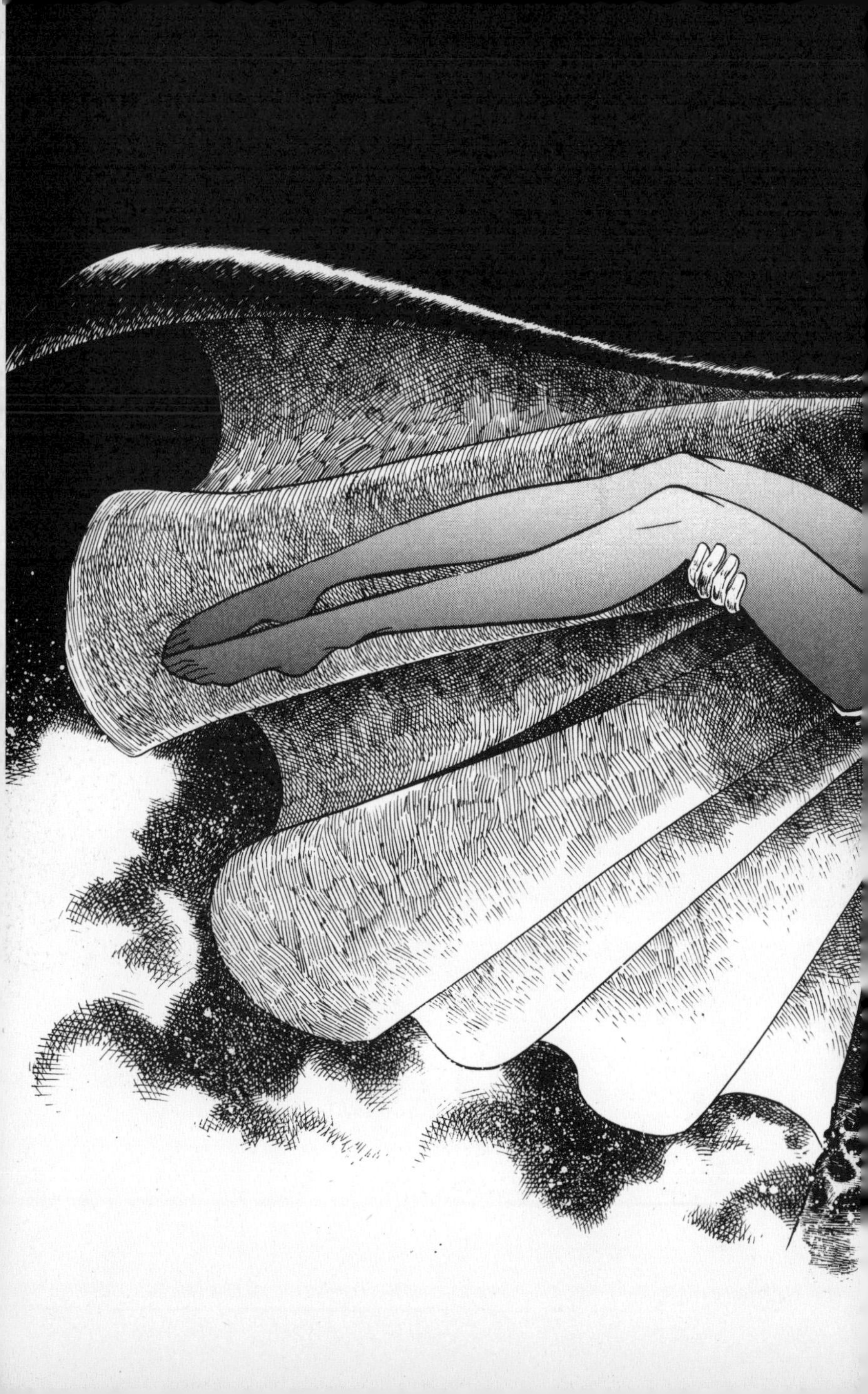

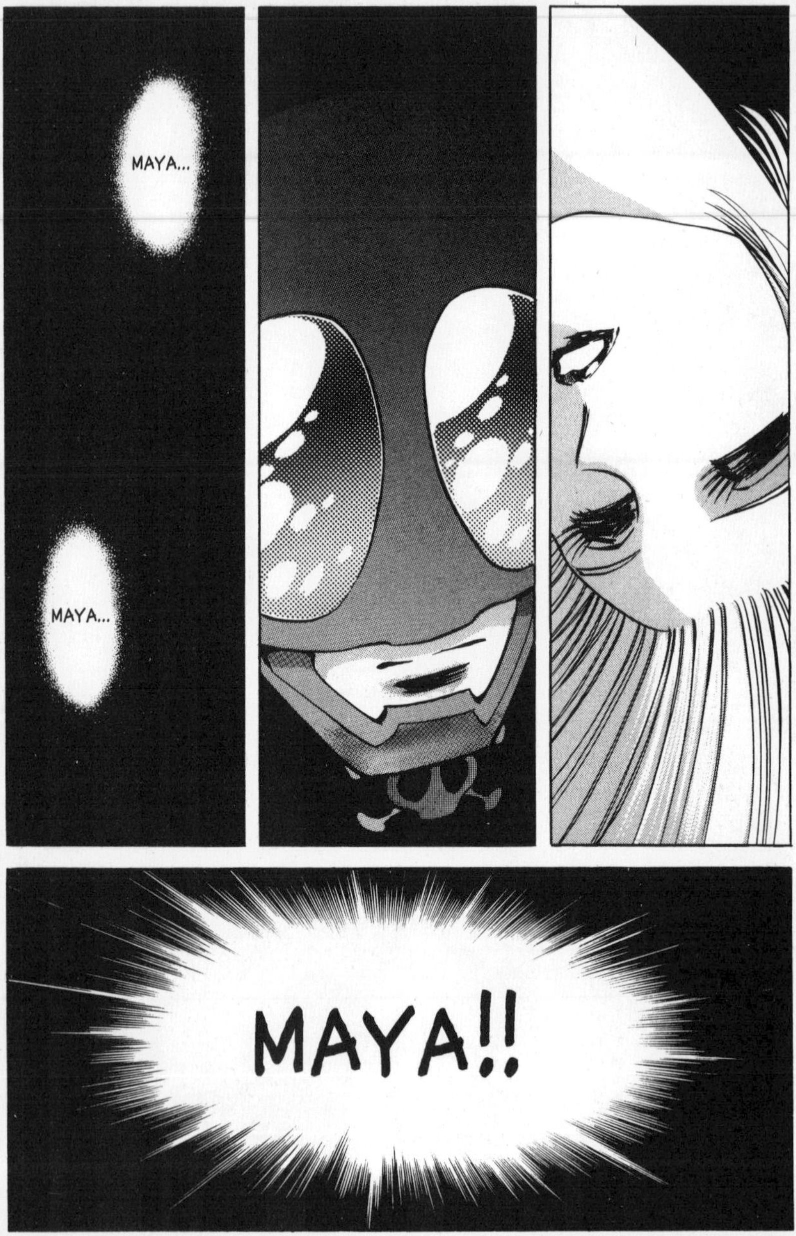
MAYA...
MAYA...
MAYA!!

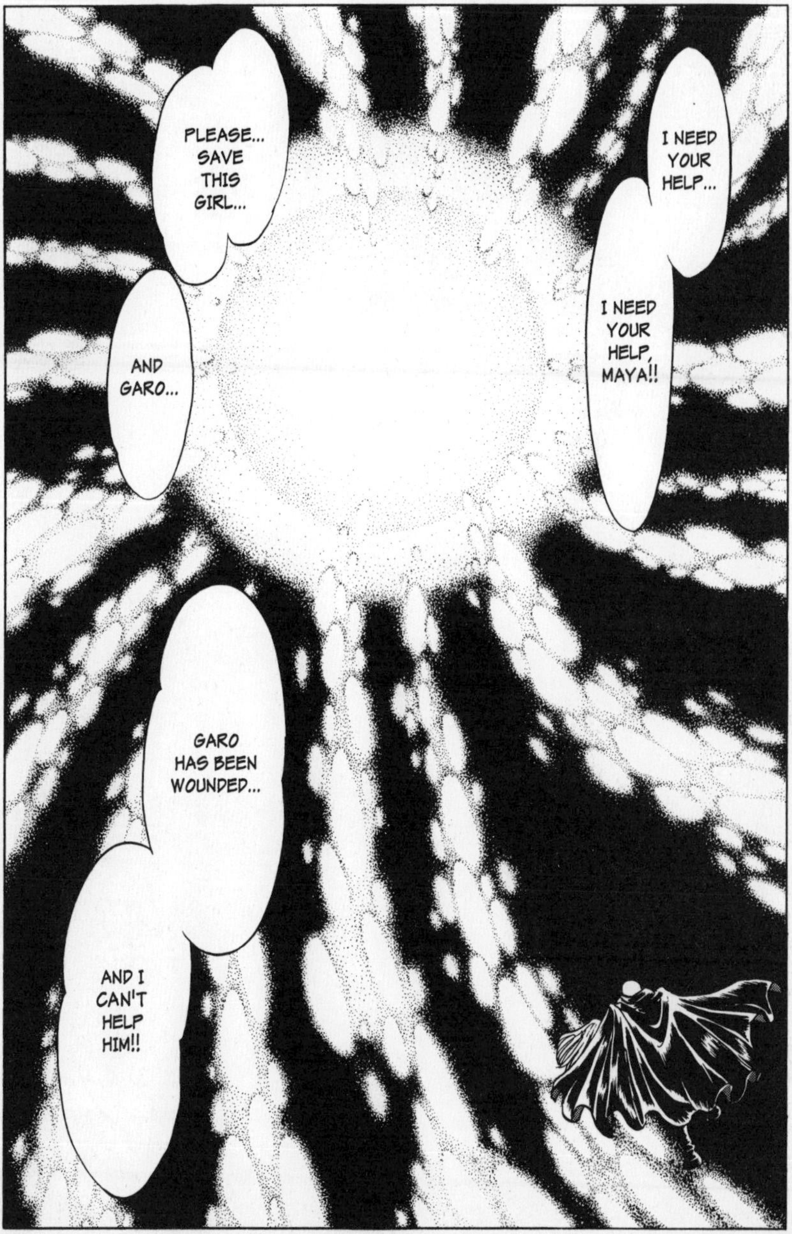
I NEED YOUR HELP...
I NEED YOUR HELP, MAYA!!
PLEASE... SAVE THIS GIRL...
AND GARO...
GARO HAS BEEN WOUNDED...
AND I CAN'T HELP HIM!!

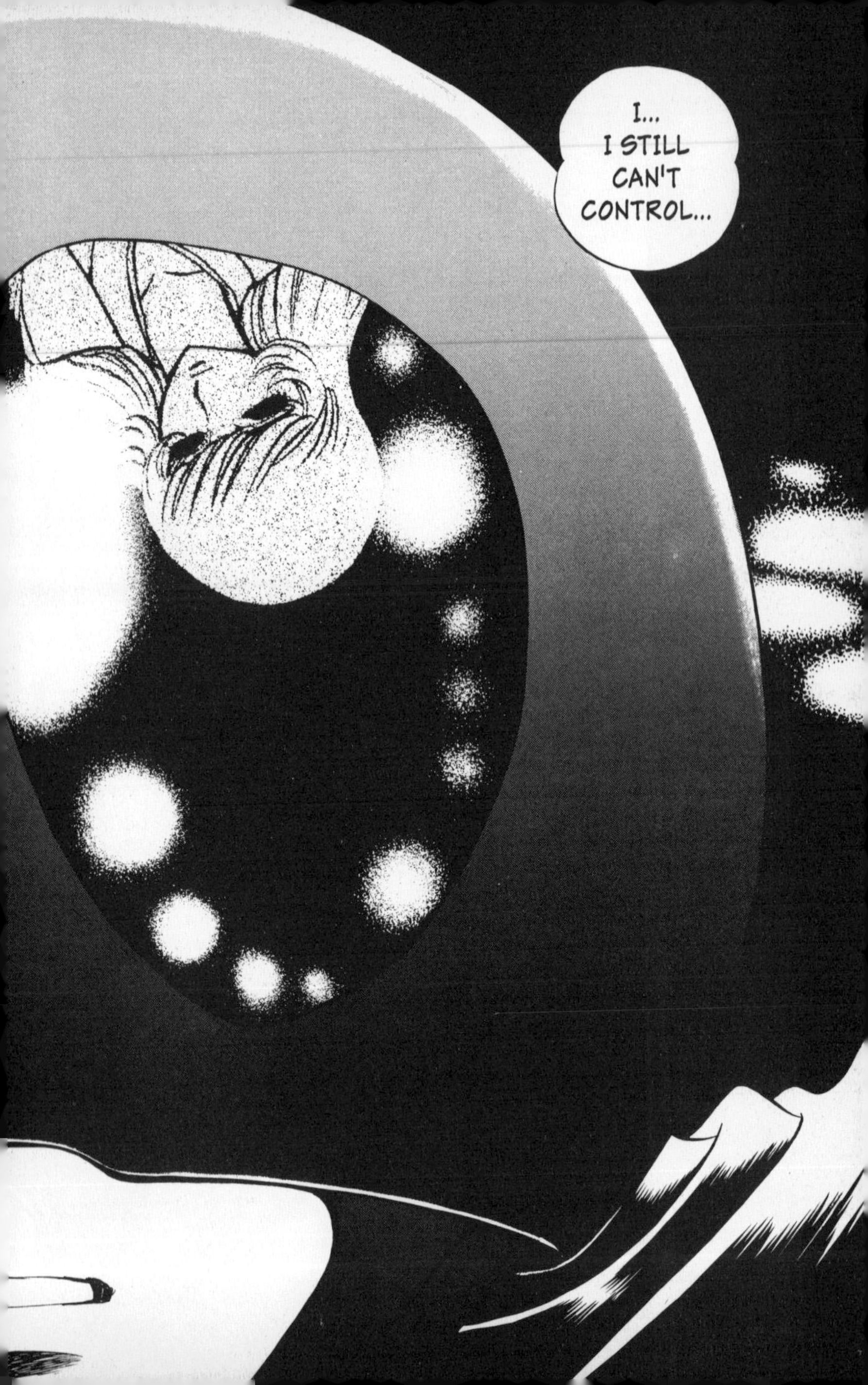
I... I STILL CAN'T CONTROL...

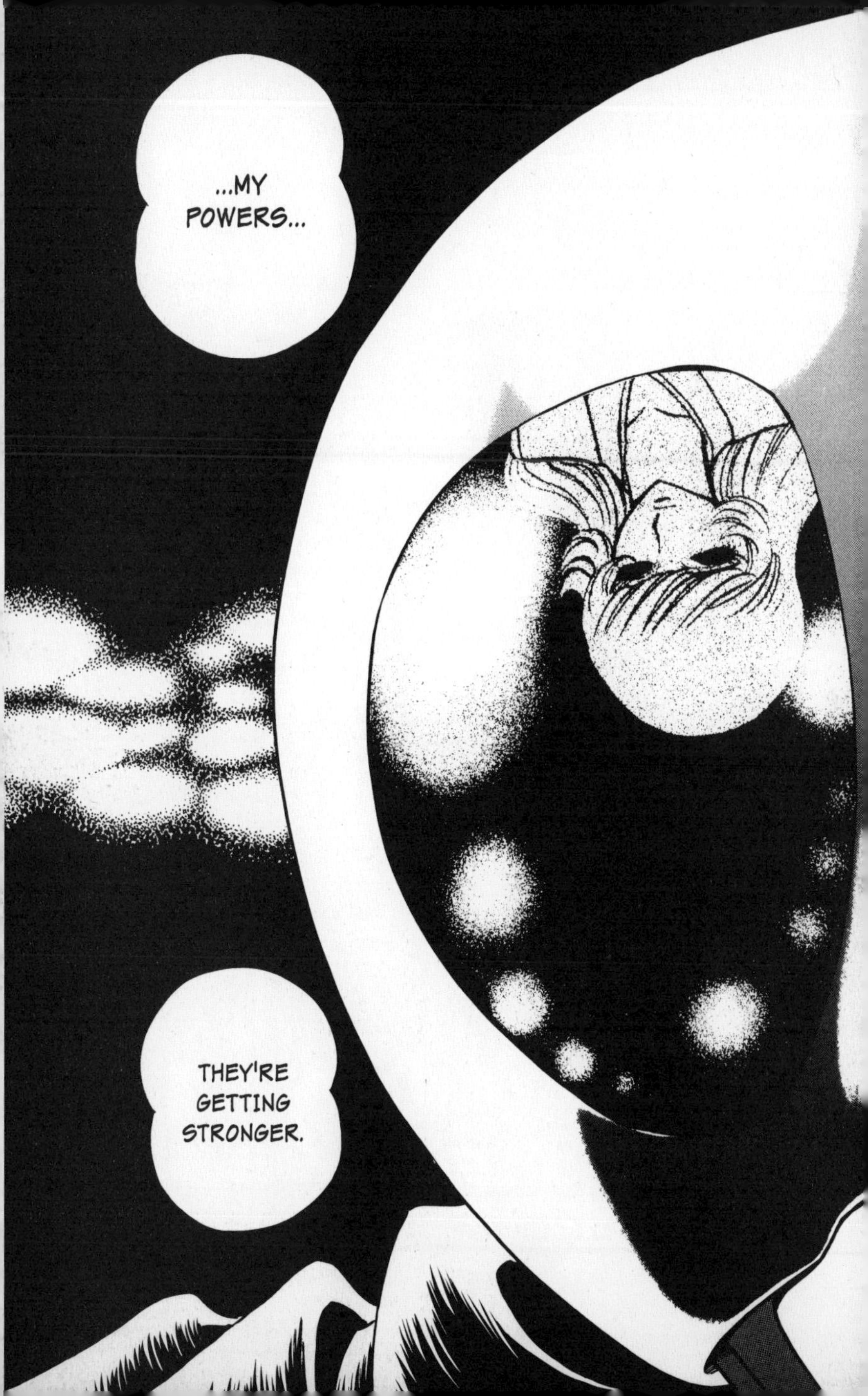
...MY POWERS...
THEY'RE GETTING STRONGER.

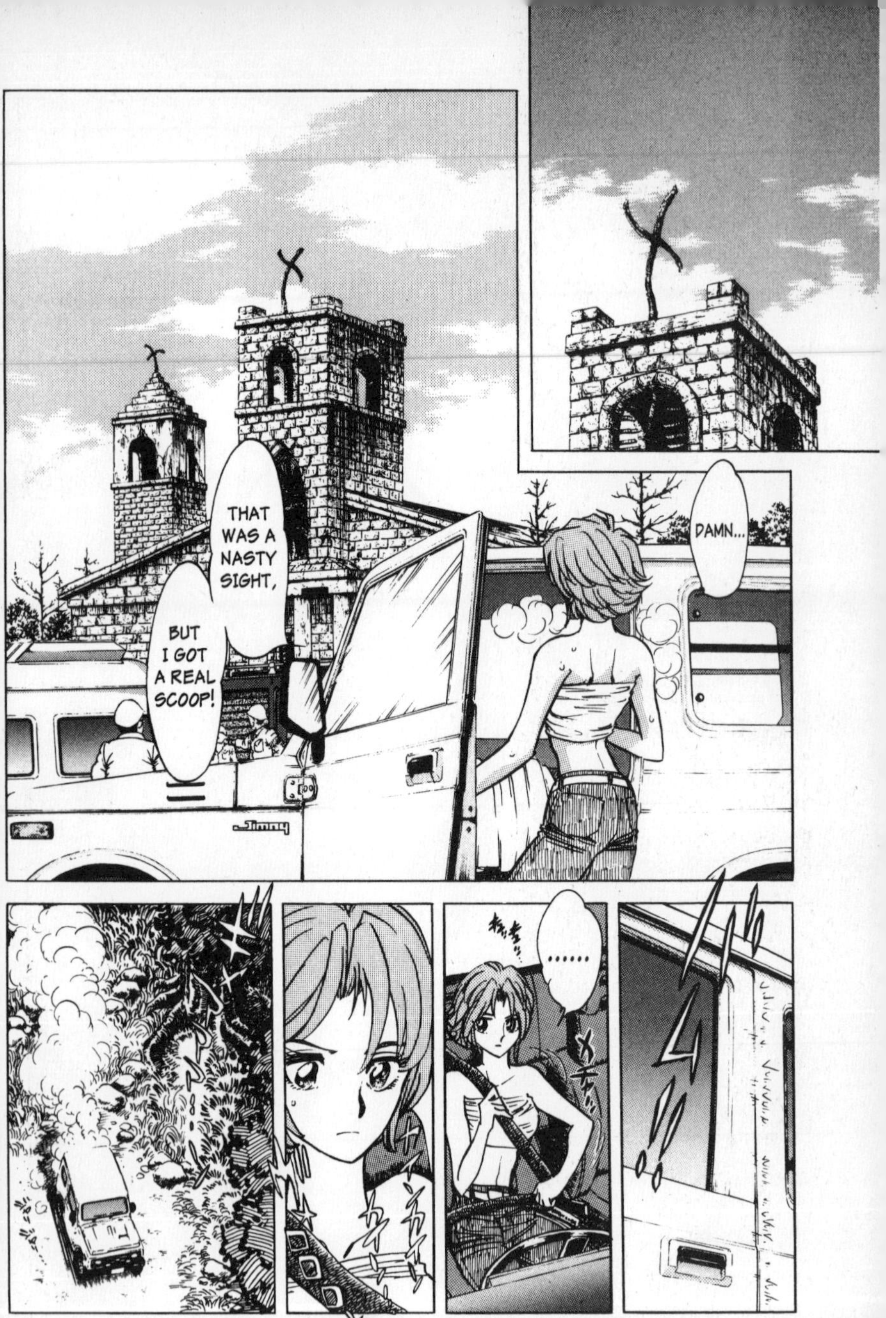
DAMN...
THAT WAS A NASTY SIGHT,
BUT I GOT A REAL SCOOP!
......

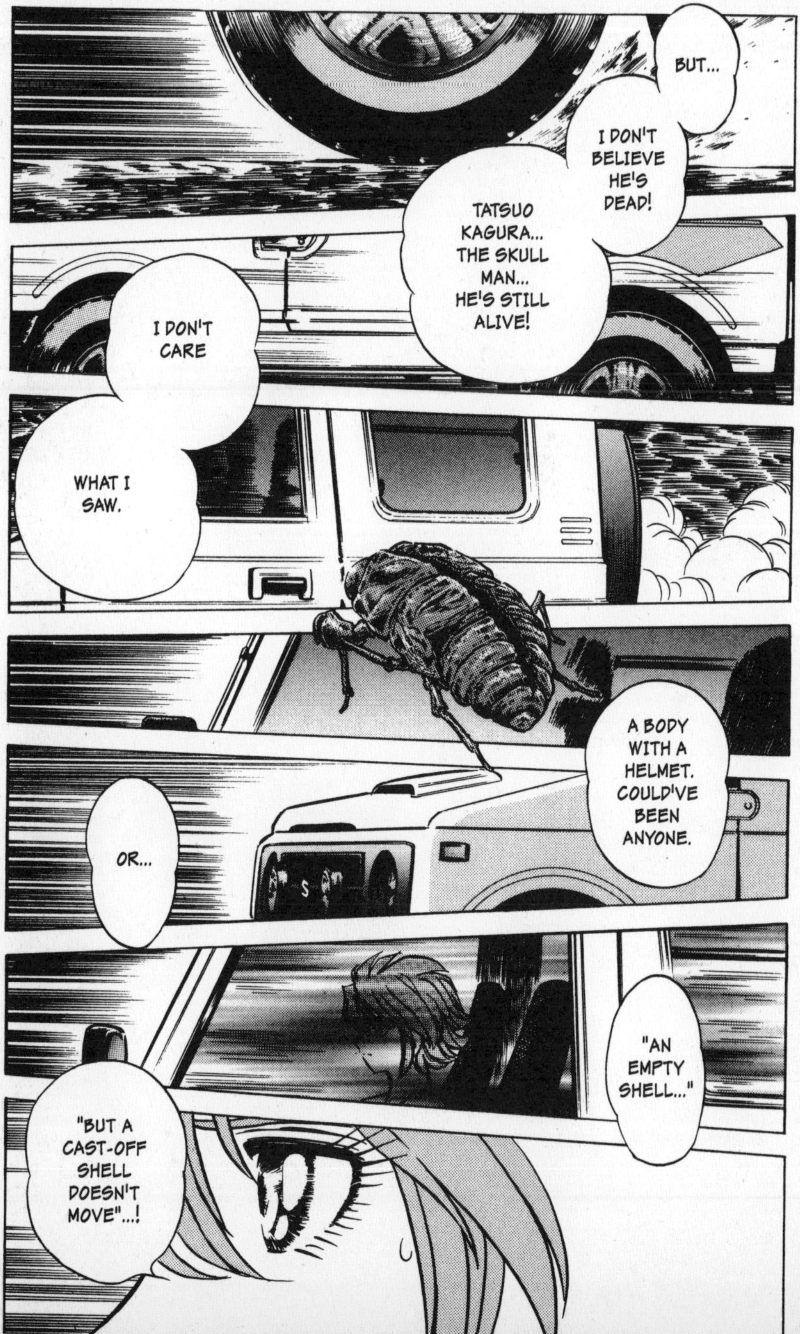
BUT...
I DON'T BELIEVE HE'S DEAD!
TATSUO KAGURA... THE SKULL MAN... HE'S STILL ALIVE!
I DON'T CARE
WHAT I SAW.
A BODY WITH A HELMET. COULD'VE BEEN ANYONE.
OR...
"AN EMPTY SHELL..."
"BUT A CAST-OFF SHELL DOESN'T MOVE"...!

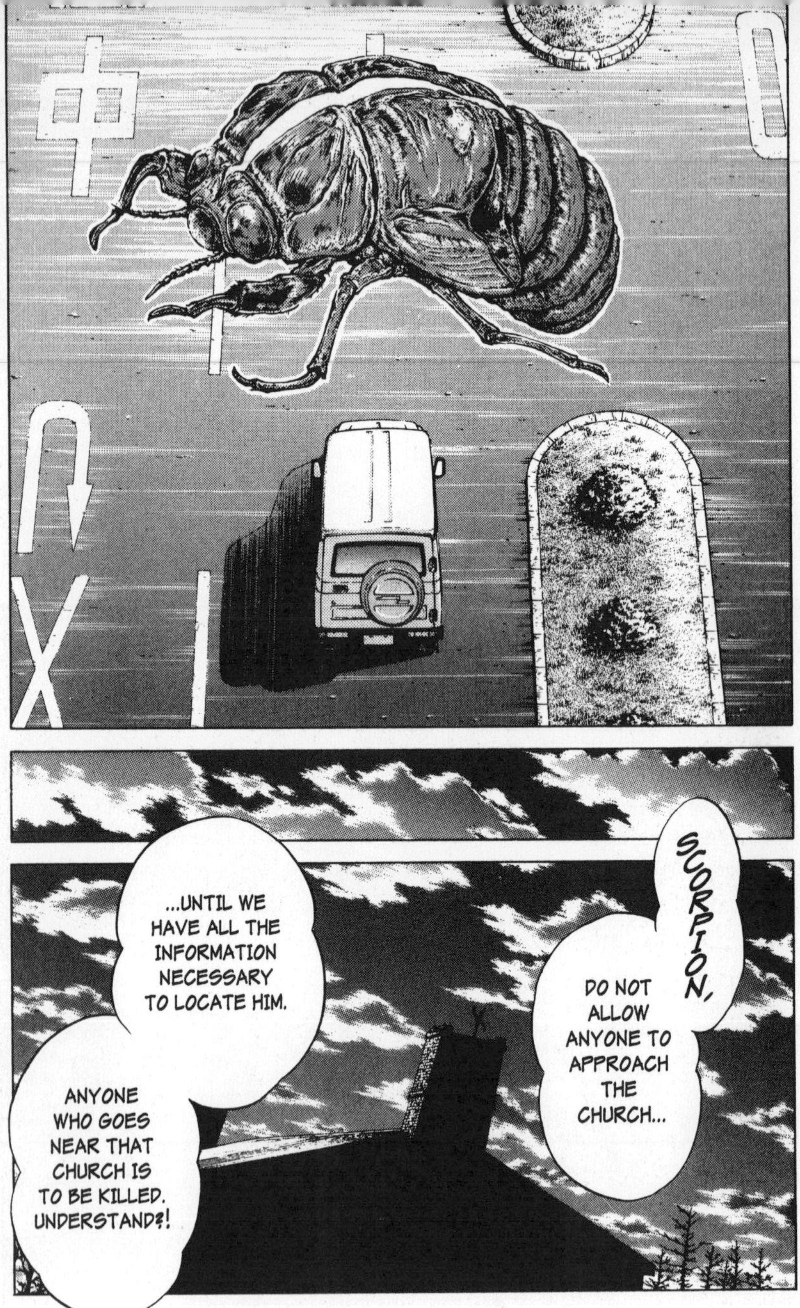
SCORPION,
DO NOT ALLOW ANYONE TO APPROACH THE CHURCH...
...UNTIL WE HAVE ALL THE INFORMATION NECESSARY TO LOCATE HIM.
ANYONE WHO GOES NEAR THAT CHURCH IS TO BE KILLED. UNDERSTAND?!

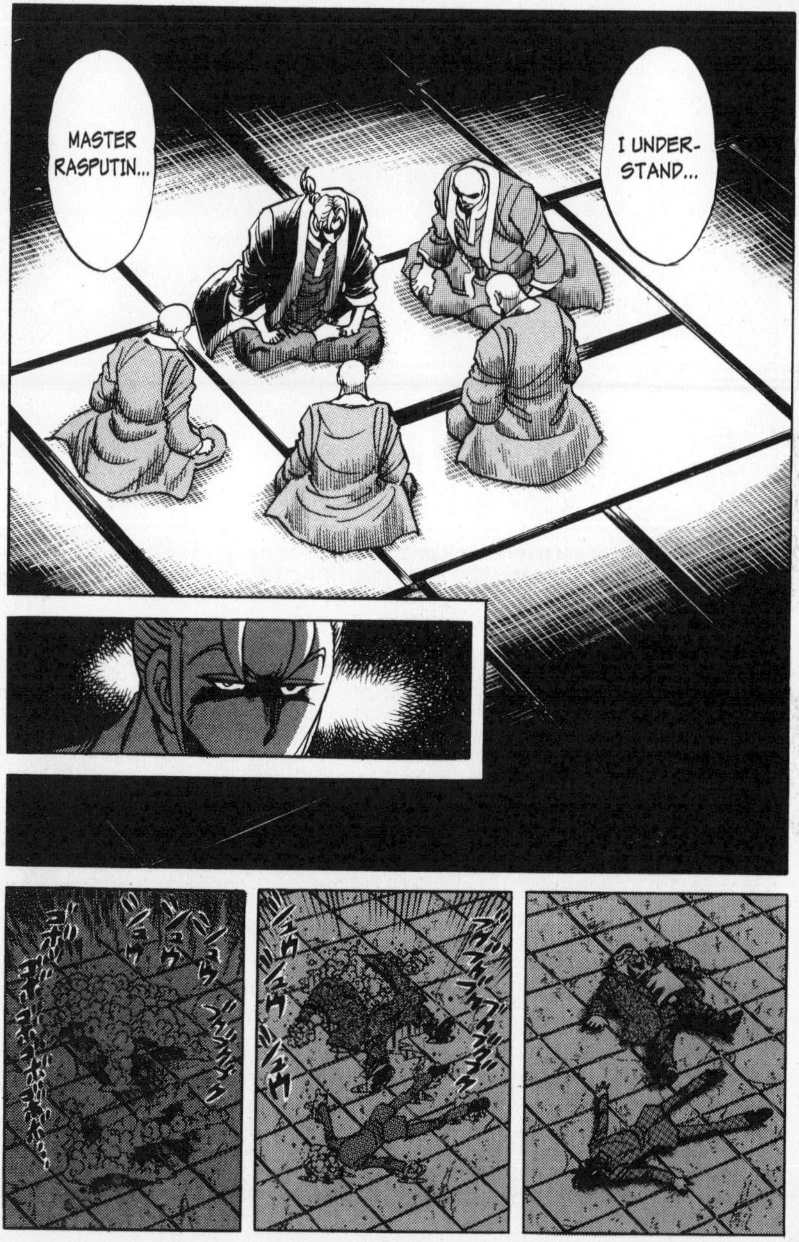
I UNDER-STAND...
MASTER RASPUTIN...

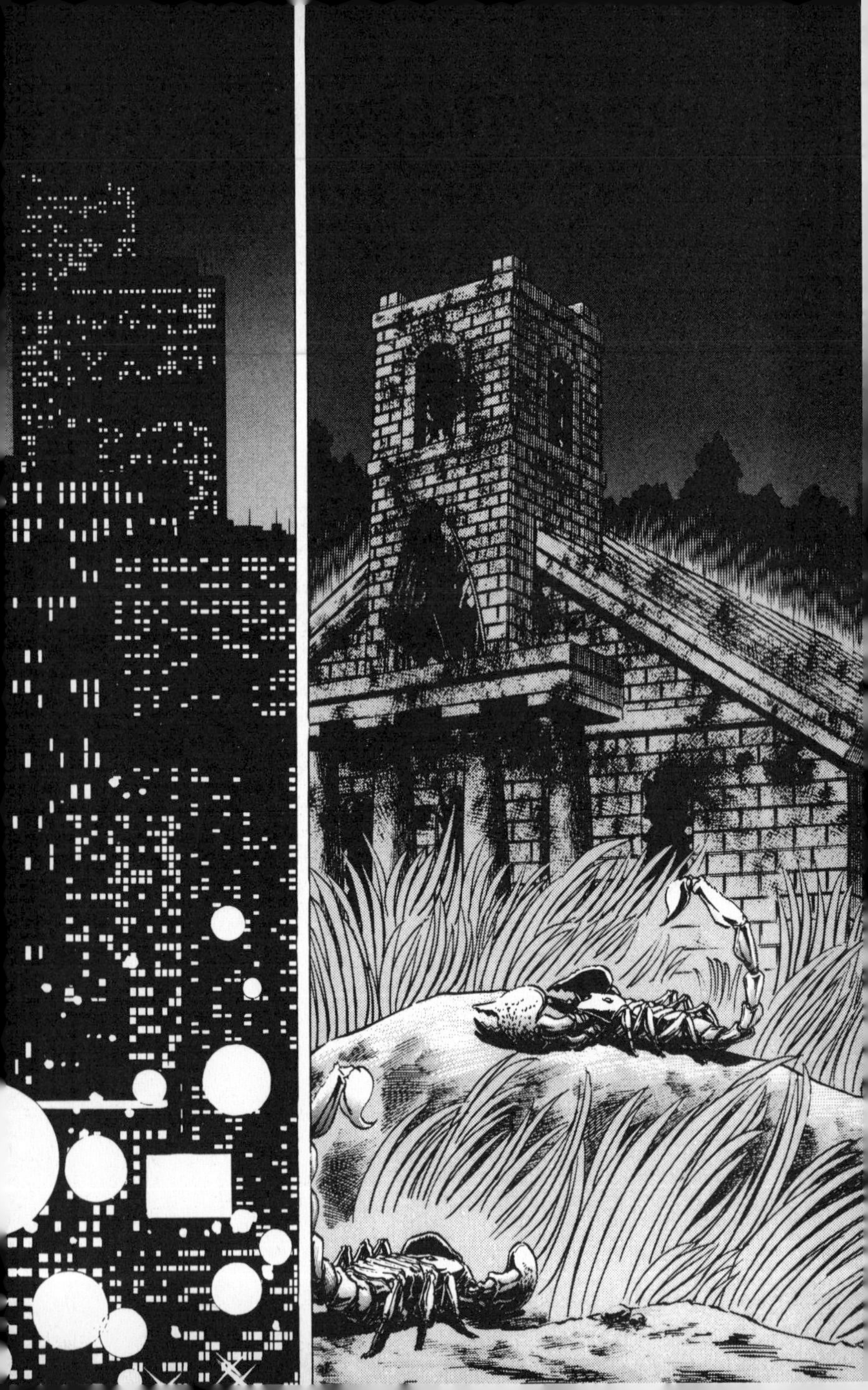

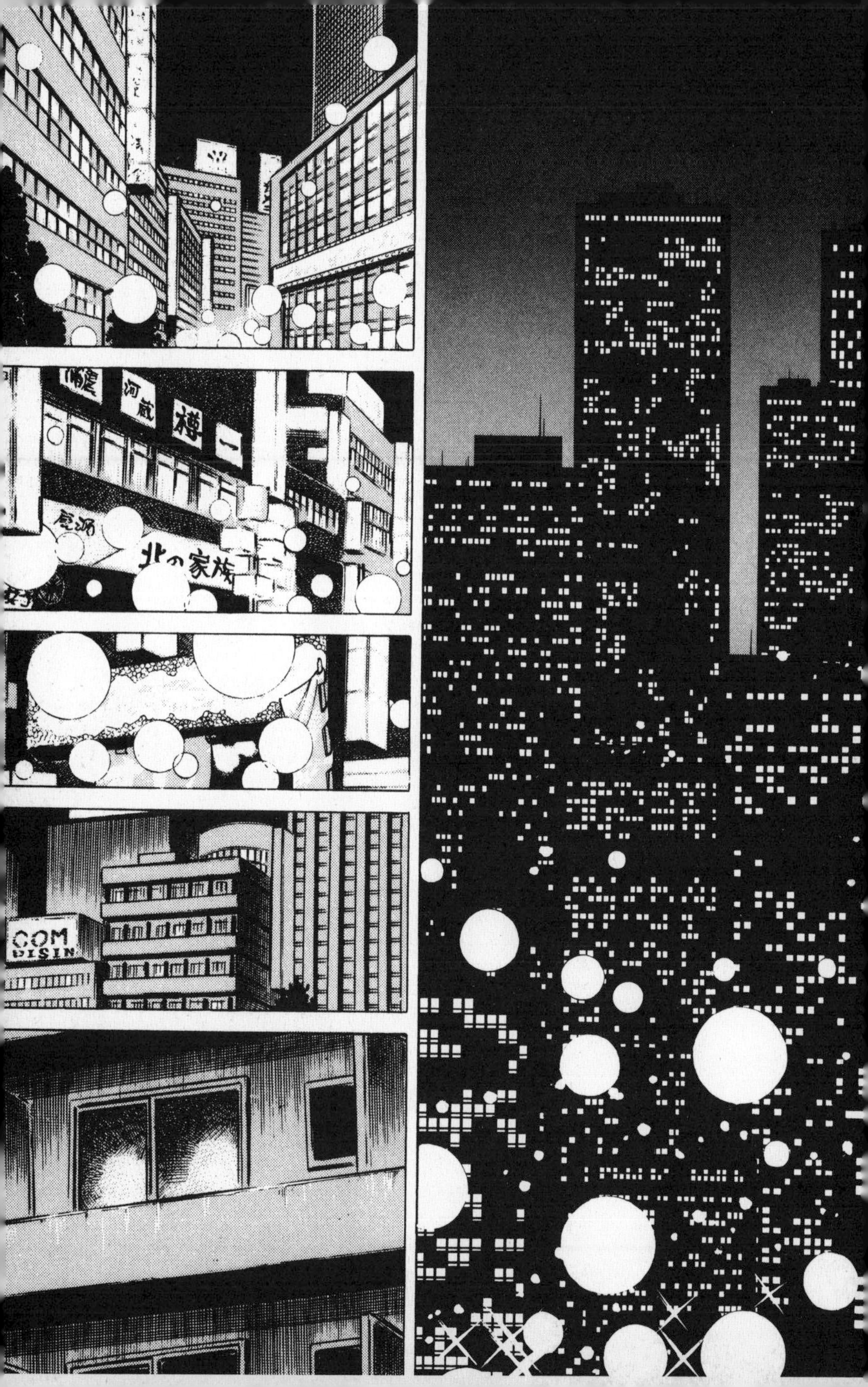
北の家族
COM

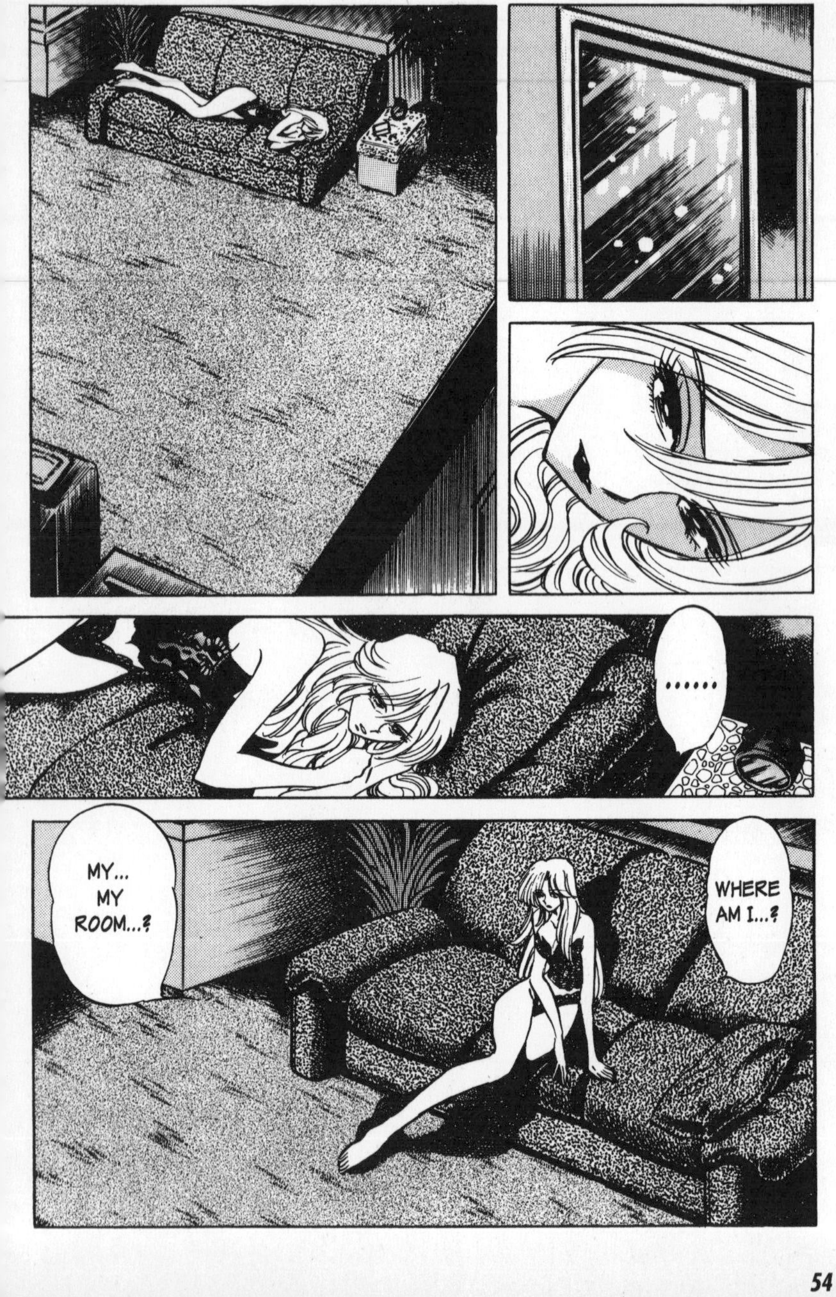
......
WHERE AM I...?
MY... MY ROOM...?

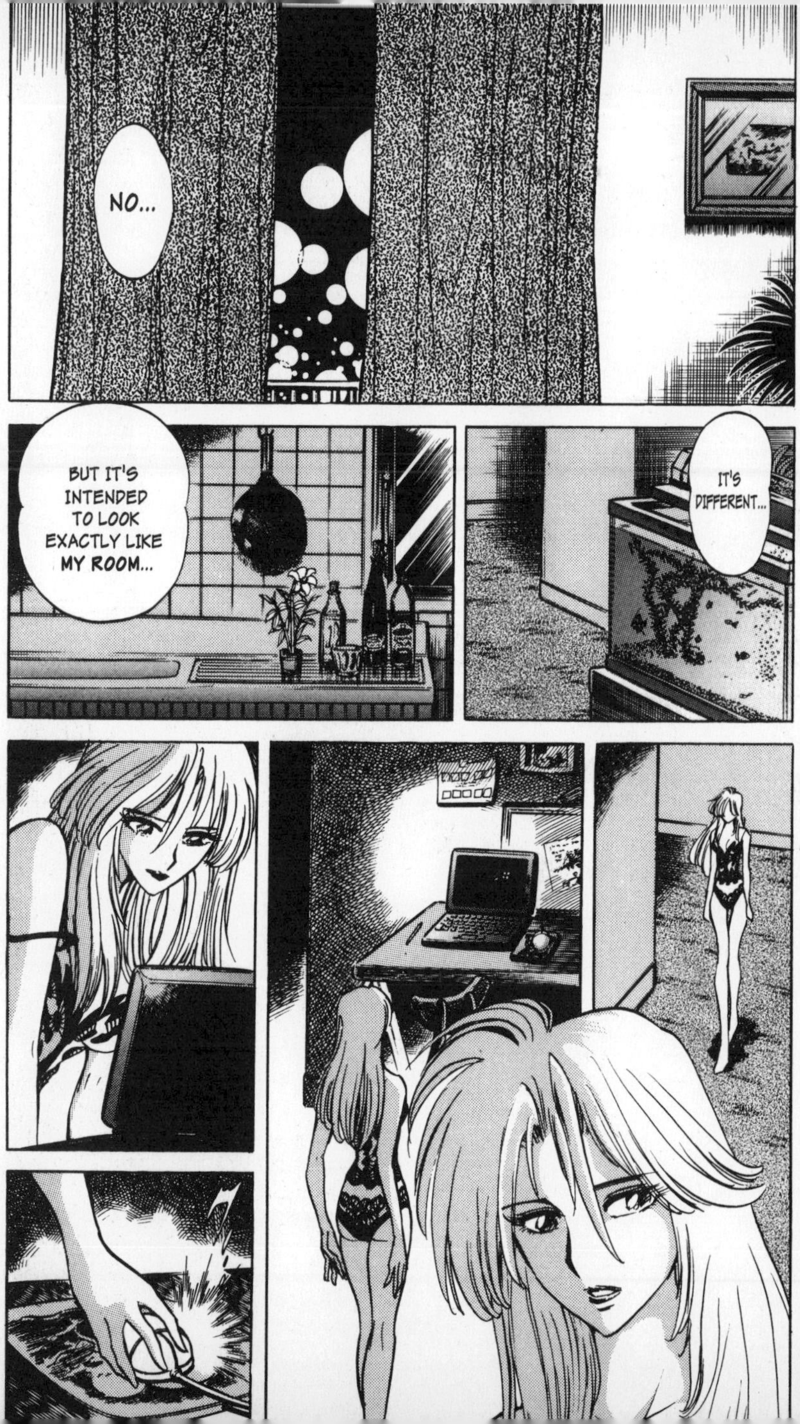
NO...
IT'S DIFFERENT...
BUT IT'S INTENDED TO LOOK EXACTLY LIKE MY ROOM...

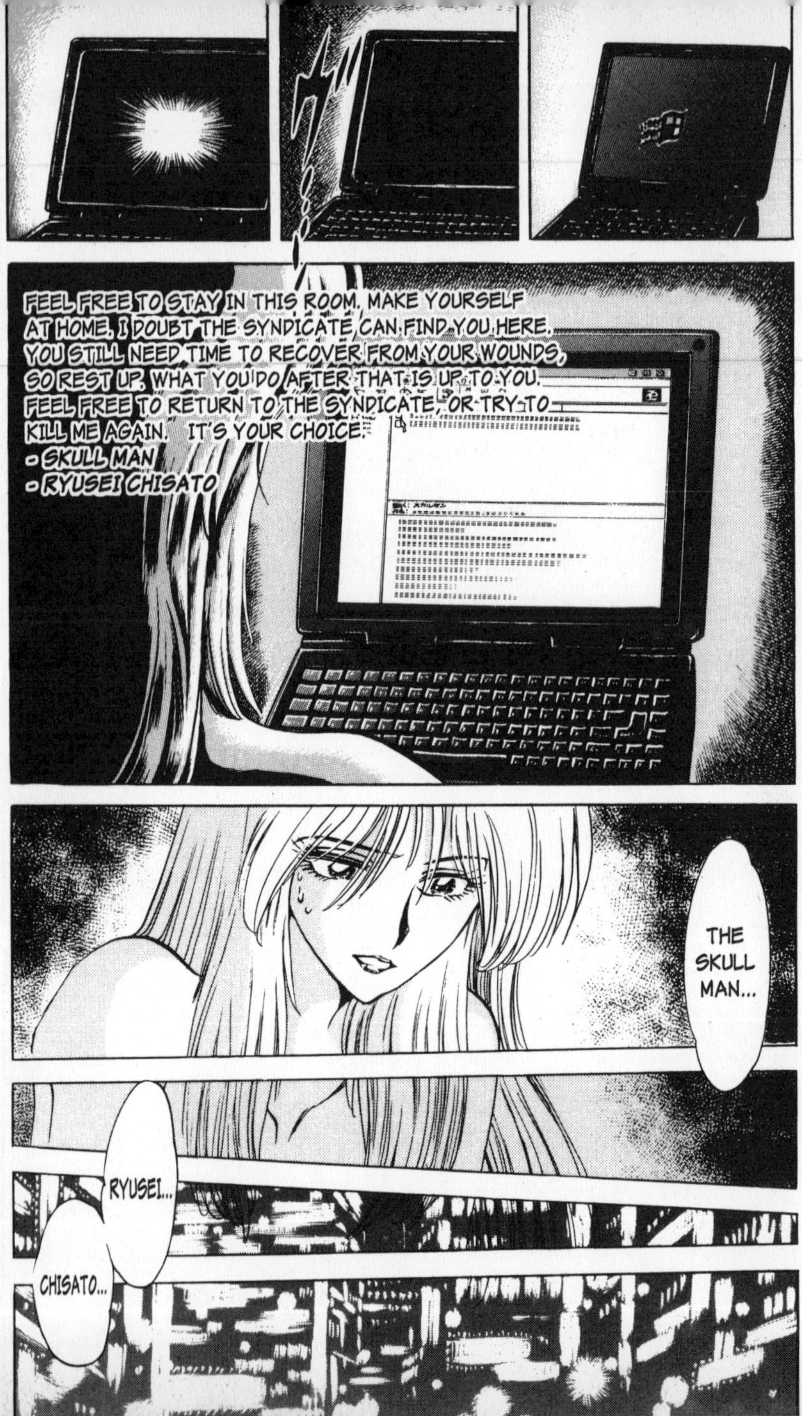
FEEL FREE TO STAY IN THIS ROOM. MAKE YOURSELF AT HOME. I DOUBT THE SYNDICATE CAN FIND YOU HERE. YOU STILL NEED TIME TO RECOVER FROM YOUR WOUNDS, SO REST UP. WHAT YOU DO AFTER THAT IS UP TO YOU. FEEL FREE TO RETURN TO THE SYNDICATE, OR TRY TO KILL ME AGAIN. IT'S YOUR CHOICE.
- SKULL MAN
- RYUSEI CHISATO
THE SKULL MAN...
RYUSEI...
CHISATO...

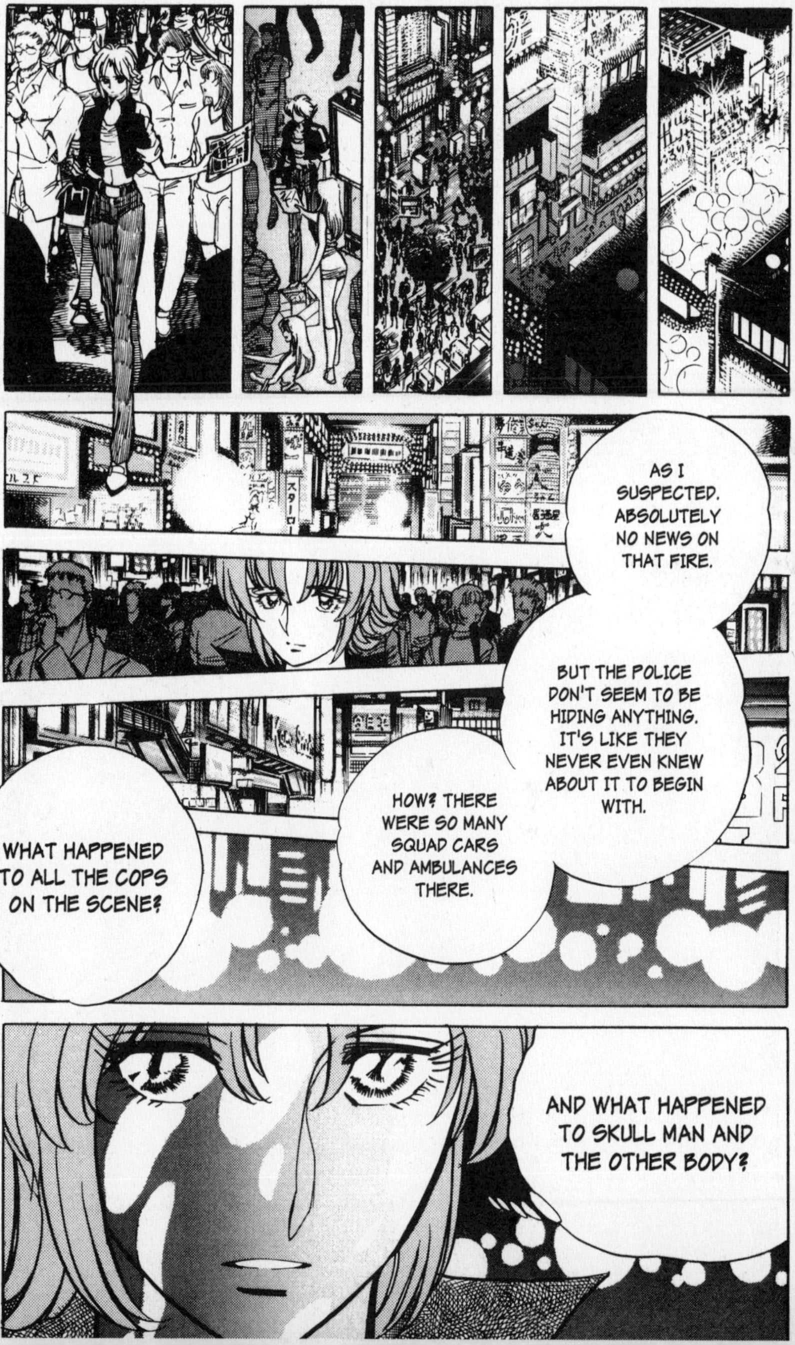
AS I SUSPECTED. ABSOLUTELY NO NEWS ON THAT FIRE.
BUT THE POLICE DON'T SEEM TO BE HIDING ANYTHING. IT'S LIKE THEY NEVER EVEN KNEW ABOUT IT TO BEGIN WITH.
HOW? THERE WERE SO MANY SQUAD CARS AND AMBULANCES THERE.
WHAT HAPPENED TO ALL THE COPS ON THE SCENE?
AND WHAT HAPPENED TO SKULL MAN AND THE OTHER BODY?

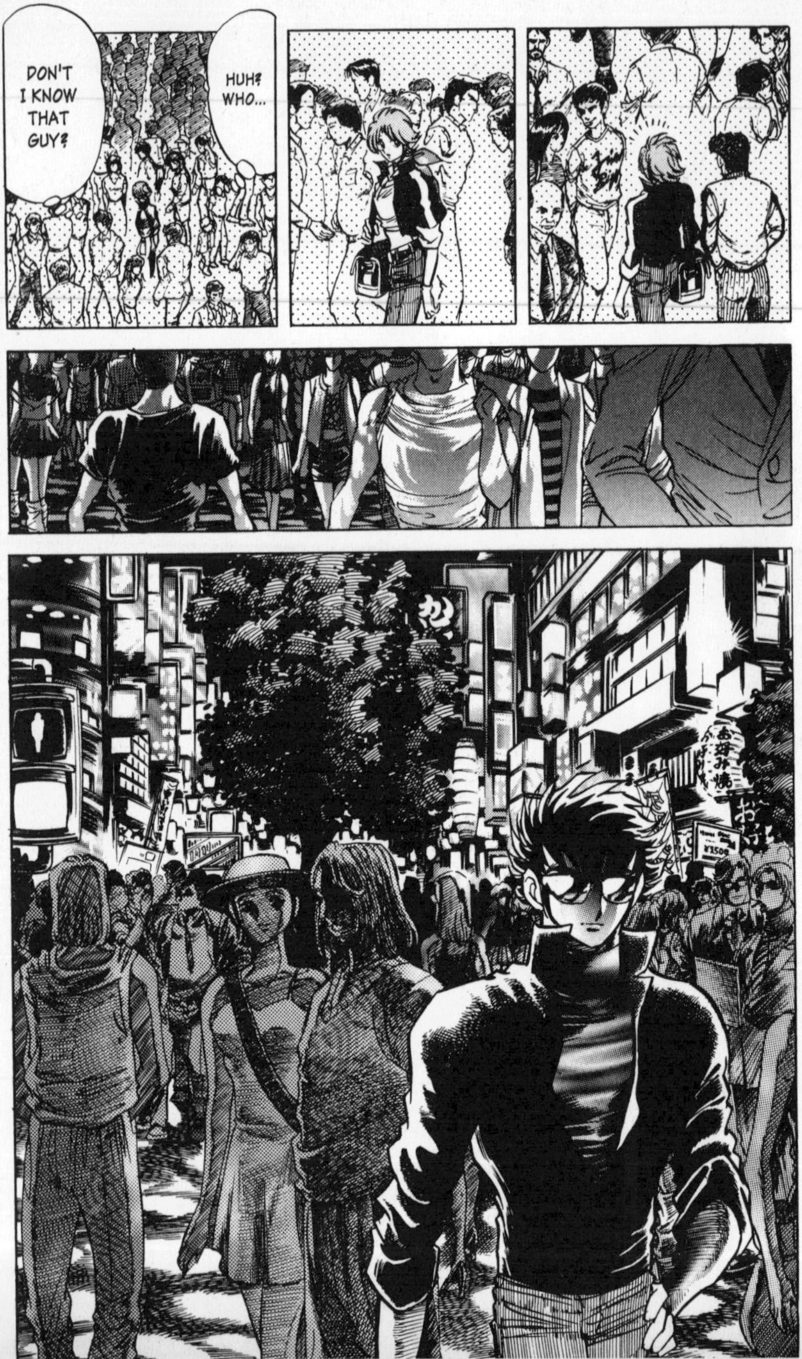
HUH? WHO...
DON'T I KNOW THAT GUY?
お好み焼

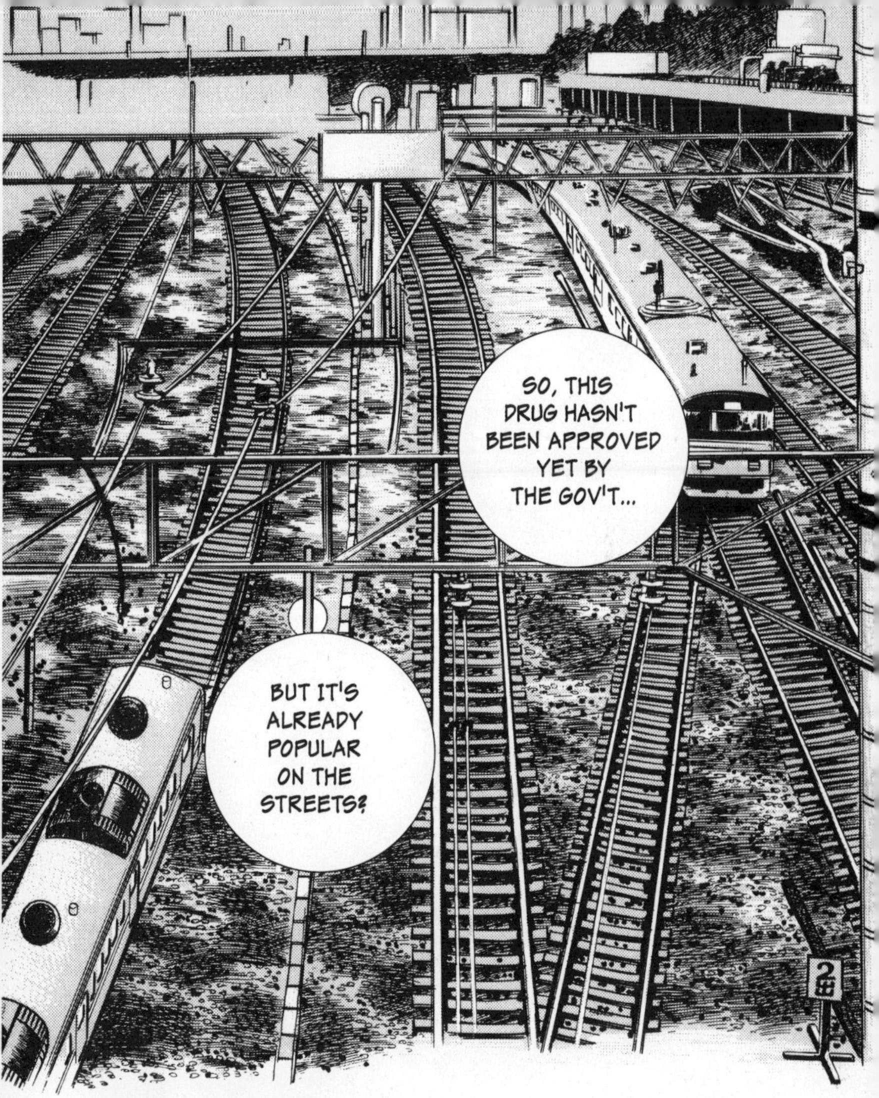
SO, THIS DRUG HASN'T BEEN APPROVED YET BY THE GOV'T...
BUT IT'S ALREADY POPULAR ON THE STREETS?
2

10 スカルマン現わる SKULL MAN EMERGES

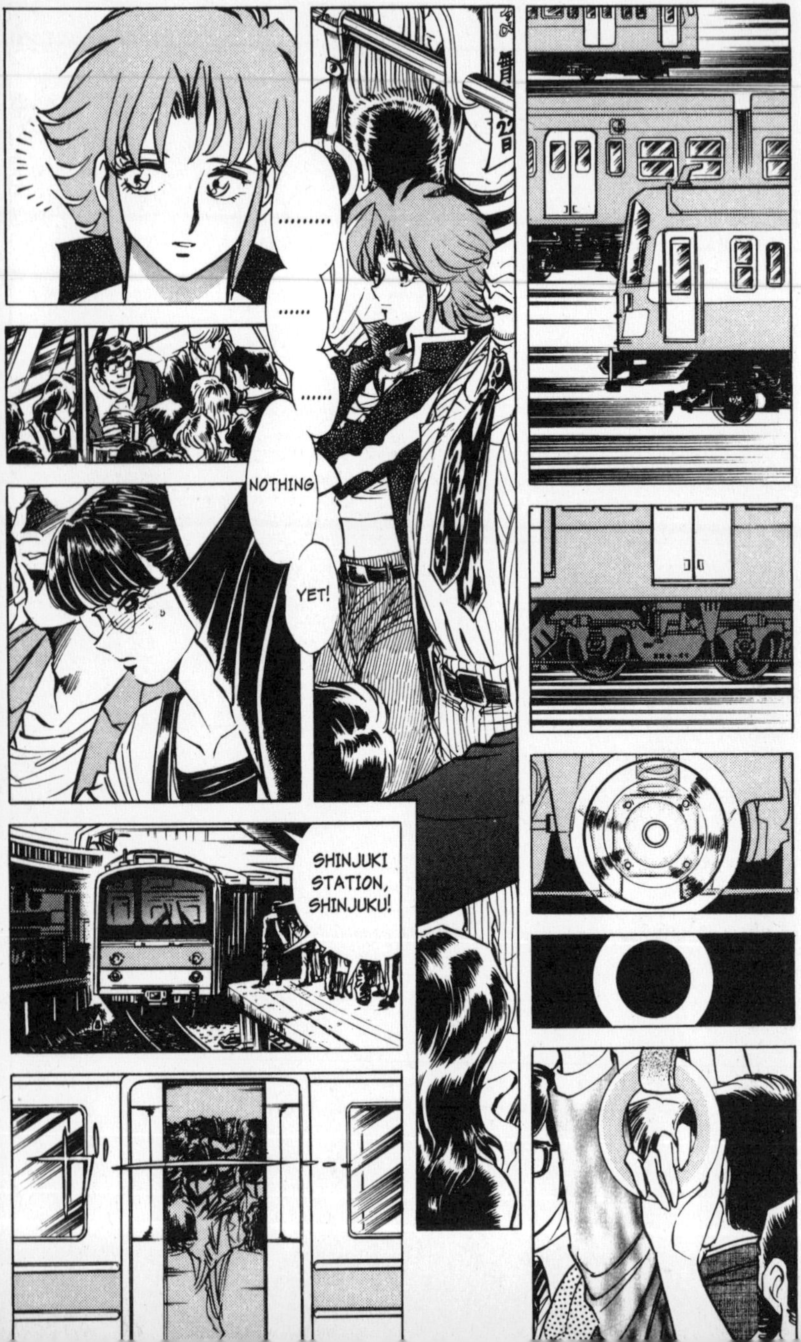
....
......
......
NOTHING
YET!
SHINJUKI STATION, SHINJUKU!

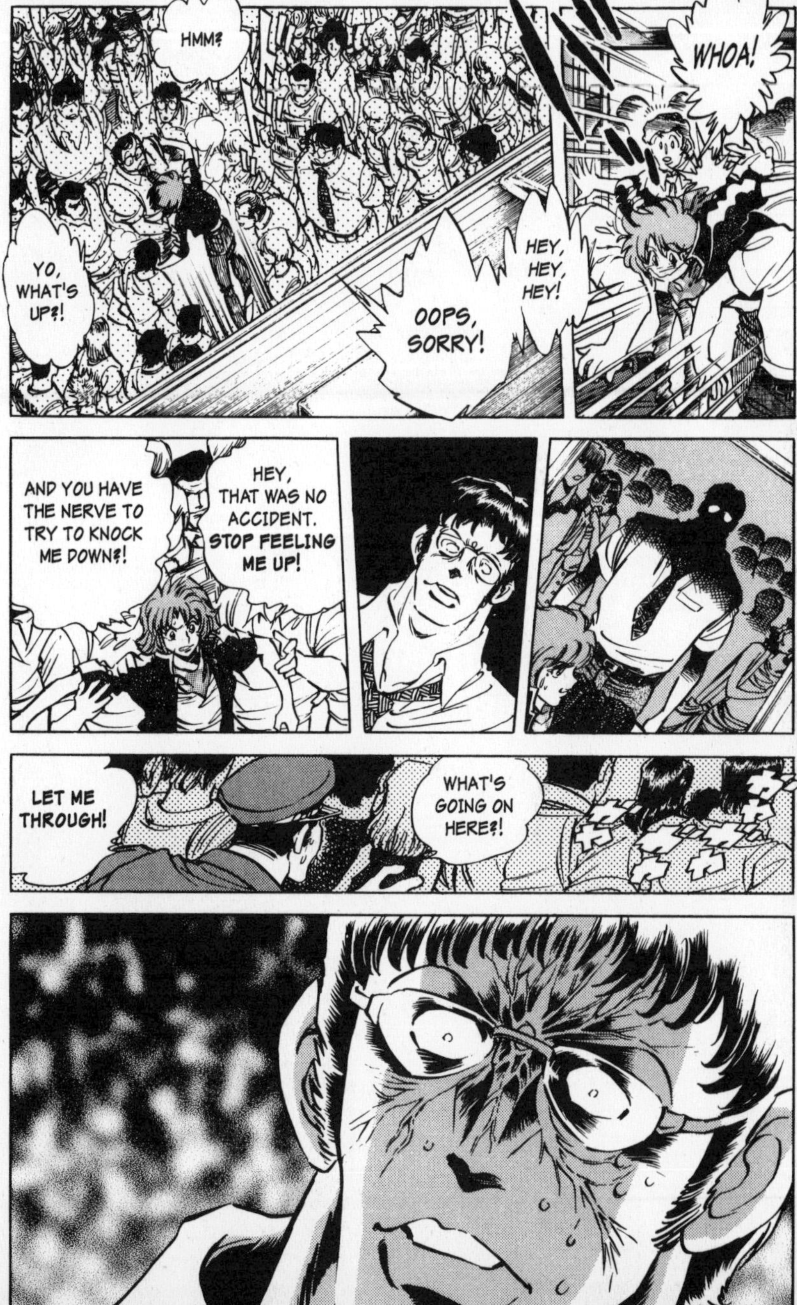
WHOA!
HEY, HEY, HEY!
OOPS, SORRY!
HMM?
YO, WHAT'S UP?!
HEY, THAT WAS NO ACCIDENT. STOP FEELING ME UP!
AND YOU HAVE THE NERVE TO TRY TO KNOCK ME DOWN?!
WHAT'S GOING ON HERE?!
LET ME THROUGH!

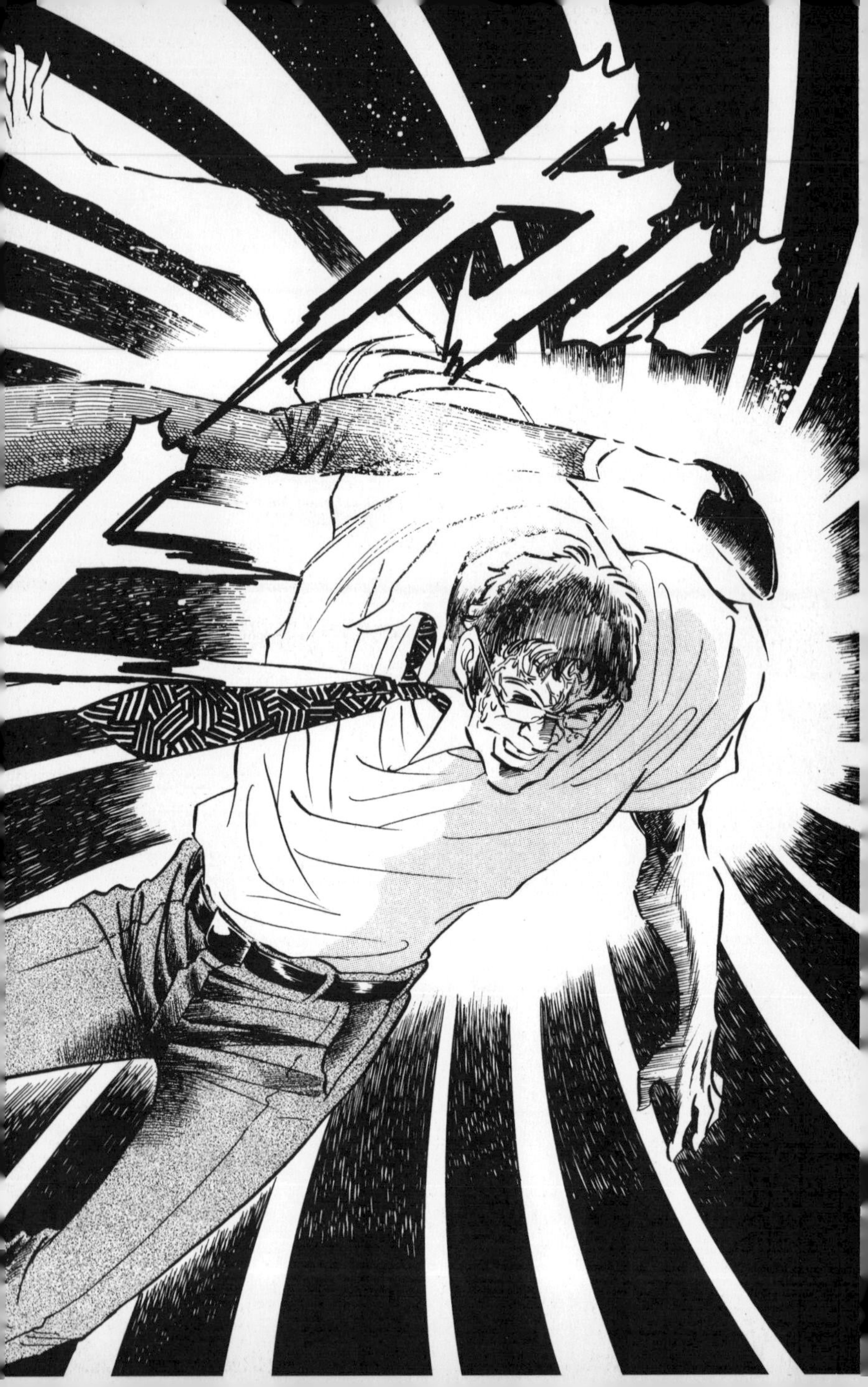

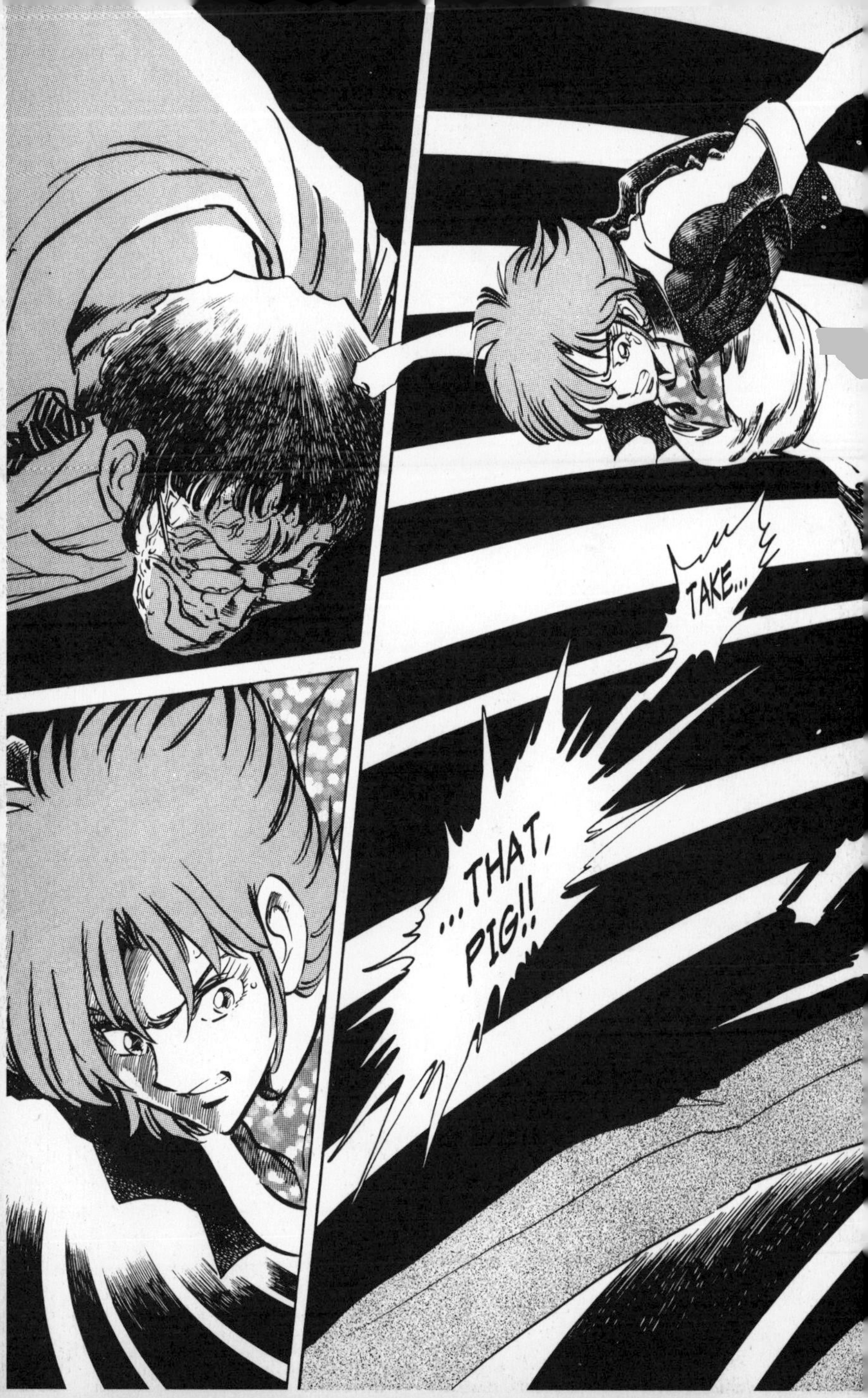
TAKE...
...THAT, PIG!!

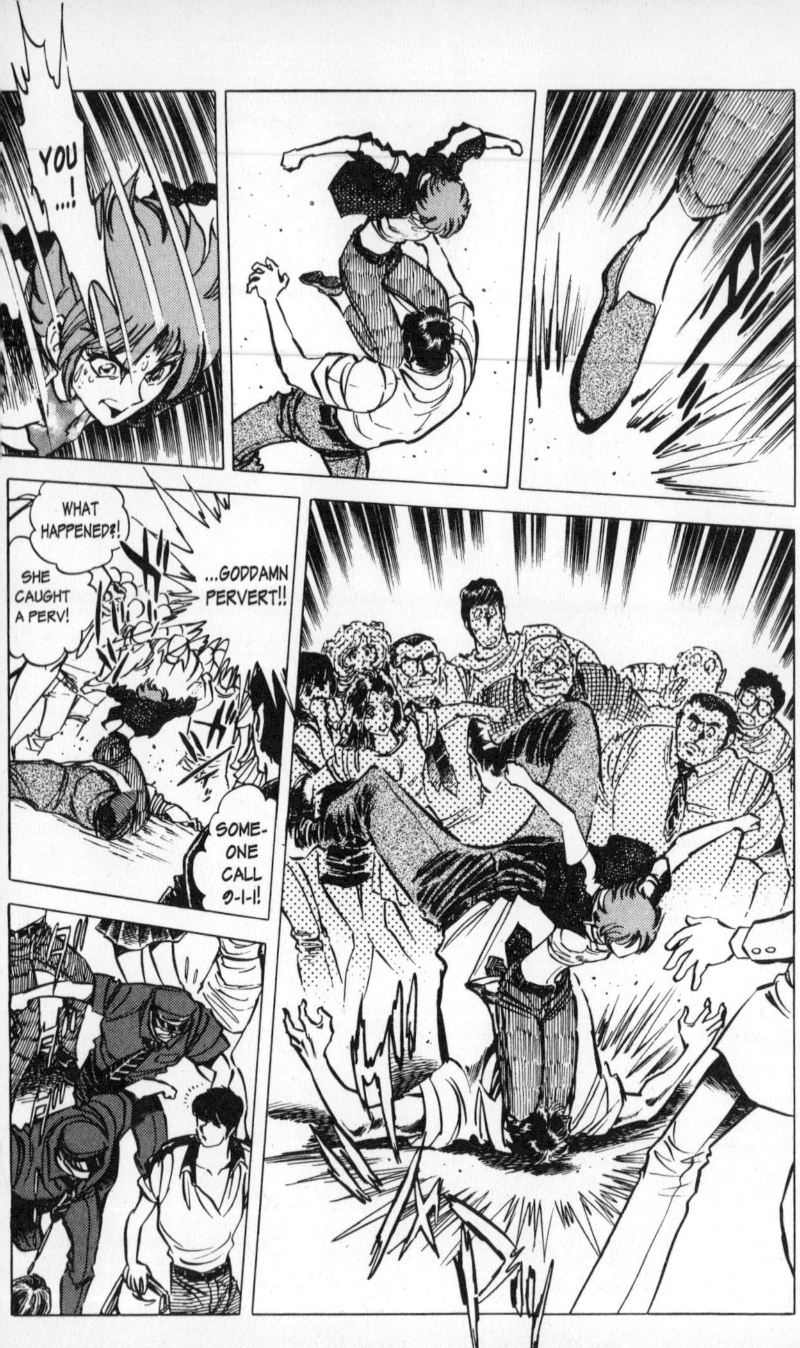
YOU ...!
...GODDAMN PERVERT!!
WHAT HAPPENED?!
SHE CAUGHT A PERV!
SOME-ONE CALL 9-1-1!

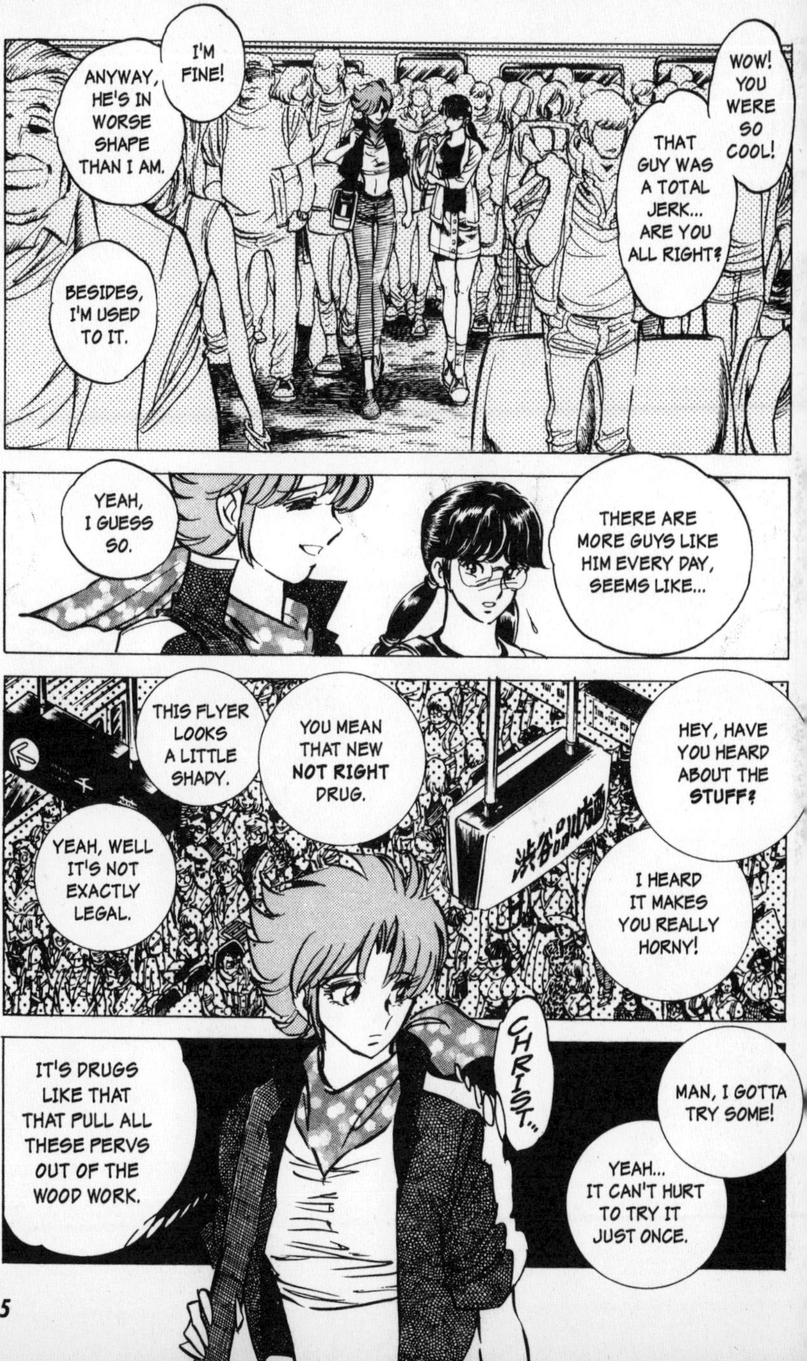
WOW! YOU WERE SO COOL!
THAT GUY WAS A TOTAL JERK... ARE YOU ALL RIGHT?
I'M FINE!
ANYWAY, HE'S IN WORSE SHAPE THAN I AM.
BESIDES, I'M USED TO IT.
THERE ARE MORE GUYS LIKE HIM EVERY DAY, SEEMS LIKE...
YEAH, I GUESS SO.
HEY, HAVE YOU HEARD ABOUT THE **STUFF**?
YOU MEAN THAT NEW **NOT RIGHT** DRUG.
I HEARD IT MAKES YOU REALLY HORNY!
THIS FLYER LOOKS A LITTLE SHADY.
YEAH, WELL IT'S NOT EXACTLY LEGAL.
MAN, I GOTTA TRY SOME!
YEAH... IT CAN'T HURT TO TRY IT JUST ONCE.
CHRIST...
IT'S DRUGS LIKE THAT THAT PULL ALL THESE PERVS OUT OF THE WOOD WORK.

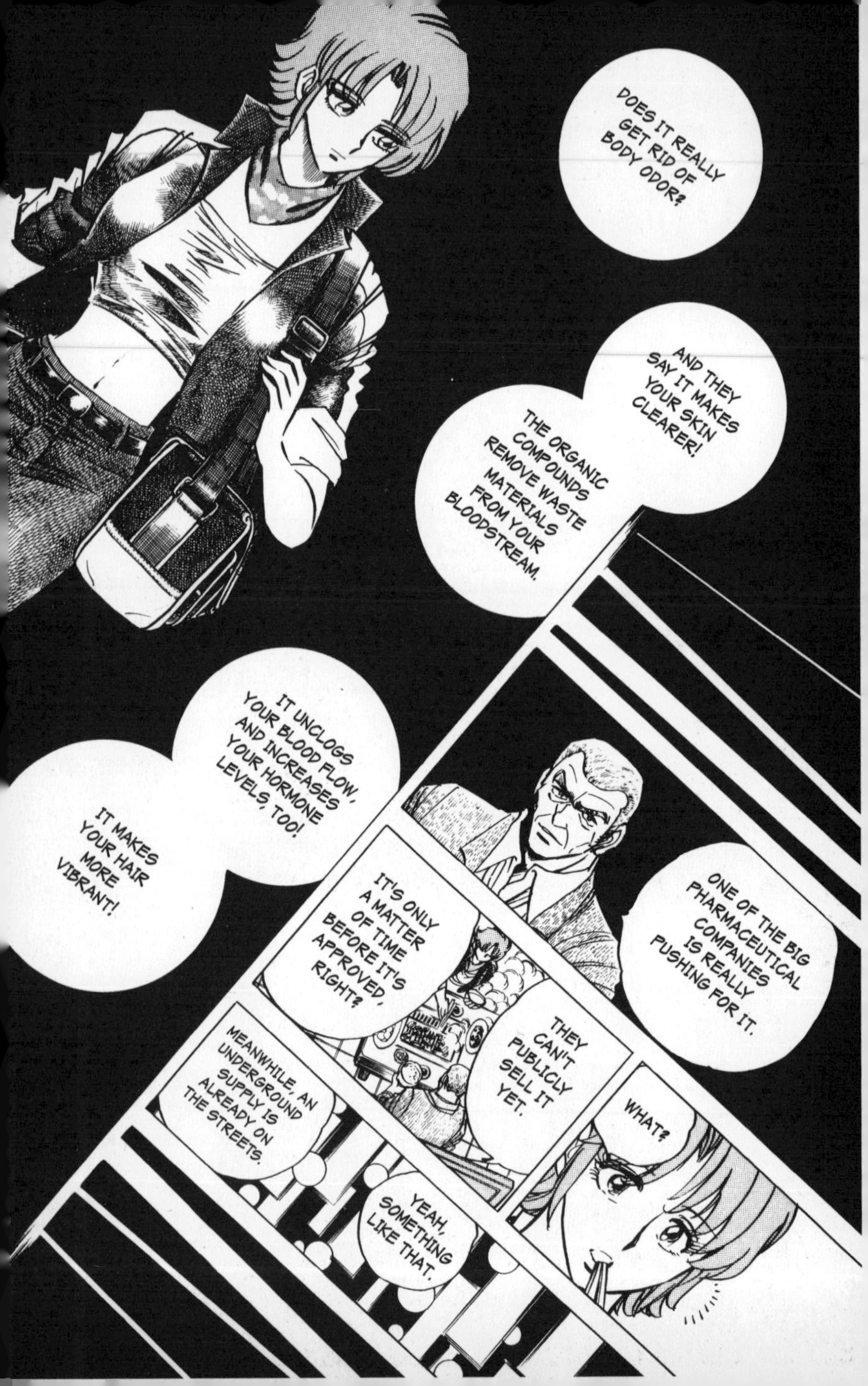
DOES IT REALLY GET RID OF BODY ODOR?
AND THEY SAY IT MAKES YOUR SKIN CLEARER!
THE ORGANIC COMPOUNDS REMOVE WASTE MATERIALS FROM YOUR BLOODSTREAM.
IT UNCLOGS YOUR BLOOD FLOW, AND INCREASES YOUR HORMONE LEVELS, TOO!
IT MAKES YOUR HAIR MORE VIBRANT!
ONE OF THE BIG PHARMACEUTICAL COMPANIES IS REALLY PUSHING FOR IT.
IT'S ONLY A MATTER OF TIME BEFORE IT'S APPROVED, RIGHT?
THEY CAN'T PUBLICLY SELL IT YET.
MEANWHILE, AN UNDERGROUND SUPPLY IS ALREADY ON THE STREETS.
WHAT?
YEAH, SOMETHING LIKE THAT.

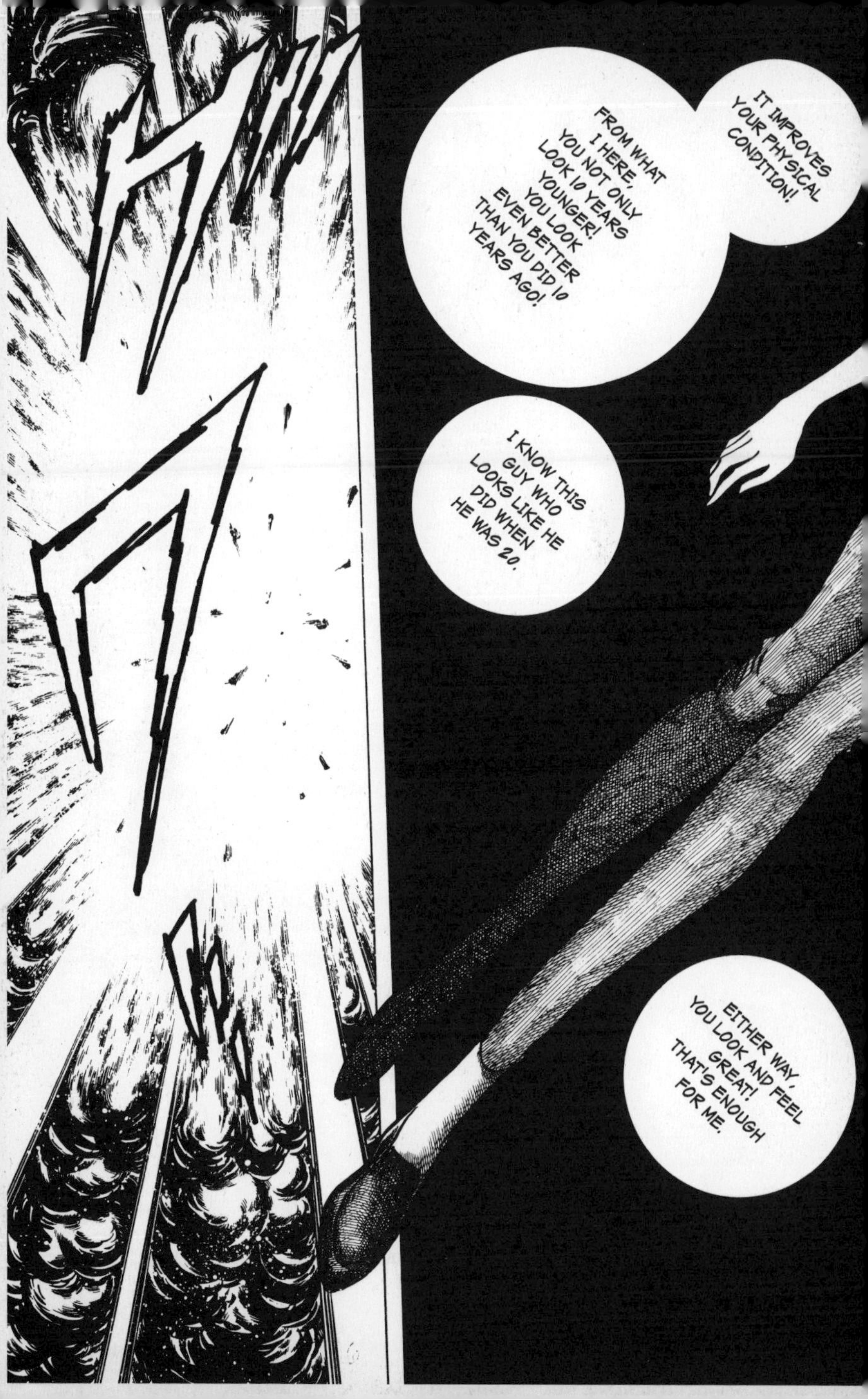
IT IMPROVES YOUR PHYSICAL CONDITION!
FROM WHAT I HERE, YOU NOT ONLY LOOK 10 YEARS YOUNGER! YOU LOOK EVEN BETTER THAN YOU DID 10 YEARS AGO!
I KNOW THIS GUY WHO LOOKS LIKE HE DID WHEN HE WAS 20.
EITHER WAY, YOU LOOK AND FEEL GREAT! THAT'S ENOUGH FOR ME.

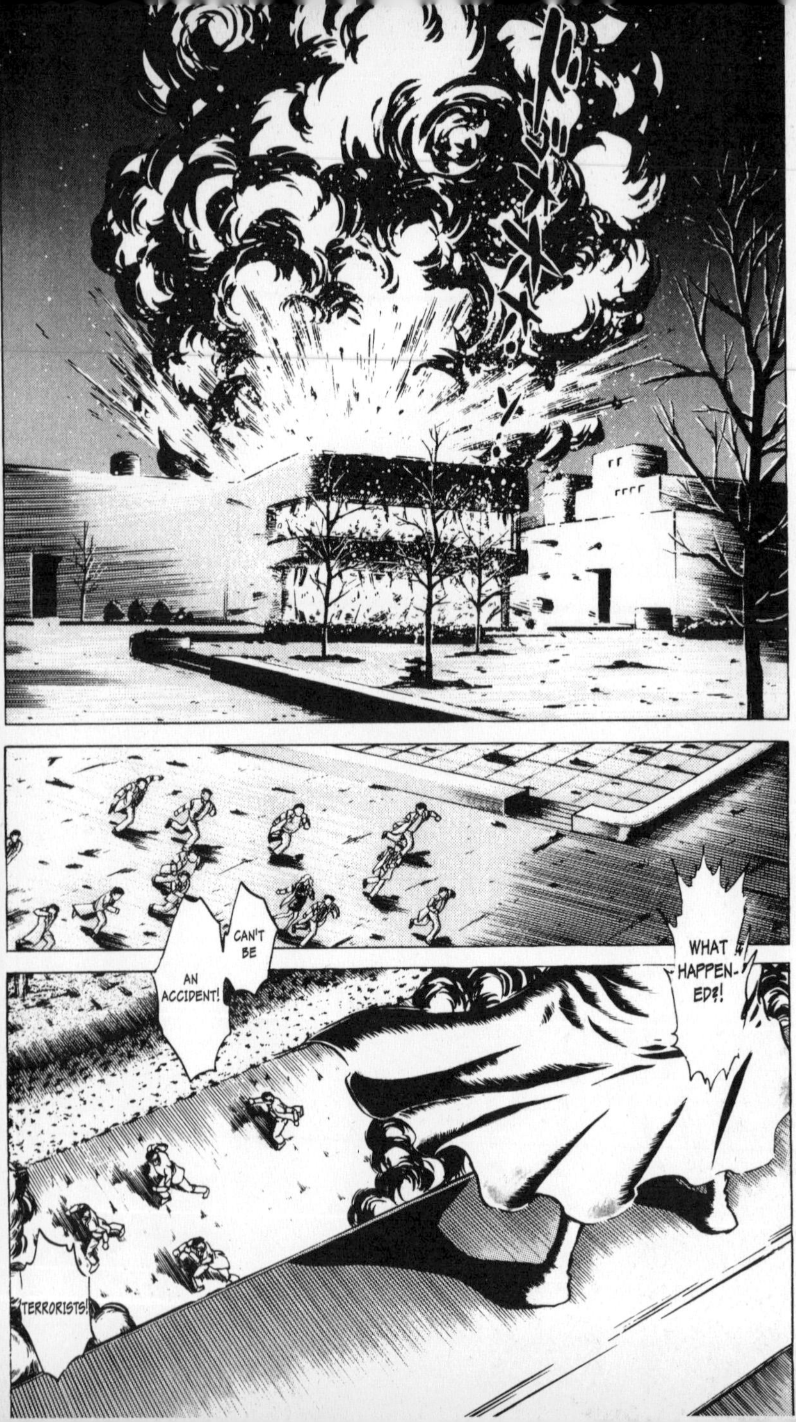
WHAT HAPPEN-ED?!
CAN'T BE AN ACCIDENT!
TERRORISTS!

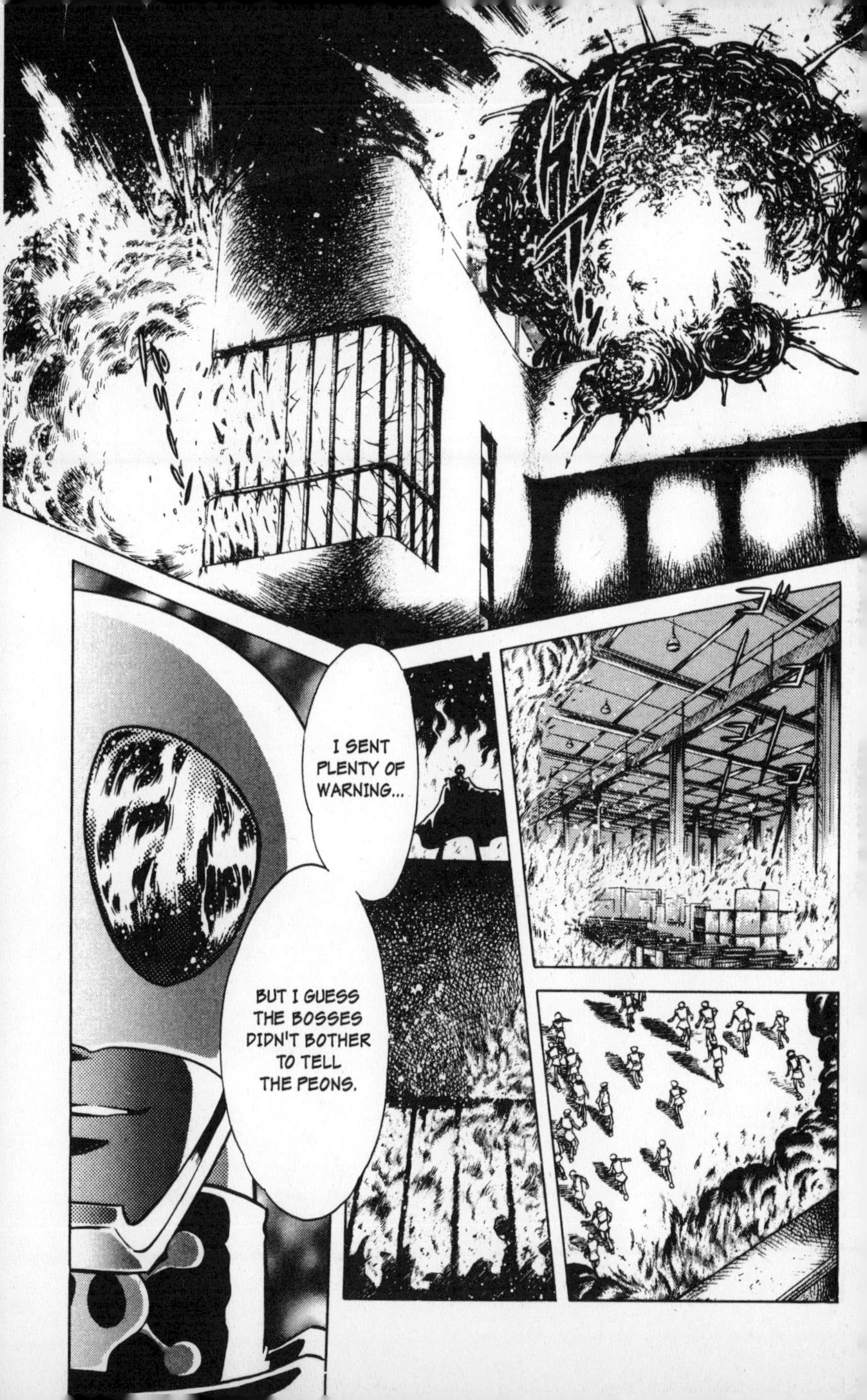
I SENT PLENTY OF WARNING...
BUT I GUESS THE BOSSES DIDN'T BOTHER TO TELL THE PEONS.

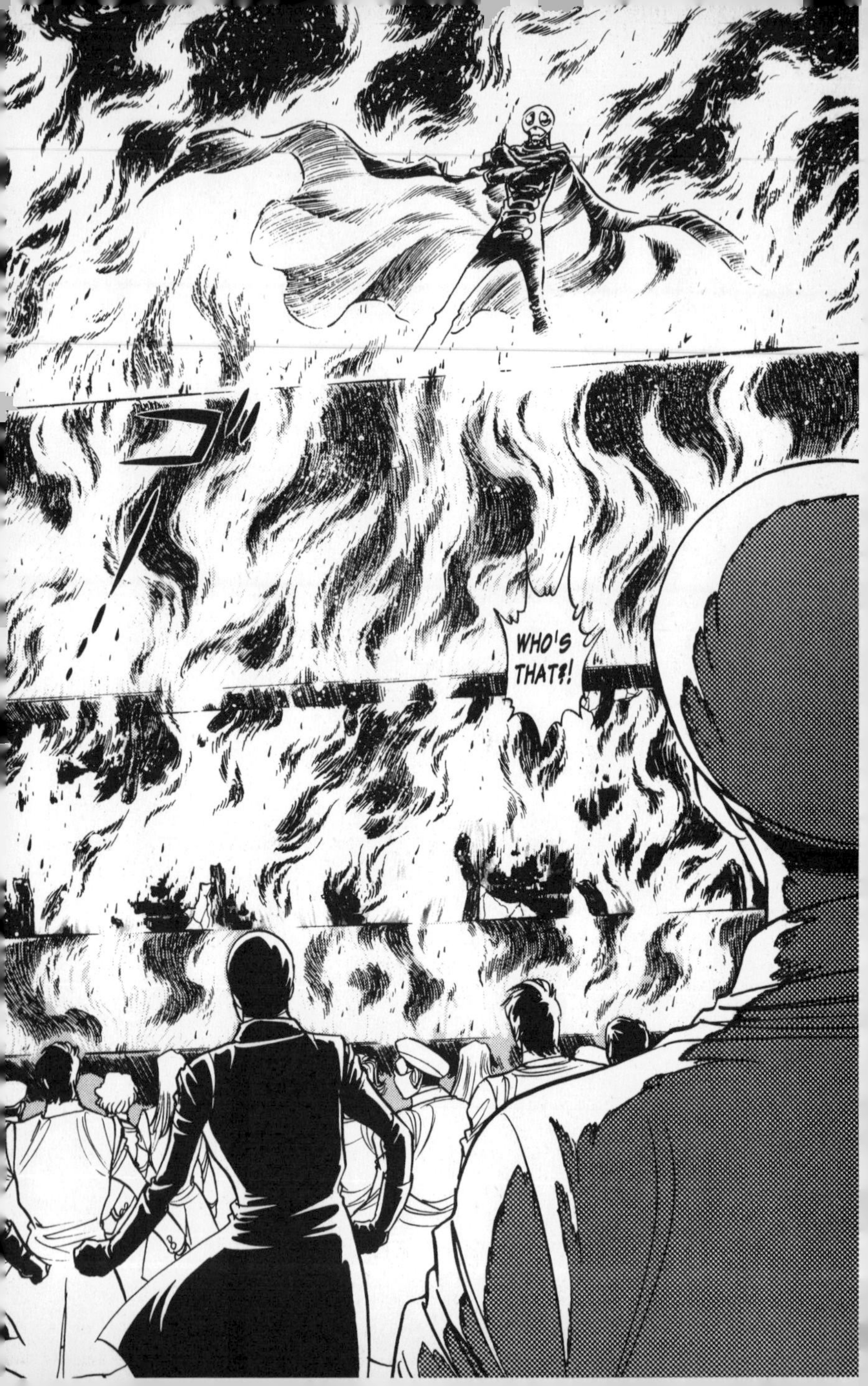
WHO'S THAT?!

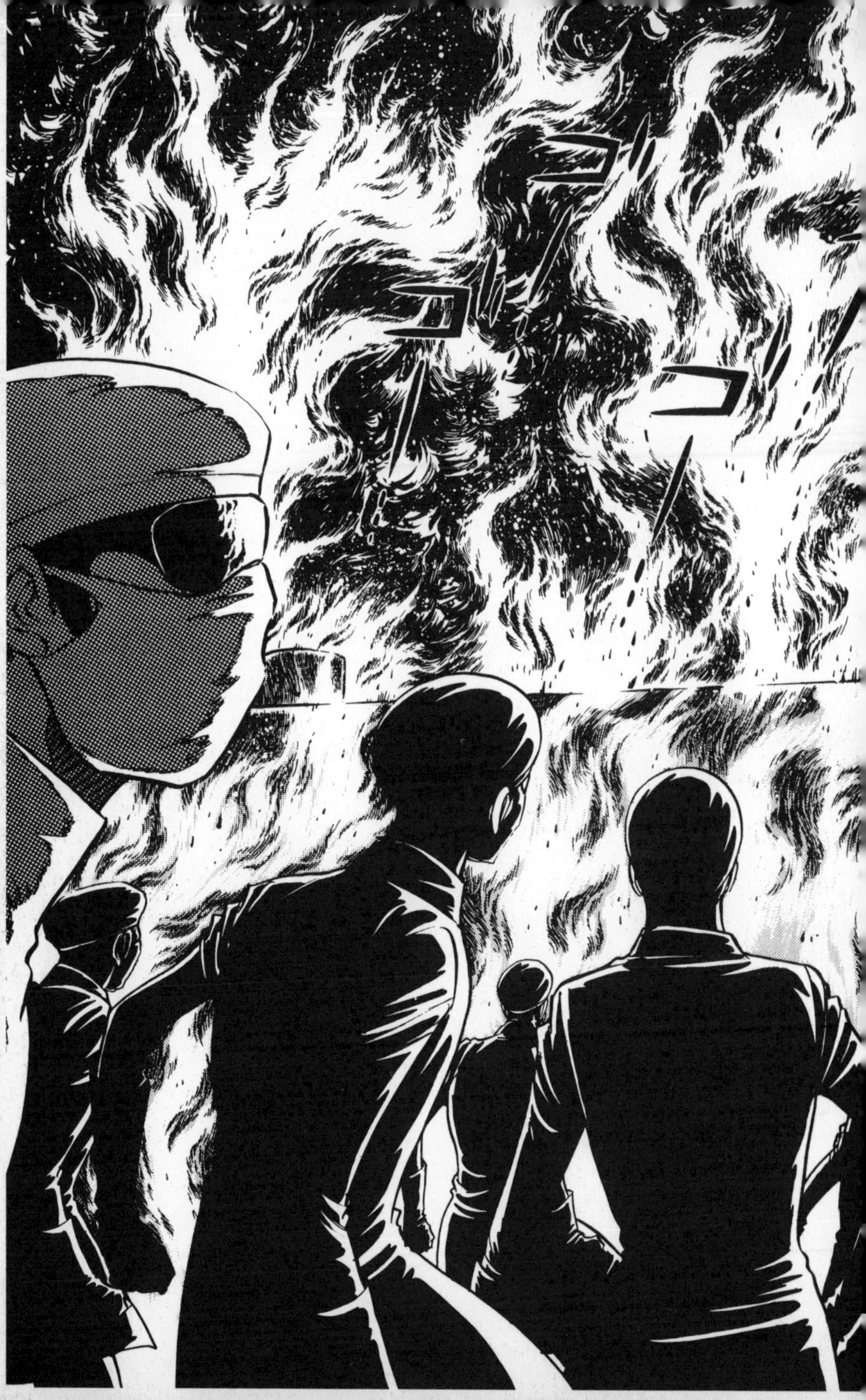
ゴゴゴ

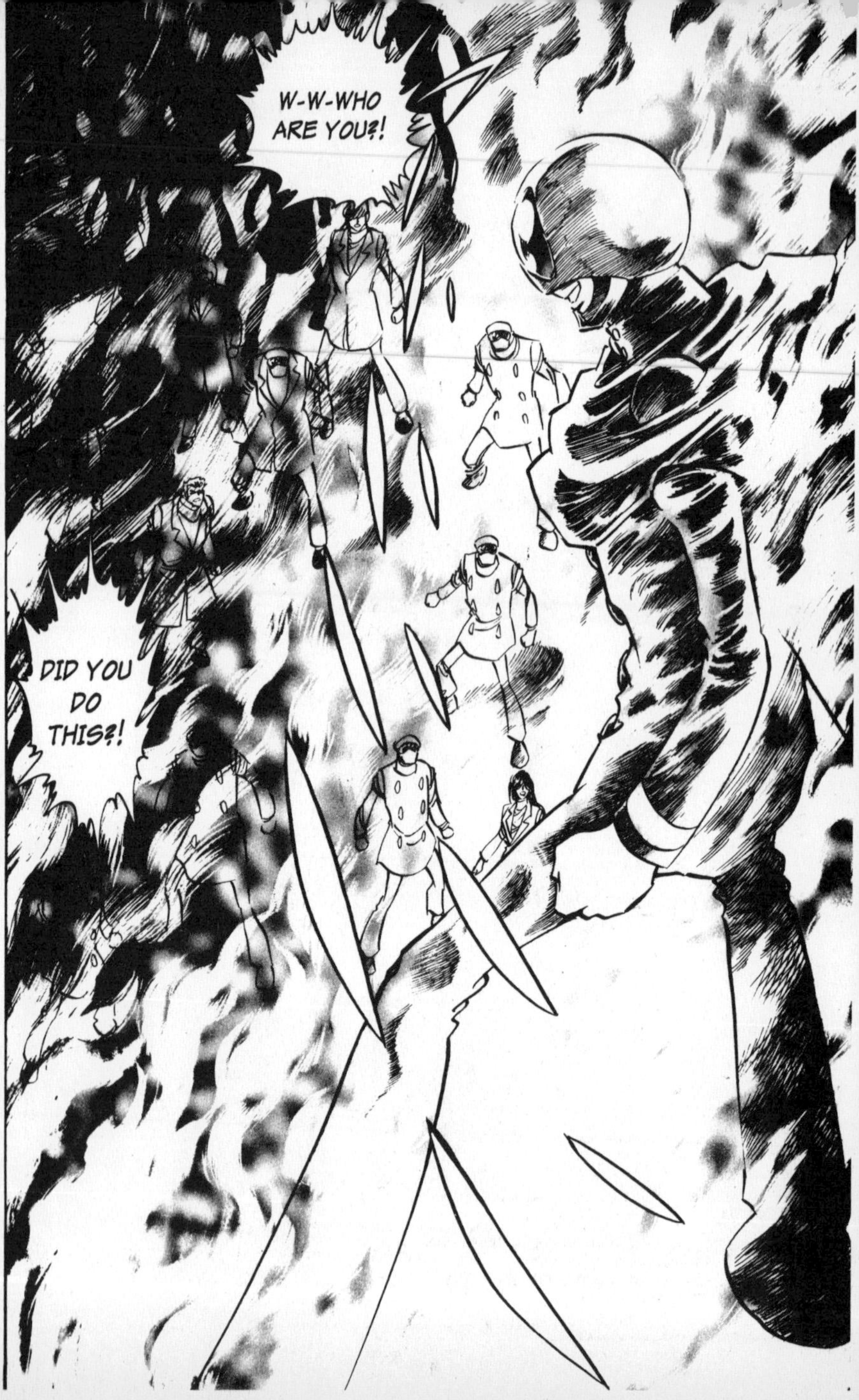
W-W-WHO ARE YOU?!
DID YOU DO THIS?!

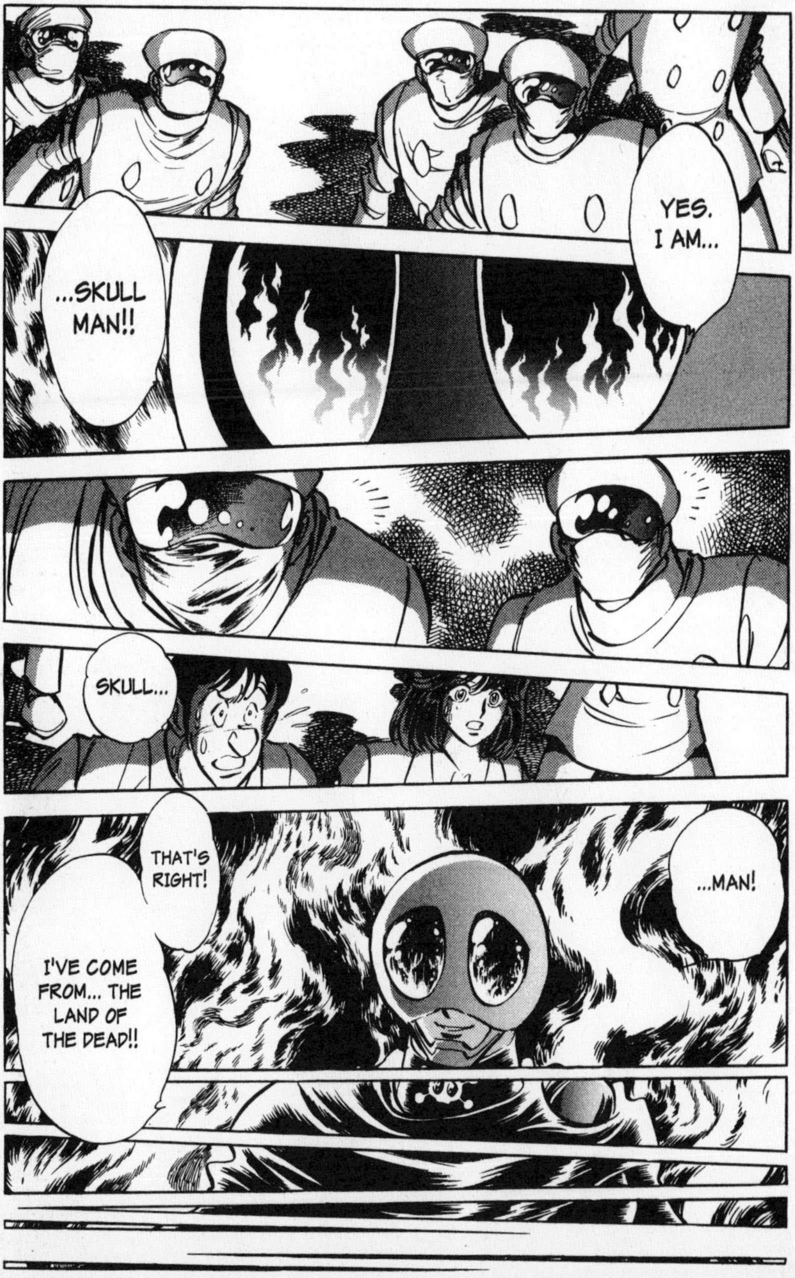
YES. I AM...
...SKULL MAN!!
SKULL...
...MAN!
THAT'S RIGHT!
I'VE COME FROM... THE LAND OF THE DEAD!!

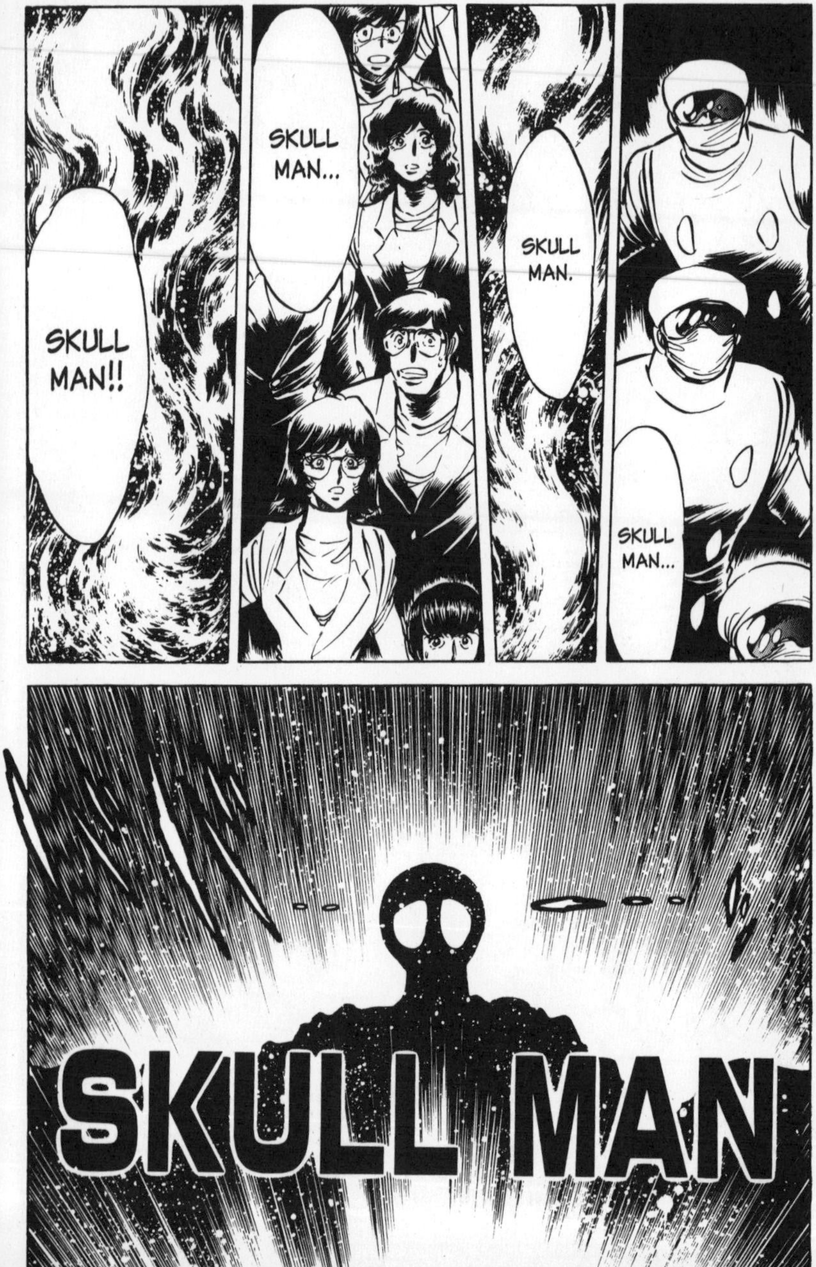
SKULL MAN...
SKULL MAN.
SKULL MAN...
SKULL MAN!!
SKULL MAN

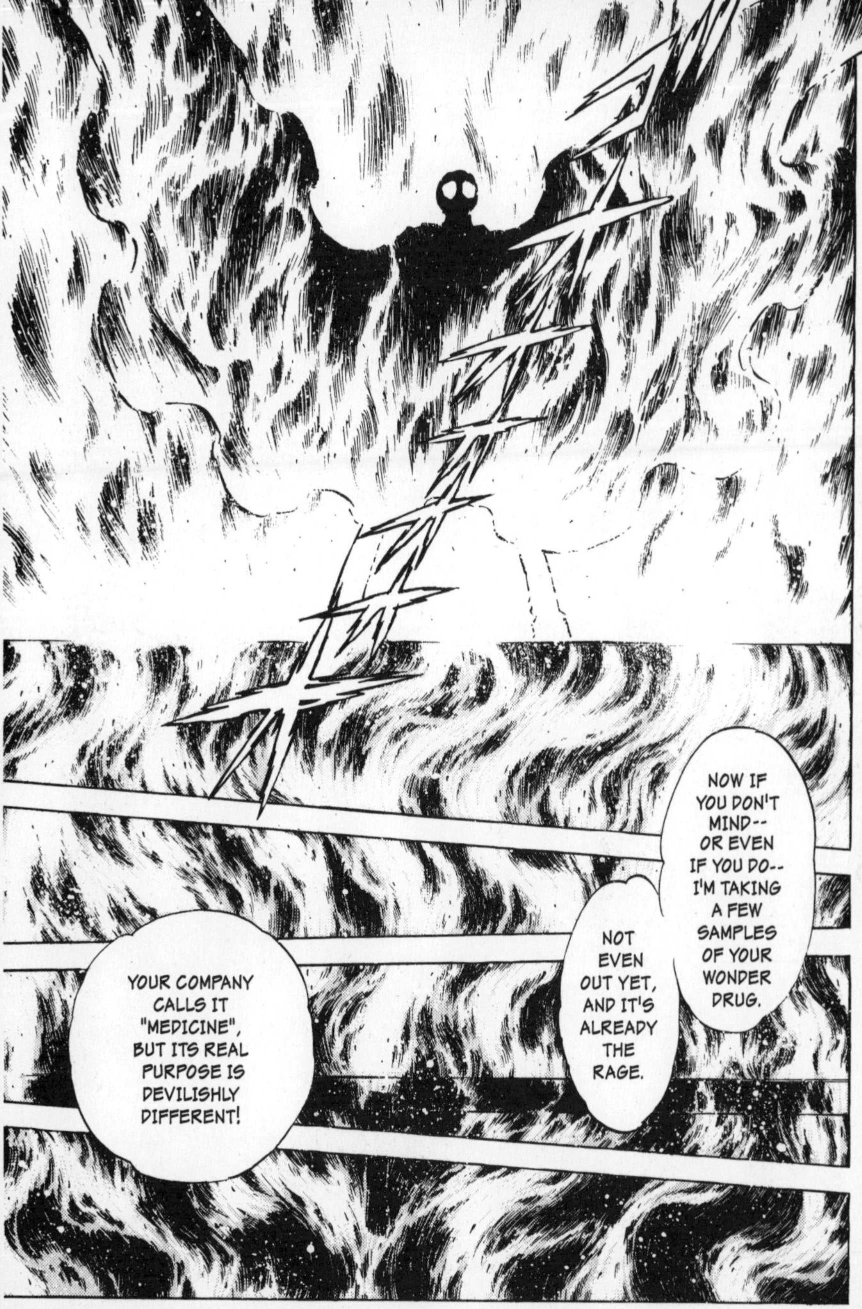
NOW IF YOU DON'T MIND-- OR EVEN IF YOU DO-- I'M TAKING A FEW SAMPLES OF YOUR WONDER DRUG.
NOT EVEN OUT YET, AND IT'S ALREADY THE RAGE.
YOUR COMPANY CALLS IT "MEDICINE", BUT ITS REAL PURPOSE IS DEVILISHLY DIFFERENT!

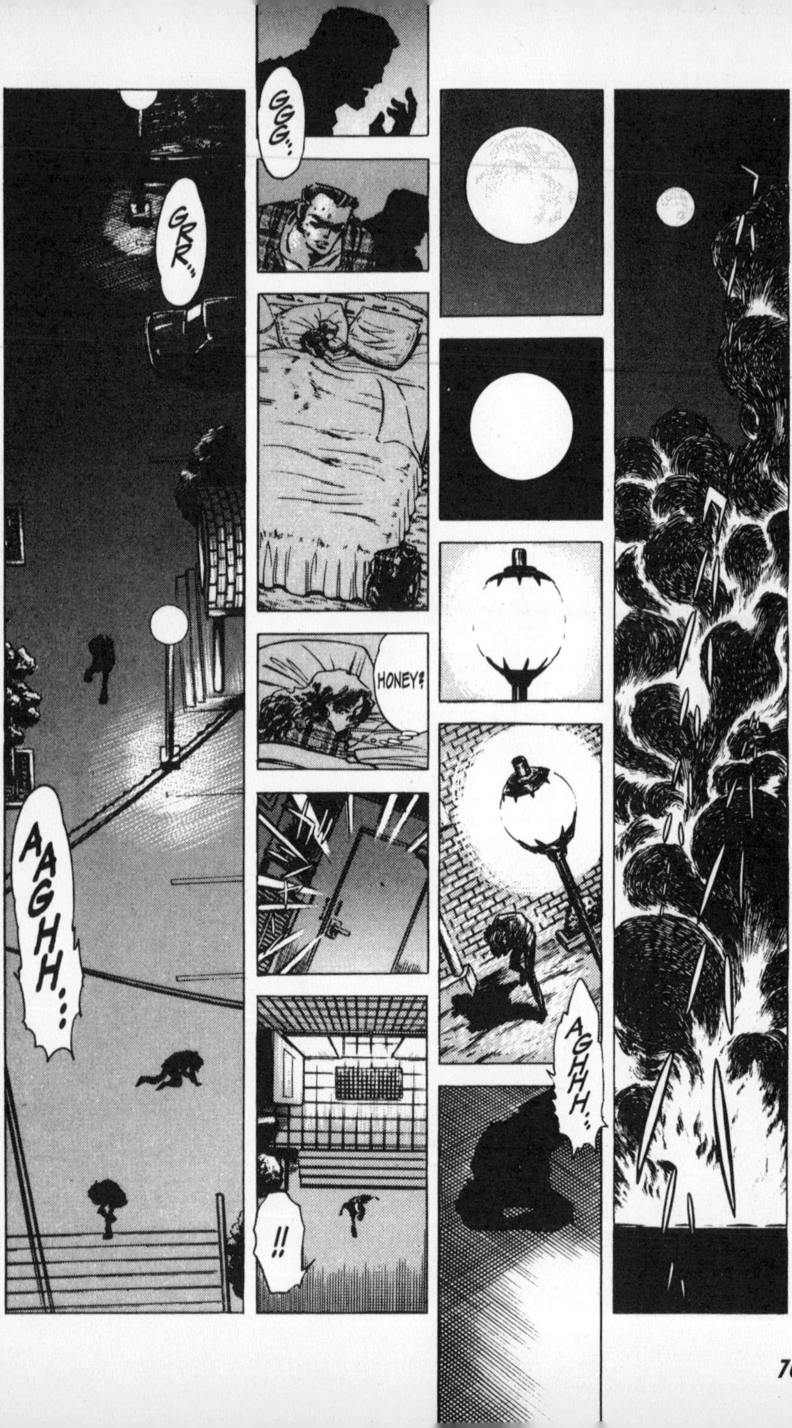
AGHHH..
GGG..
HONEY?
!!
GRR..
AAGHH...

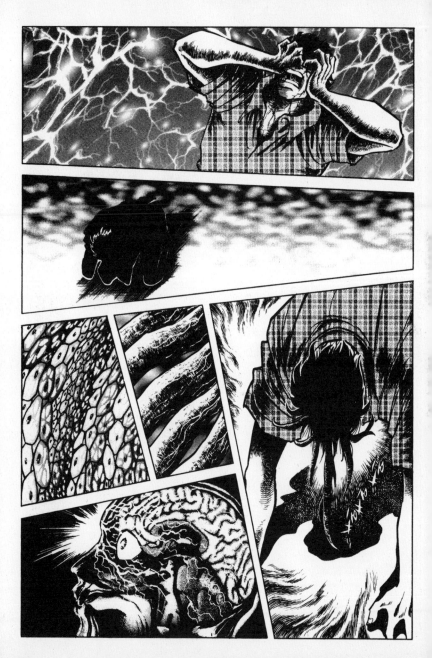

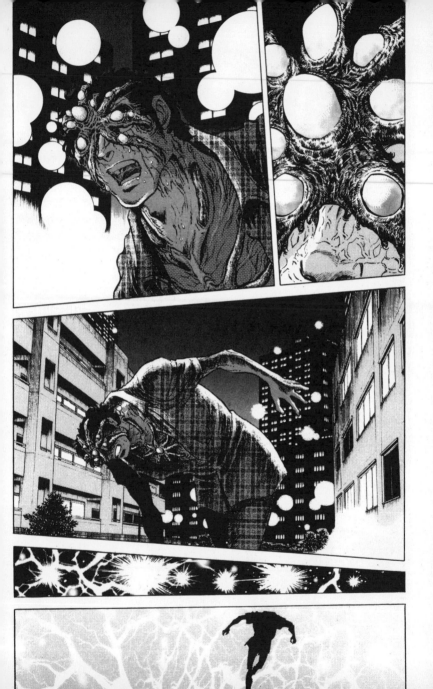

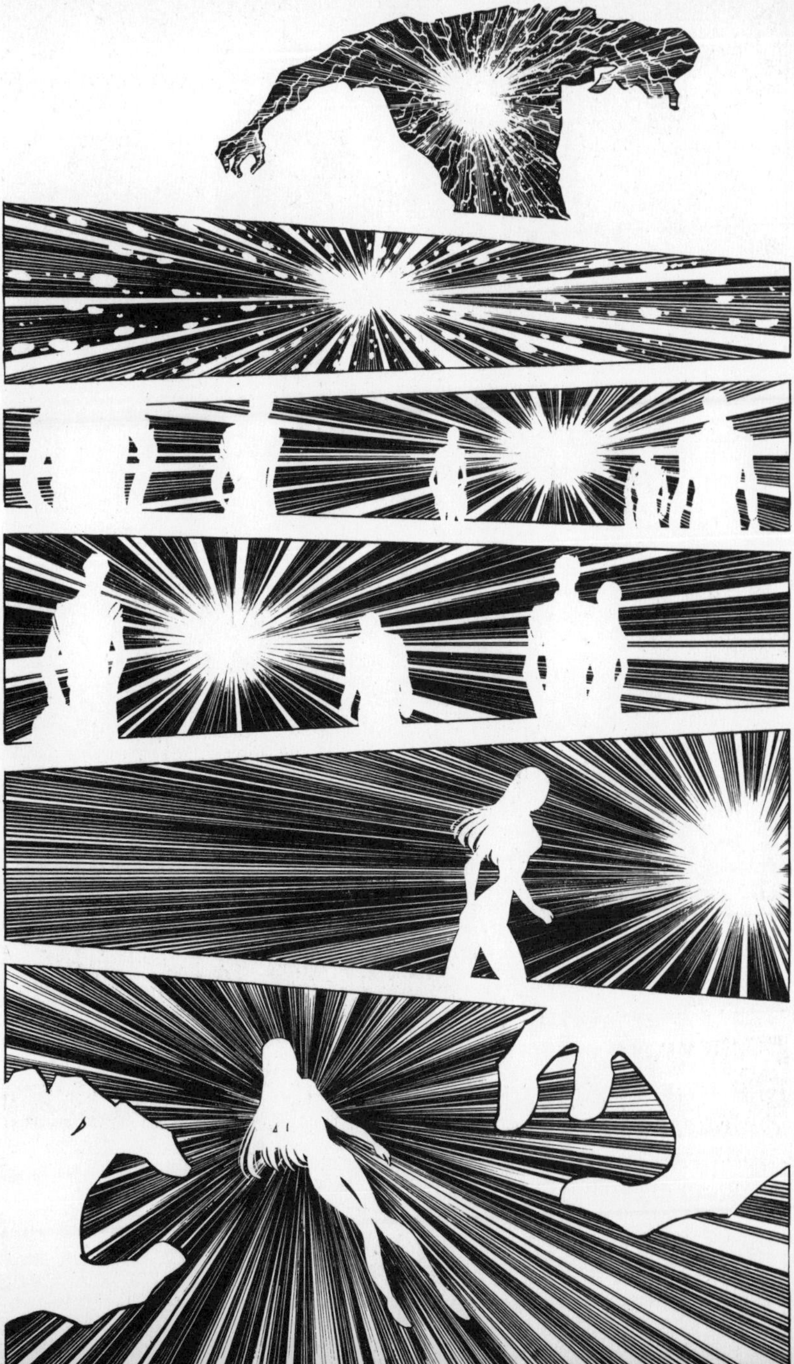

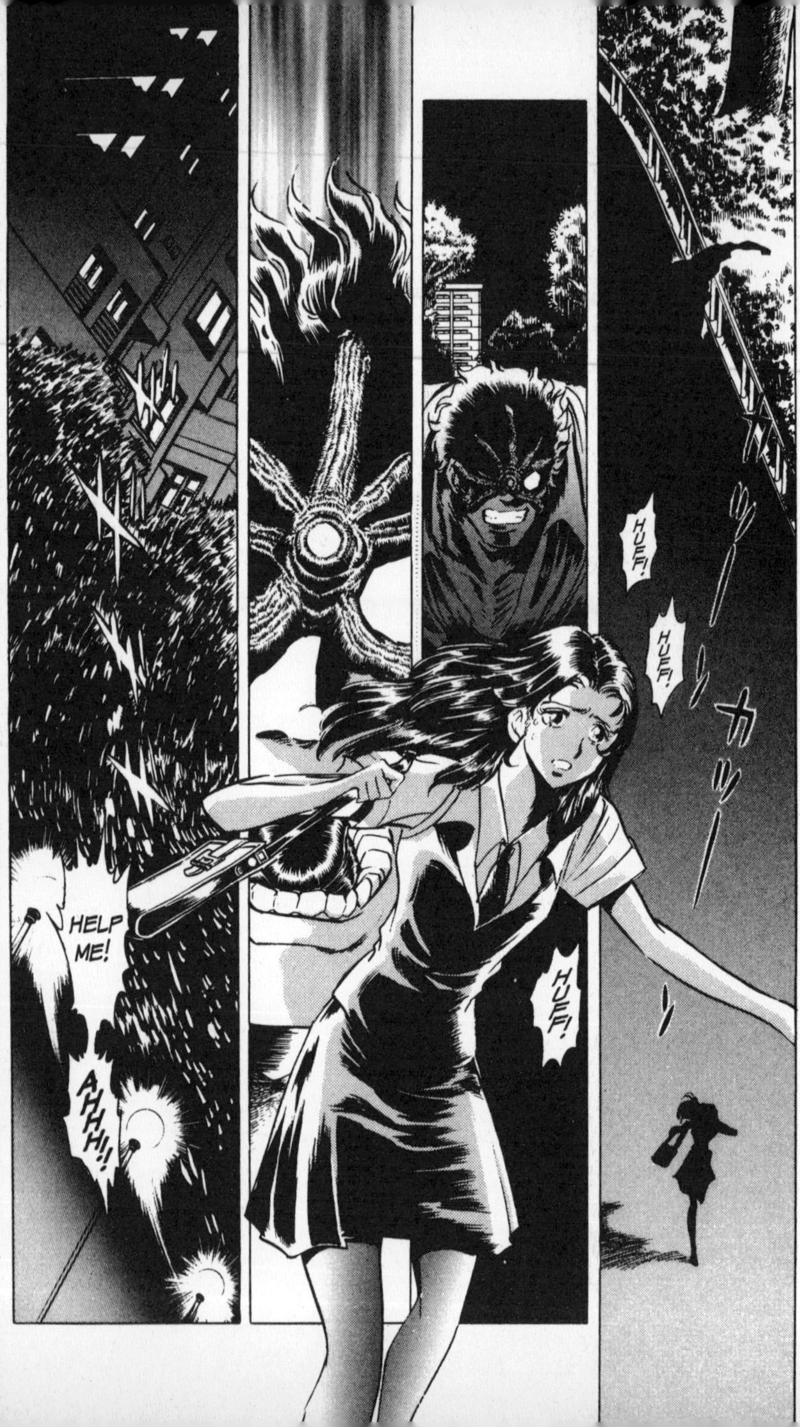
HUFF!
HUFF!
HUFF!
HELP ME!
AHHH!!

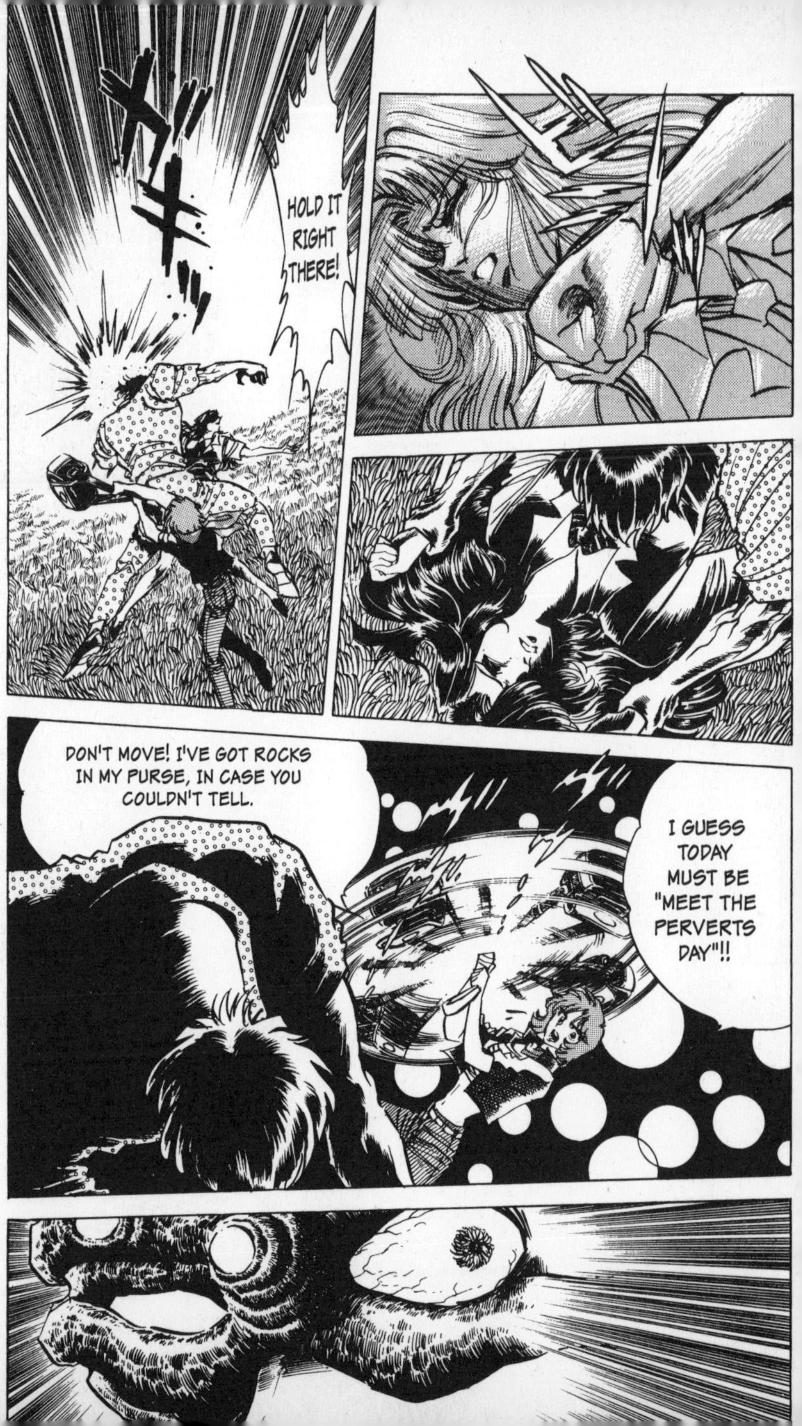
HOLD IT RIGHT THERE!
DON'T MOVE! I'VE GOT ROCKS IN MY PURSE, IN CASE YOU COULDN'T TELL.
I GUESS TODAY MUST BE "MEET THE PERVERTS DAY"!!

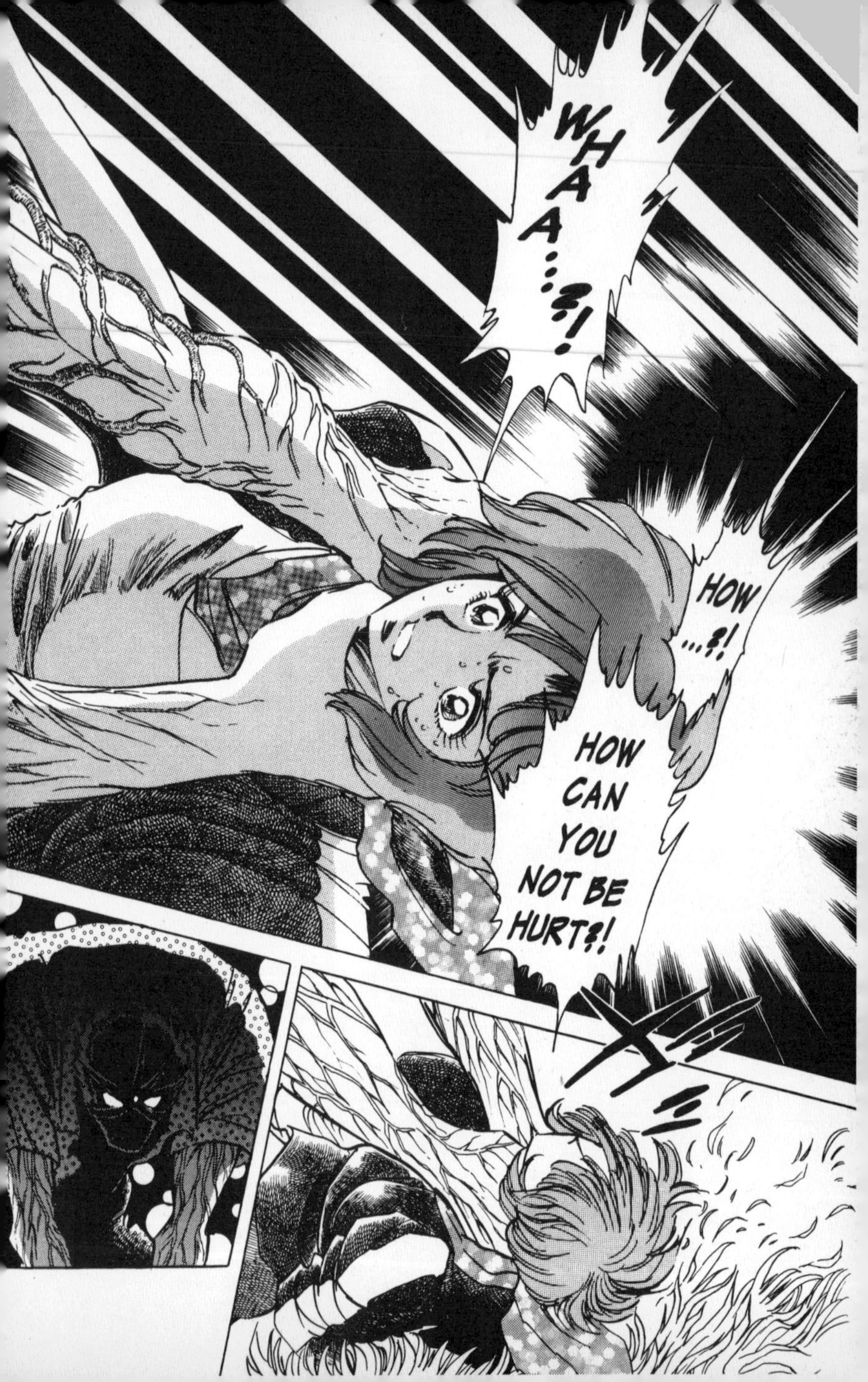
WHAA...?!
HOW...?!
HOW CAN YOU NOT BE HURT?!

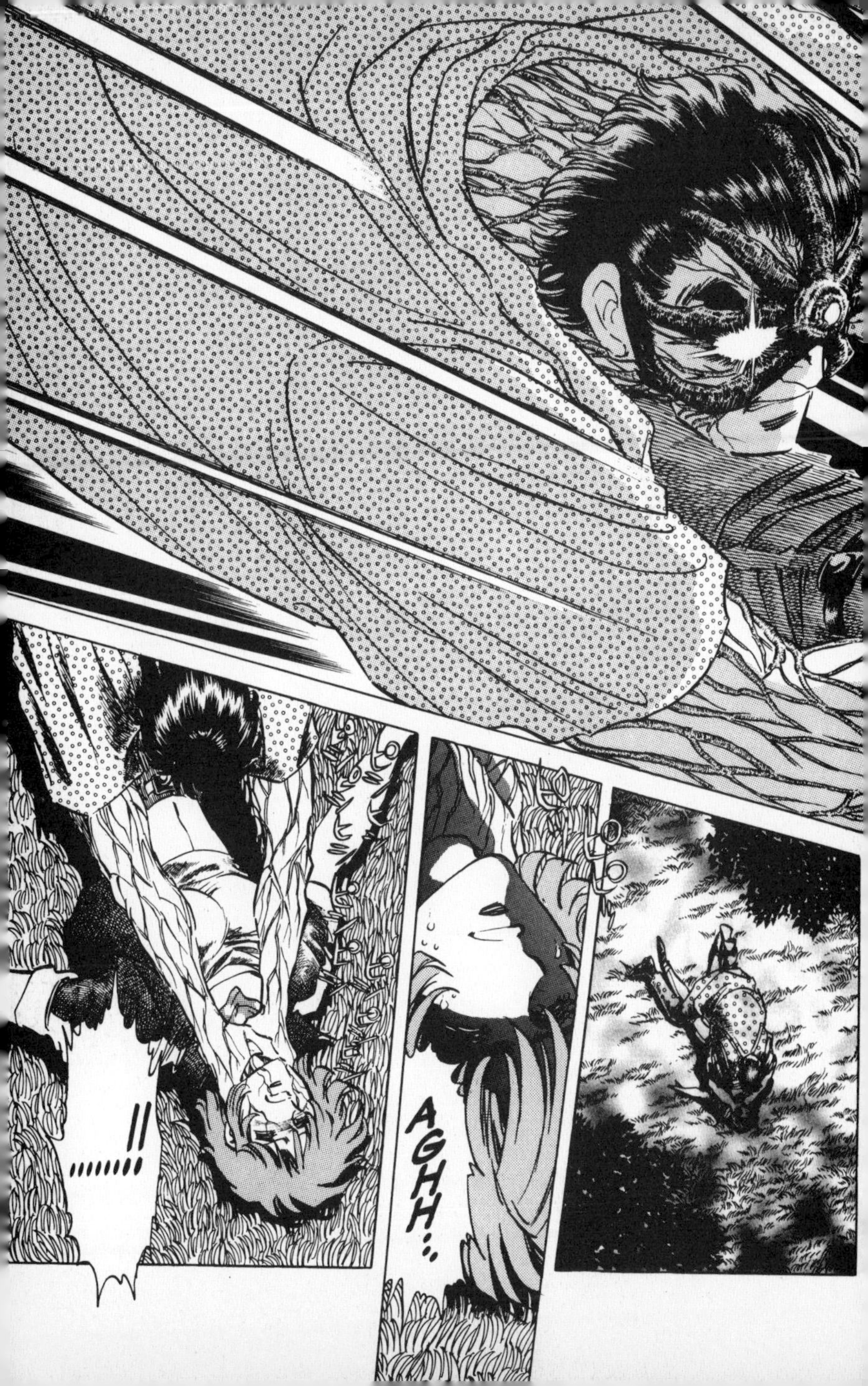
AGHH...
......!!

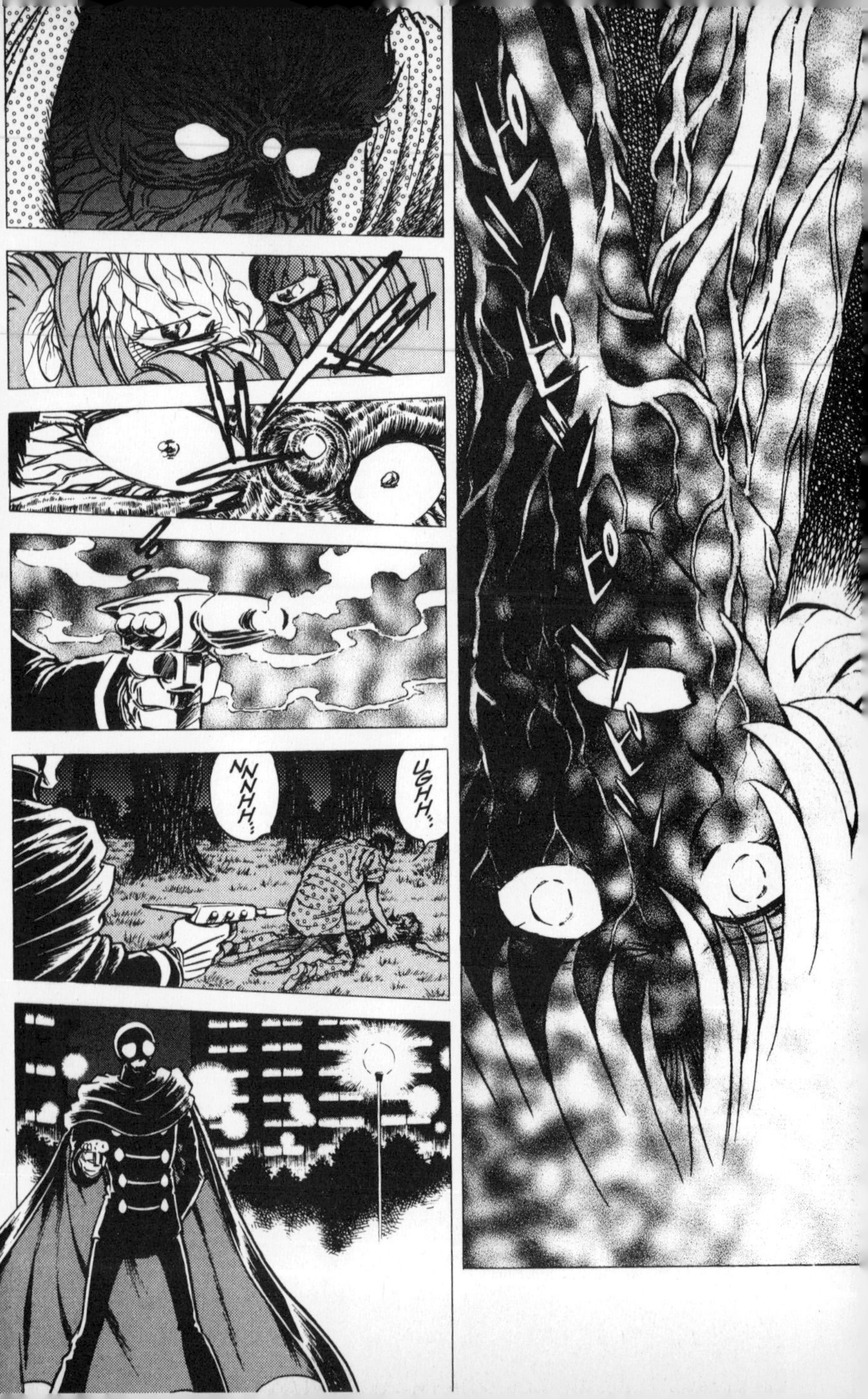
UGHH...
NNNHH...

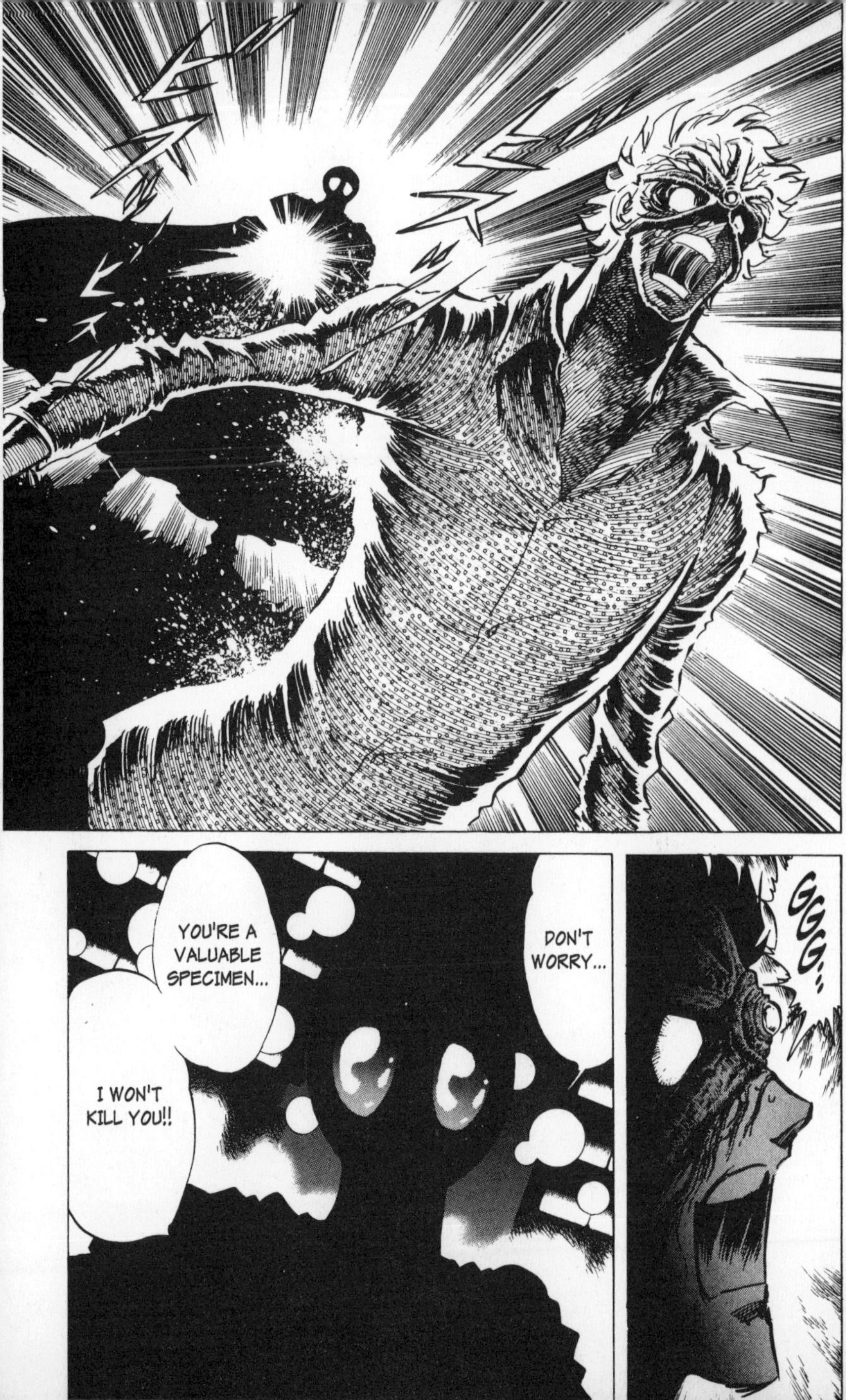
GGG..
DON'T WORRY...
YOU'RE A VALUABLE SPECIMEN...
I WON'T KILL YOU!!

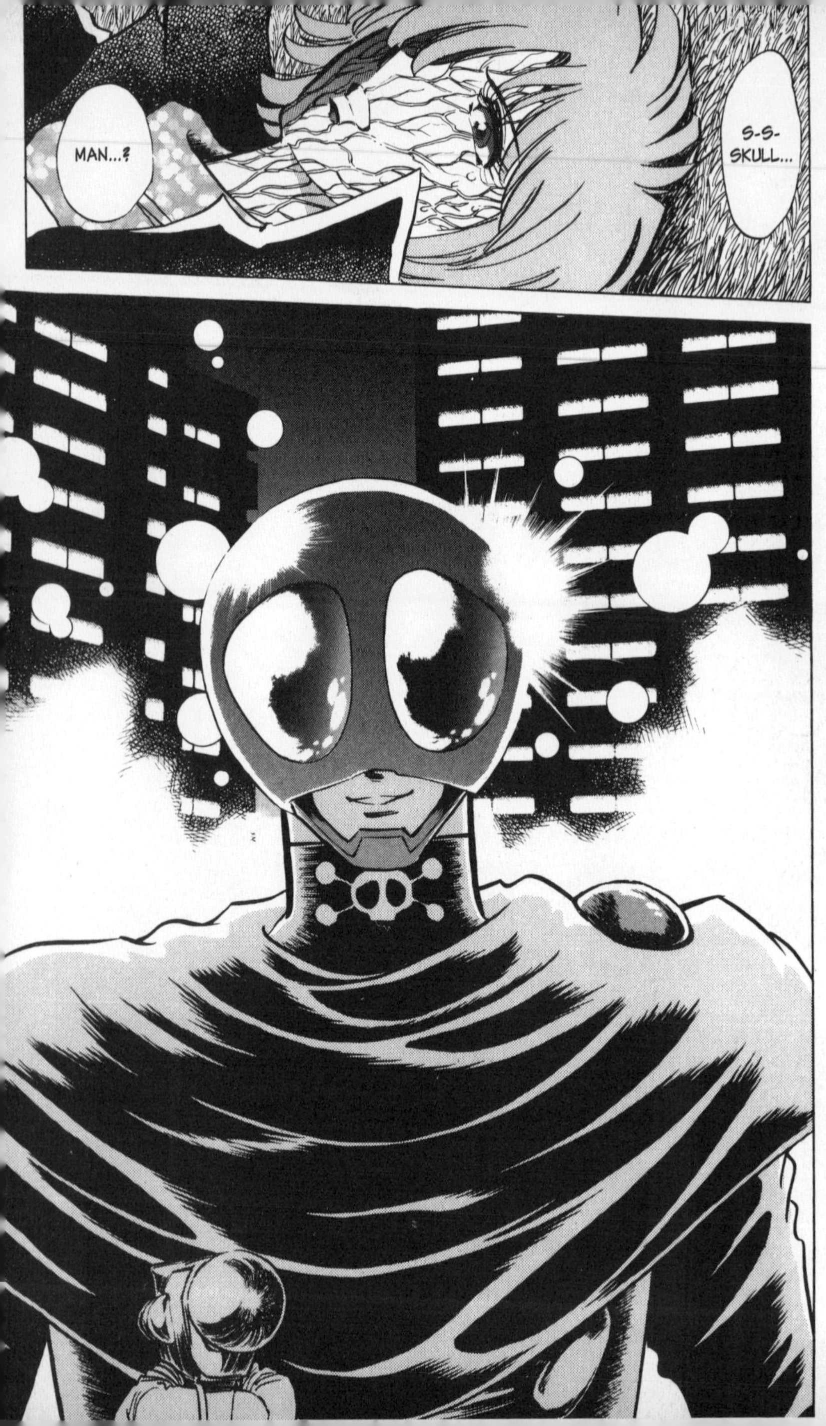
S-S-SKULL...
MAN...?

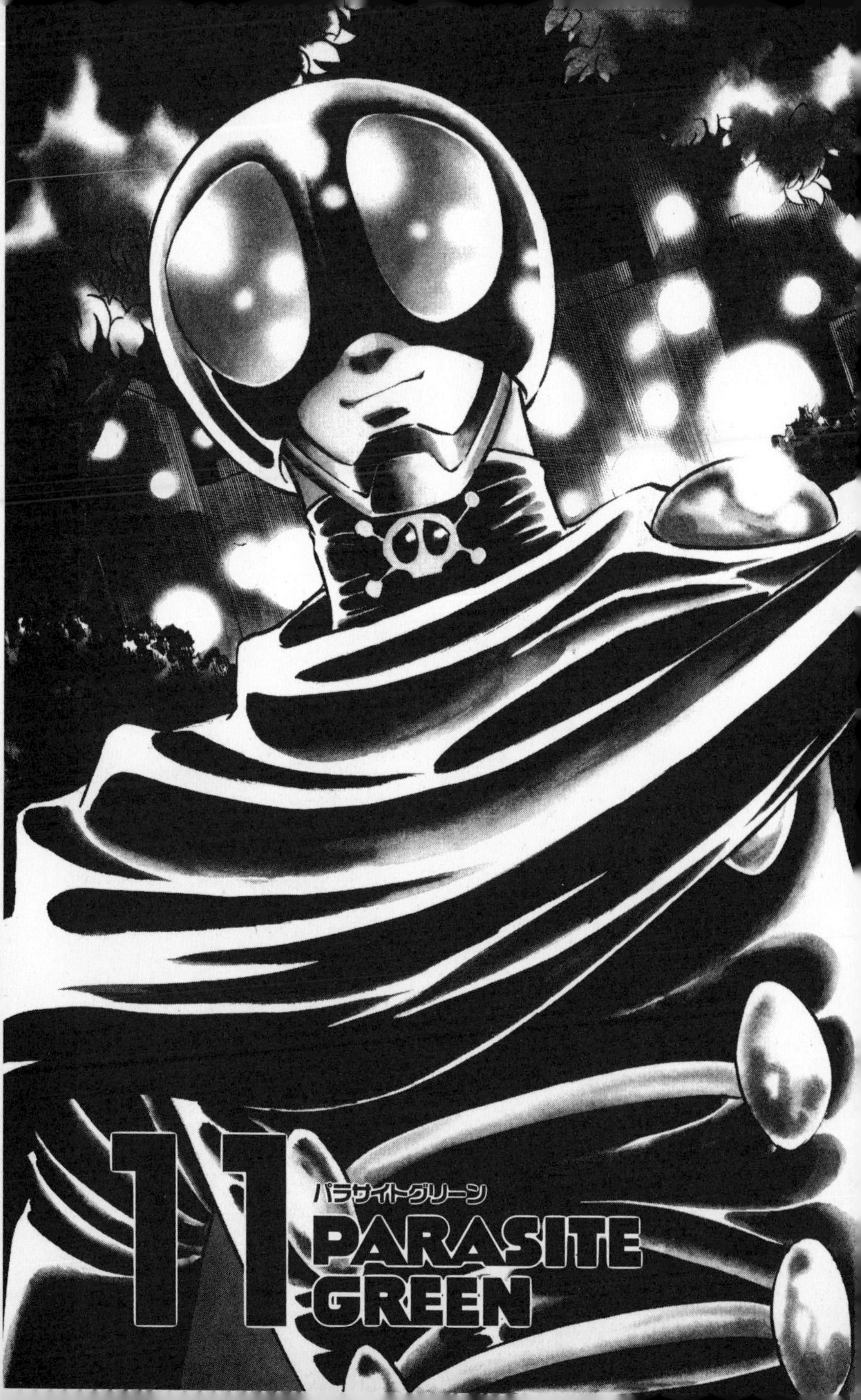
11
パラサイトグリーン
PARASITE GREEN

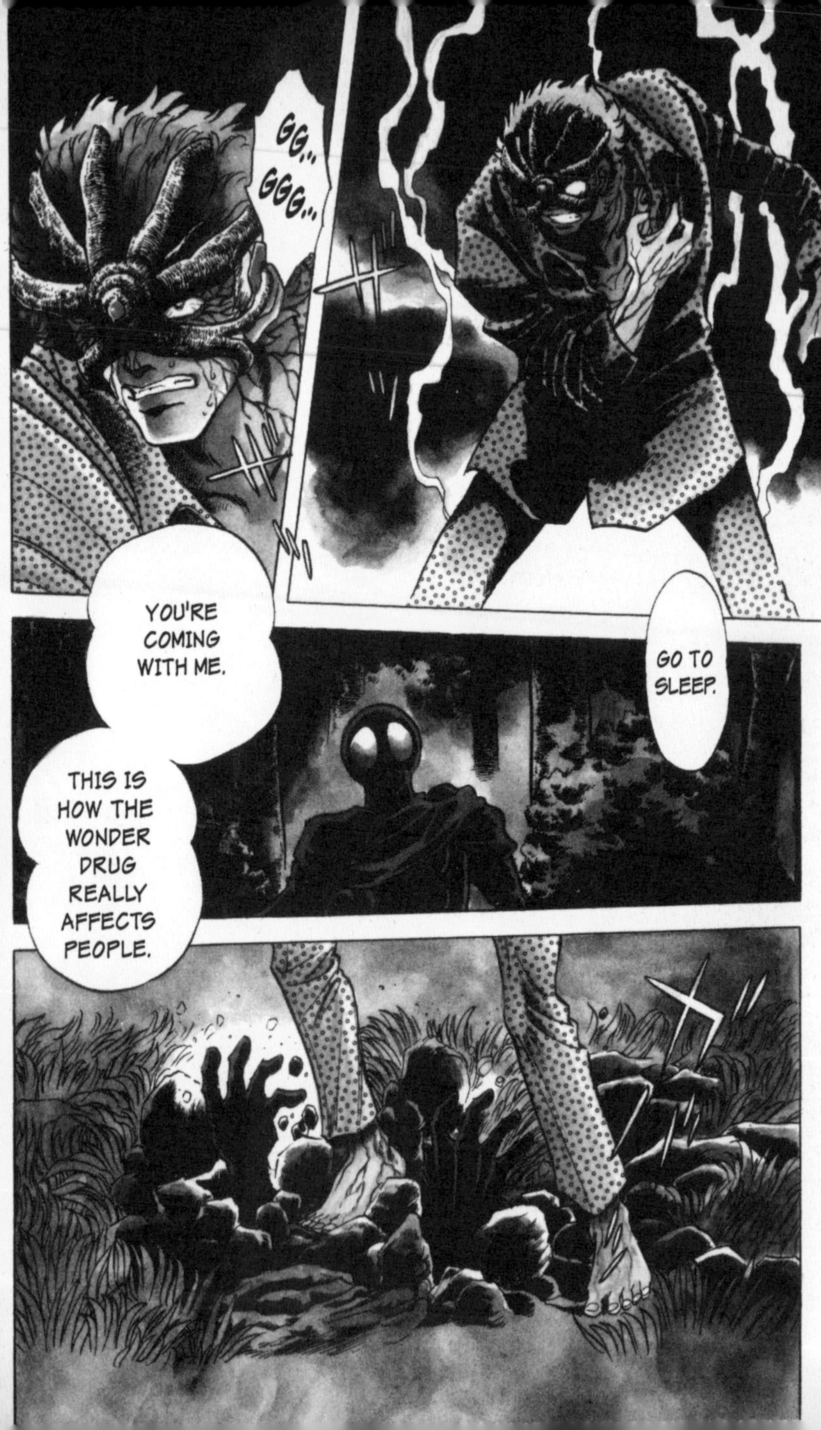
GG... GGG...
GO TO SLEEP.
YOU'RE COMING WITH ME.
THIS IS HOW THE WONDER DRUG REALLY AFFECTS PEOPLE.

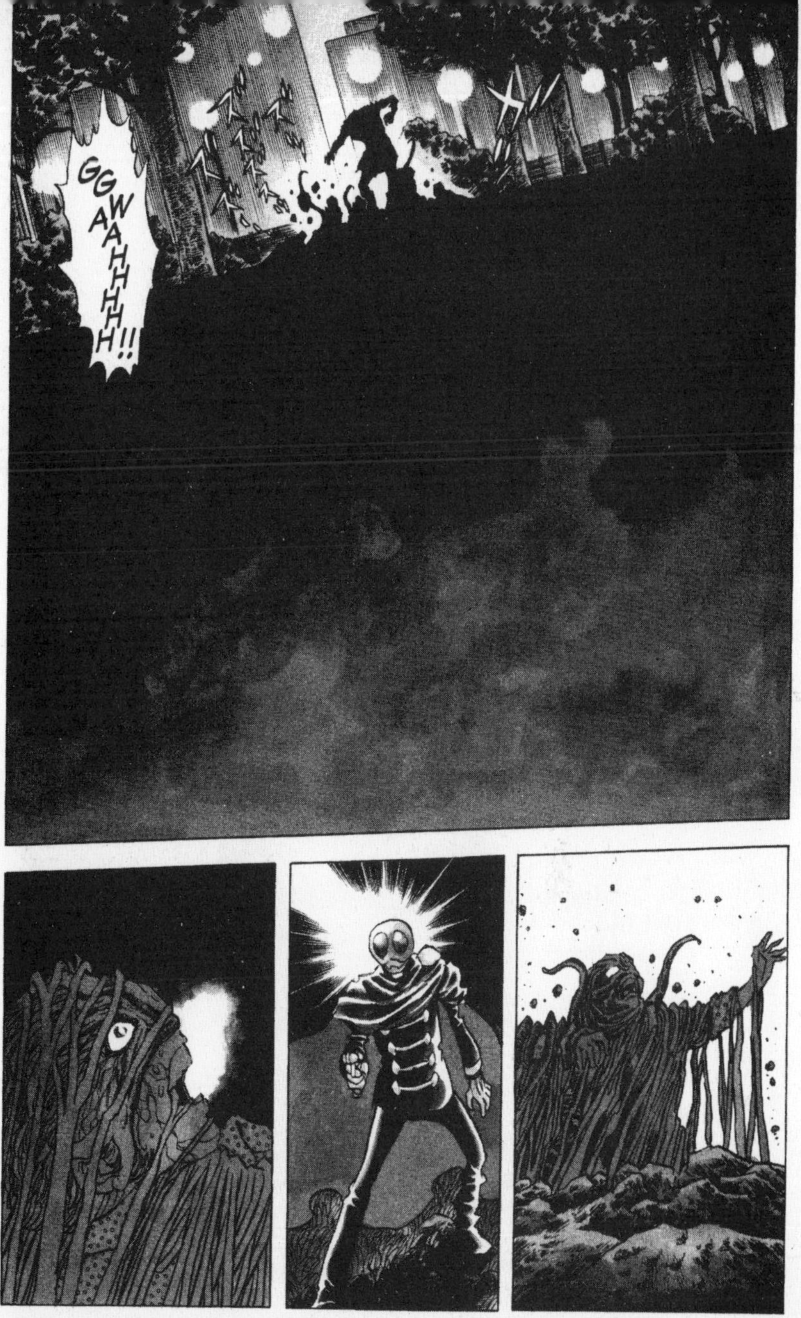
GGWAAHHHHH!!

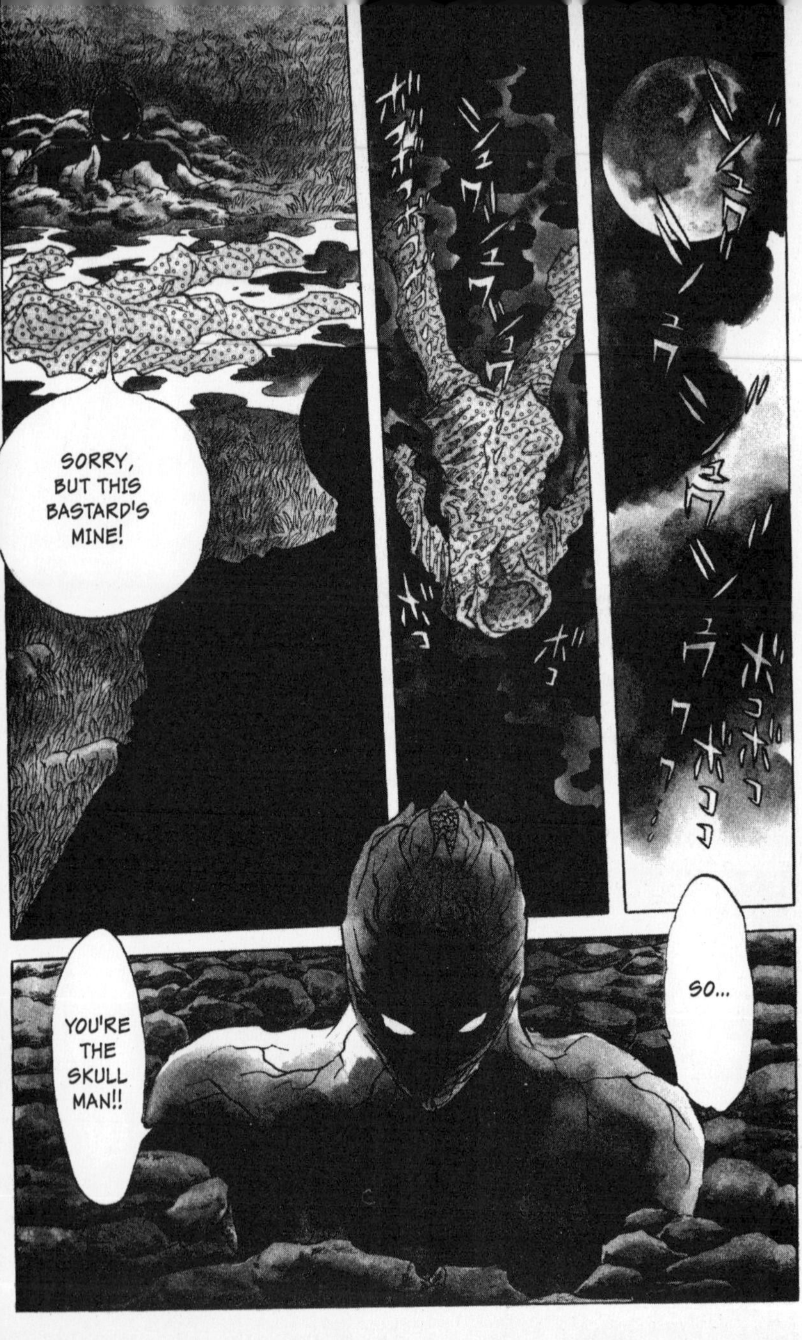
SORRY, BUT THIS BASTARD'S MINE!
SO...
YOU'RE THE SKULL MAN!!

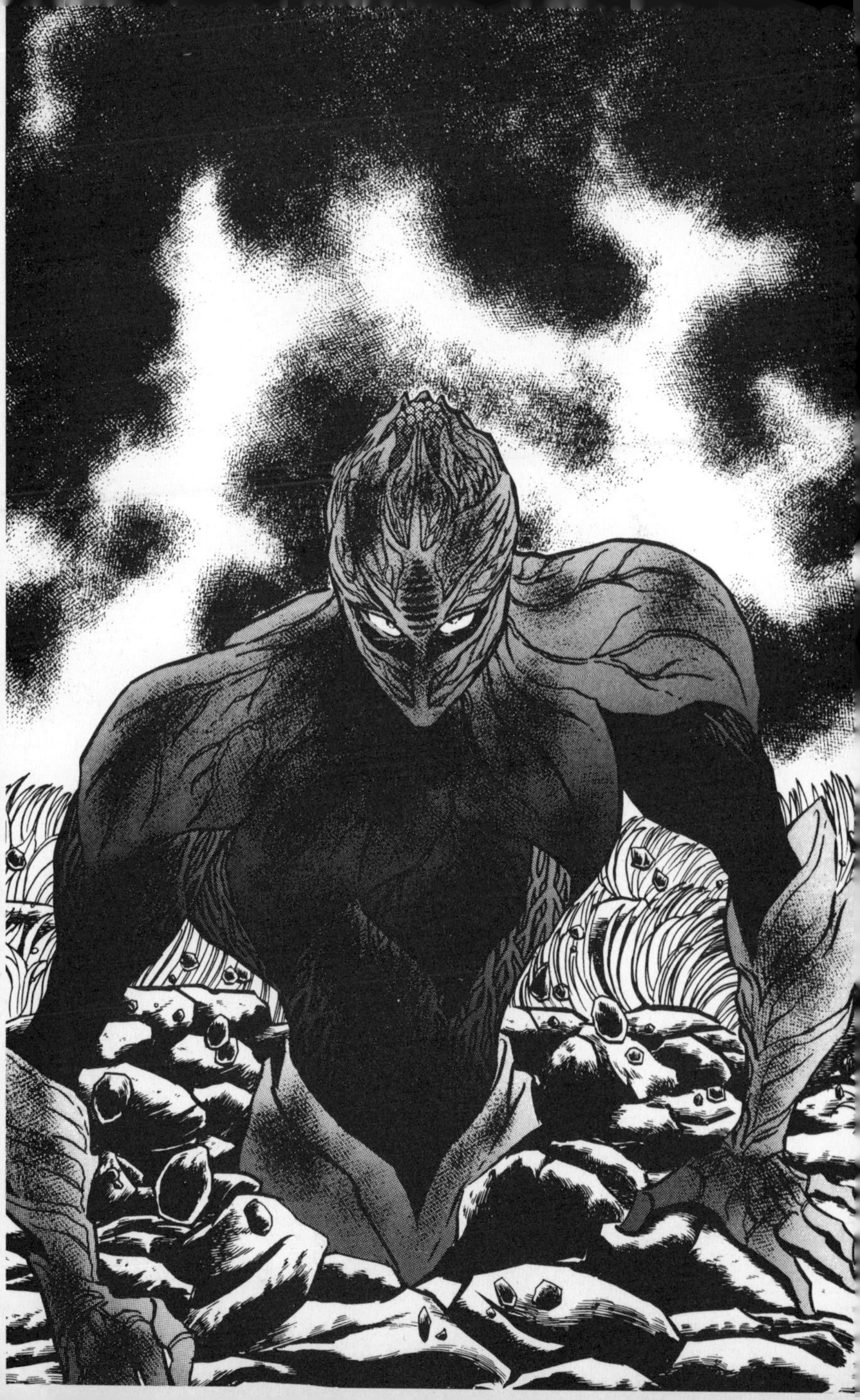

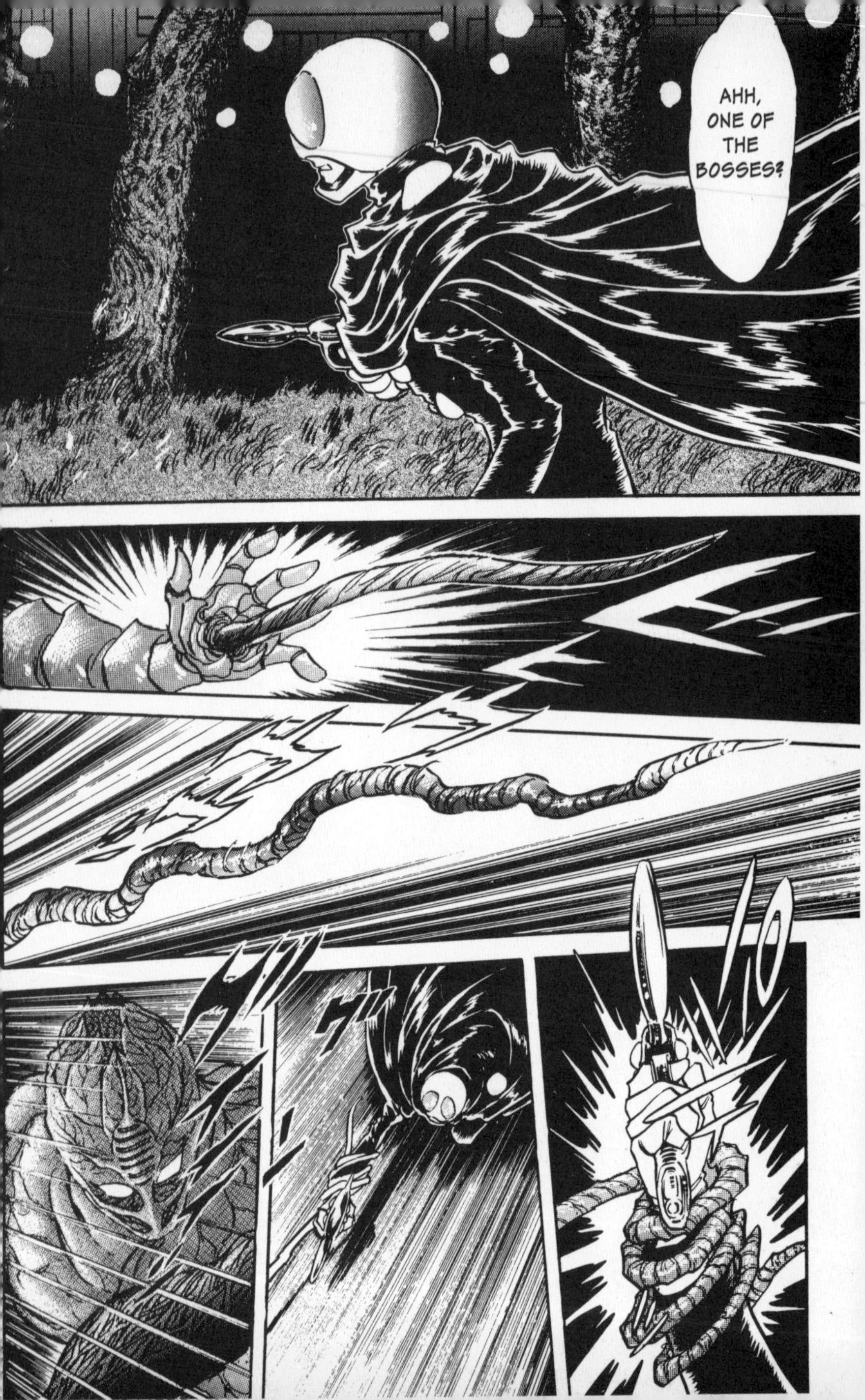
AHH, ONE OF THE BOSSES?

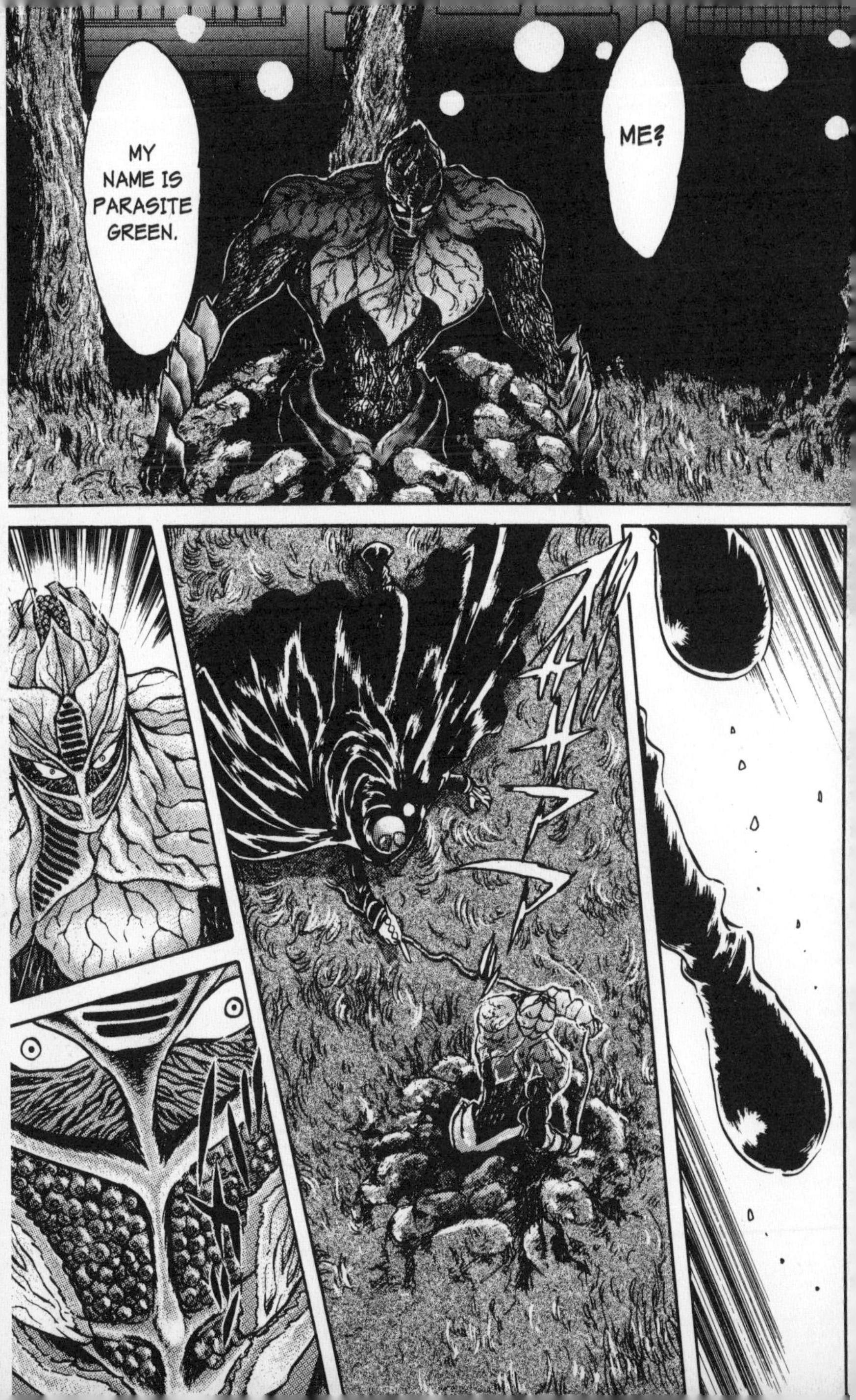
ME?
MY NAME IS PARASITE GREEN.

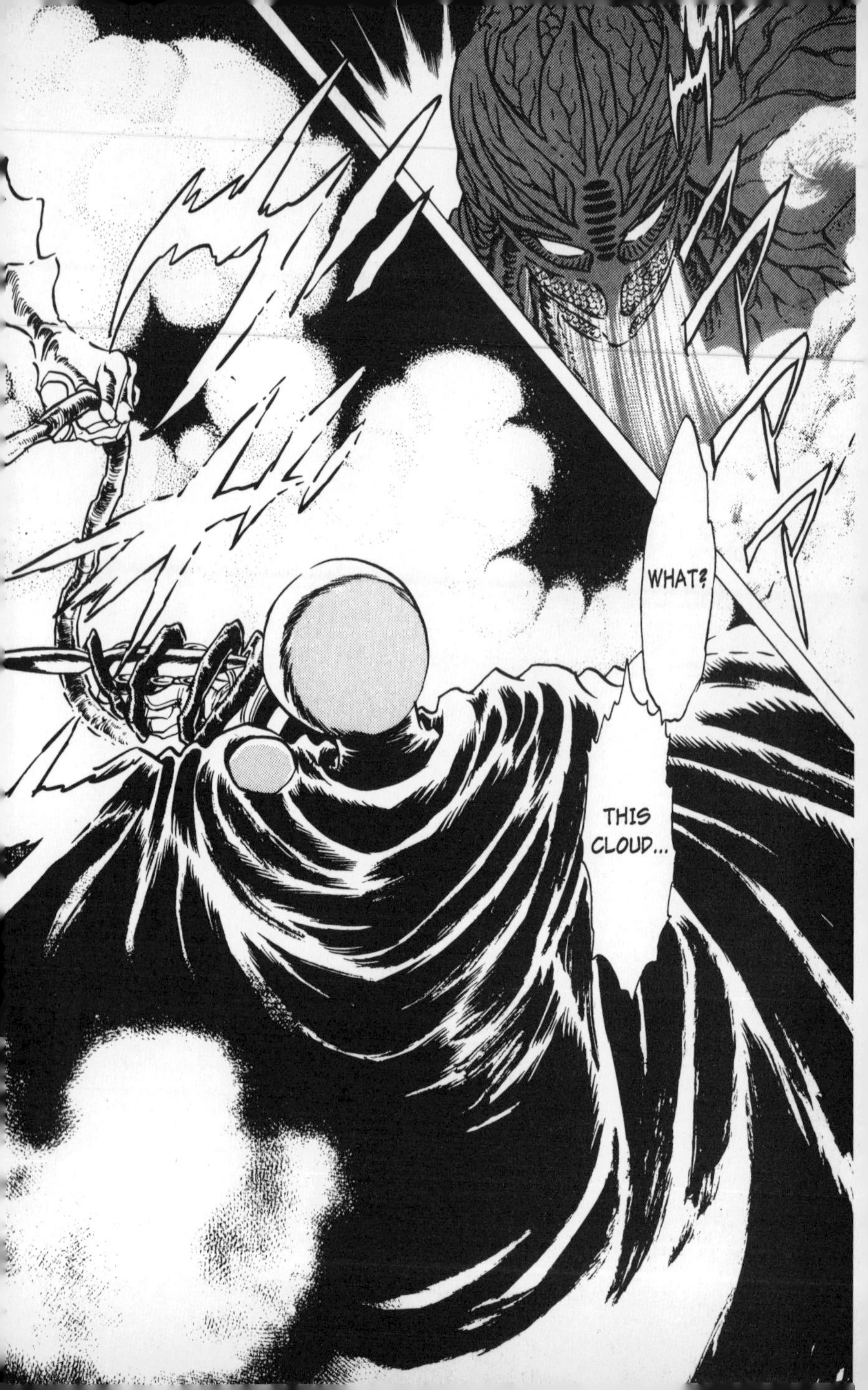
WHAT?
THIS CLOUD...

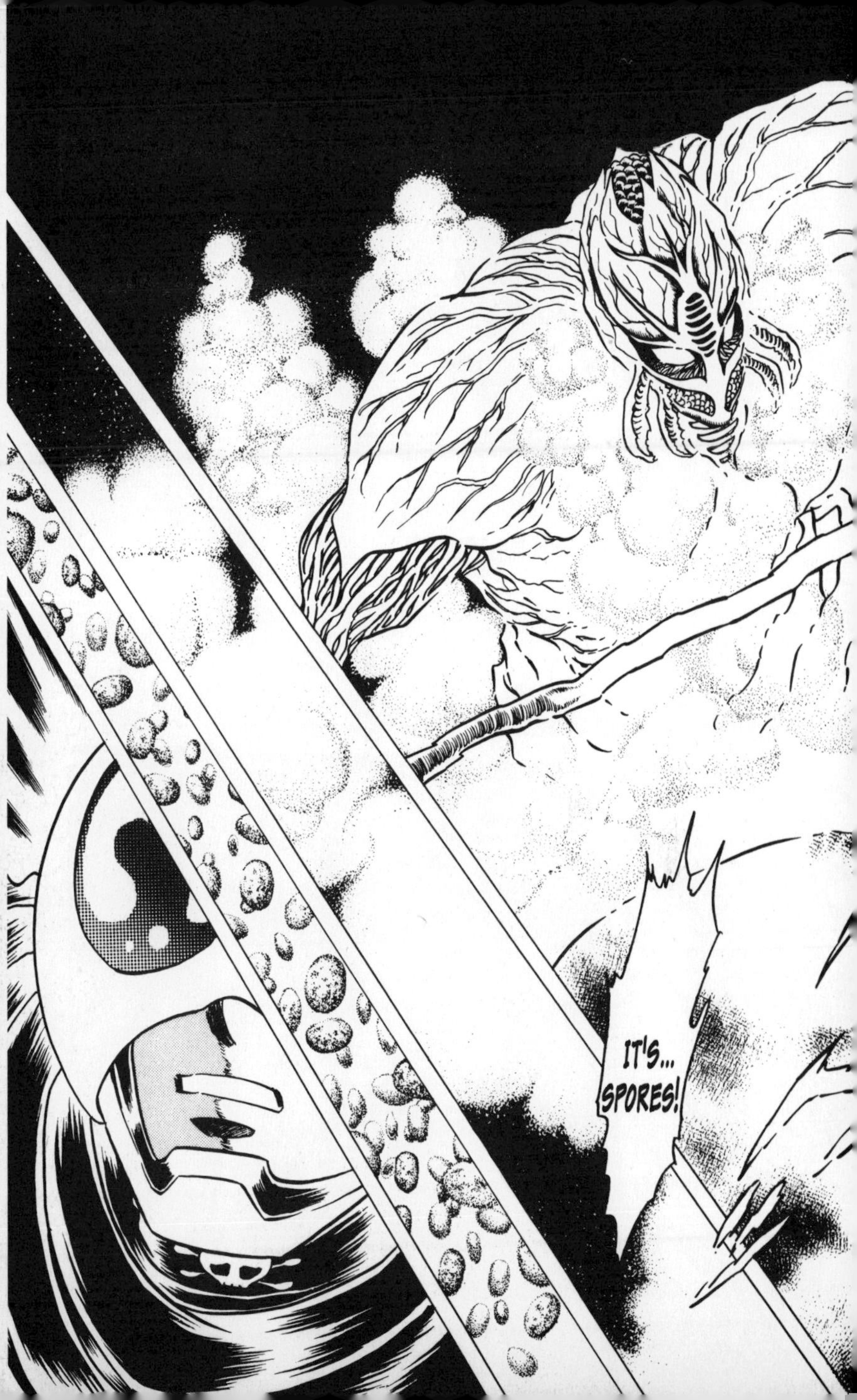
IT'S... SPORES!

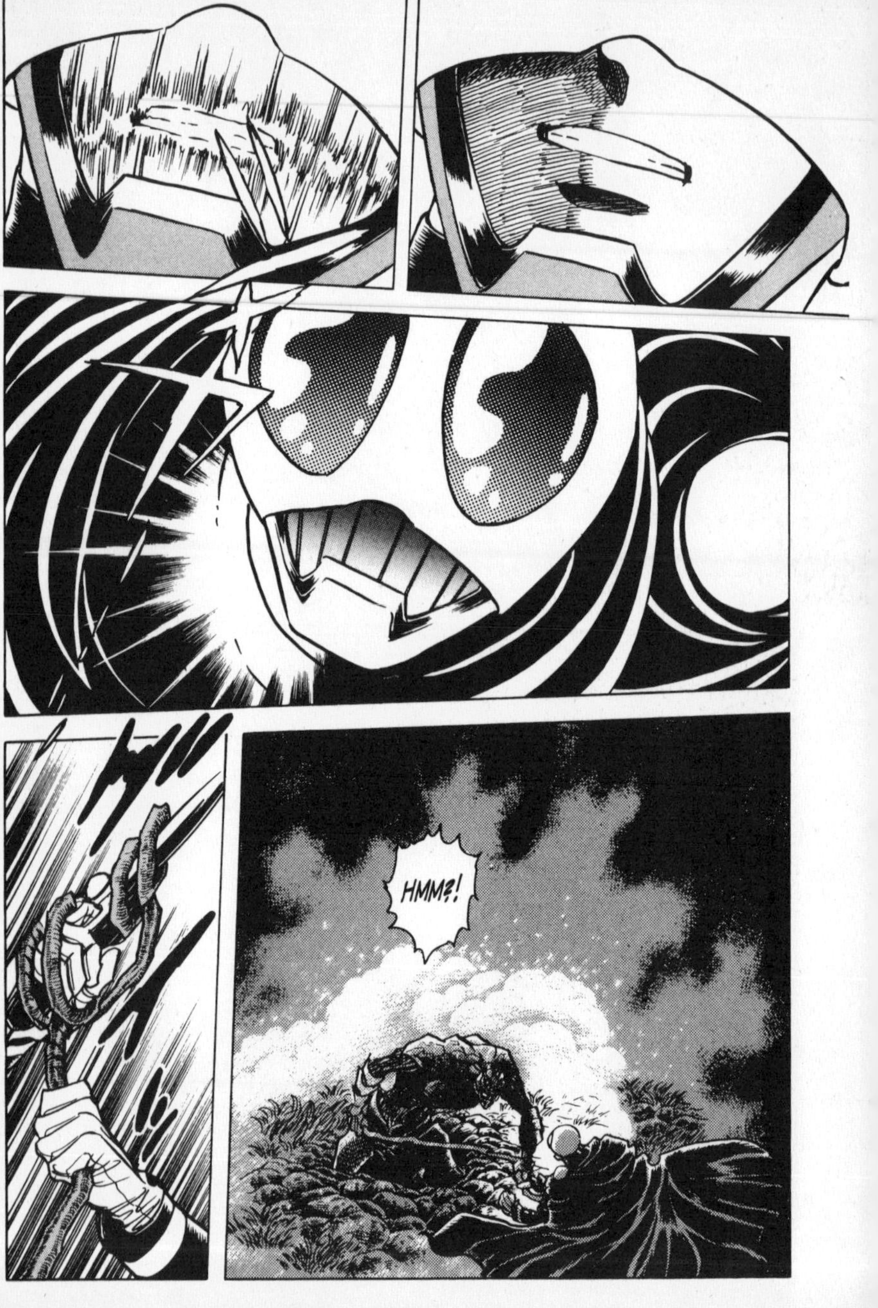
HMM?!

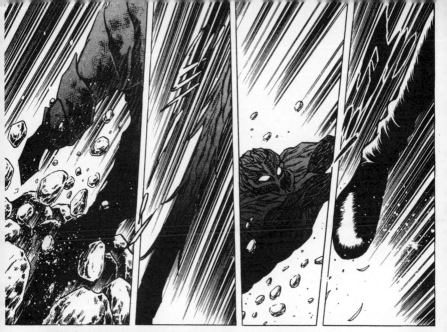

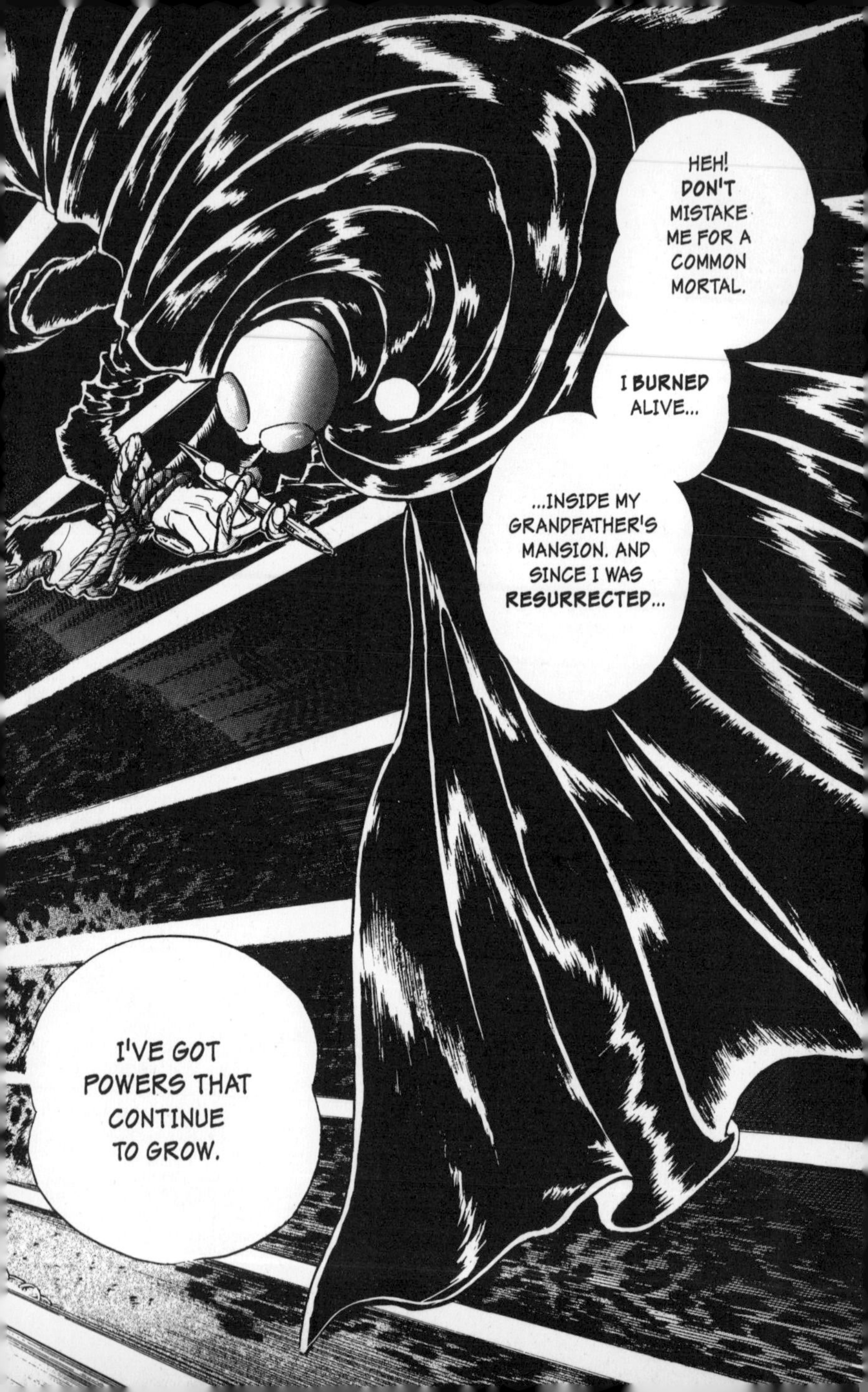
HEH! DON'T MISTAKE ME FOR A COMMON MORTAL.
I BURNED ALIVE...
...INSIDE MY GRANDFATHER'S MANSION. AND SINCE I WAS RESURRECTED...
I'VE GOT POWERS THAT CONTINUE TO GROW.

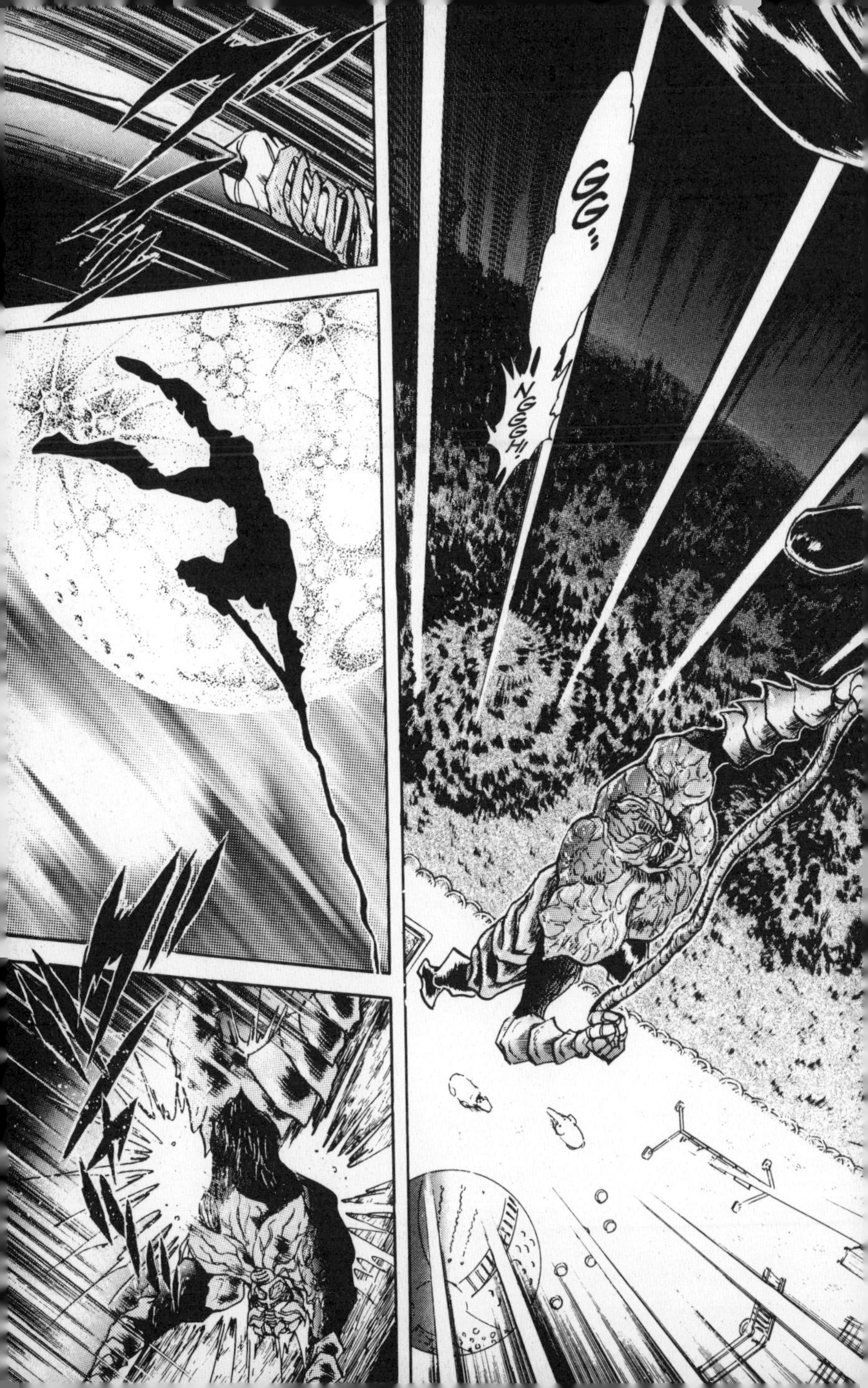

GG...
NGGGH!

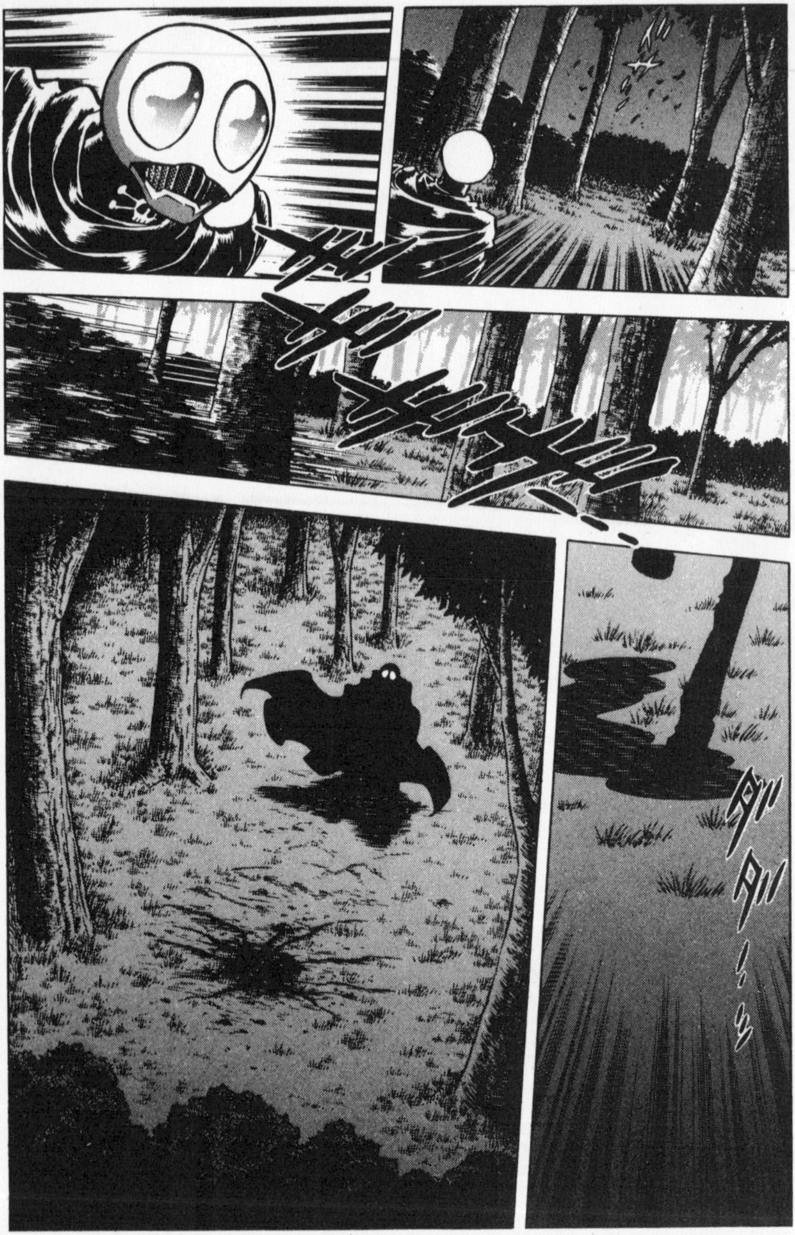

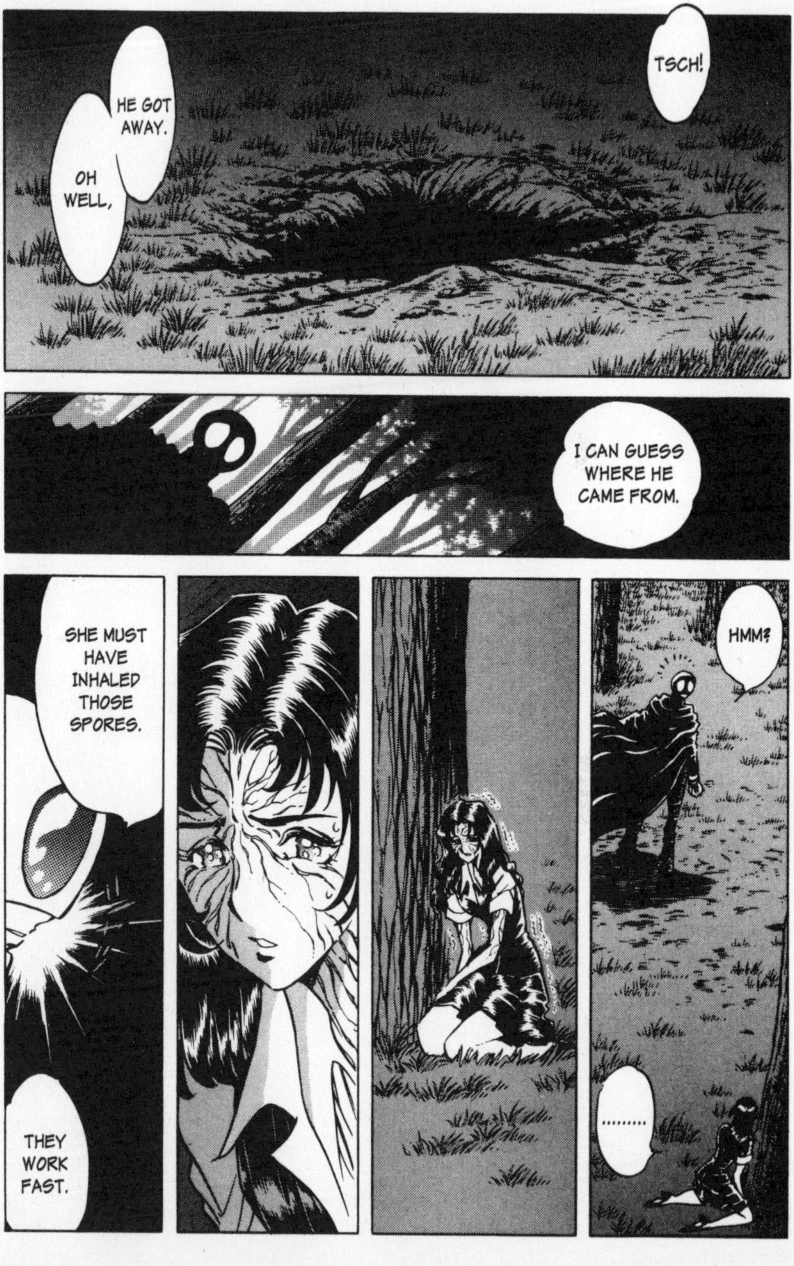
TSCH!
HE GOT AWAY.
OH WELL,
I CAN GUESS WHERE HE CAME FROM.
HMM?
....
SHE MUST HAVE INHALED THOSE SPORES.
THEY WORK FAST.

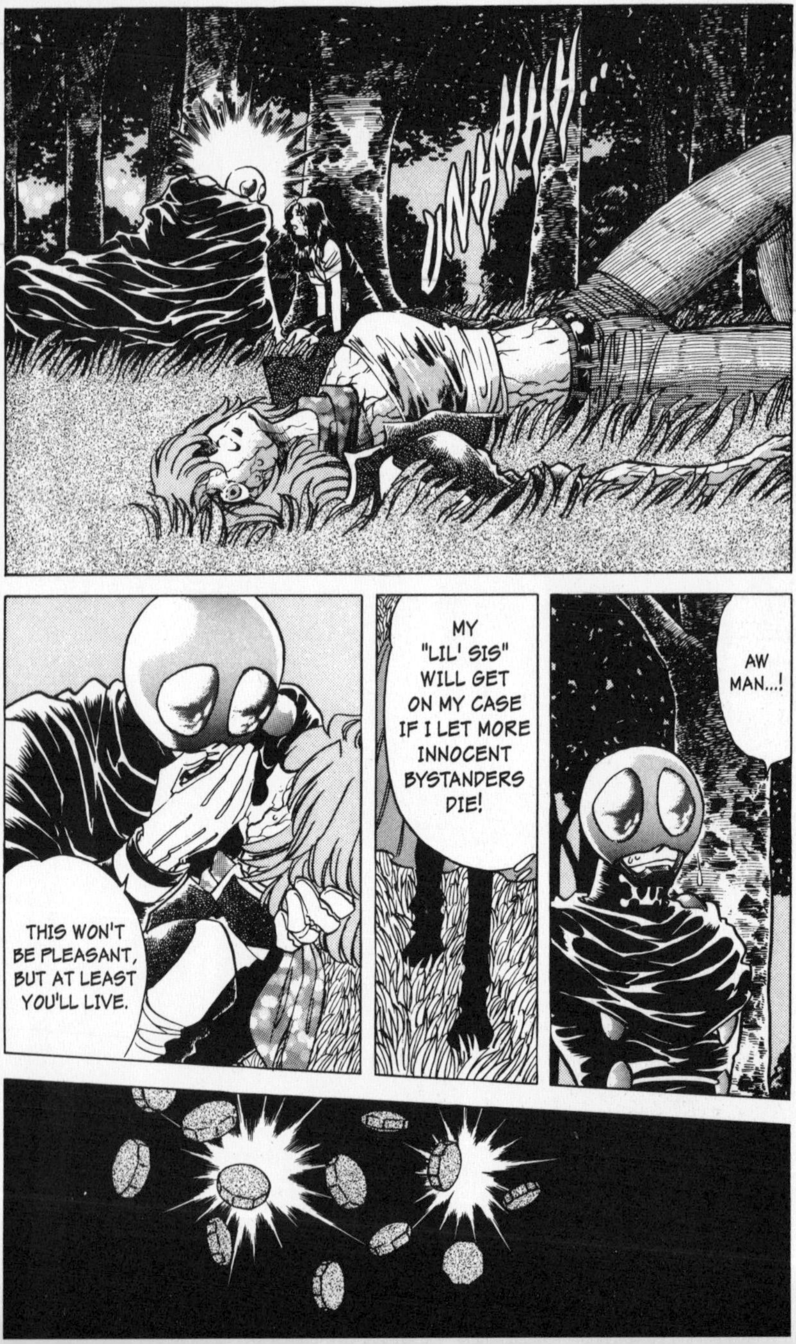
UNAHHH...
AW MAN...!
MY "LIL' SIS" WILL GET ON MY CASE IF I LET MORE INNOCENT BYSTANDERS DIE!
THIS WON'T BE PLEASANT, BUT AT LEAST YOU'LL LIVE.

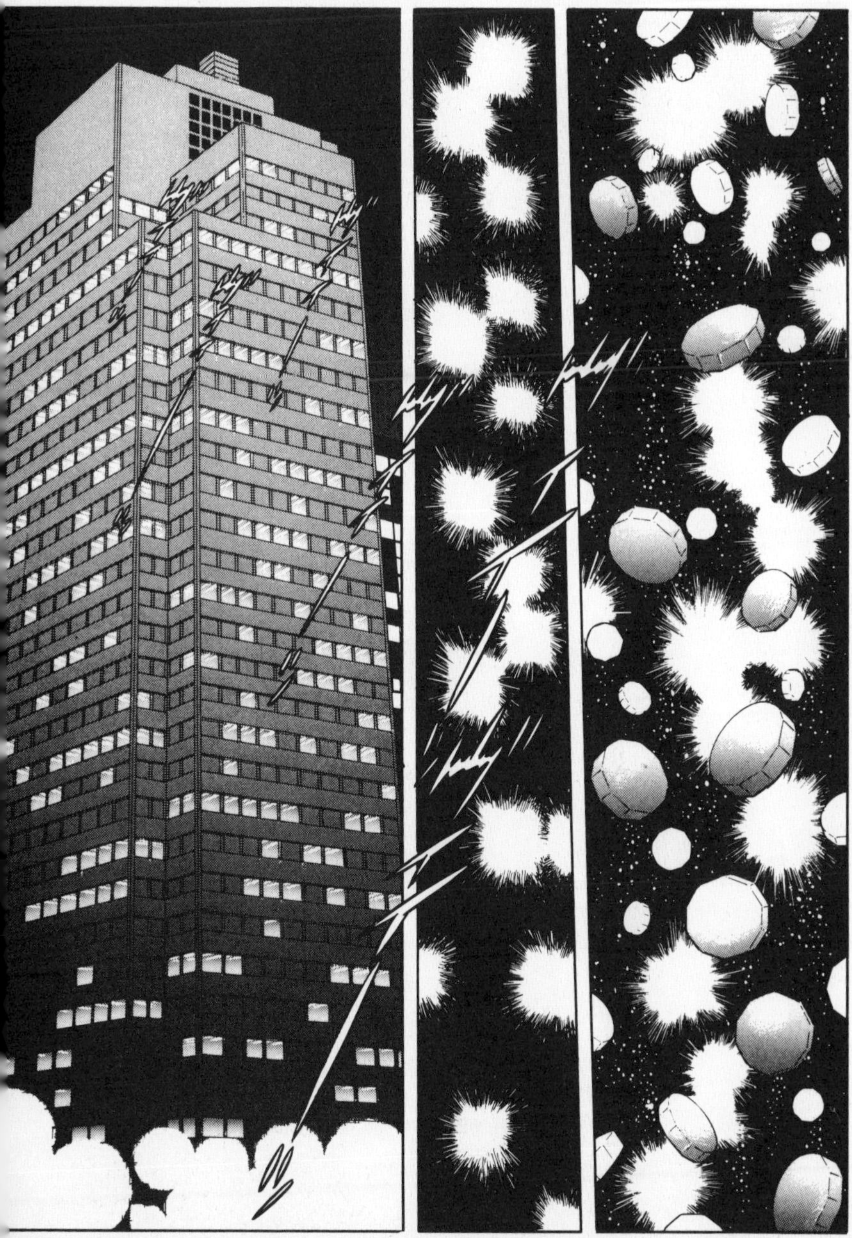

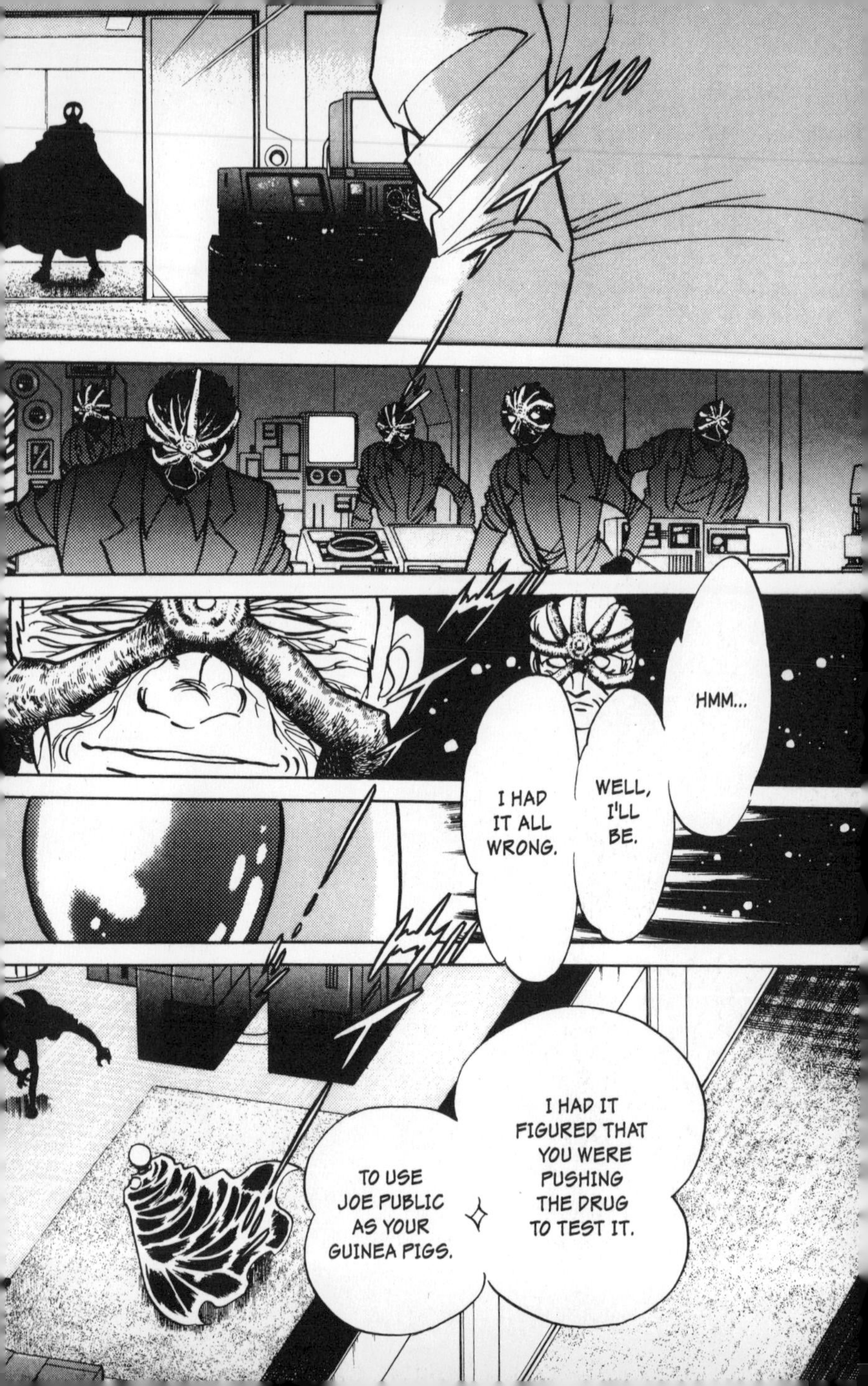
HMM...
WELL, I'LL BE.
I HAD IT ALL WRONG.
I HAD IT FIGURED THAT YOU WERE PUSHING THE DRUG TO TEST IT.
TO USE JOE PUBLIC AS YOUR GUINEA PIGS.

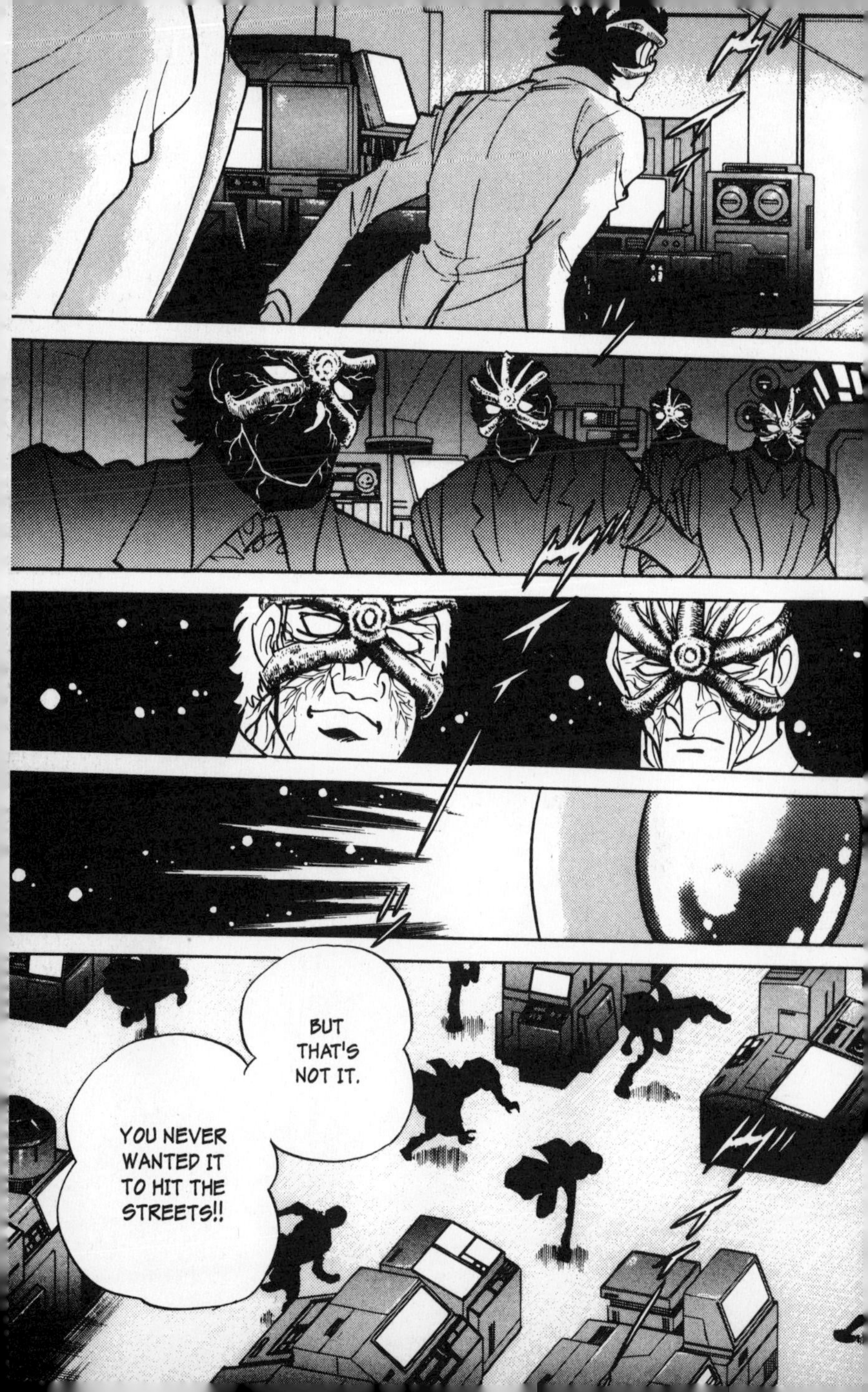
BUT THAT'S NOT IT.
YOU NEVER WANTED IT TO HIT THE STREETS!!

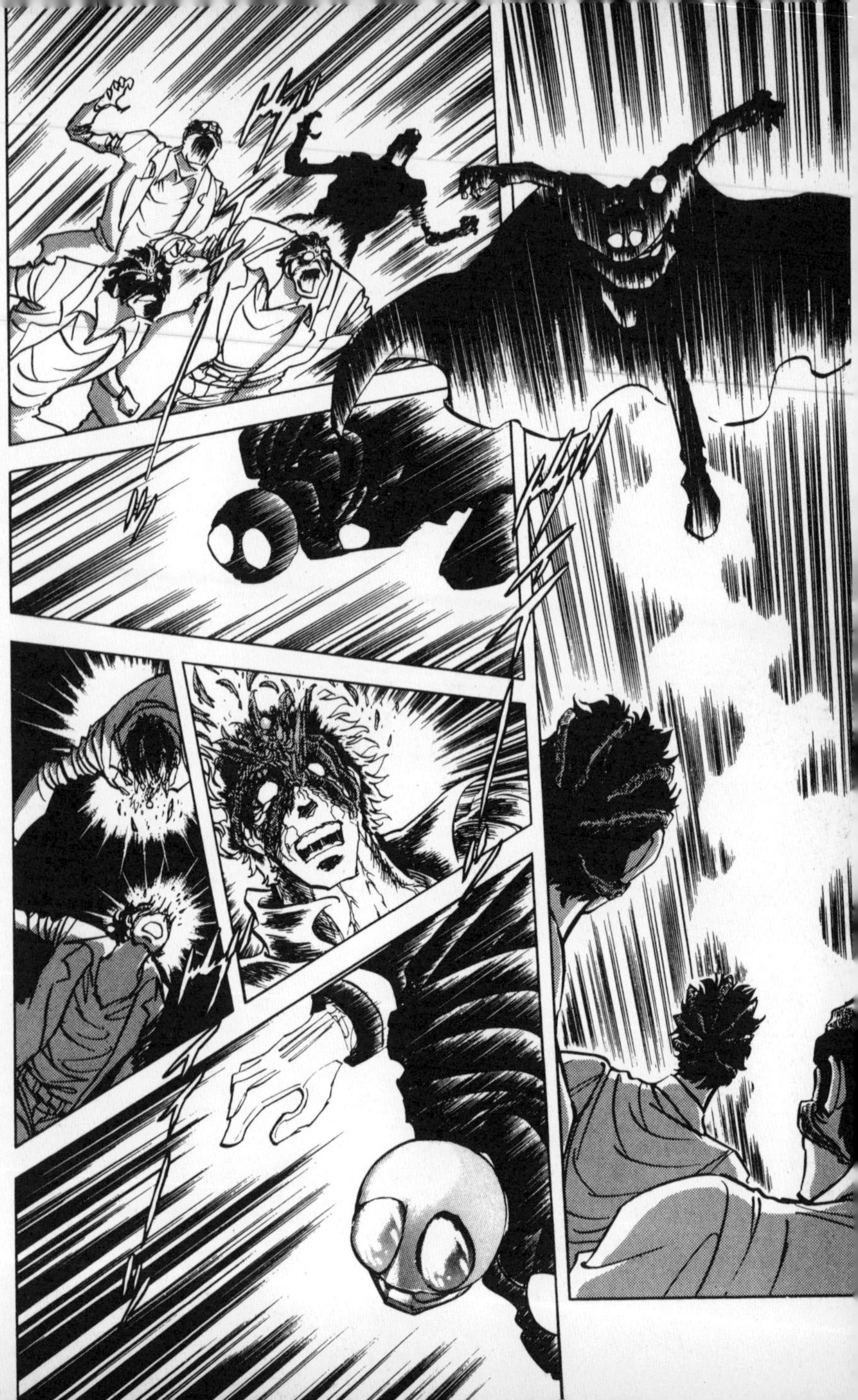

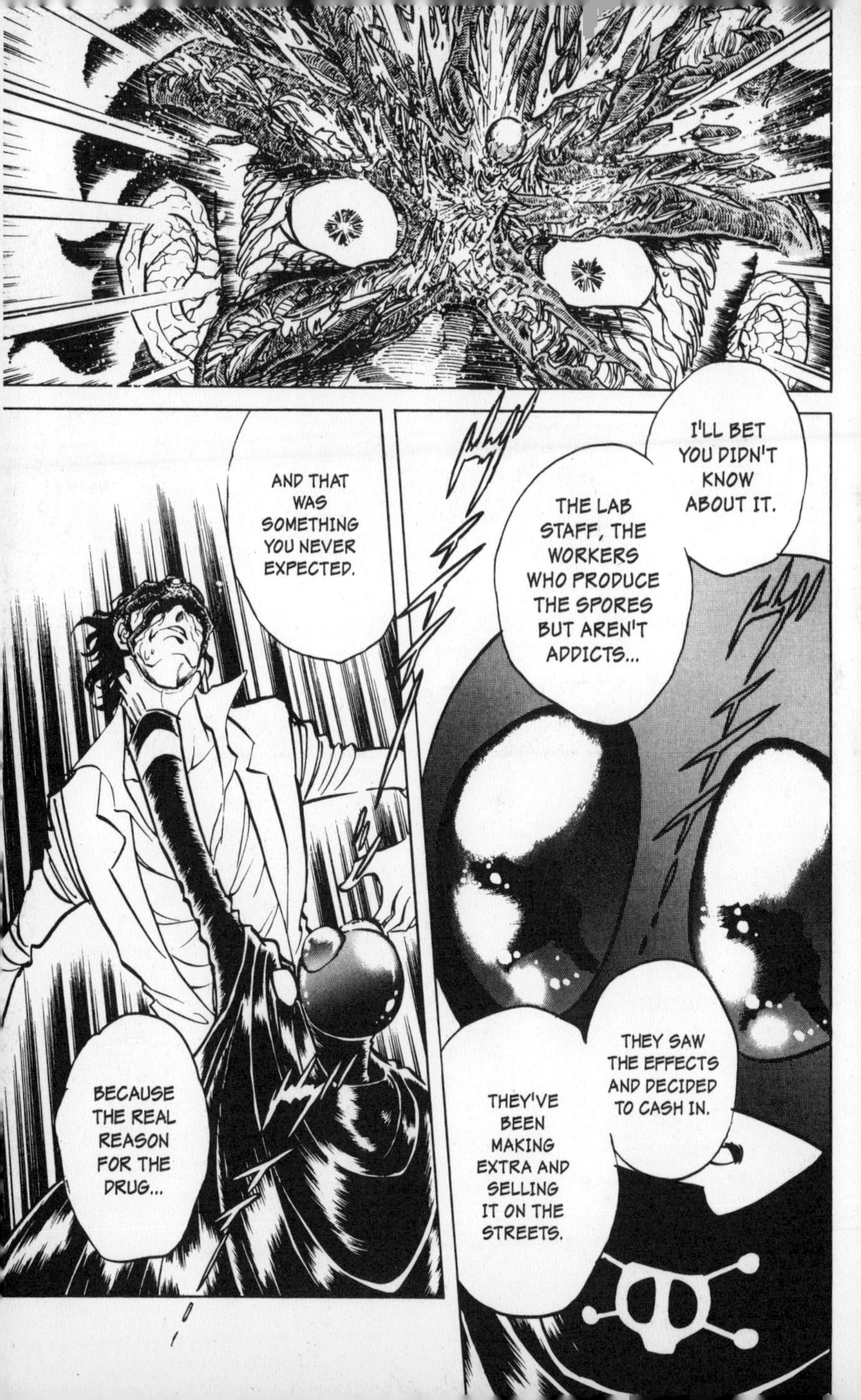
I'LL BET YOU DIDN'T KNOW ABOUT IT.
THE LAB STAFF, THE WORKERS WHO PRODUCE THE SPORES BUT AREN'T ADDICTS...
THEY SAW THE EFFECTS AND DECIDED TO CASH IN.
THEY'VE BEEN MAKING EXTRA AND SELLING IT ON THE STREETS.
AND THAT WAS SOMETHING YOU NEVER EXPECTED.
BECAUSE THE REAL REASON FOR THE DRUG...

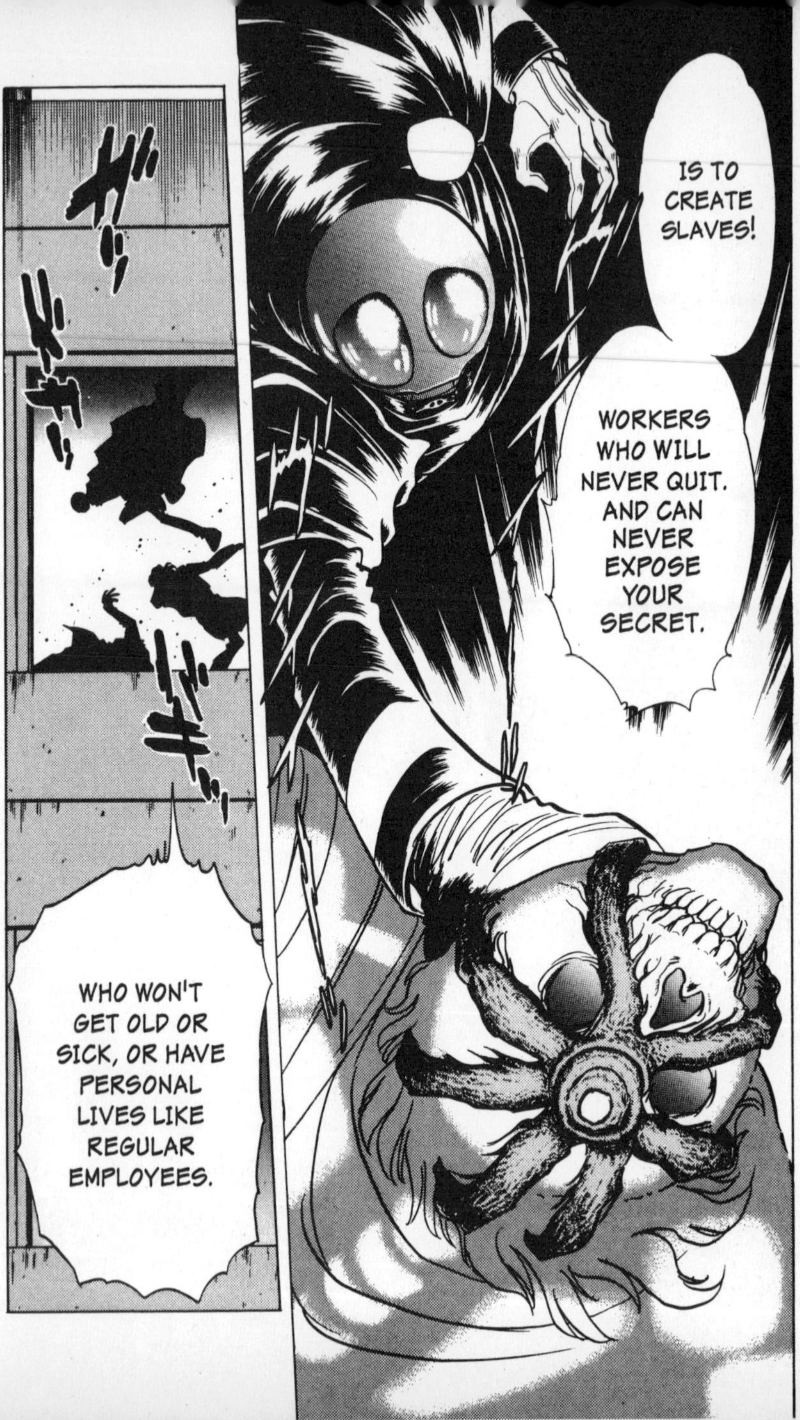
IS TO CREATE SLAVES!
WORKERS WHO WILL NEVER QUIT. AND CAN NEVER EXPOSE YOUR SECRET.
WHO WON'T GET OLD OR SICK, OR HAVE PERSONAL LIVES LIKE REGULAR EMPLOYEES.

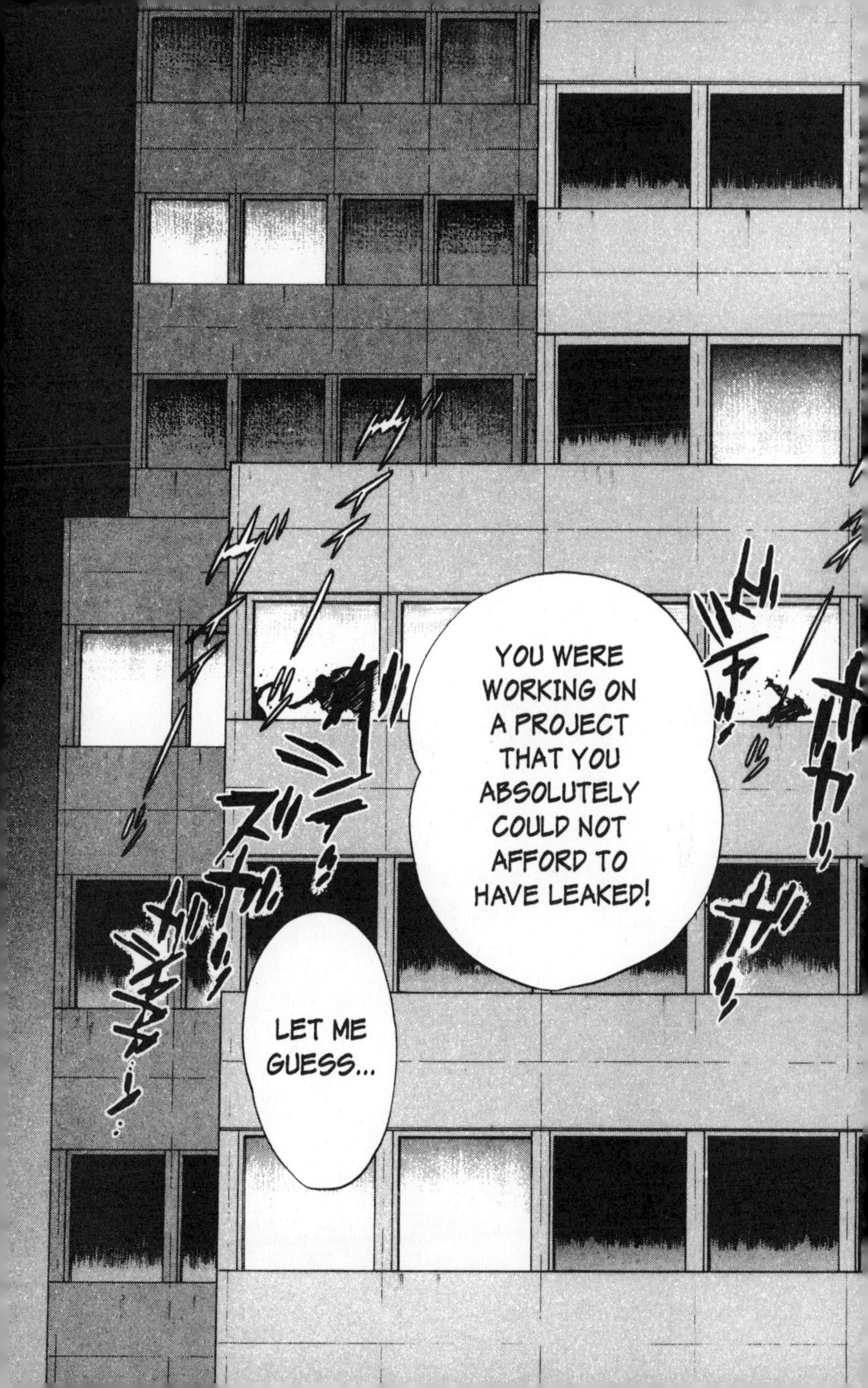
YOU WERE WORKING ON A PROJECT THAT YOU ABSOLUTELY COULD NOT AFFORD TO HAVE LEAKED!
LET ME GUESS...

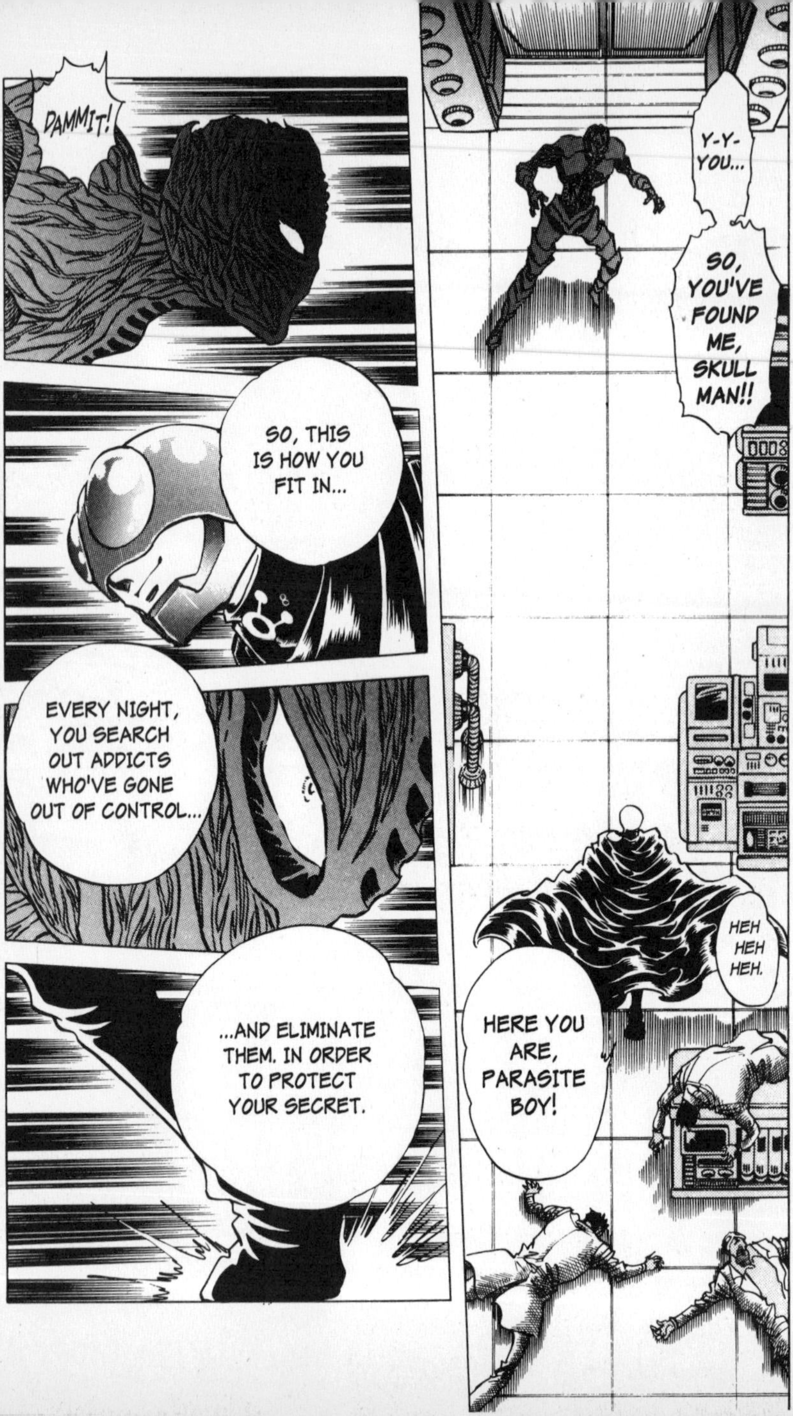
Y-Y-YOU...
SO, YOU'VE FOUND ME, SKULL MAN!!
HEH HEH HEH.
HERE YOU ARE, PARASITE BOY!
DAMMIT!
SO, THIS IS HOW YOU FIT IN...
EVERY NIGHT, YOU SEARCH OUT ADDICTS WHO'VE GONE OUT OF CONTROL...
...AND ELIMINATE THEM. IN ORDER TO PROTECT YOUR SECRET.

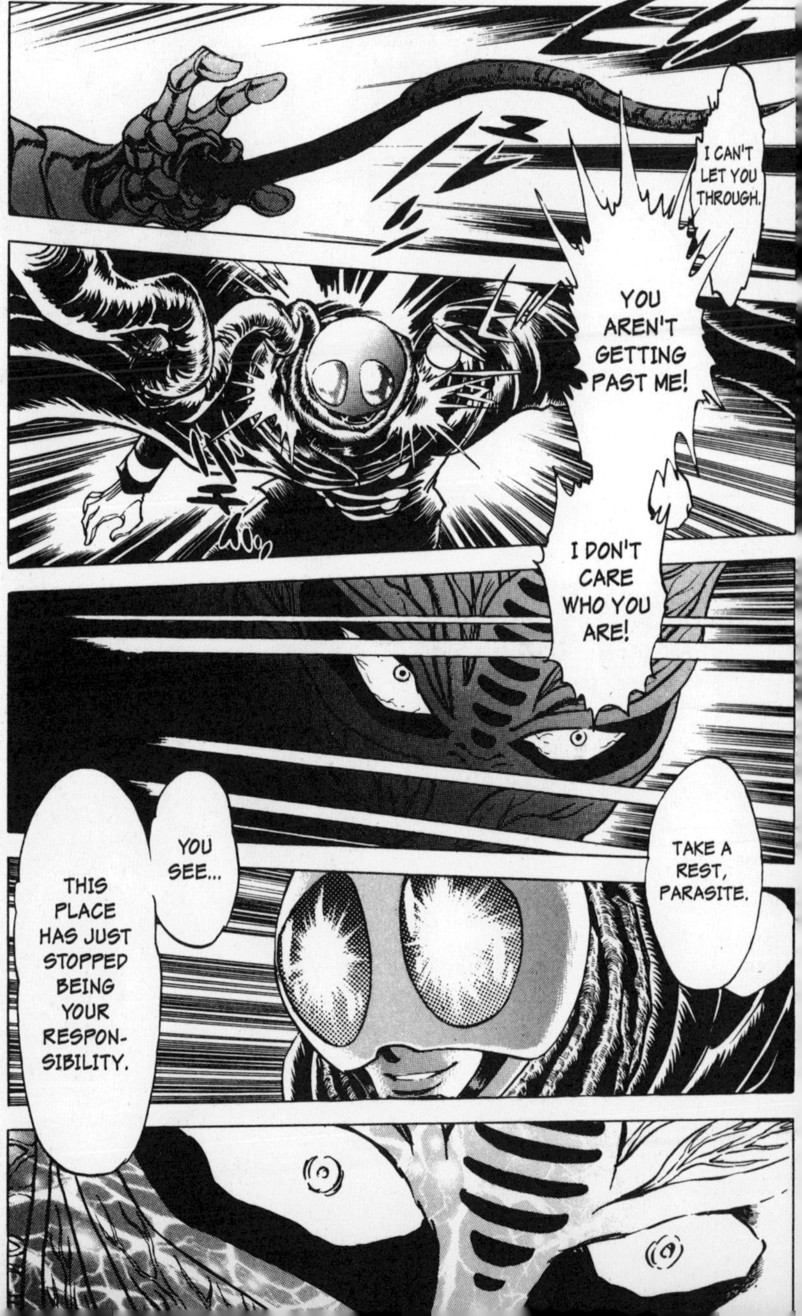
I CAN'T LET YOU THROUGH.
YOU AREN'T GETTING PAST ME!
I DON'T CARE WHO YOU ARE!
TAKE A REST, PARASITE.
YOU SEE...
THIS PLACE HAS JUST STOPPED BEING YOUR RESPON-SIBILITY.

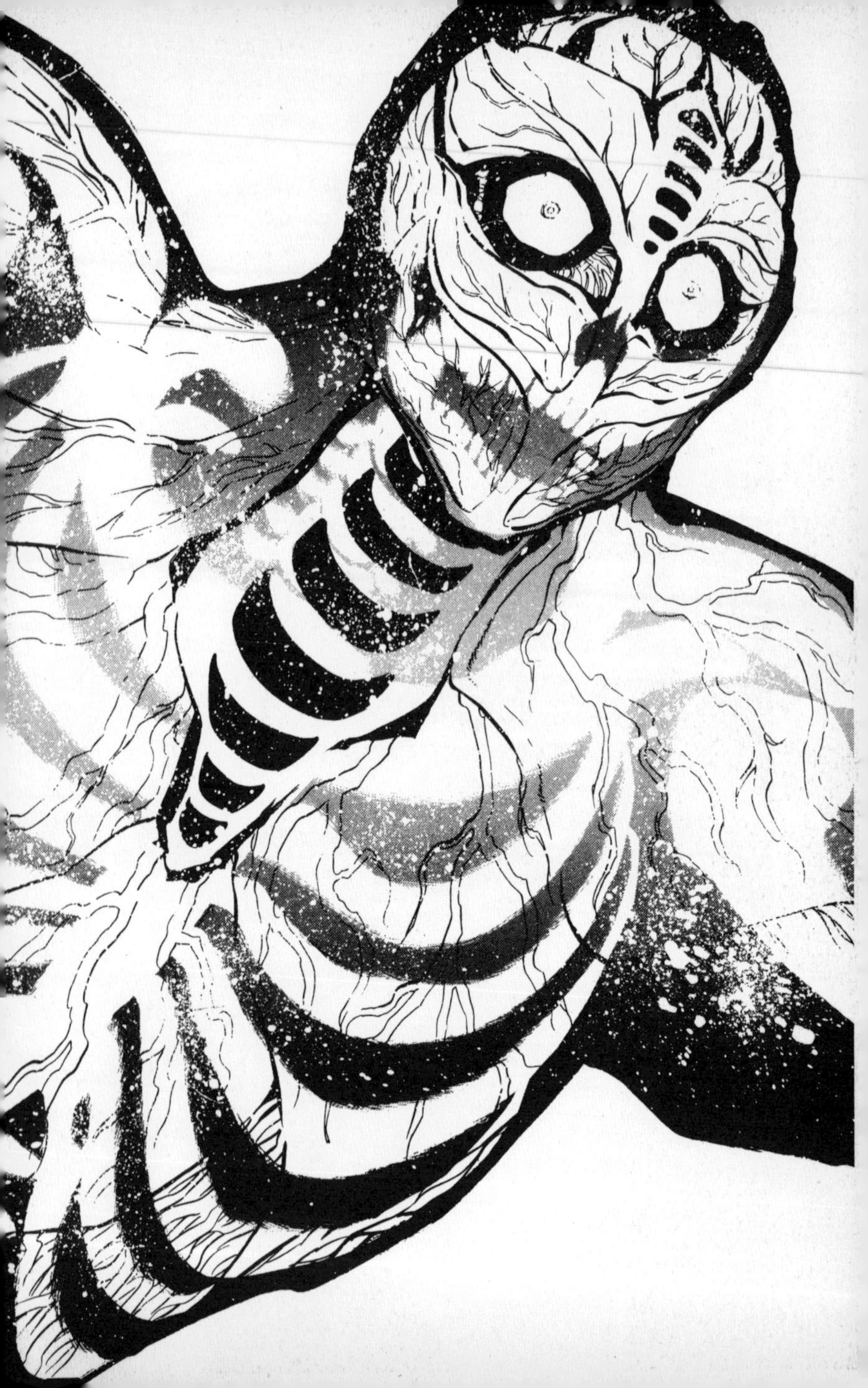

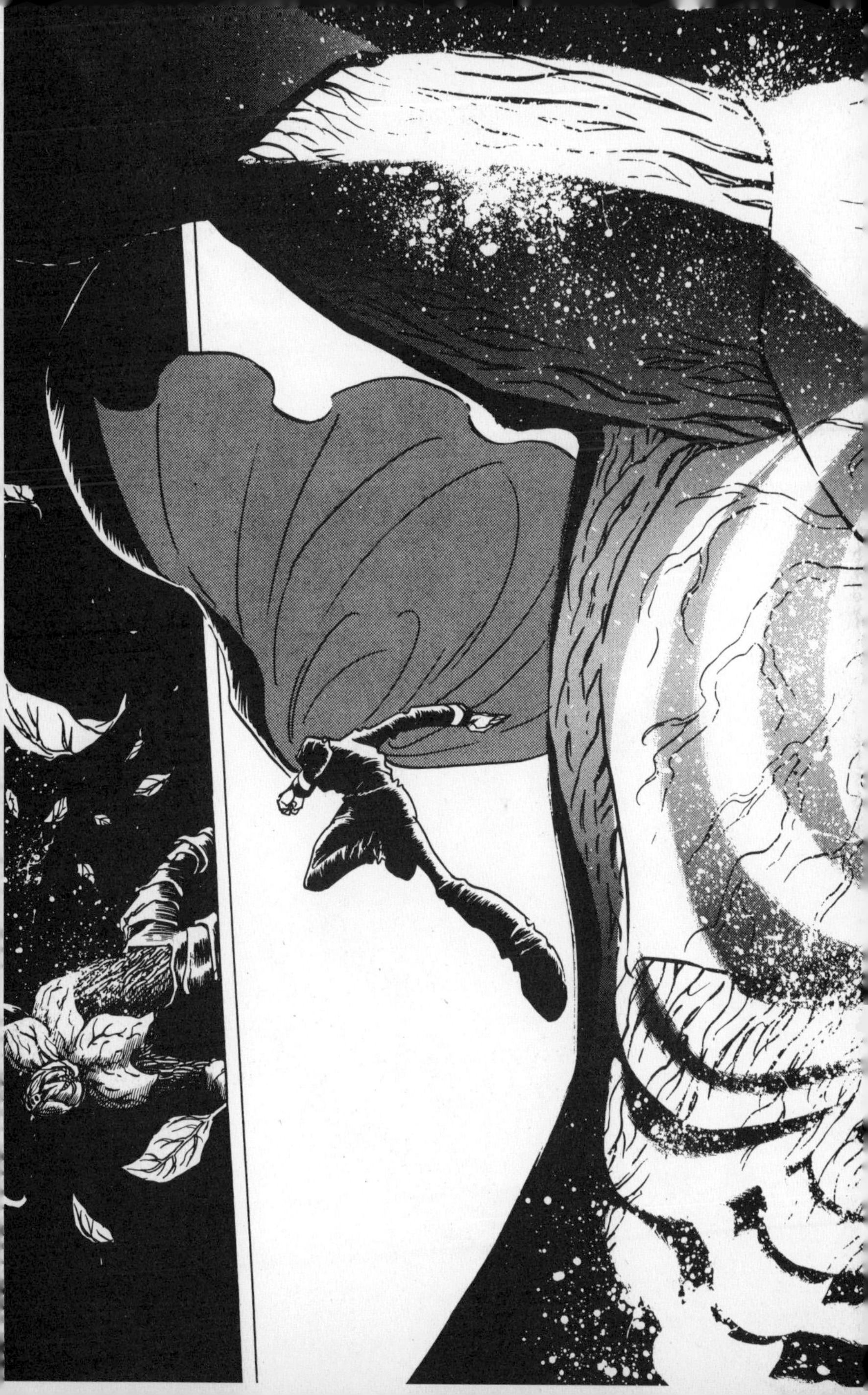

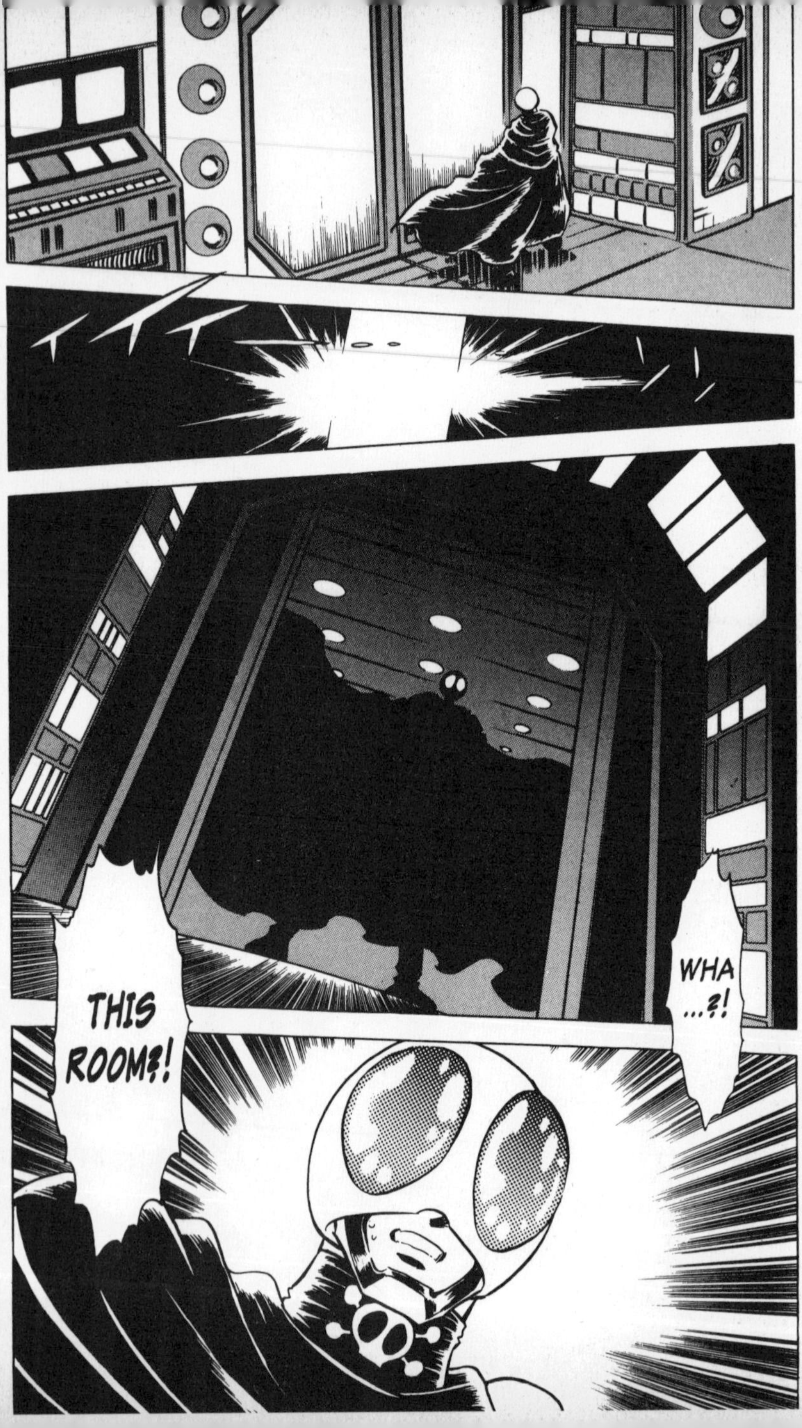
WHA ...?!
THIS ROOM?!

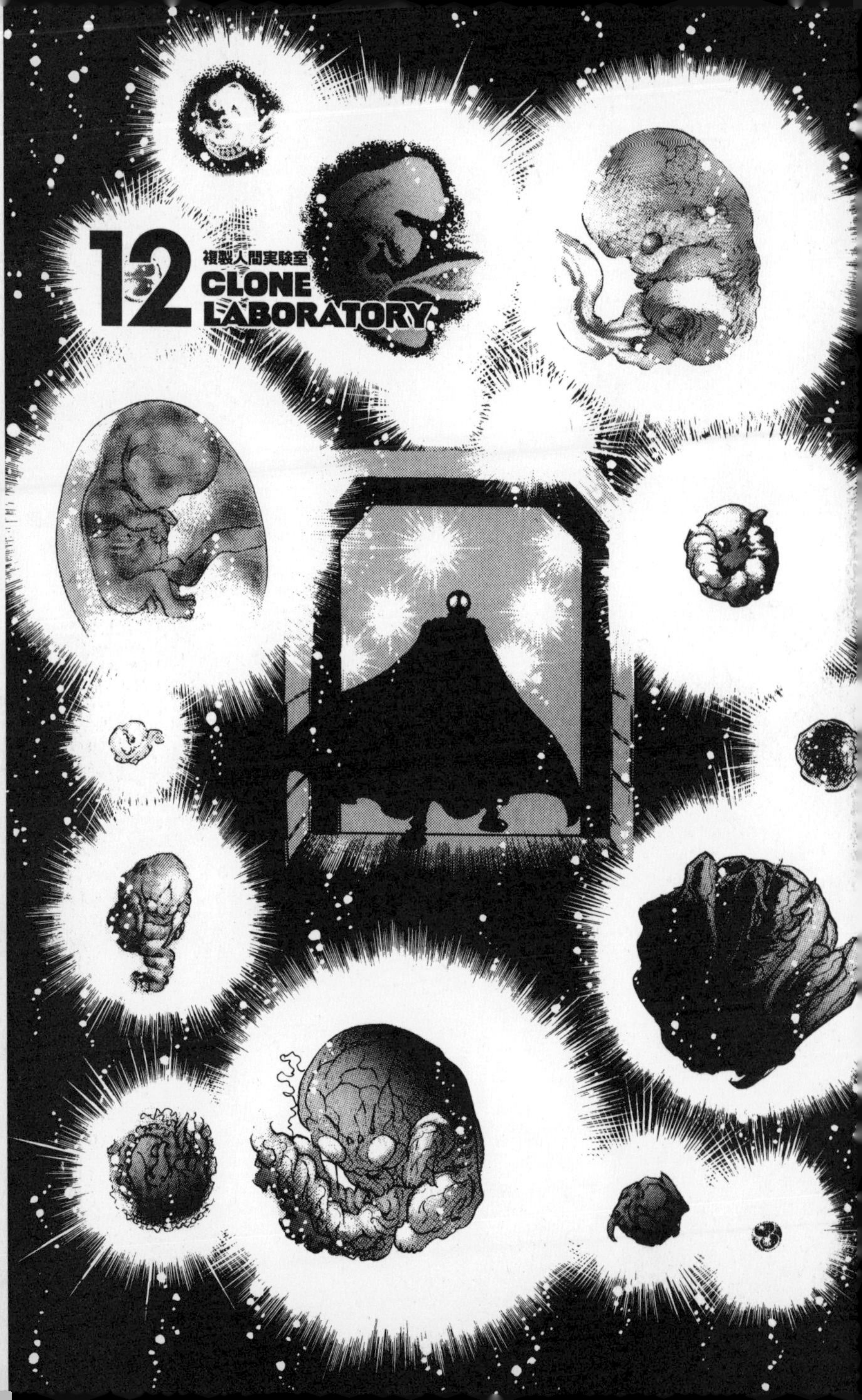
12
複製人間実験室
CLONE
LABORATORY

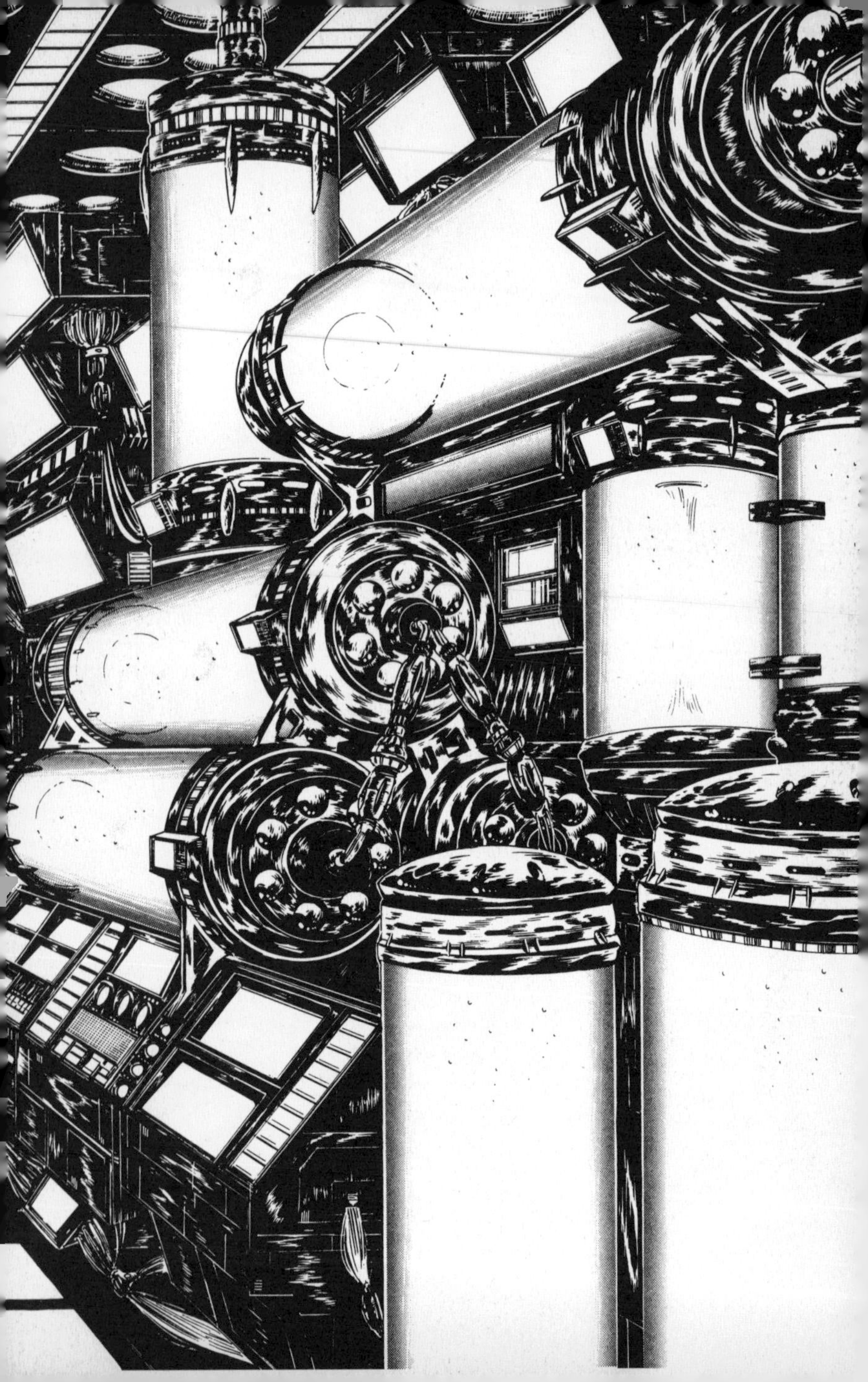

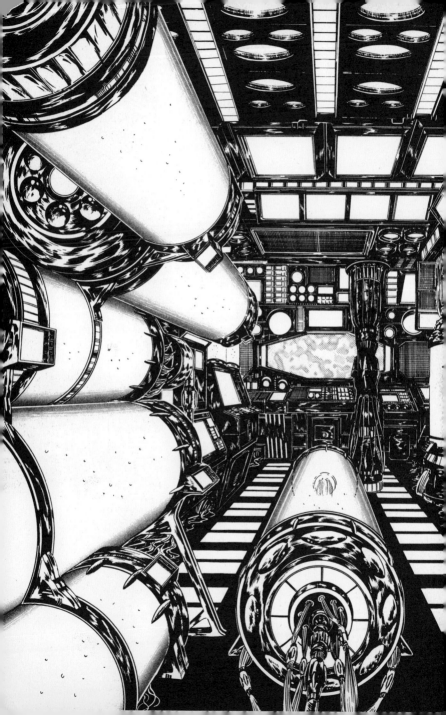

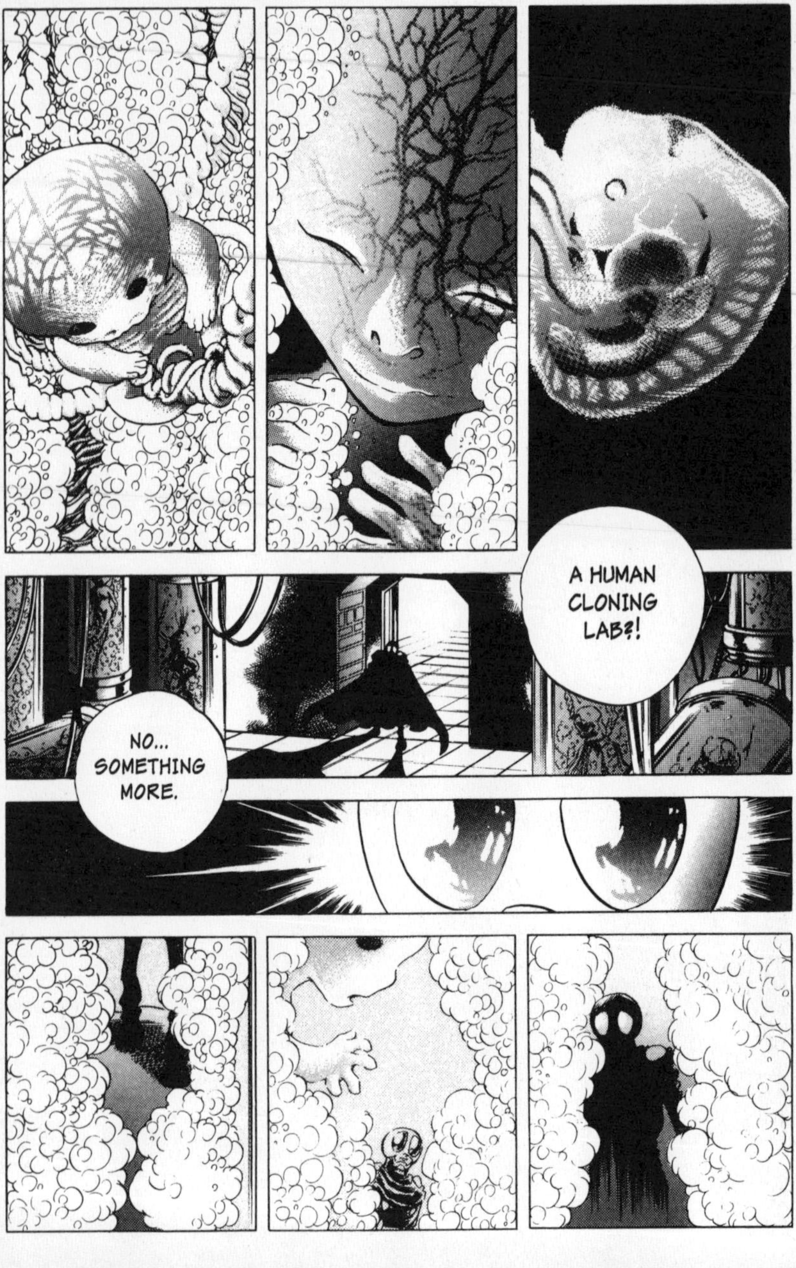
A HUMAN CLONING LAB?!
NO... SOMETHING MORE.

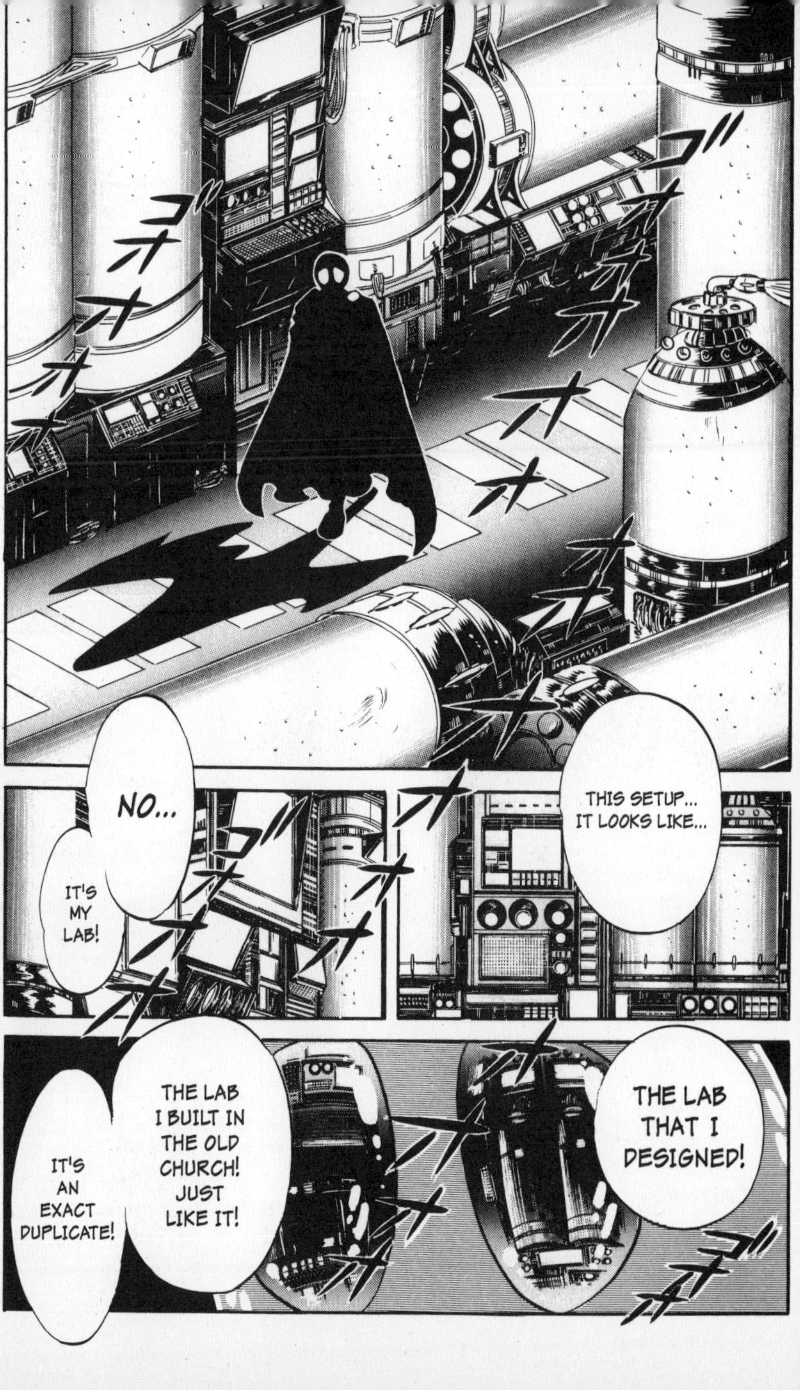
THIS SETUP... IT LOOKS LIKE...
NO...
IT'S MY LAB!
THE LAB THAT I DESIGNED!
THE LAB I BUILT IN THE OLD CHURCH! JUST LIKE IT!
IT'S AN EXACT DUPLICATE!

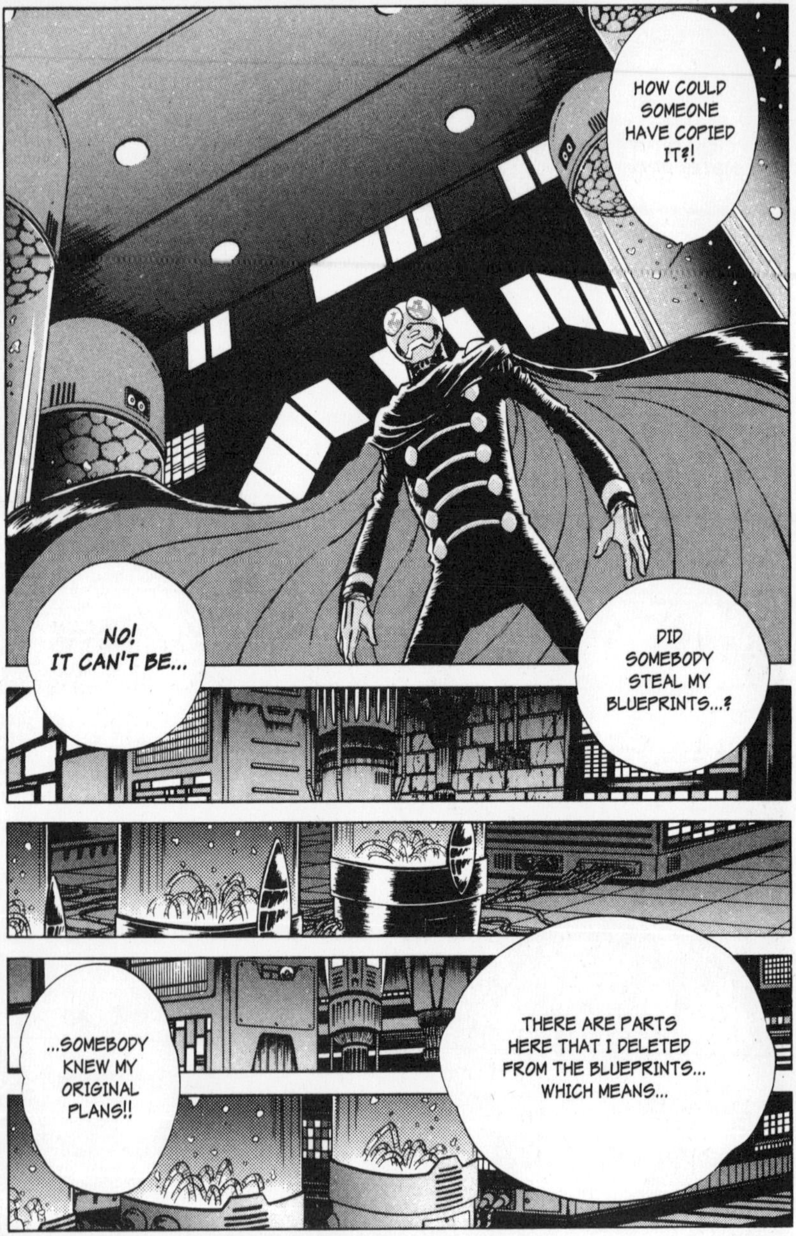
HOW COULD SOMEONE HAVE COPIED IT?!
NO! IT CAN'T BE...
DID SOMEBODY STEAL MY BLUEPRINTS...?
THERE ARE PARTS HERE THAT I DELETED FROM THE BLUEPRINTS... WHICH MEANS...
...SOMEBODY KNEW MY ORIGINAL PLANS!!

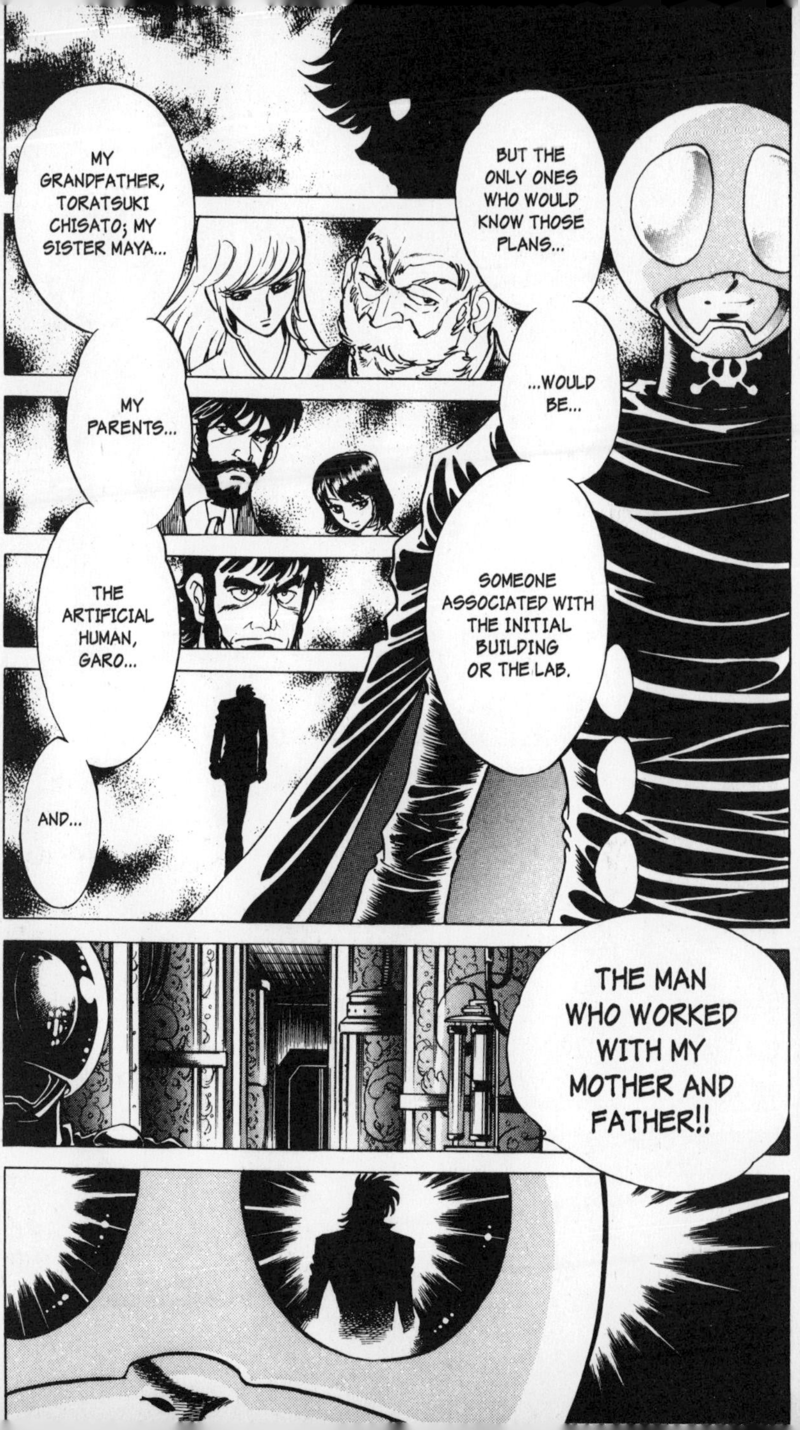
BUT THE ONLY ONES WHO WOULD KNOW THOSE PLANS...
...WOULD BE...
SOMEONE ASSOCIATED WITH THE INITIAL BUILDING OR THE LAB.
MY GRANDFATHER, TORATSUKI CHISATO; MY SISTER MAYA...
MY PARENTS...
THE ARTIFICIAL HUMAN, GARO...
AND...
THE MAN WHO WORKED WITH MY MOTHER AND FATHER!!

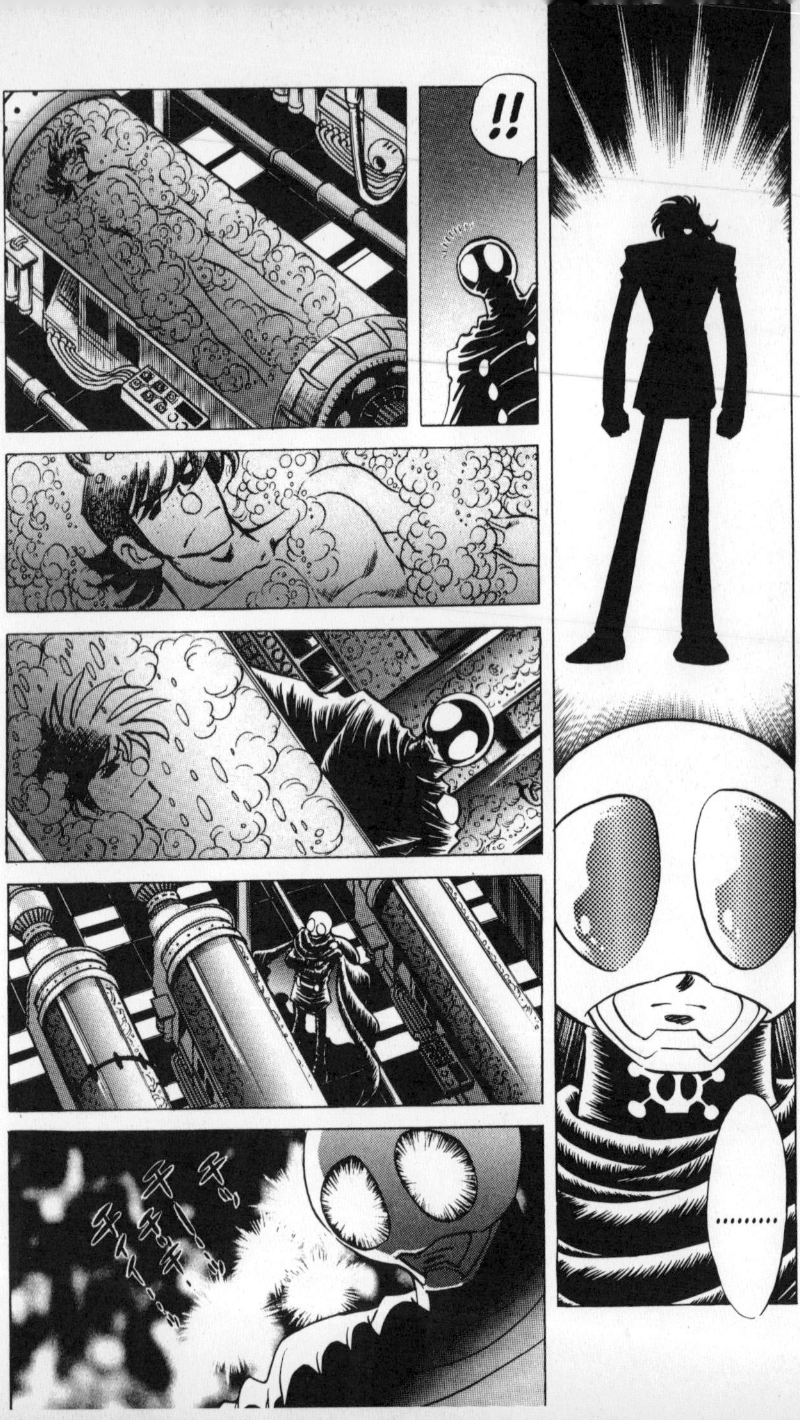
!!
……
チッ
チー…ッ
チッチ…
チィィ…ッ

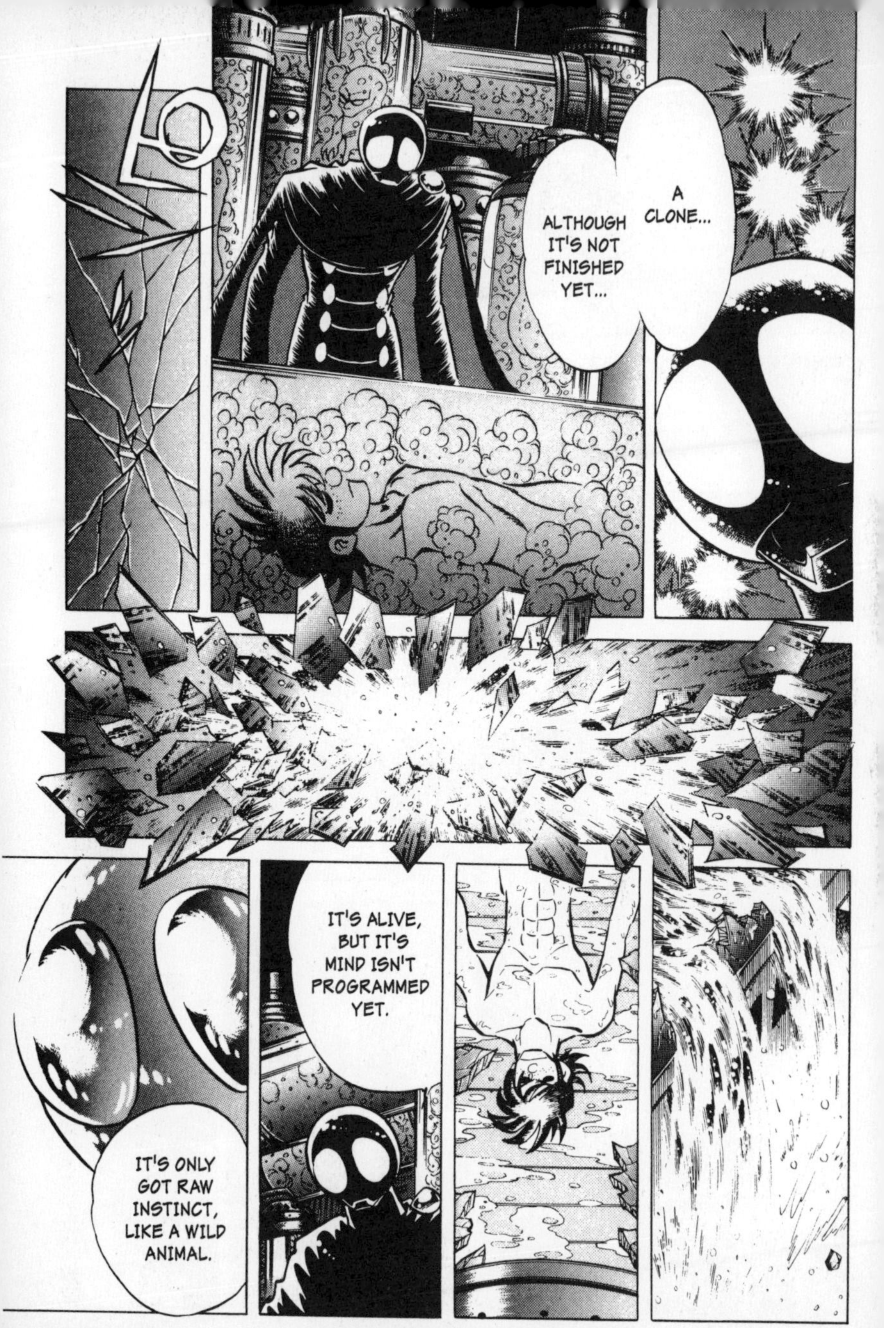
A CLONE...
ALTHOUGH IT'S NOT FINISHED YET...
IT'S ALIVE, BUT IT'S MIND ISN'T PROGRAMMED YET.
IT'S ONLY GOT RAW INSTINCT, LIKE A WILD ANIMAL.

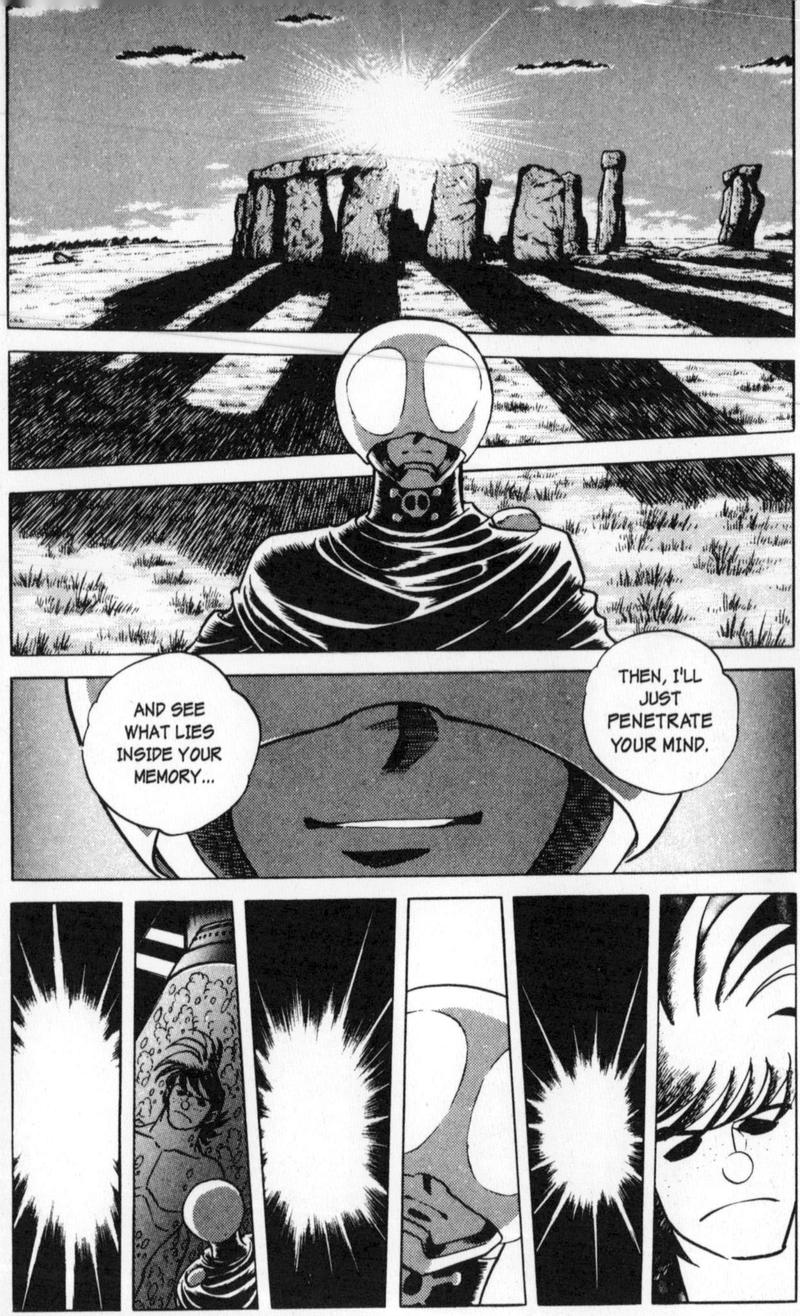
THEN, I'LL JUST PENETRATE YOUR MIND.
AND SEE WHAT LIES INSIDE YOUR MEMORY...

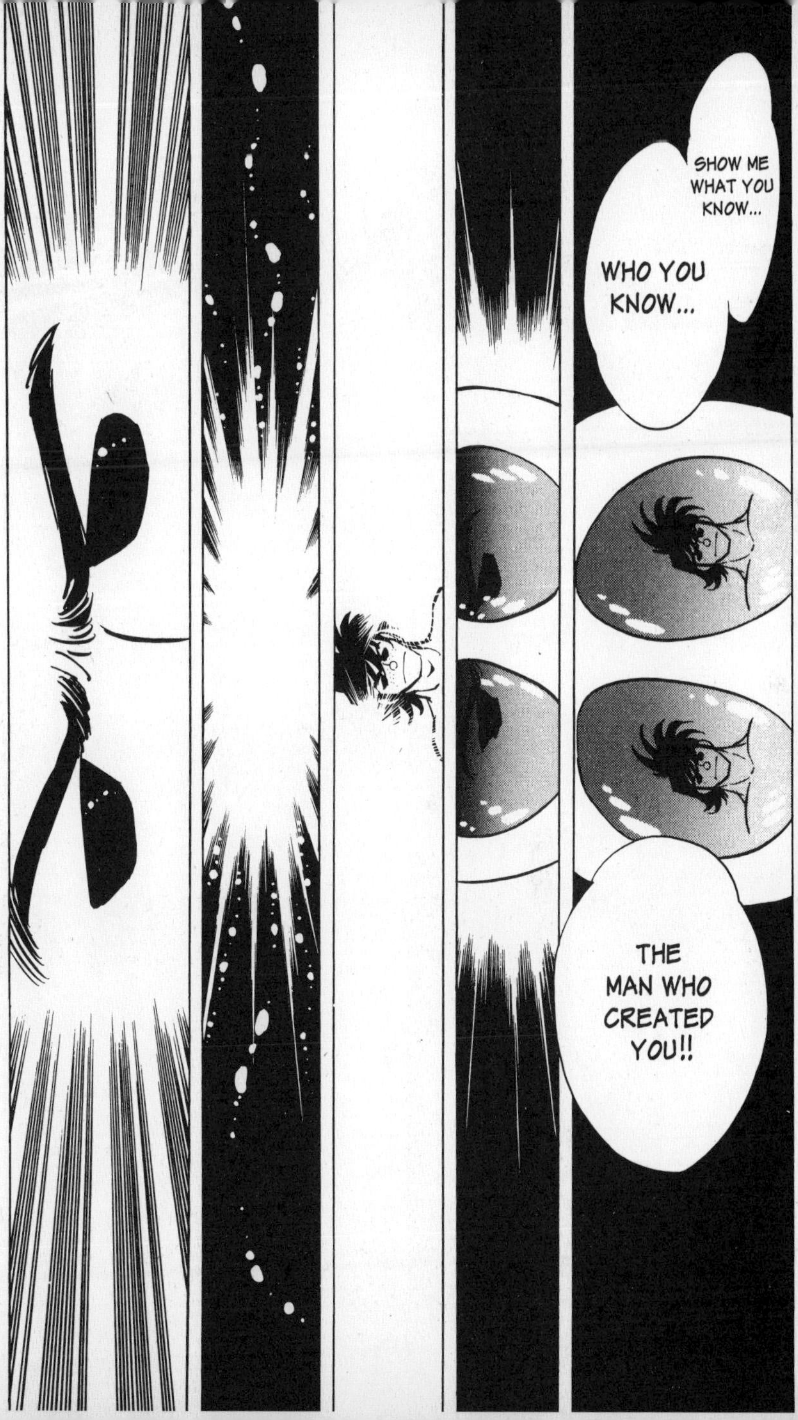
SHOW ME WHAT YOU KNOW...
WHO YOU KNOW...
THE MAN WHO CREATED YOU!!

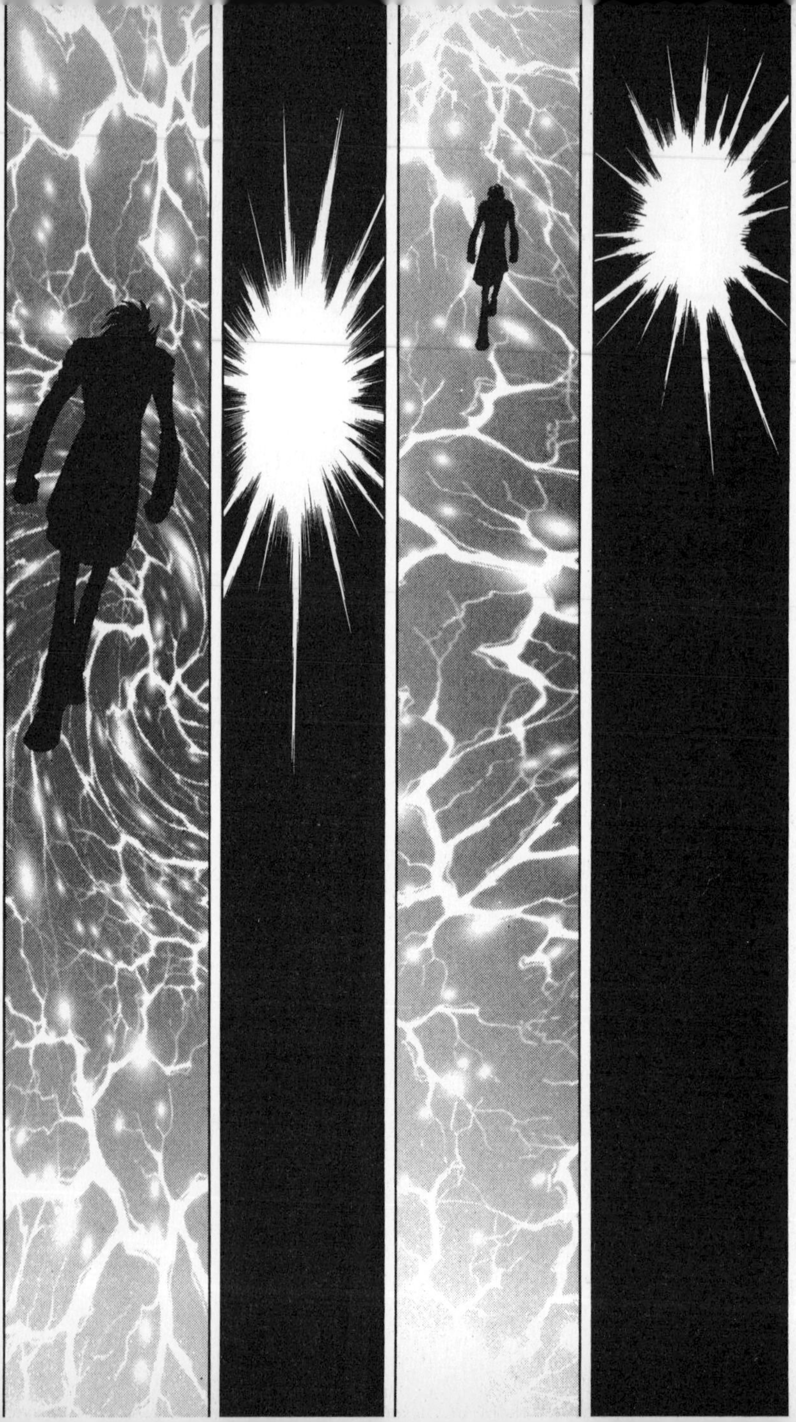

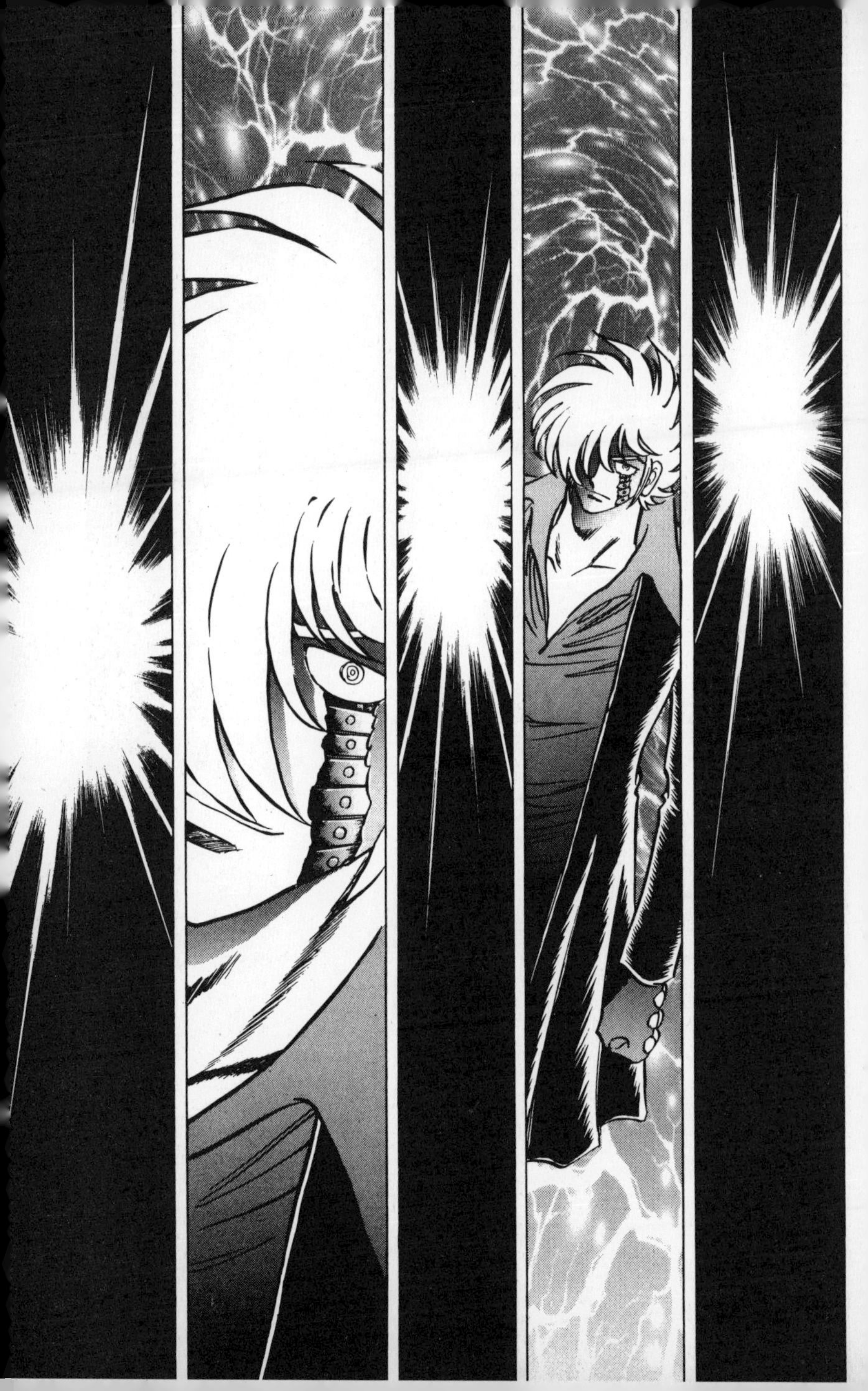

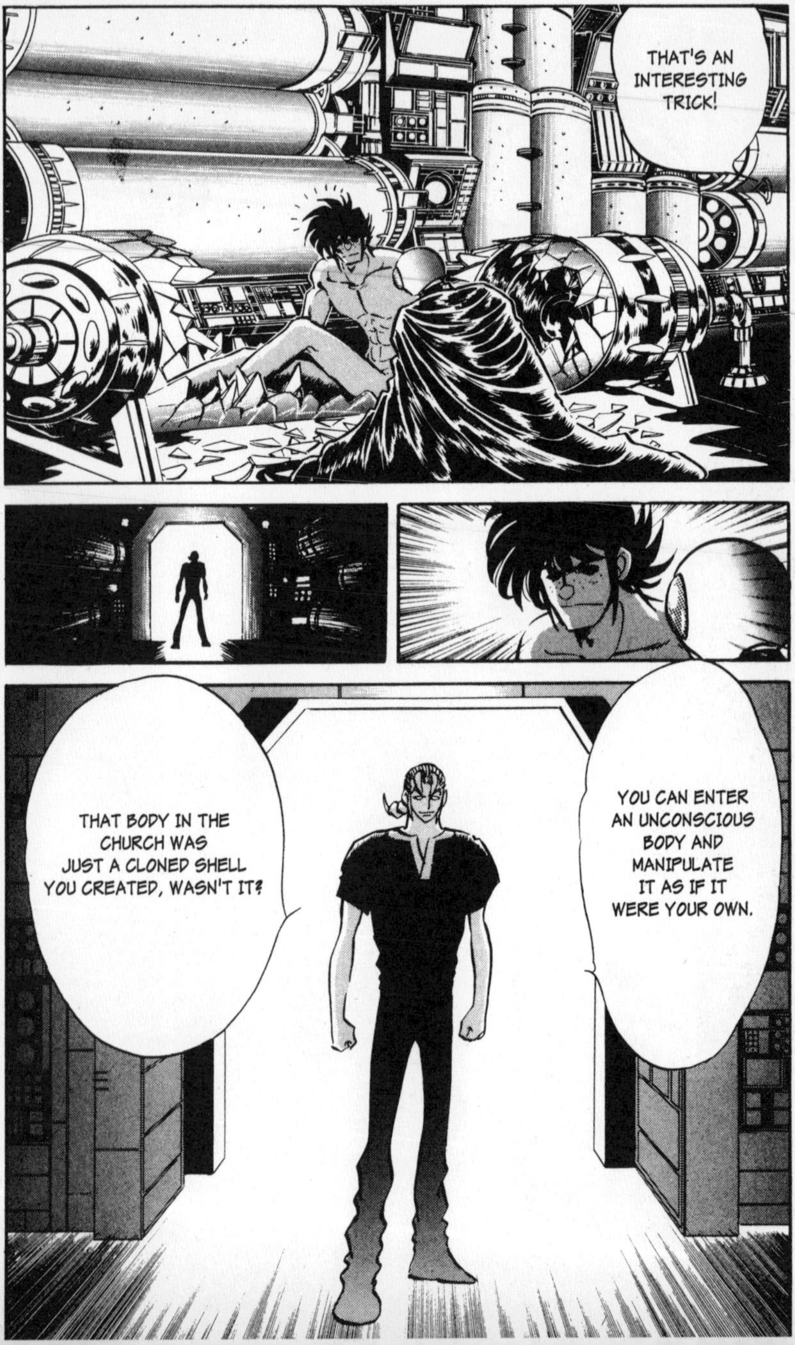
THAT'S AN INTERESTING TRICK!
YOU CAN ENTER AN UNCONSCIOUS BODY AND MANIPULATE IT AS IF IT WERE YOUR OWN.
THAT BODY IN THE CHURCH WAS JUST A CLONED SHELL YOU CREATED, WASN'T IT?

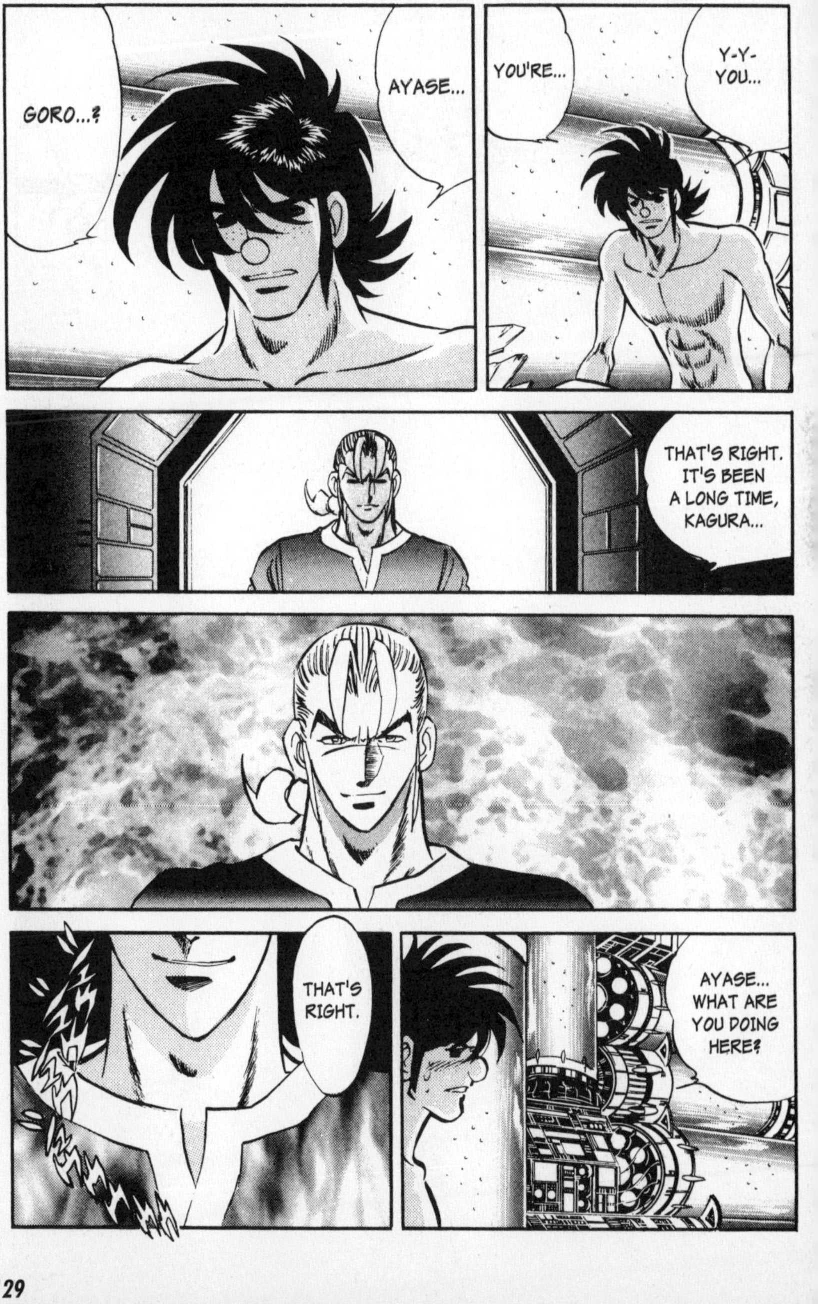
Y-Y-YOU...
YOU'RE...
AYASE...
GORO...?
THAT'S RIGHT. IT'S BEEN A LONG TIME, KAGURA...
AYASE... WHAT ARE YOU DOING HERE?
THAT'S RIGHT.

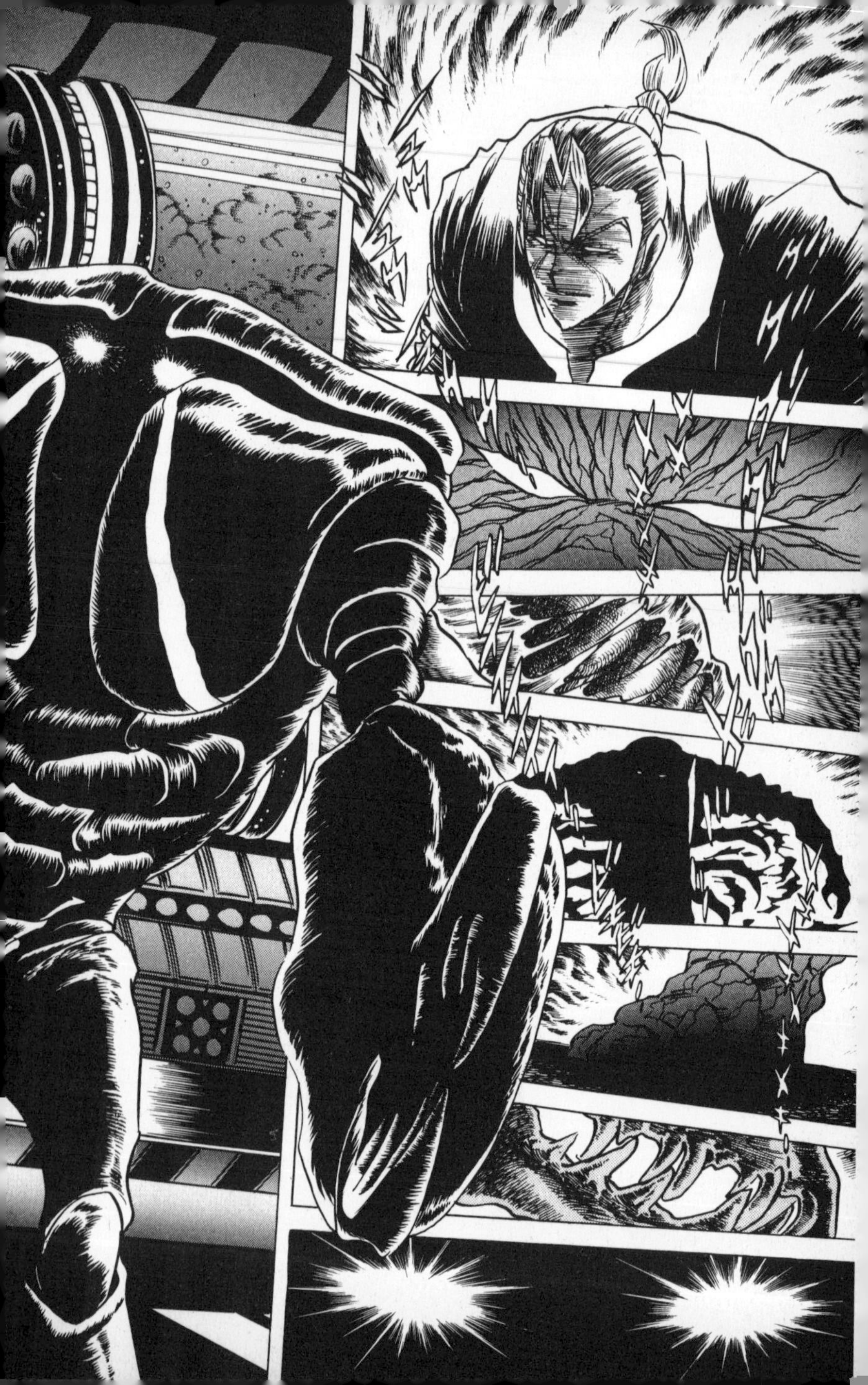

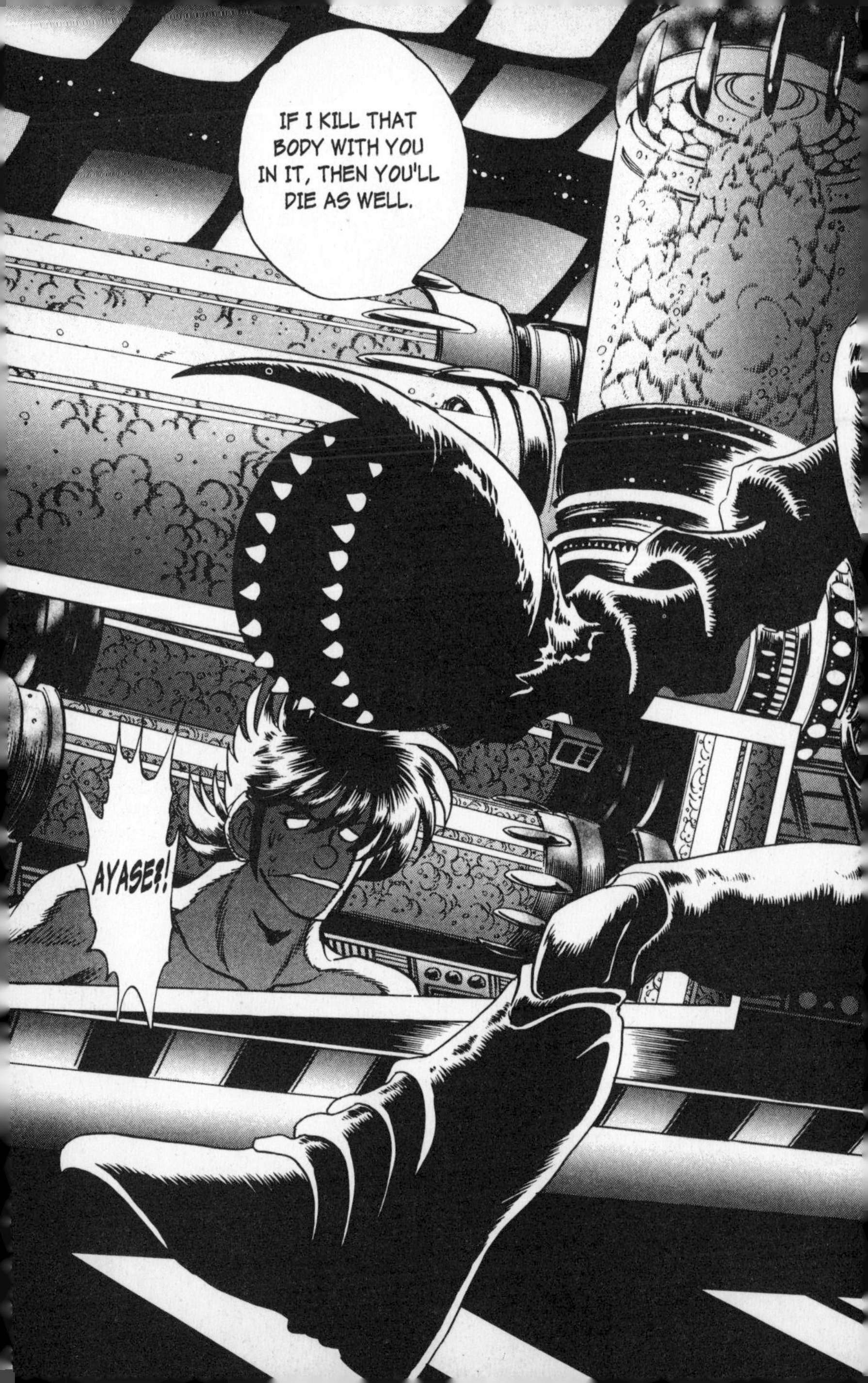
IF I KILL THAT BODY WITH YOU IN IT, THEN YOU'LL DIE AS WELL.
AYASE?!

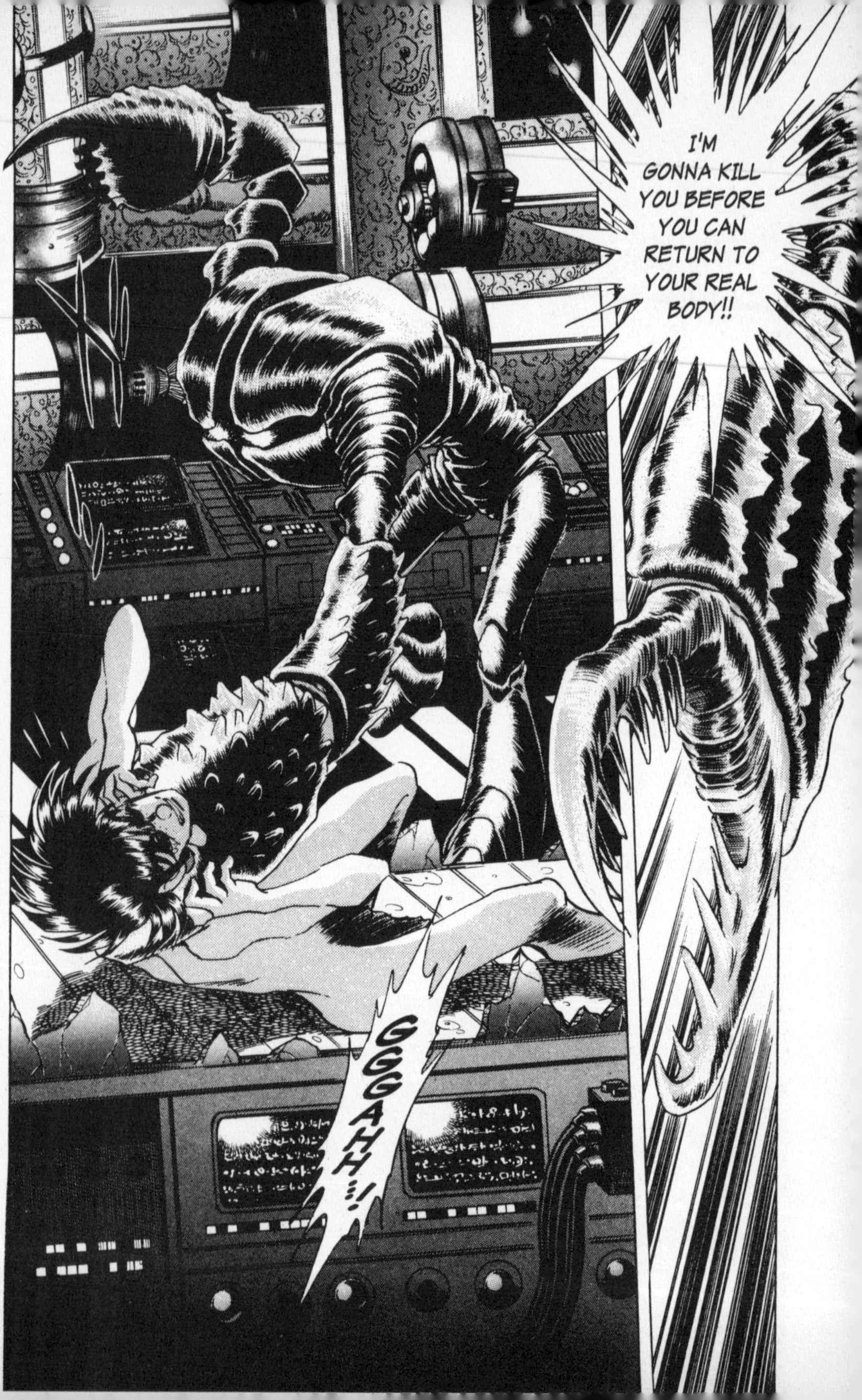
I'M GONNA KILL YOU BEFORE YOU CAN RETURN TO YOUR REAL BODY!!
GGGAHH!!

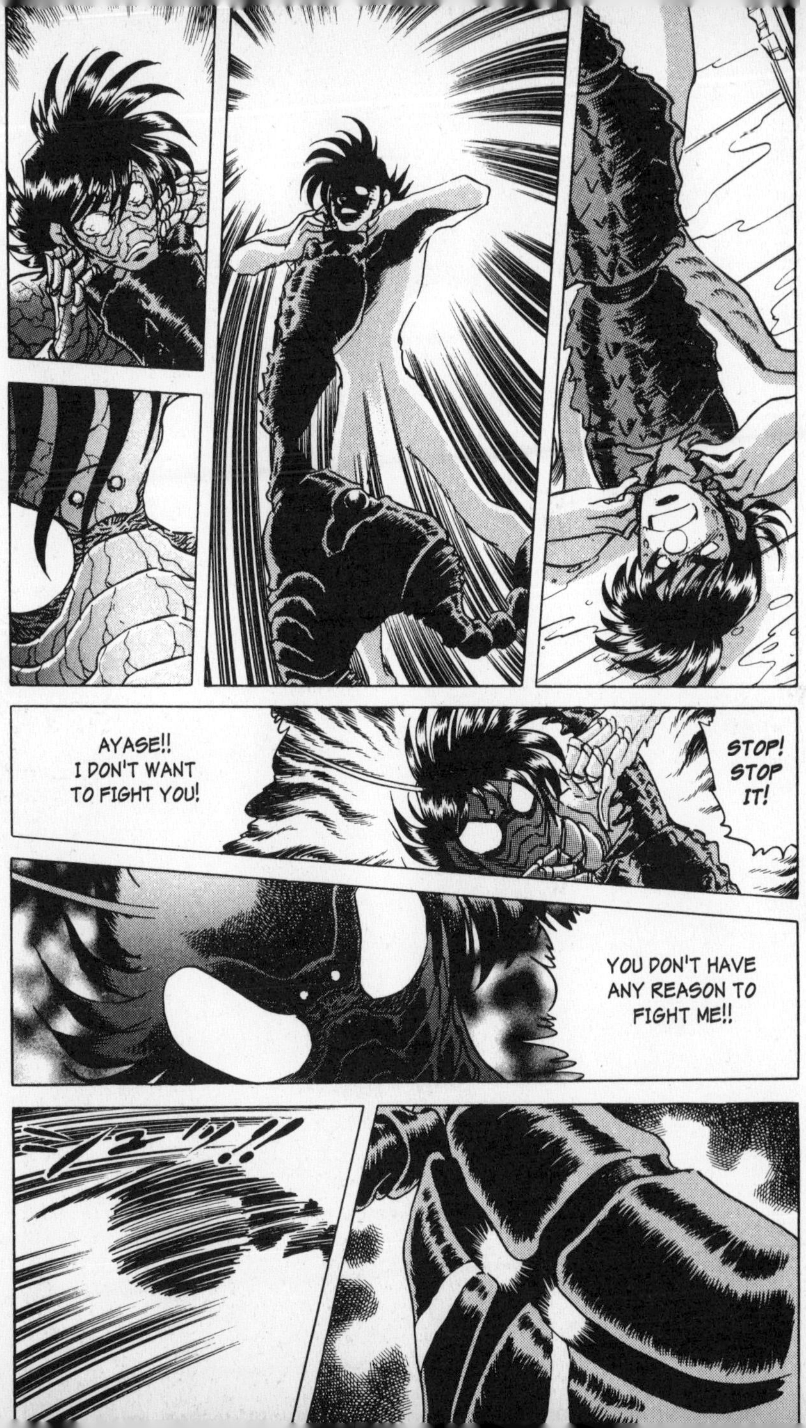
STOP! STOP IT!
AYASE!! I DON'T WANT TO FIGHT YOU!
YOU DON'T HAVE ANY REASON TO FIGHT ME!!

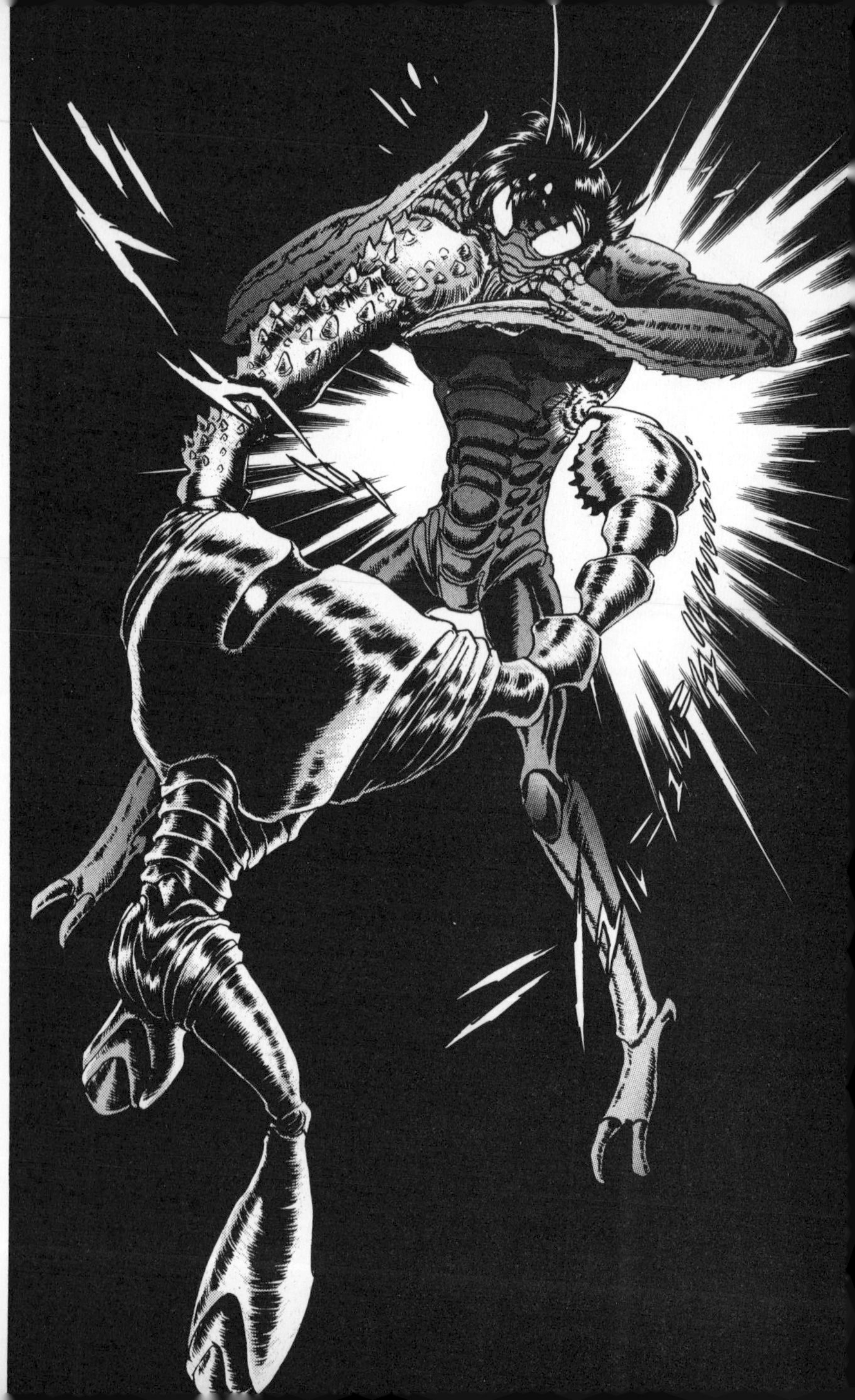

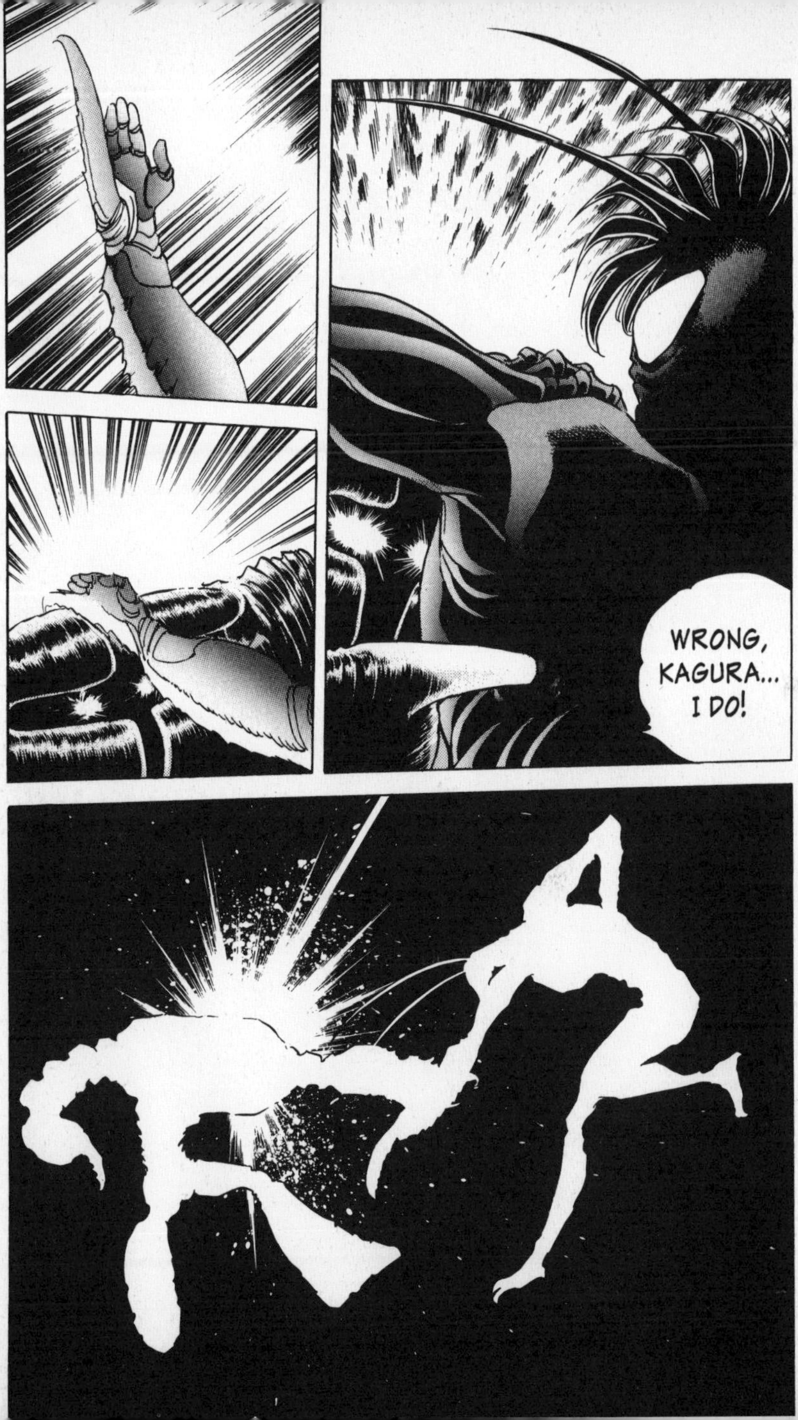
WRONG, KAGURA... I DO!

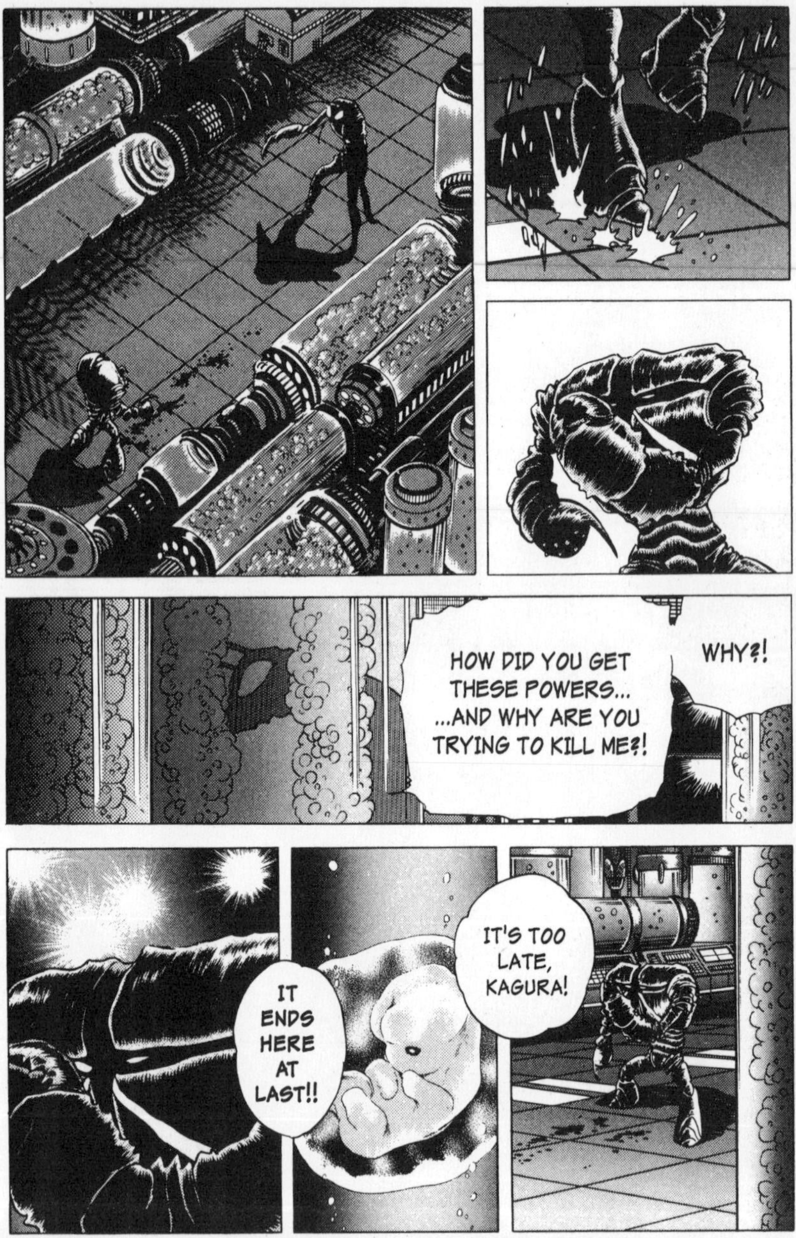
WHY?!
HOW DID YOU GET THESE POWERS... ...AND WHY ARE YOU TRYING TO KILL ME?!
IT'S TOO LATE, KAGURA!
IT ENDS HERE AT LAST!!

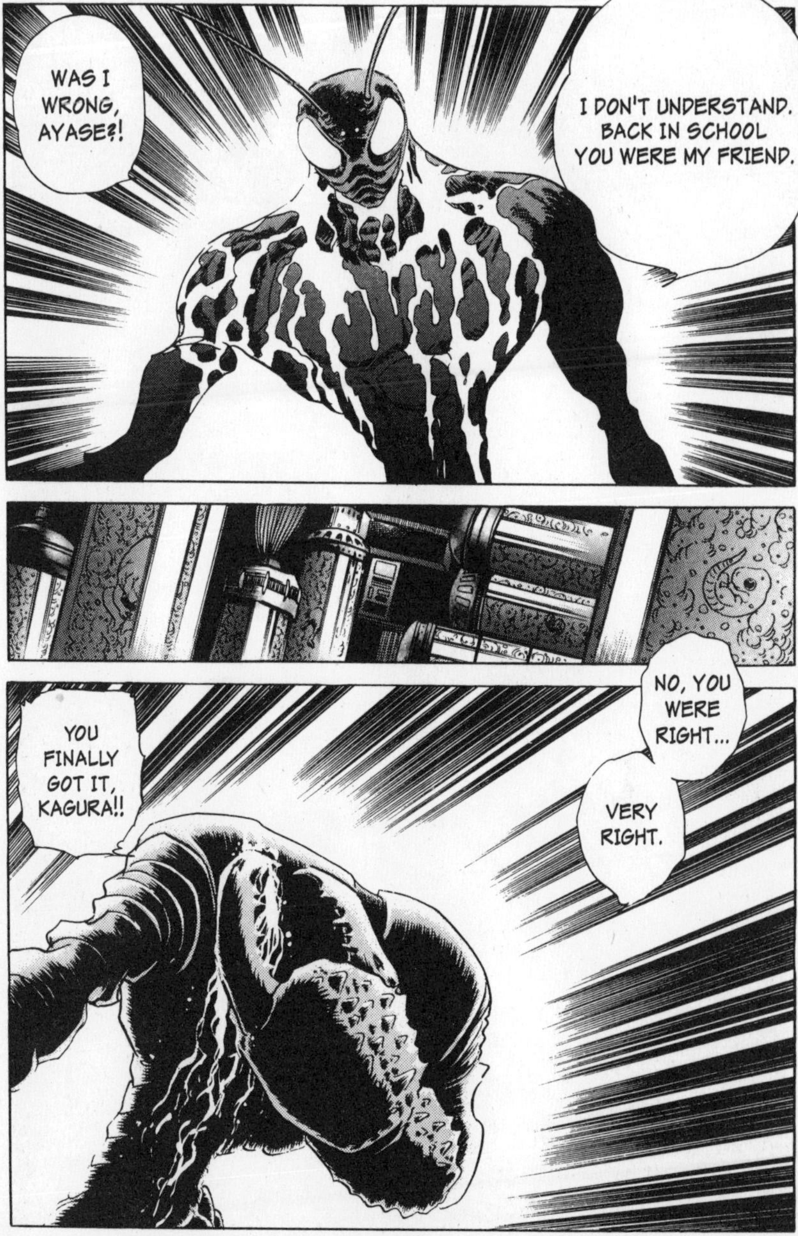
I DON'T UNDERSTAND. BACK IN SCHOOL YOU WERE MY FRIEND.
WAS I WRONG, AYASE?!
NO, YOU WERE RIGHT...
VERY RIGHT.
YOU FINALLY GOT IT, KAGURA!!

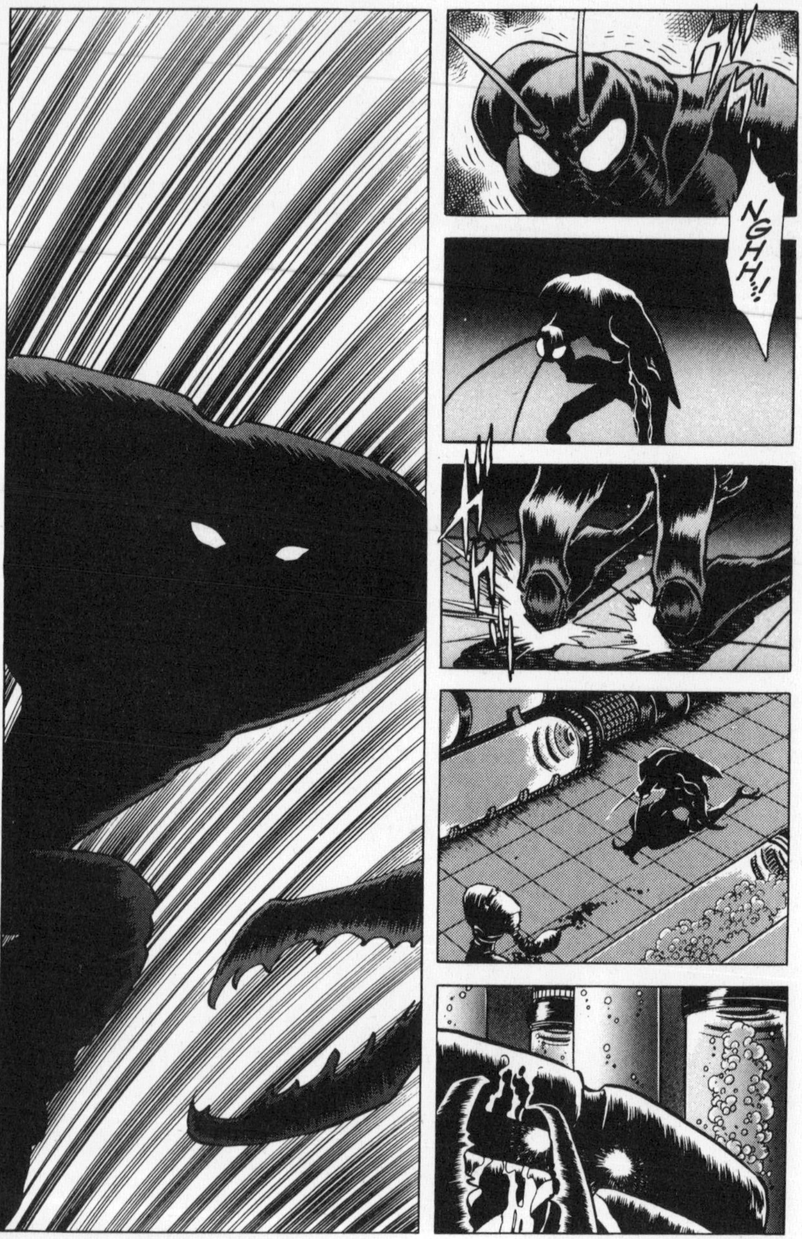
NGHH...!

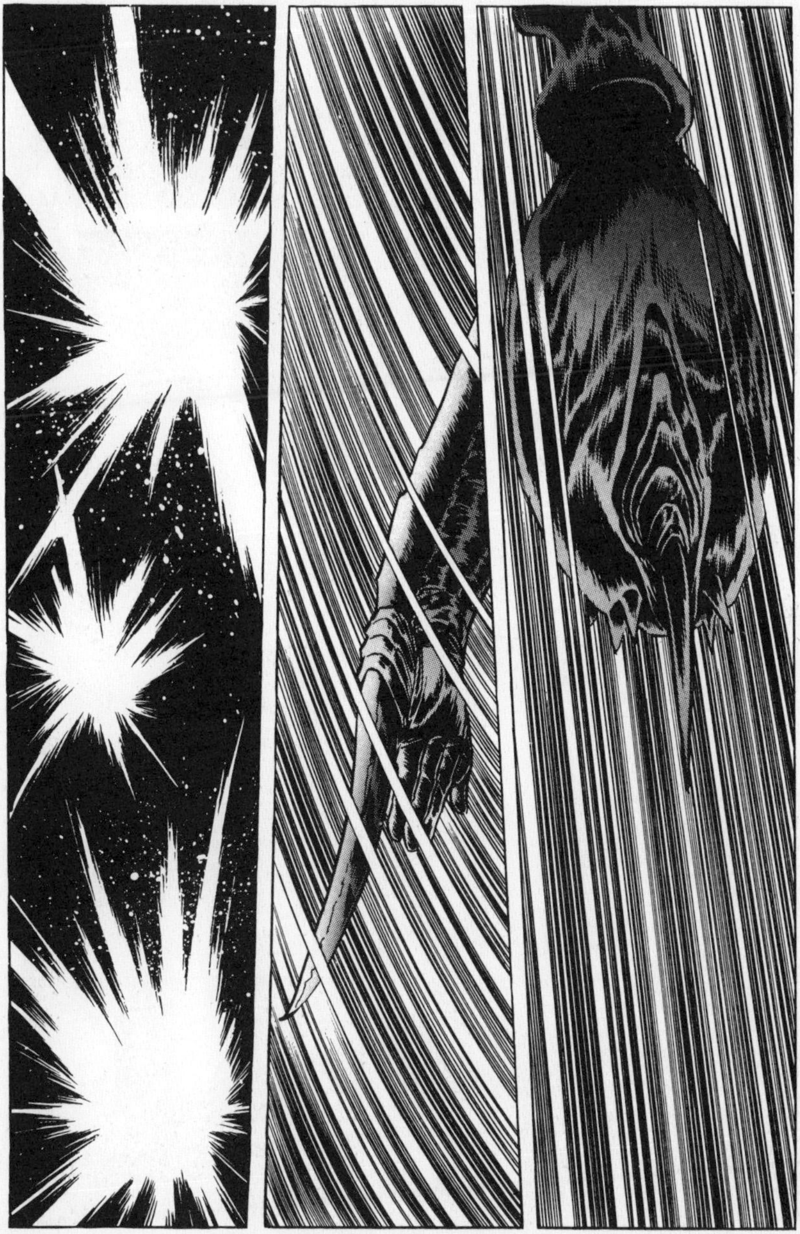

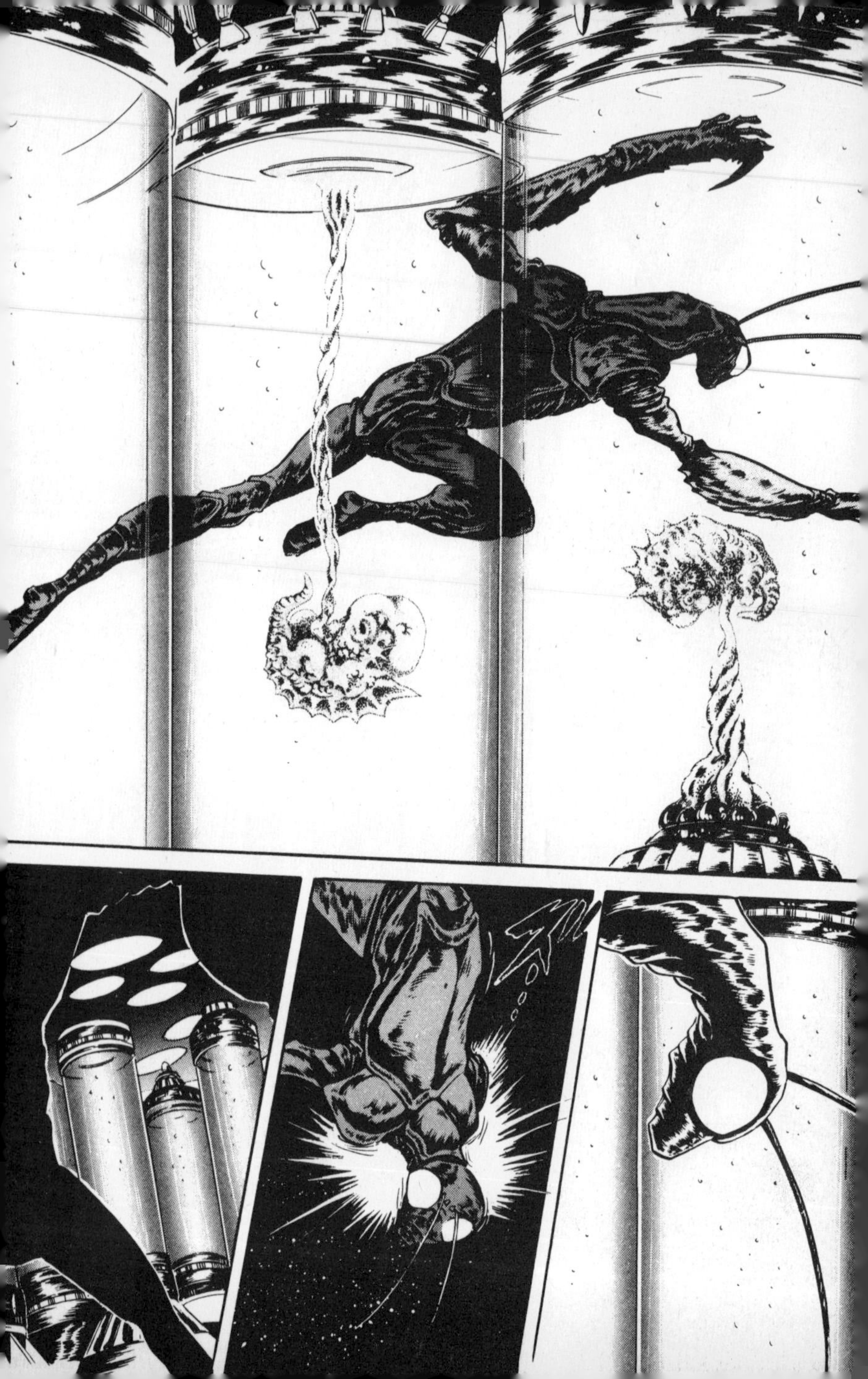

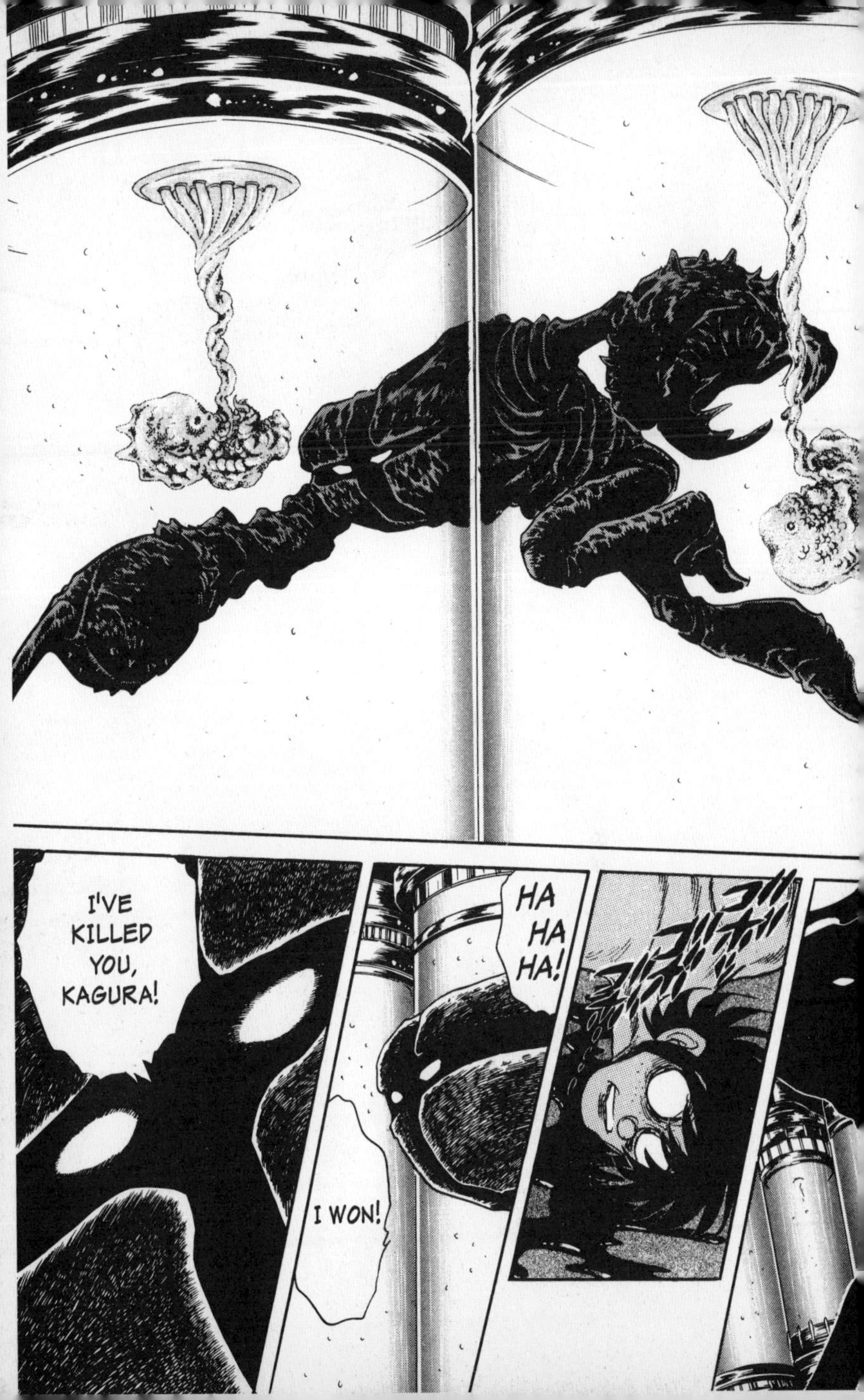
HA HA HA!
I WON!
I'VE KILLED YOU, KAGURA!

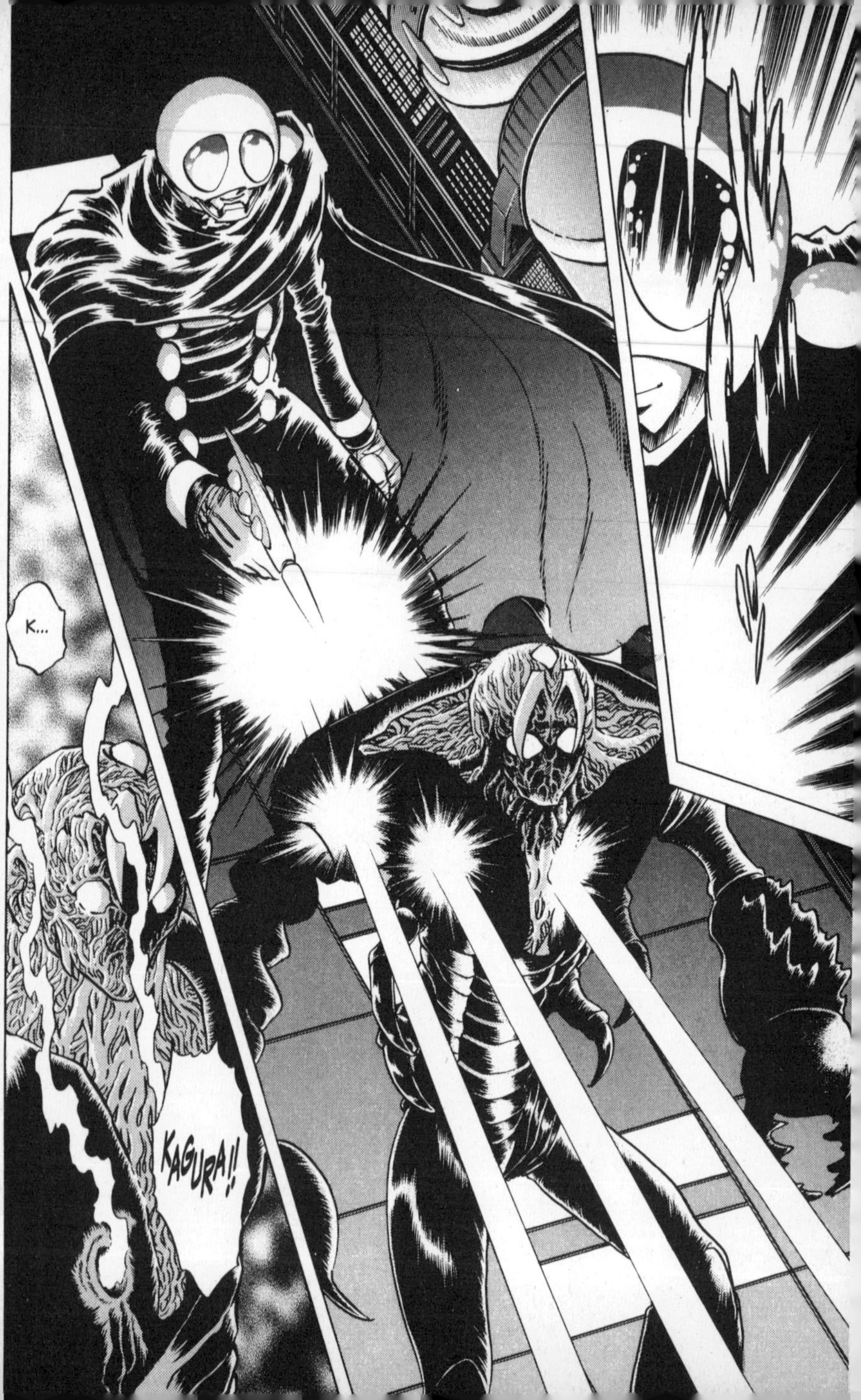
K...
KAGURA!!

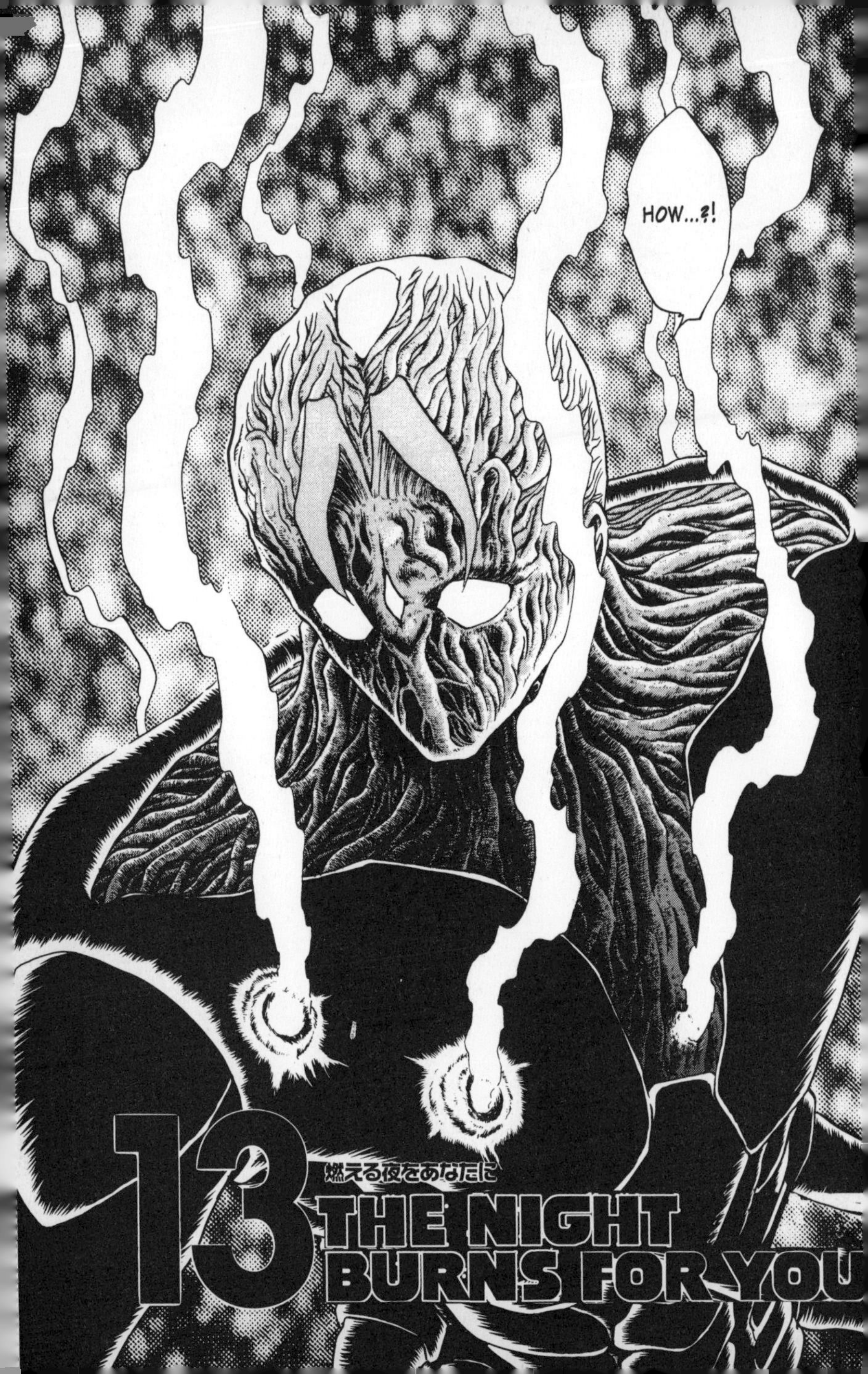
HOW...?!
13
燃える夜をあなたに
THE NIGHT BURNS FOR YOU

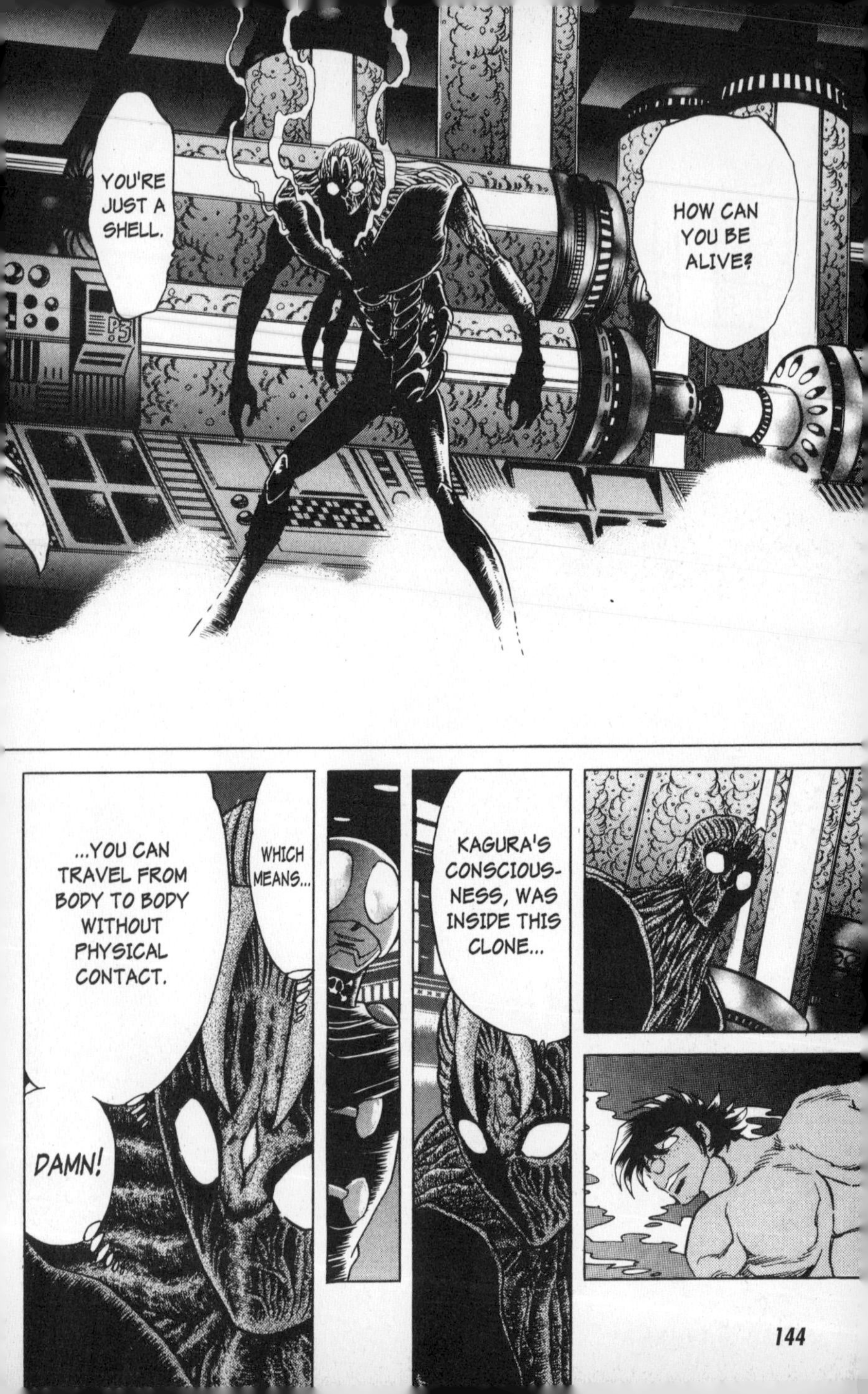
HOW CAN YOU BE ALIVE?
YOU'RE JUST A SHELL.
KAGURA'S CONSCIOUSNESS, WAS INSIDE THIS CLONE...
WHICH MEANS...
...YOU CAN TRAVEL FROM BODY TO BODY WITHOUT PHYSICAL CONTACT.
DAMN!

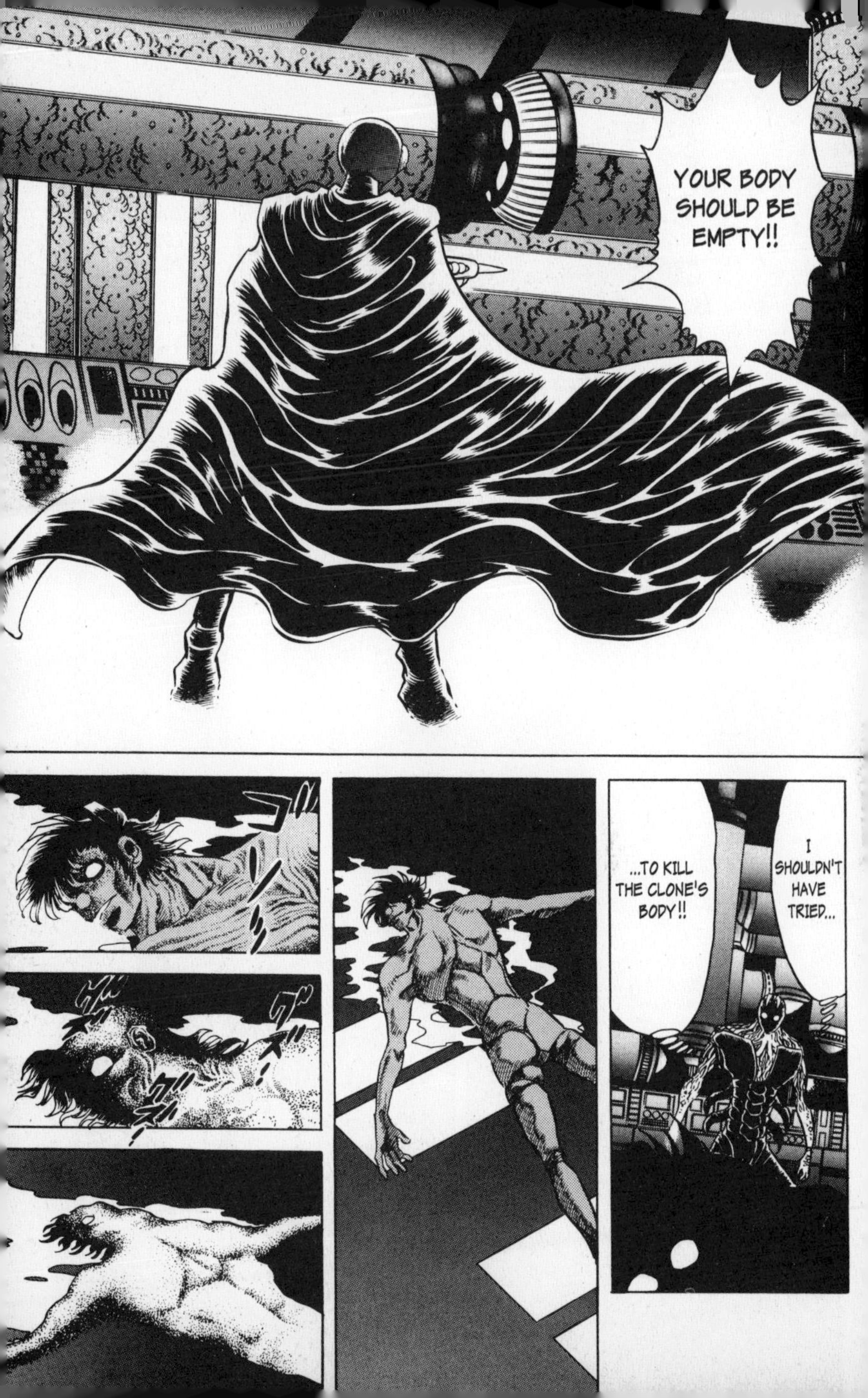
YOUR BODY SHOULD BE EMPTY!!
I SHOULDN'T HAVE TRIED...
...TO KILL THE CLONE'S BODY!!

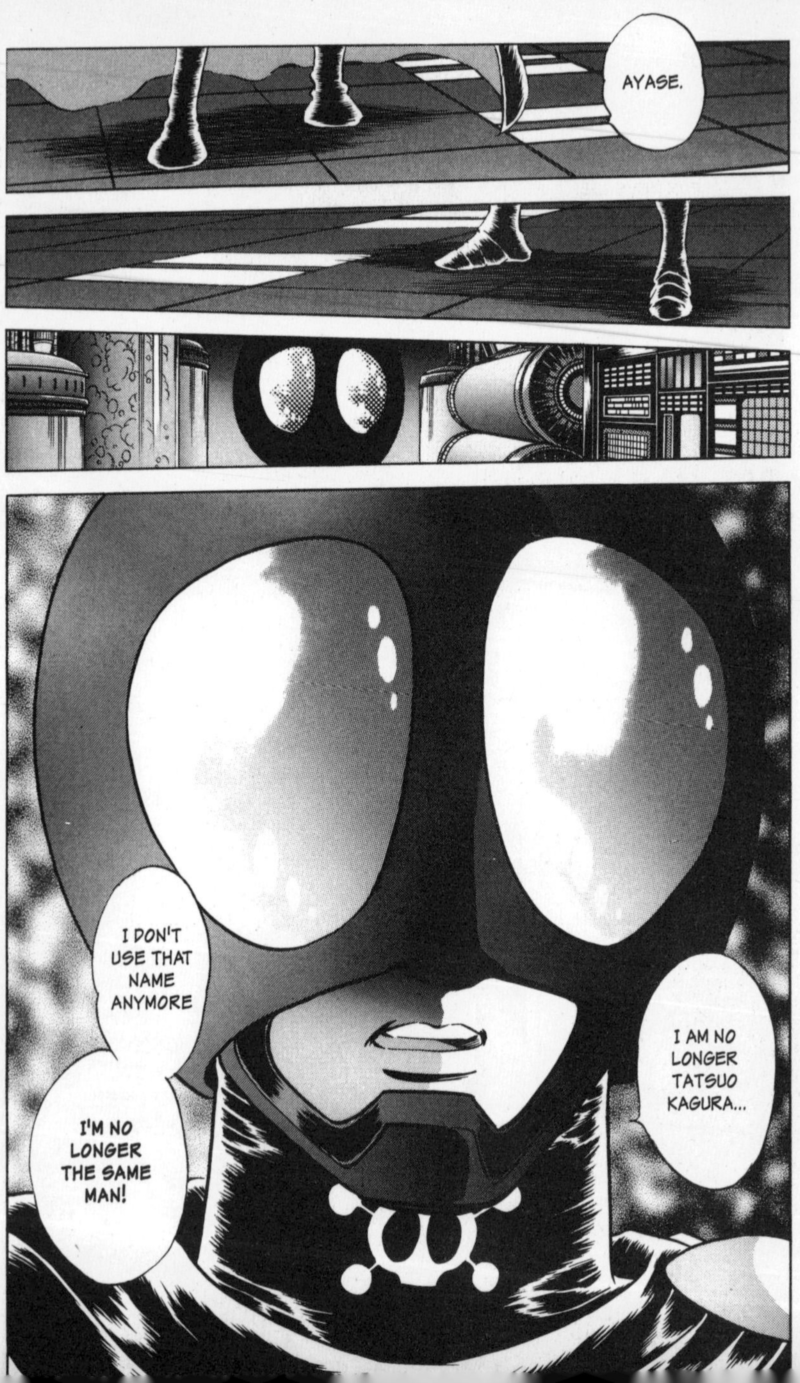
AYASE.
I AM NO LONGER TATSUO KAGURA...
I DON'T USE THAT NAME ANYMORE
I'M NO LONGER THE SAME MAN!

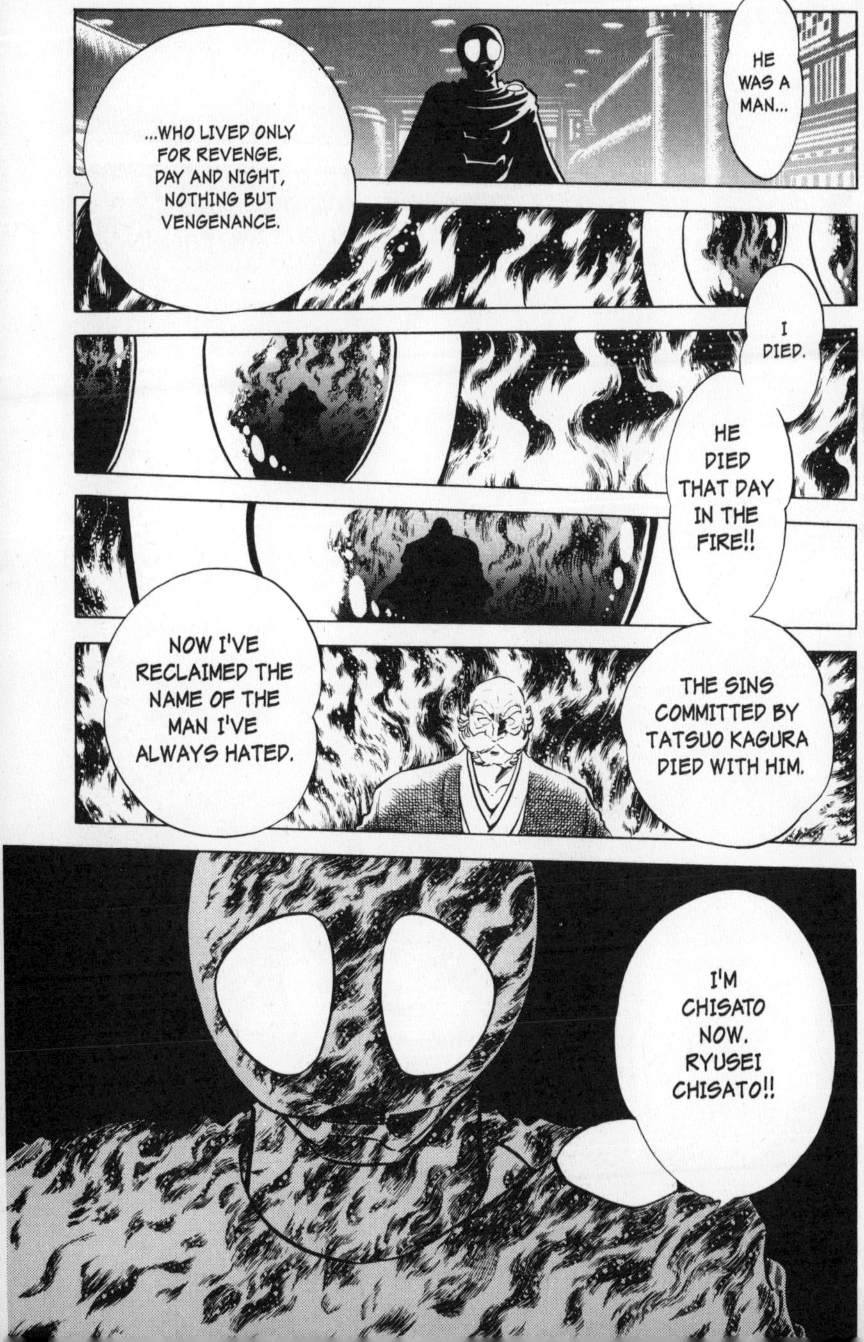
HE WAS A MAN...
...WHO LIVED ONLY FOR REVENGE. DAY AND NIGHT, NOTHING BUT VENGENANCE.
I DIED.
HE DIED THAT DAY IN THE FIRE!!
THE SINS COMMITTED BY TATSUO KAGURA DIED WITH HIM.
NOW I'VE RECLAIMED THE NAME OF THE MAN I'VE ALWAYS HATED.
I'M CHISATO NOW. RYUSEI CHISATO!!

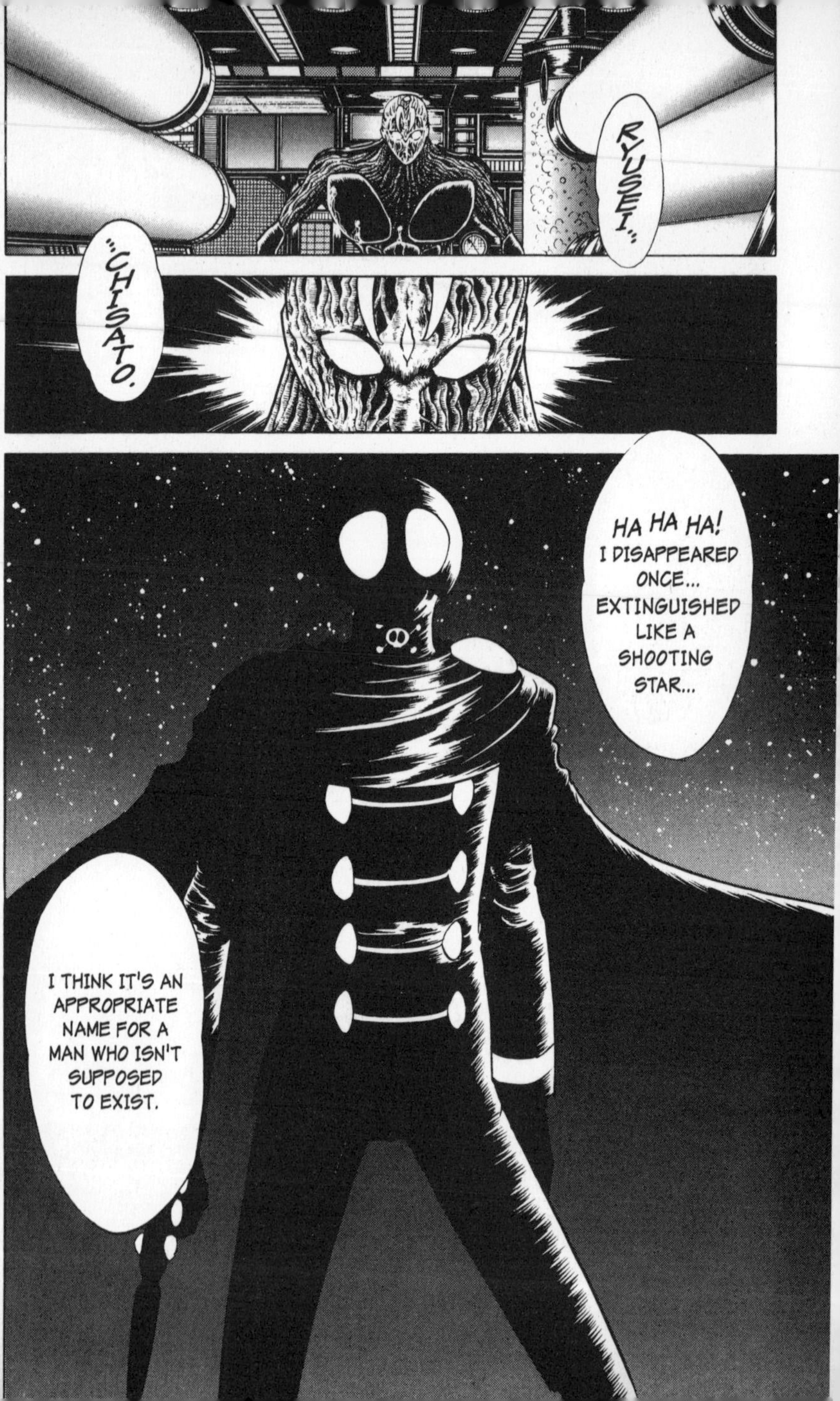
RYUSEI...
...CHISATO.
HA HA HA! I DISAPPEARED ONCE... EXTINGUISHED LIKE A SHOOTING STAR...
I THINK IT'S AN APPROPRIATE NAME FOR A MAN WHO ISN'T SUPPOSED TO EXIST.

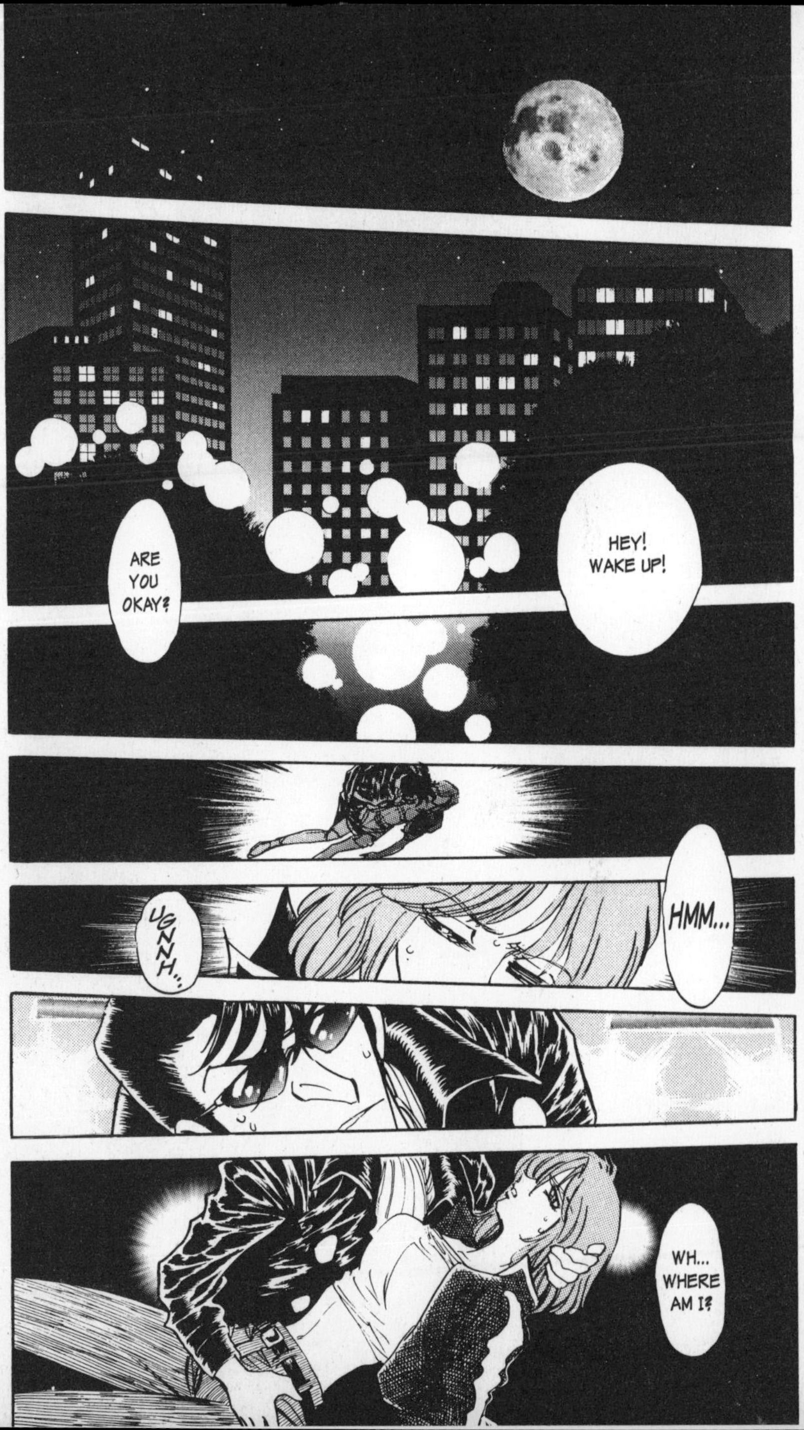
HEY! WAKE UP!
ARE YOU OKAY?
HMM...
UGNNH..
WH... WHERE AM I?

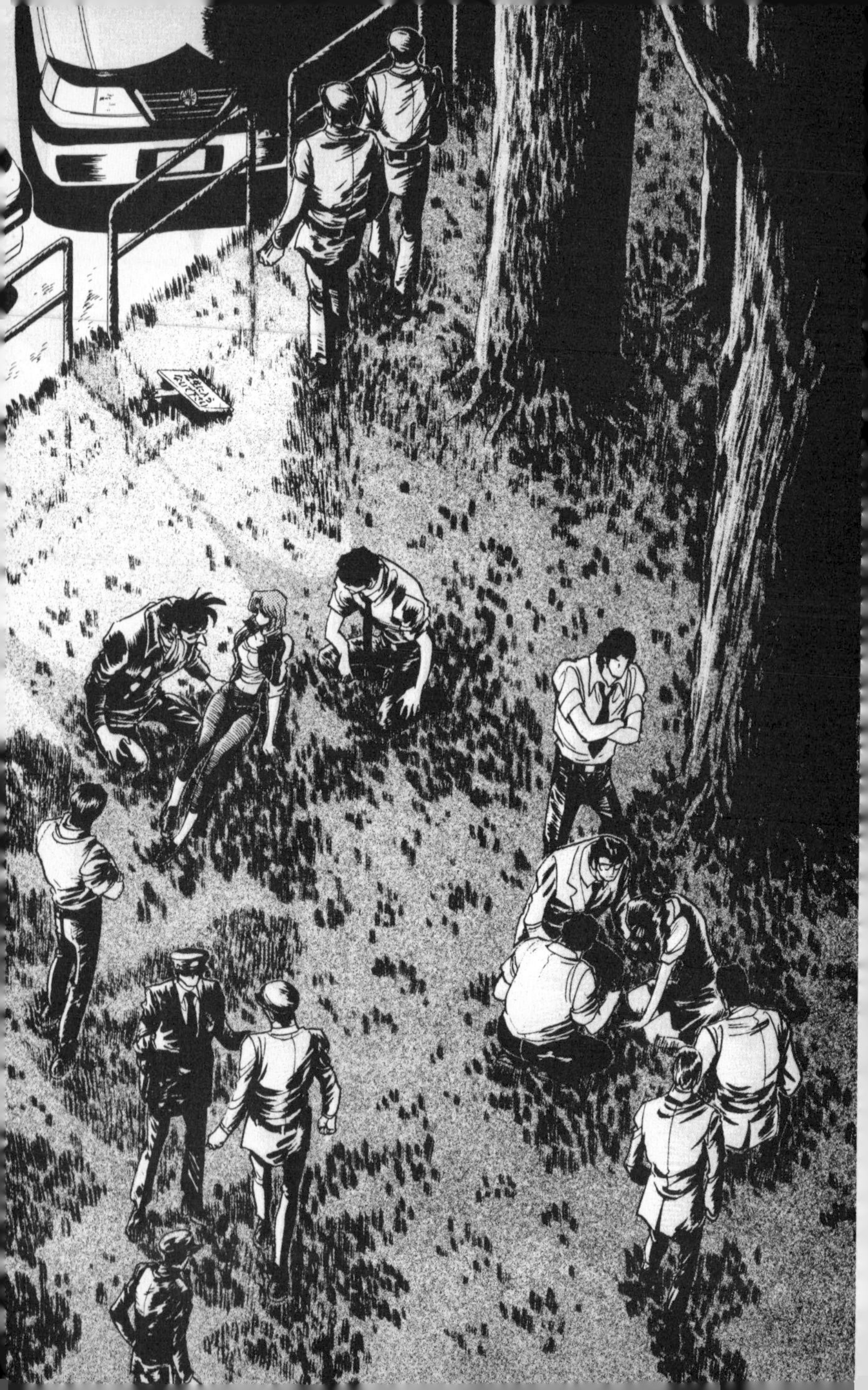

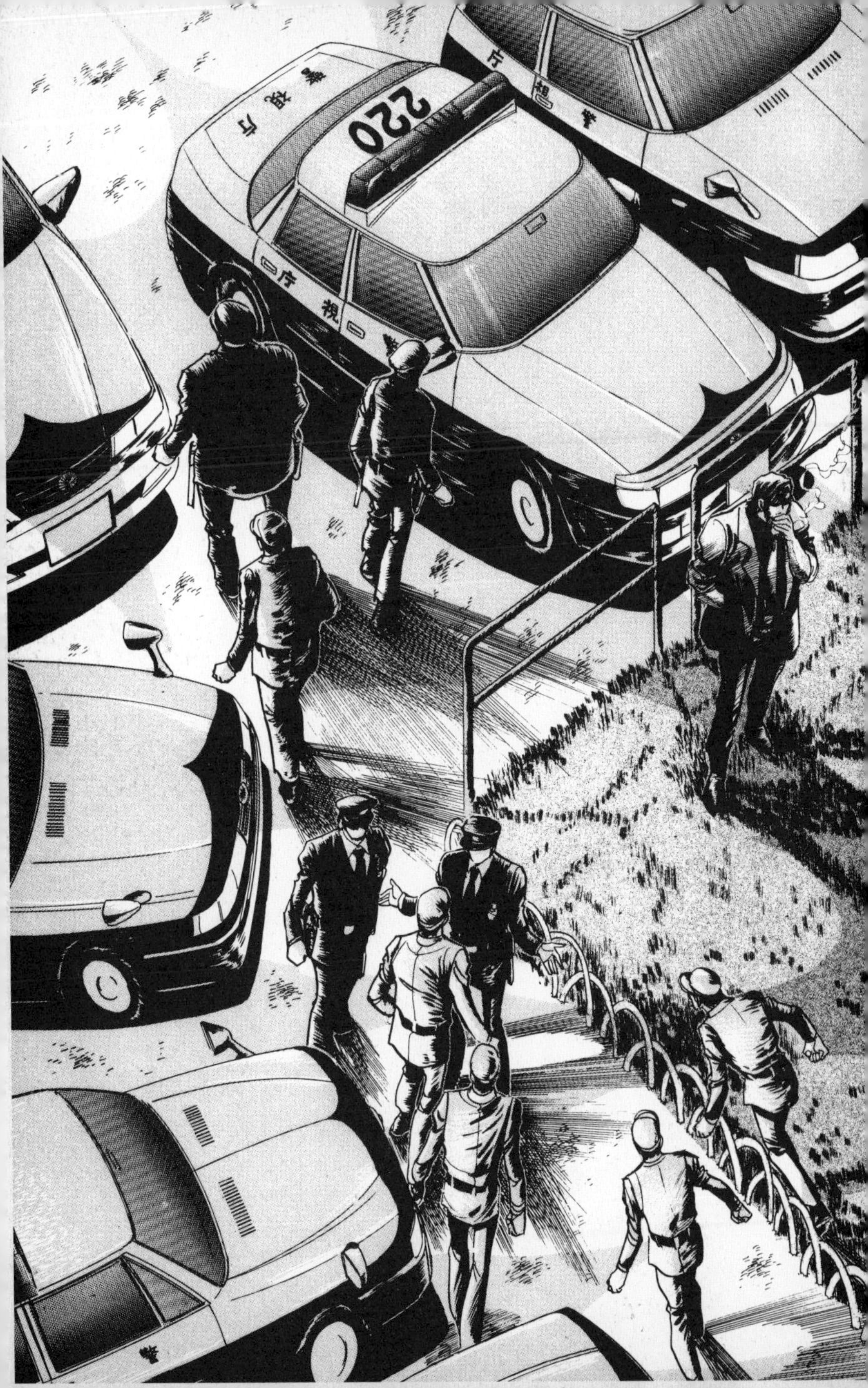
警視庁
220

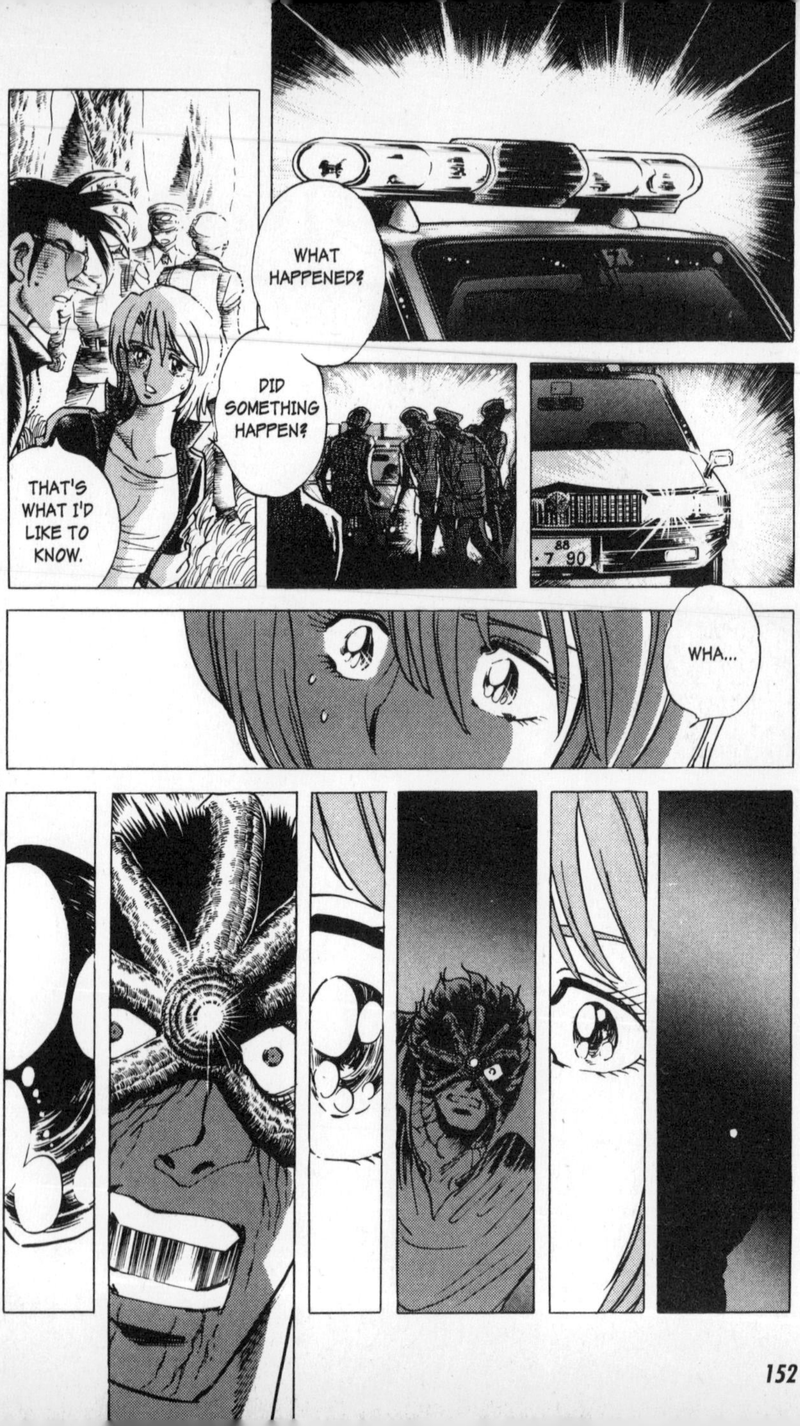
WHAT HAPPENED?
DID SOMETHING HAPPEN?
THAT'S WHAT I'D LIKE TO KNOW.
WHA...

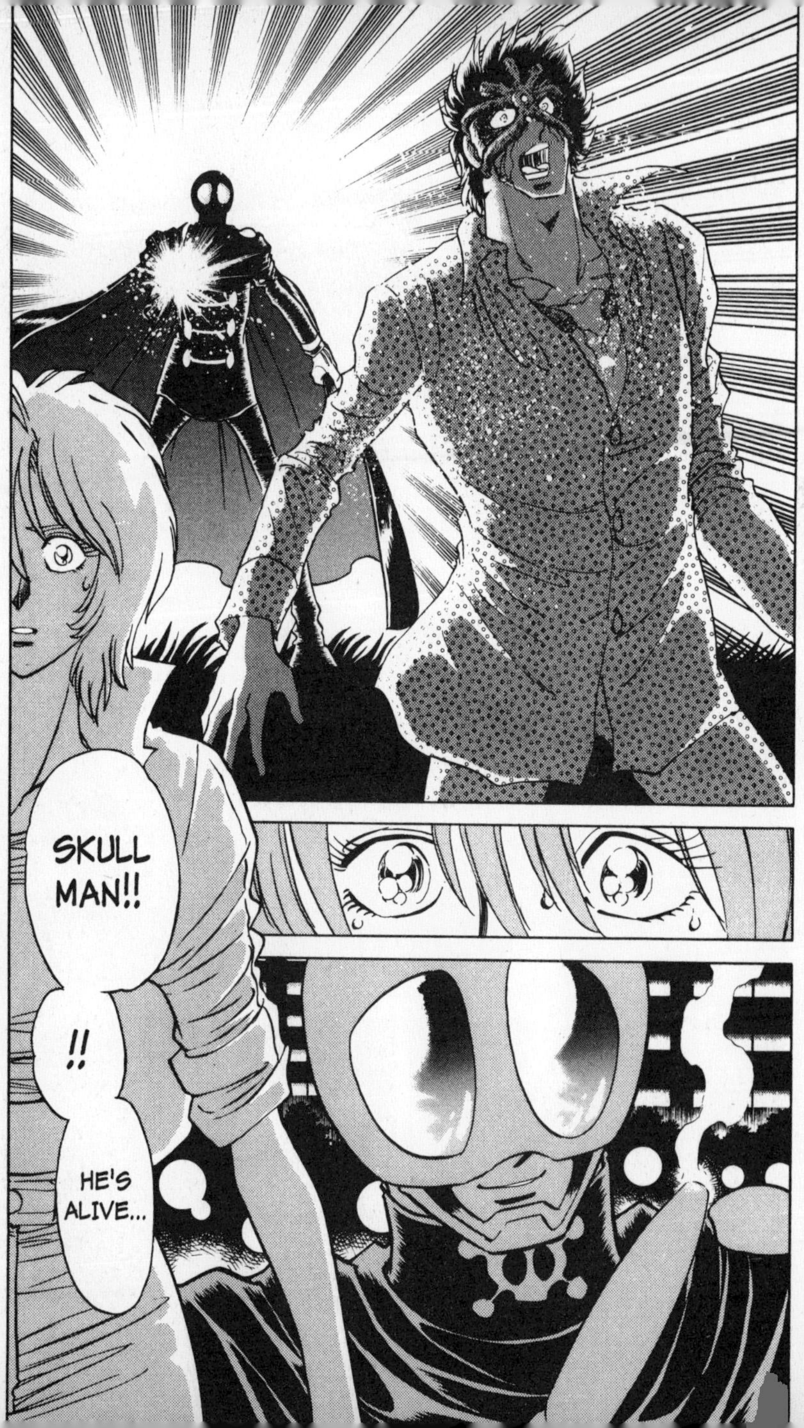
SKULL MAN!!
!!
HE'S ALIVE...

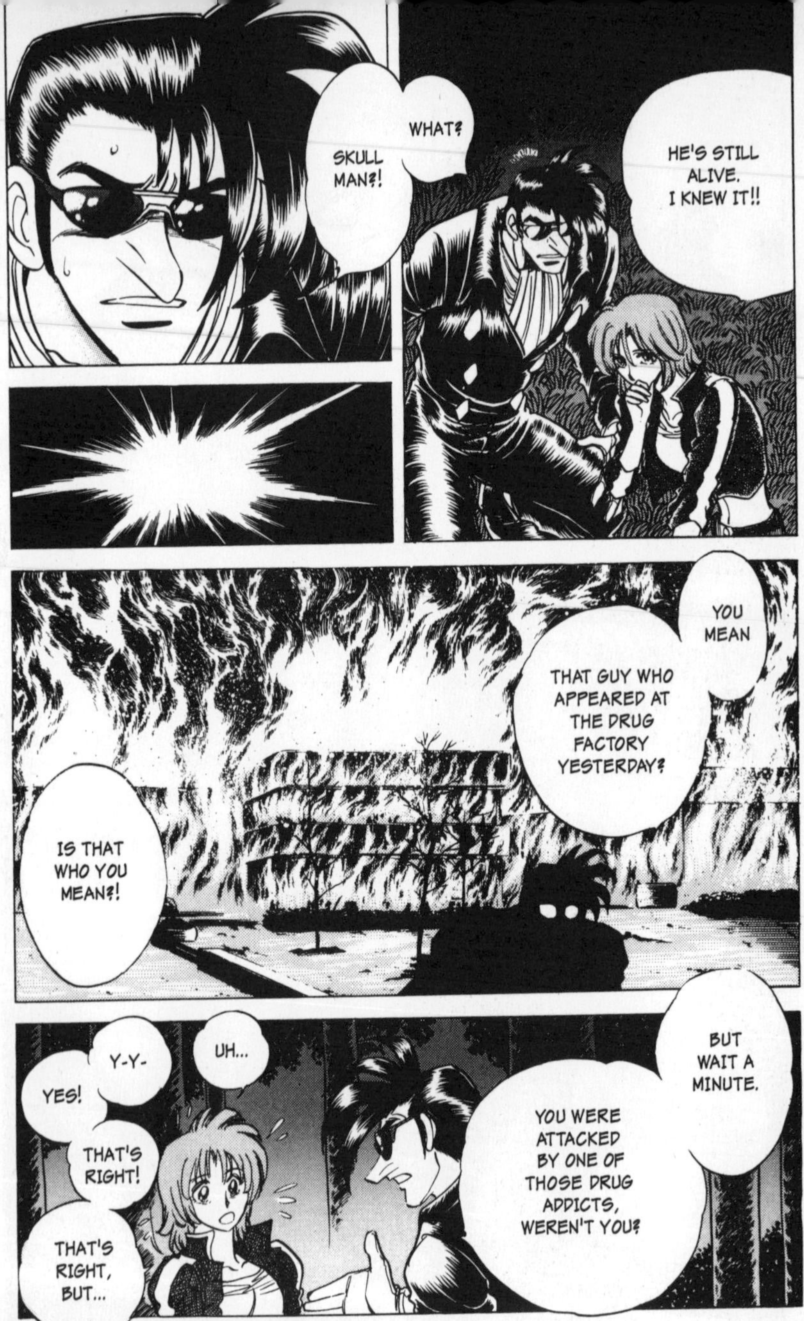
HE'S STILL ALIVE. I KNEW IT!!
WHAT?
SKULL MAN?!
YOU MEAN
THAT GUY WHO APPEARED AT THE DRUG FACTORY YESTERDAY?
IS THAT WHO YOU MEAN?!
BUT WAIT A MINUTE.
YOU WERE ATTACKED BY ONE OF THOSE DRUG ADDICTS, WEREN'T YOU?
UH...
Y-Y-
YES!
THAT'S RIGHT!
THAT'S RIGHT, BUT...

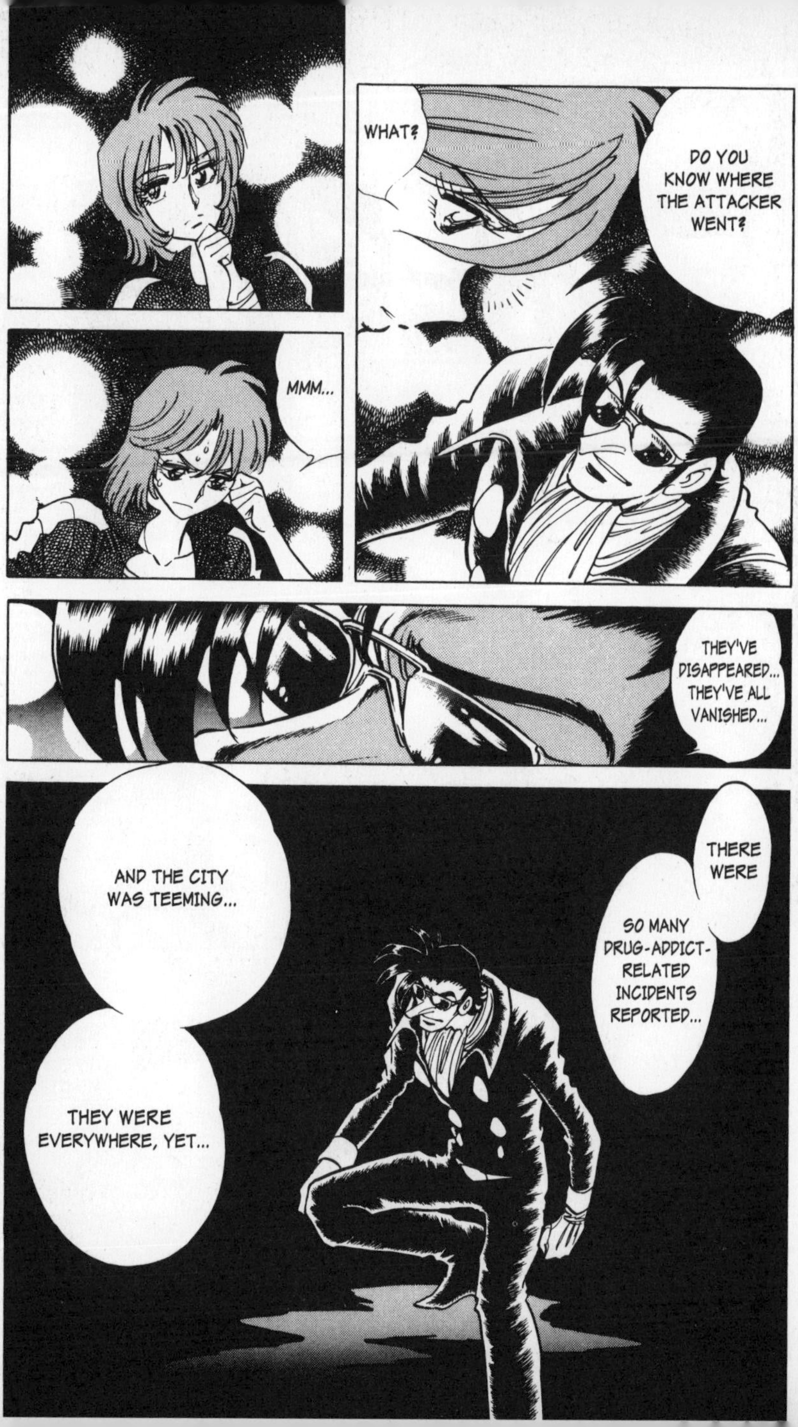
DO YOU KNOW WHERE THE ATTACKER WENT?
WHAT?
MMM...
THEY'VE DISAPPEARED... THEY'VE ALL VANISHED...
THERE WERE
SO MANY DRUG-ADDICT-RELATED INCIDENTS REPORTED...
AND THE CITY WAS TEEMING...
THEY WERE EVERYWHERE, YET...

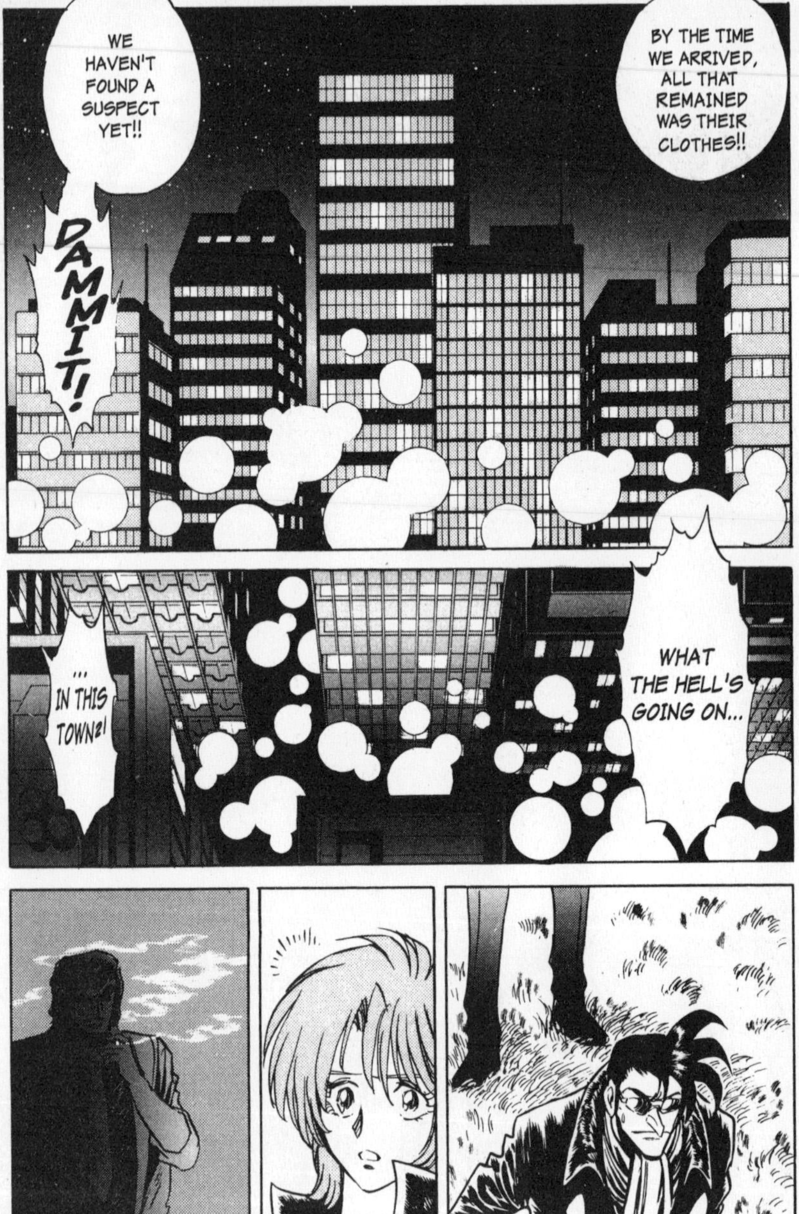
BY THE TIME WE ARRIVED, ALL THAT REMAINED WAS THEIR CLOTHES!!
WE HAVEN'T FOUND A SUSPECT YET!!
DAMMIT!
WHAT THE HELL'S GOING ON...
... IN THIS TOWN?!

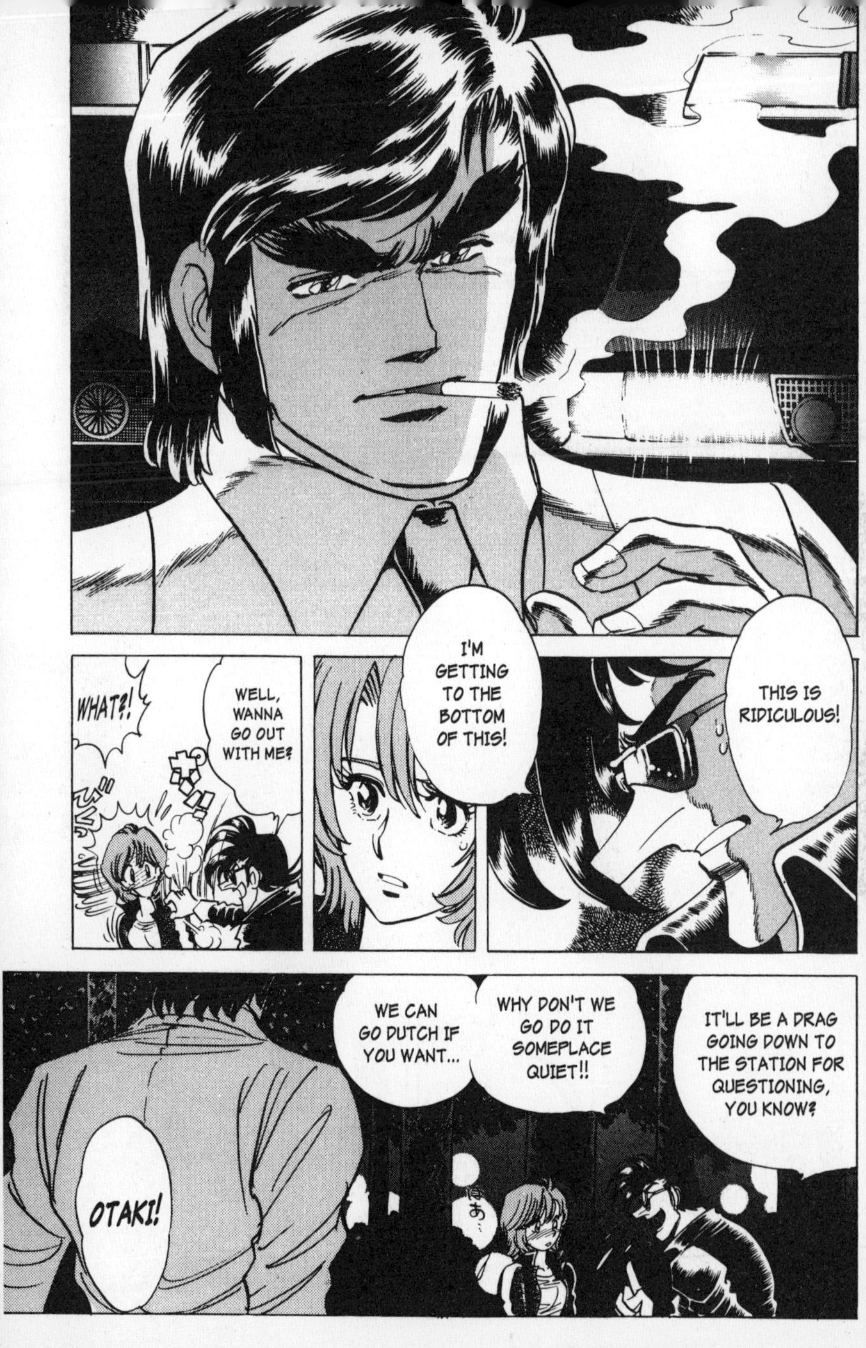
THIS IS RIDICULOUS!
I'M GETTING TO THE BOTTOM OF THIS!
WELL, WANNA GO OUT WITH ME?
WHAT?!
IT'LL BE A DRAG GOING DOWN TO THE STATION FOR QUESTIONING, YOU KNOW?
WHY DON'T WE GO DO IT SOMEPLACE QUIET!!
WE CAN GO DUTCH IF YOU WANT...
はあ…
OTAKI!

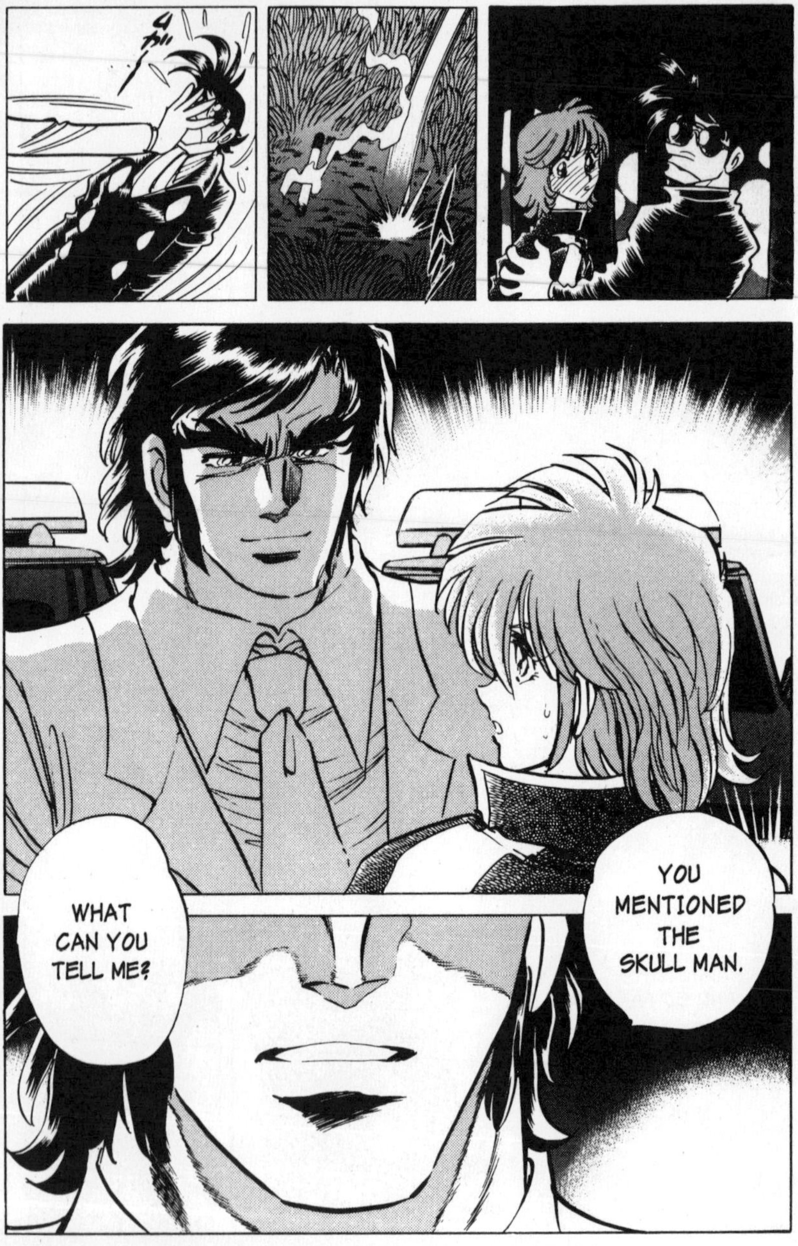
YOU MENTIONED THE SKULL MAN.
WHAT CAN YOU TELL ME?

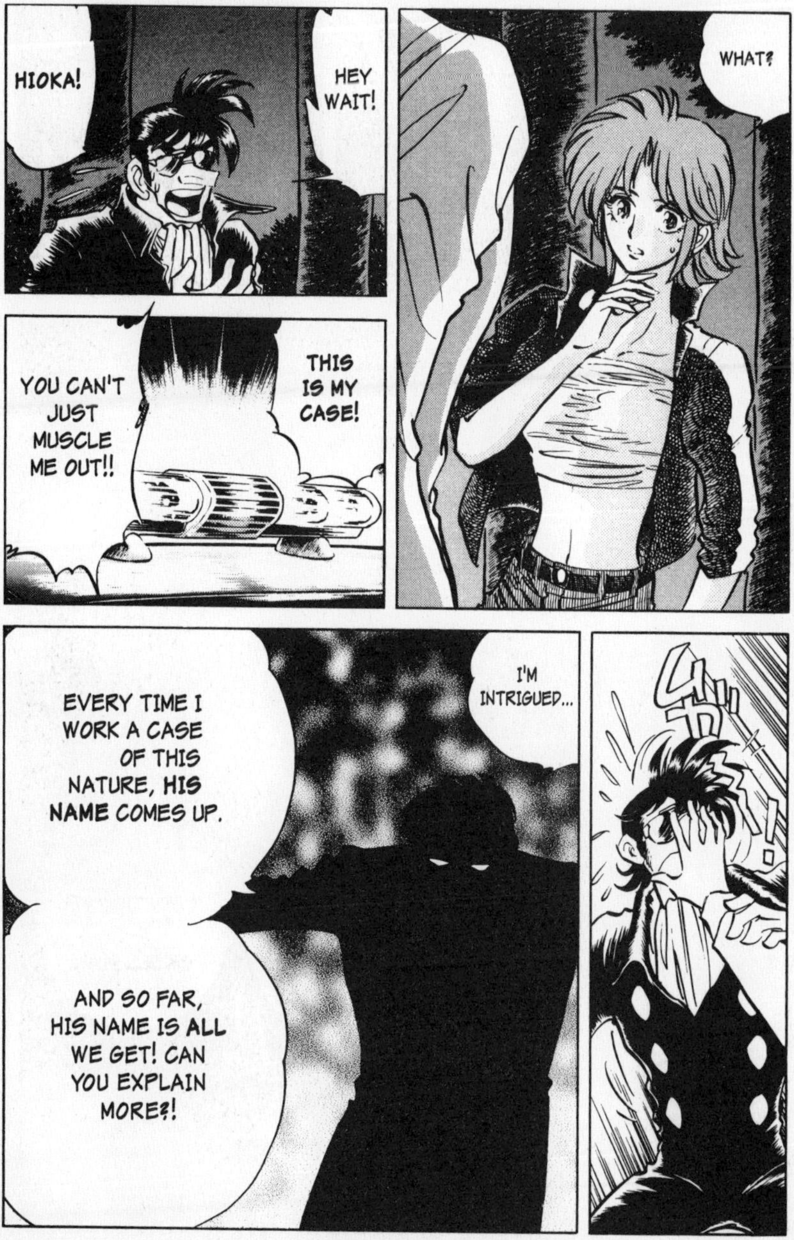
WHAT?
HEY WAIT!
HIOKA!
THIS IS MY CASE!
YOU CAN'T JUST MUSCLE ME OUT!!
I'M INTRIGUED...
EVERY TIME I WORK A CASE OF THIS NATURE, HIS NAME COMES UP.
AND SO FAR, HIS NAME IS ALL WE GET! CAN YOU EXPLAIN MORE?!

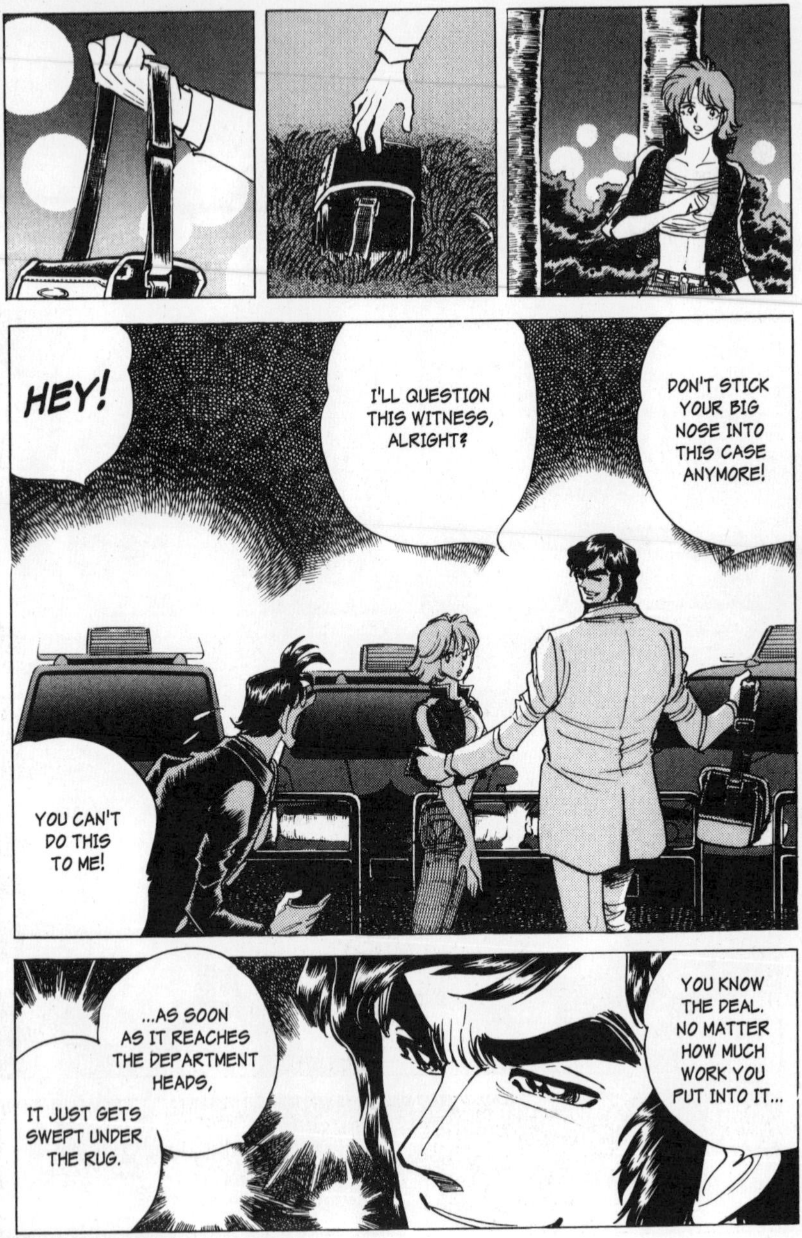
DON'T STICK YOUR BIG NOSE INTO THIS CASE ANYMORE!
I'LL QUESTION THIS WITNESS, ALRIGHT?
HEY!
YOU CAN'T DO THIS TO ME!
YOU KNOW THE DEAL. NO MATTER HOW MUCH WORK YOU PUT INTO IT...
...AS SOON AS IT REACHES THE DEPARTMENT HEADS,
IT JUST GETS SWEPT UNDER THE RUG.

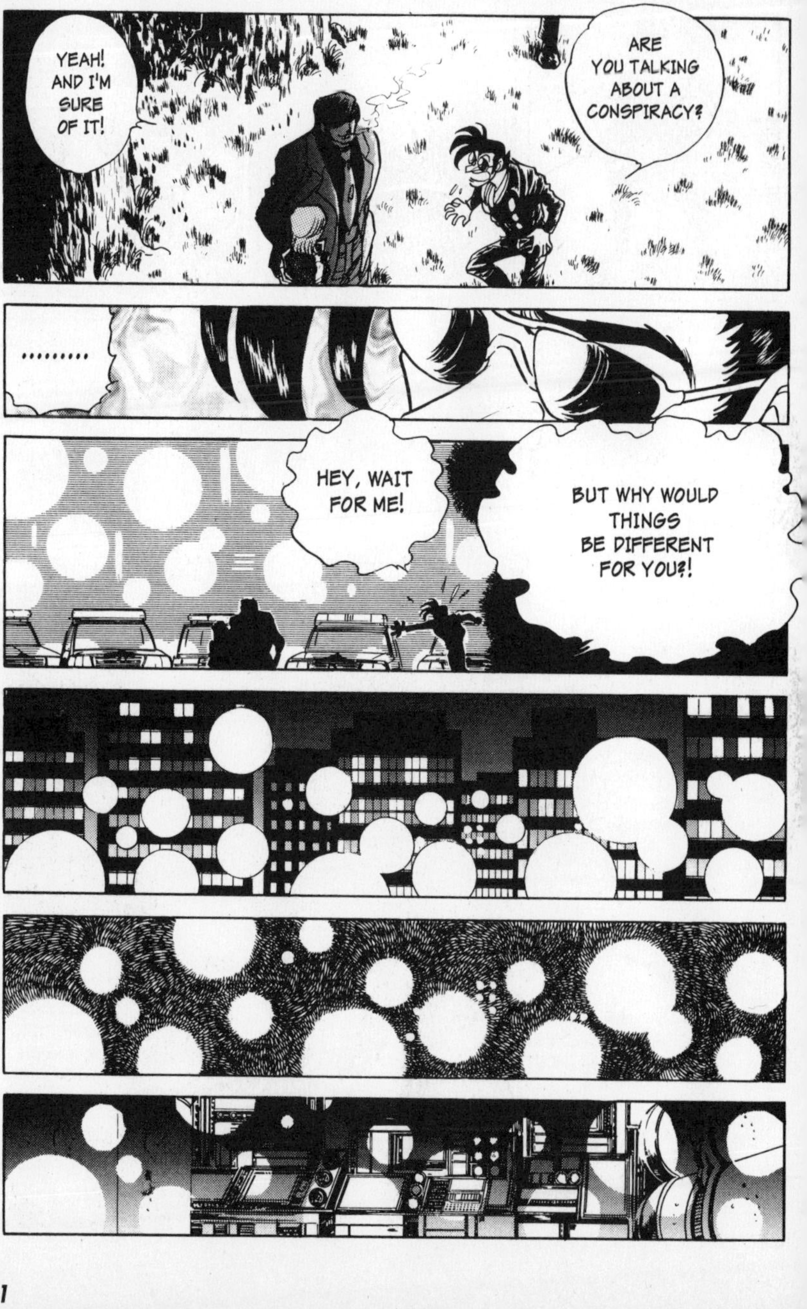
ARE YOU TALKING ABOUT A CONSPIRACY?
YEAH! AND I'M SURE OF IT!
....
BUT WHY WOULD THINGS BE DIFFERENT FOR YOU?!
HEY, WAIT FOR ME!

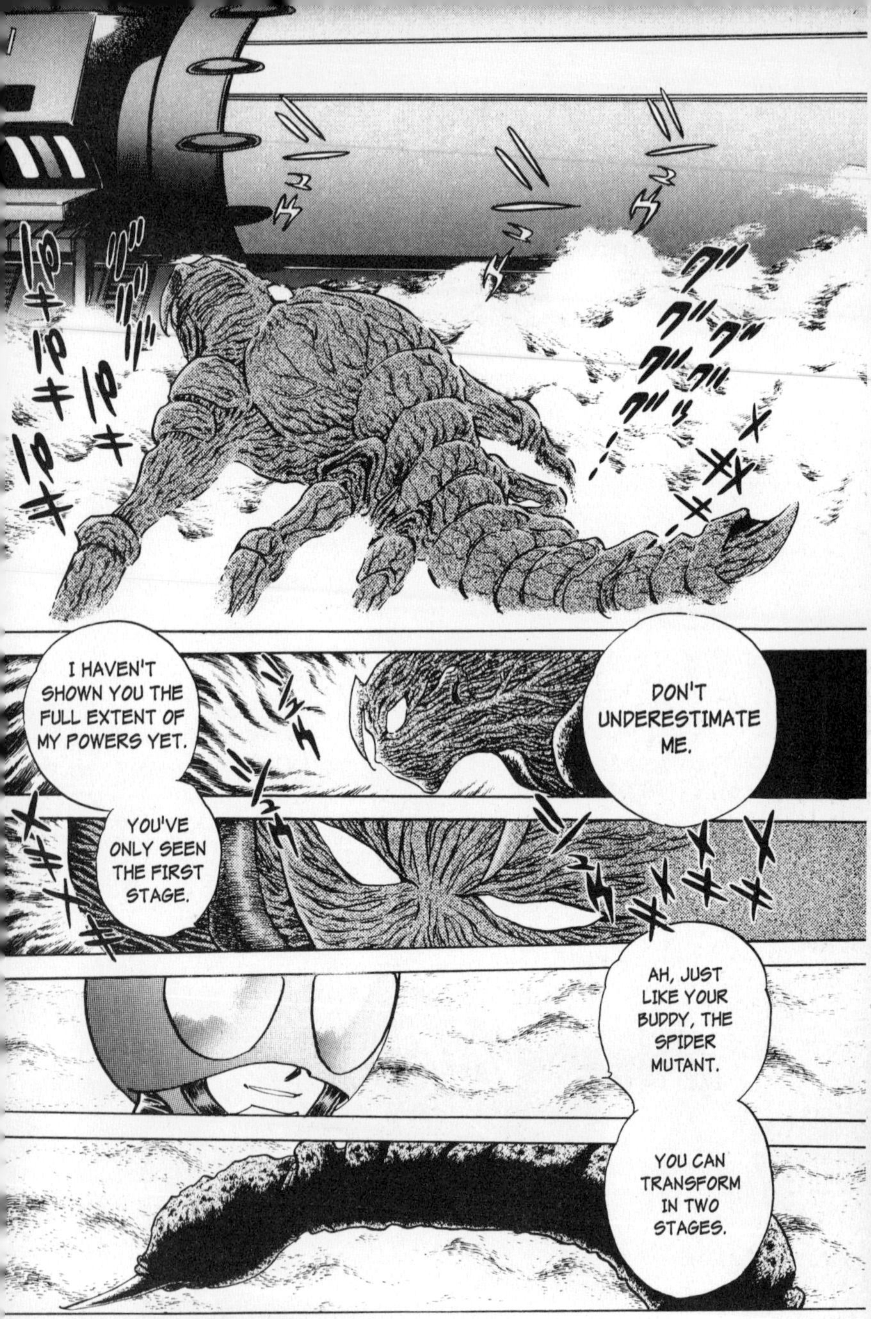
DON'T UNDERESTIMATE ME.
I HAVEN'T SHOWN YOU THE FULL EXTENT OF MY POWERS YET.
YOU'VE ONLY SEEN THE FIRST STAGE.
AH, JUST LIKE YOUR BUDDY, THE SPIDER MUTANT.
YOU CAN TRANSFORM IN TWO STAGES.

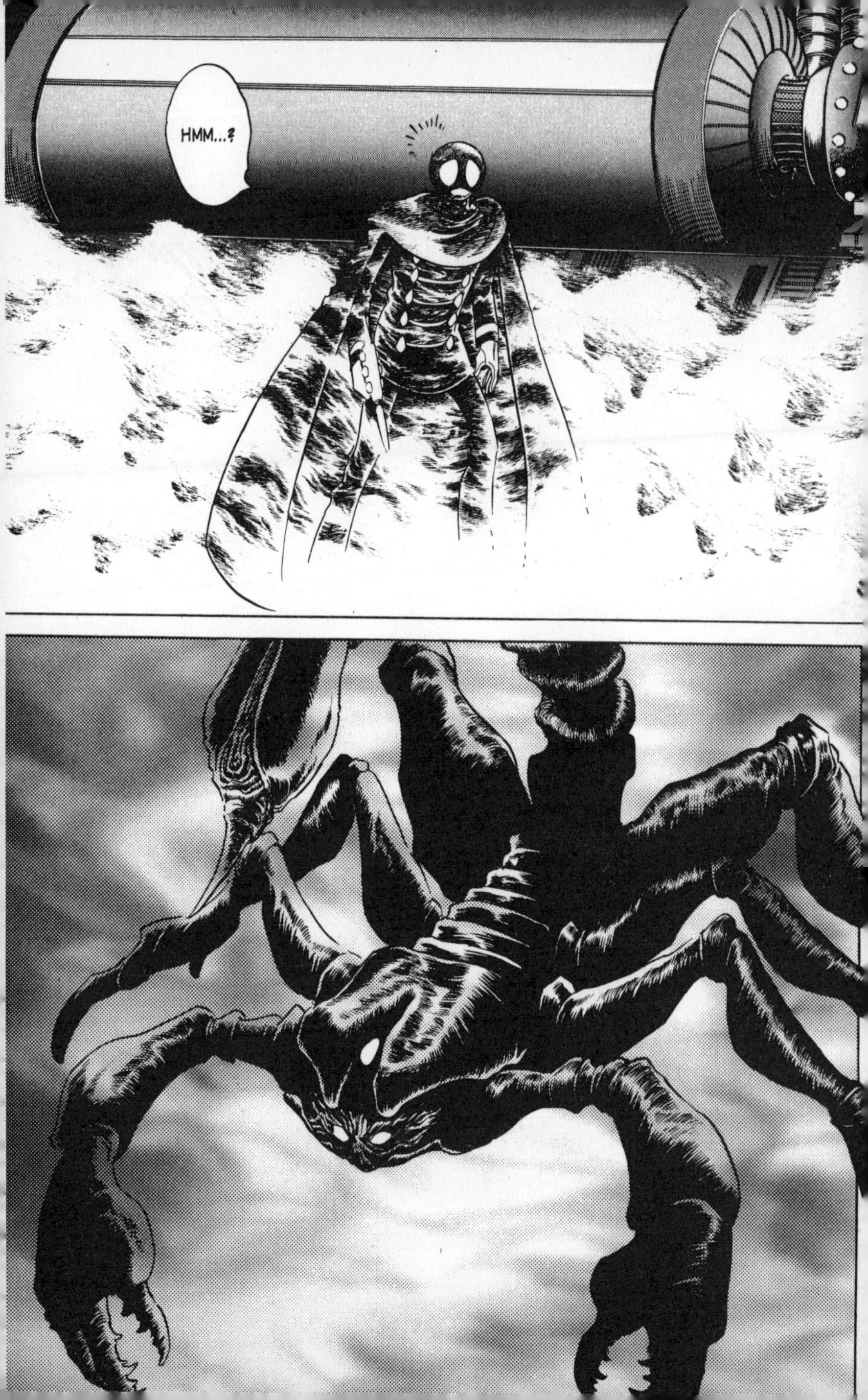
HMM...?

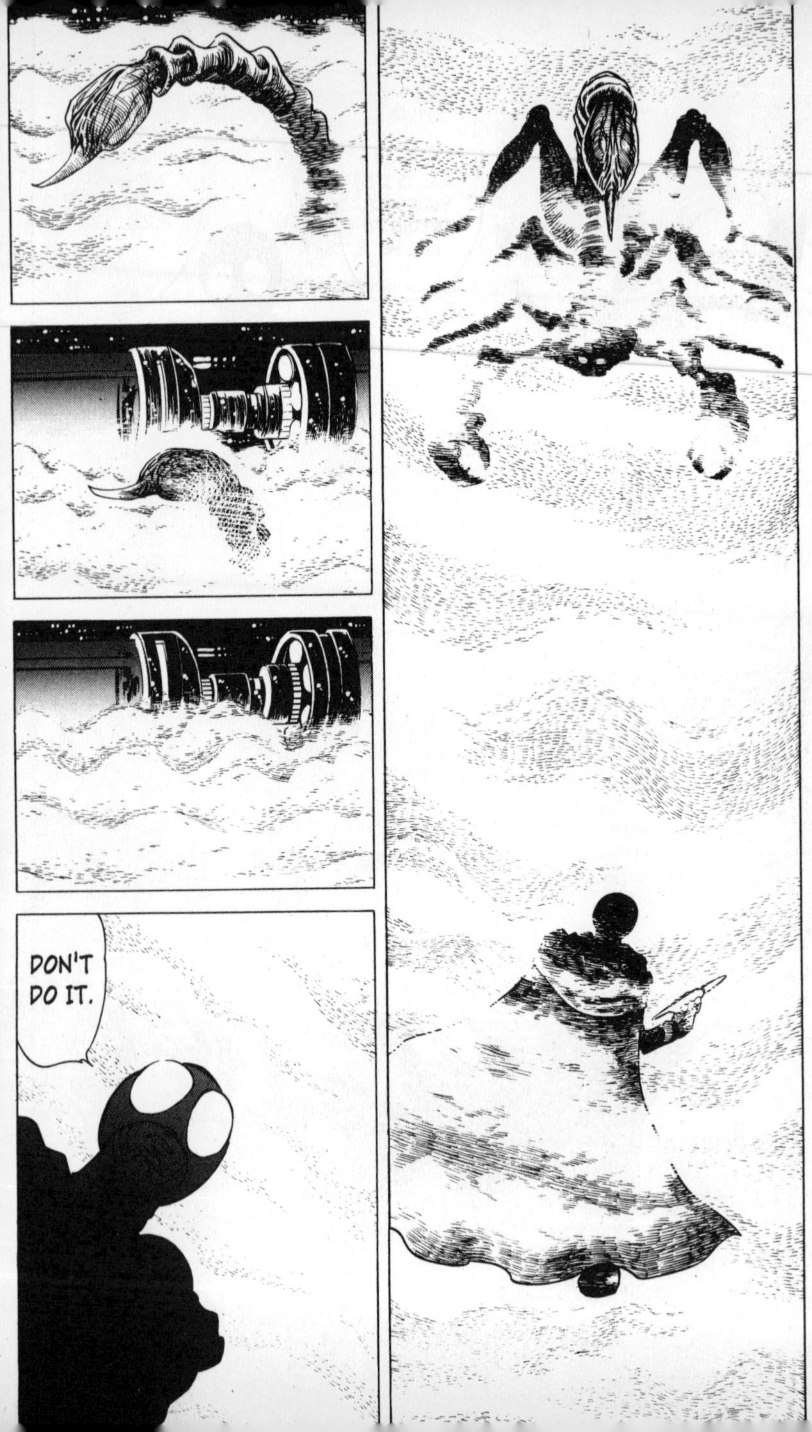
DON'T DO IT.

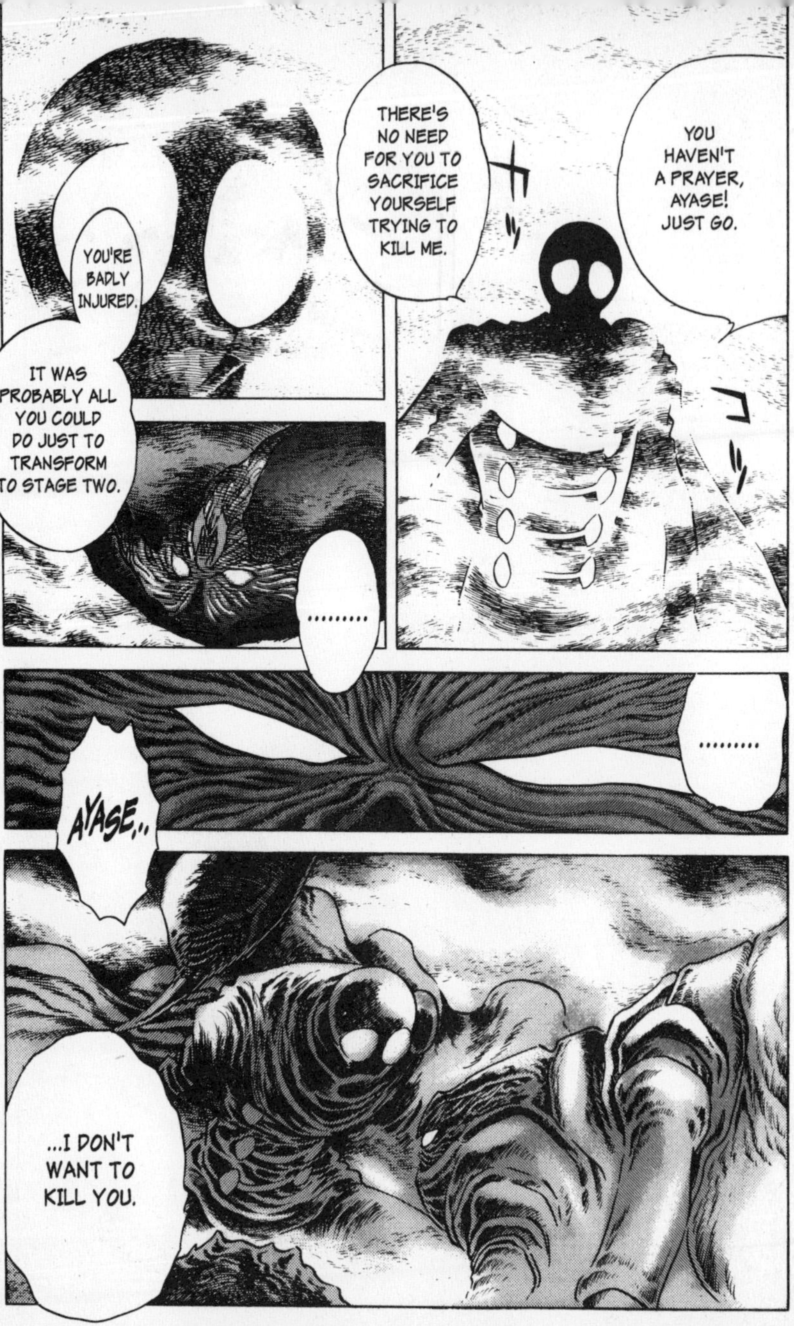

YOU HAVEN'T A PRAYER, AYASE! JUST GO.
THERE'S NO NEED FOR YOU TO SACRIFICE YOURSELF TRYING TO KILL ME.
YOU'RE BADLY INJURED.
IT WAS PROBABLY ALL YOU COULD DO JUST TO TRANSFORM TO STAGE TWO.
....
....
AYASE...
...I DON'T WANT TO KILL YOU.

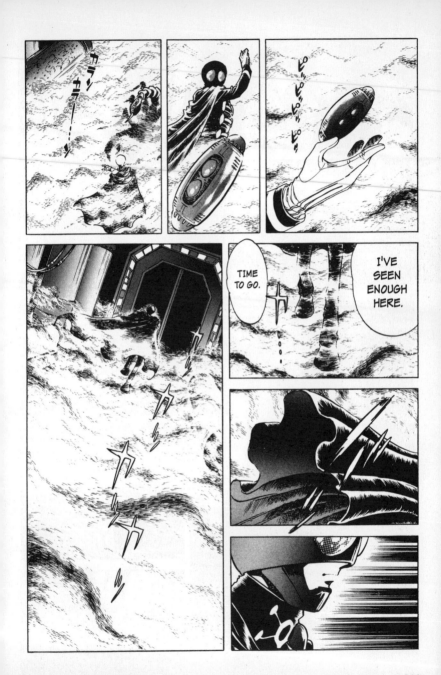

TIME TO GO.

I'VE SEEN ENOUGH HERE.

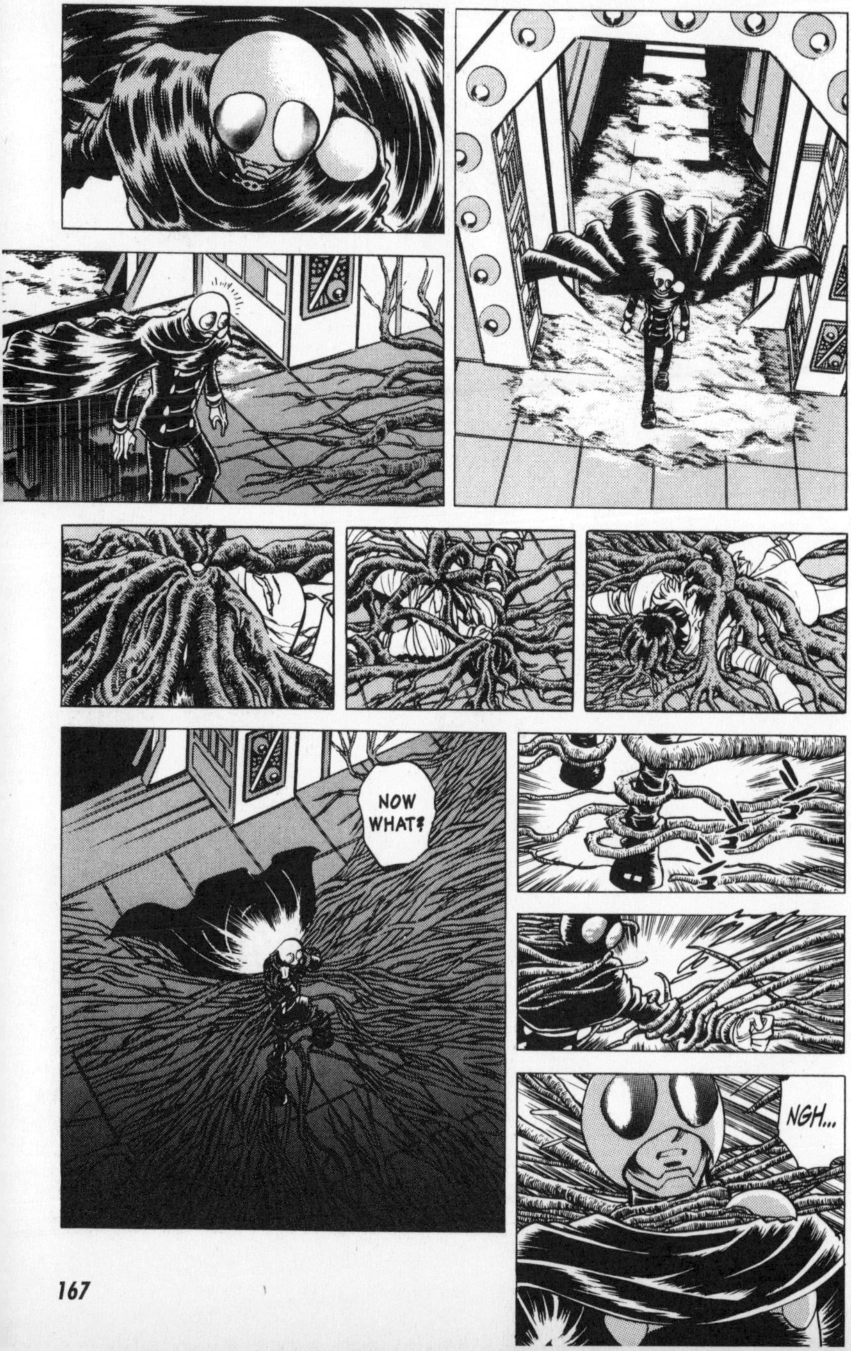
NGH...
NOW WHAT?

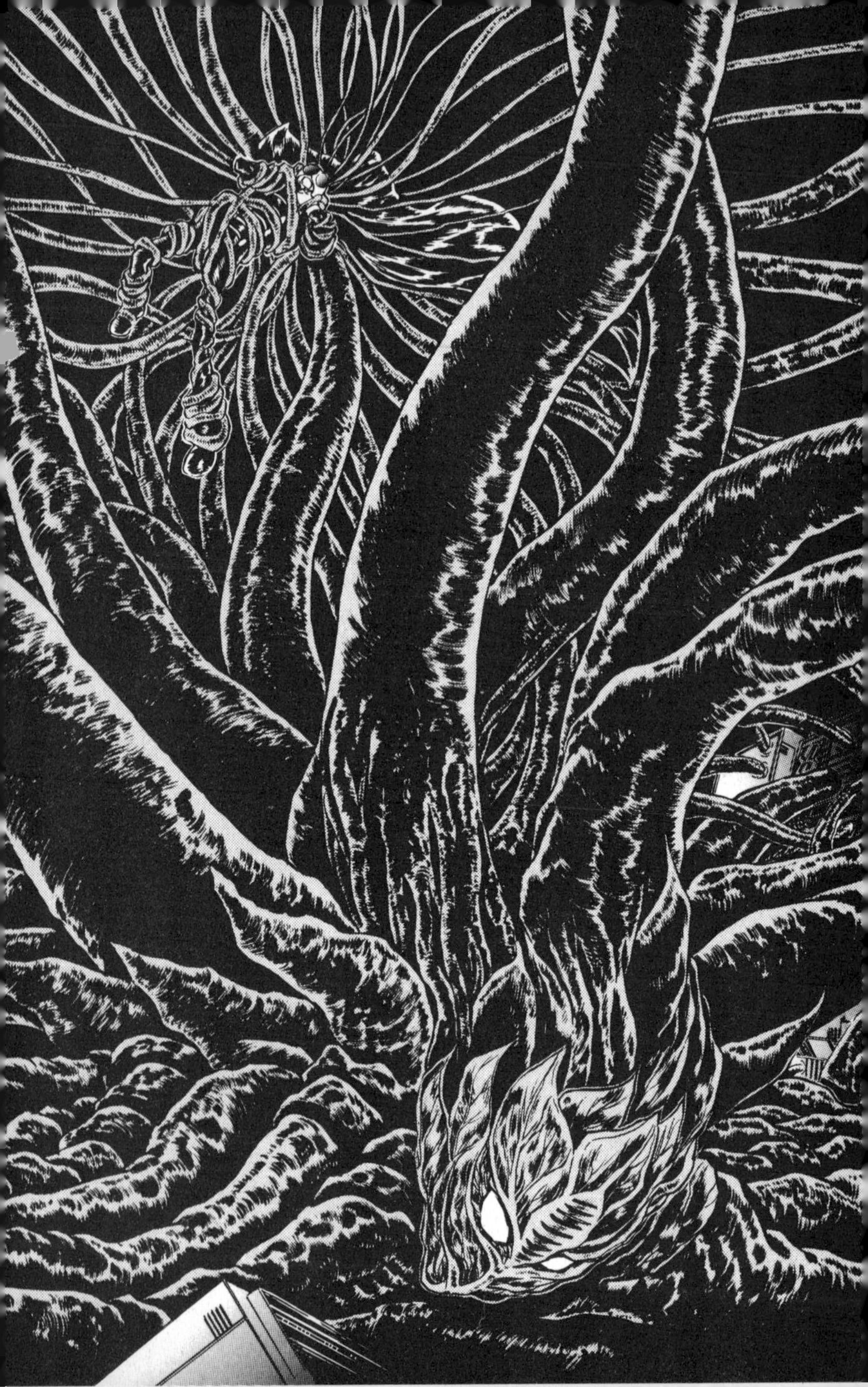

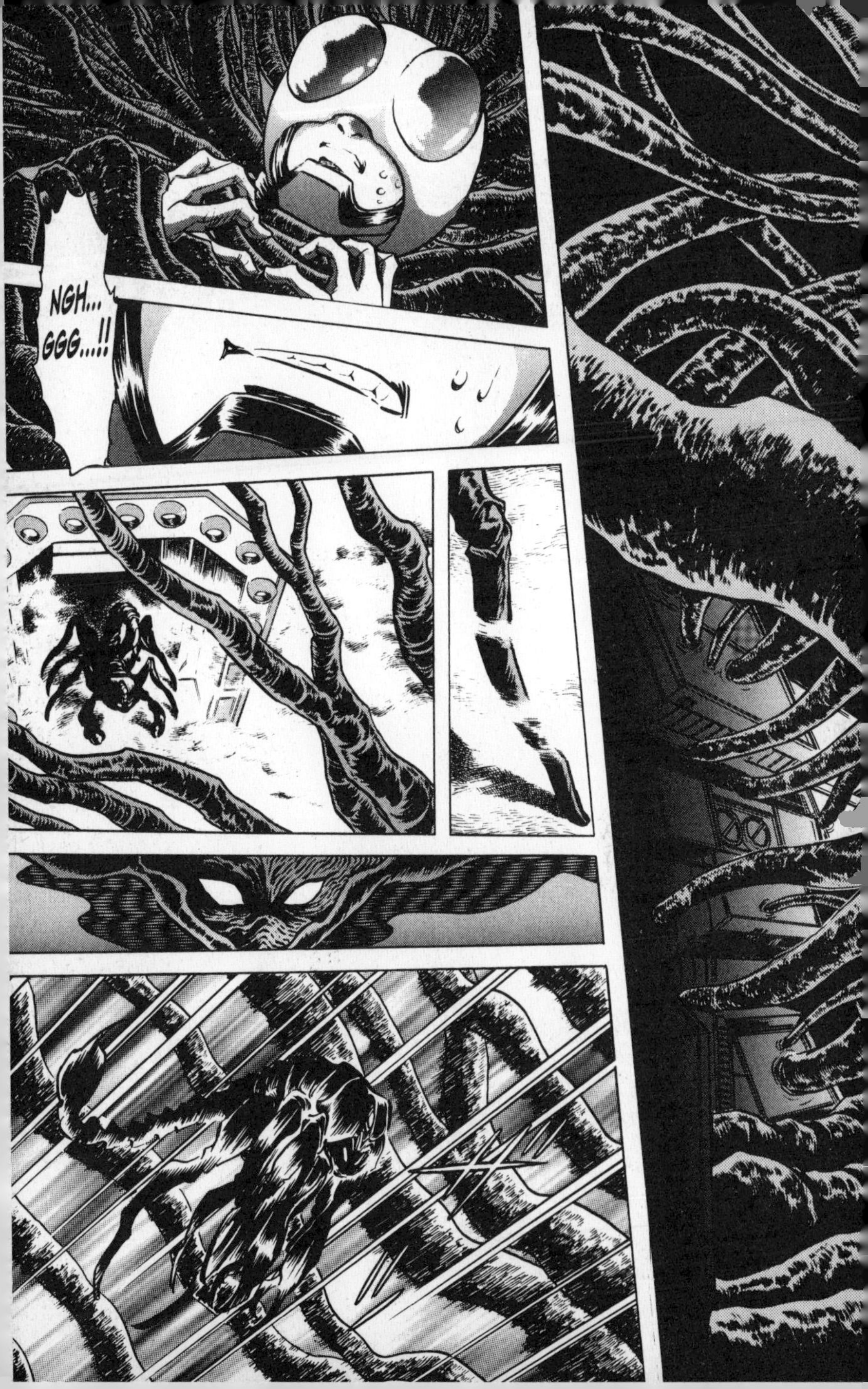
NGH... GGG...!!

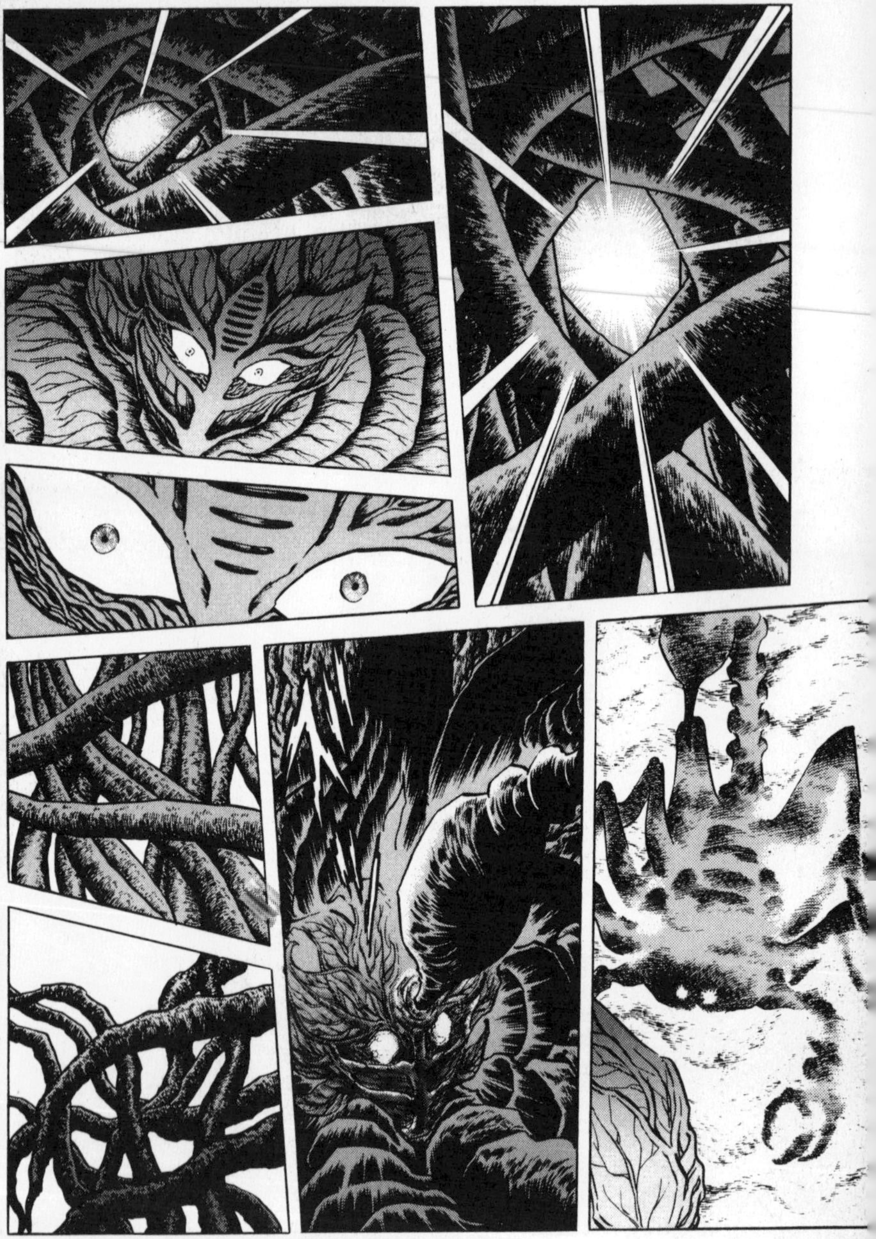

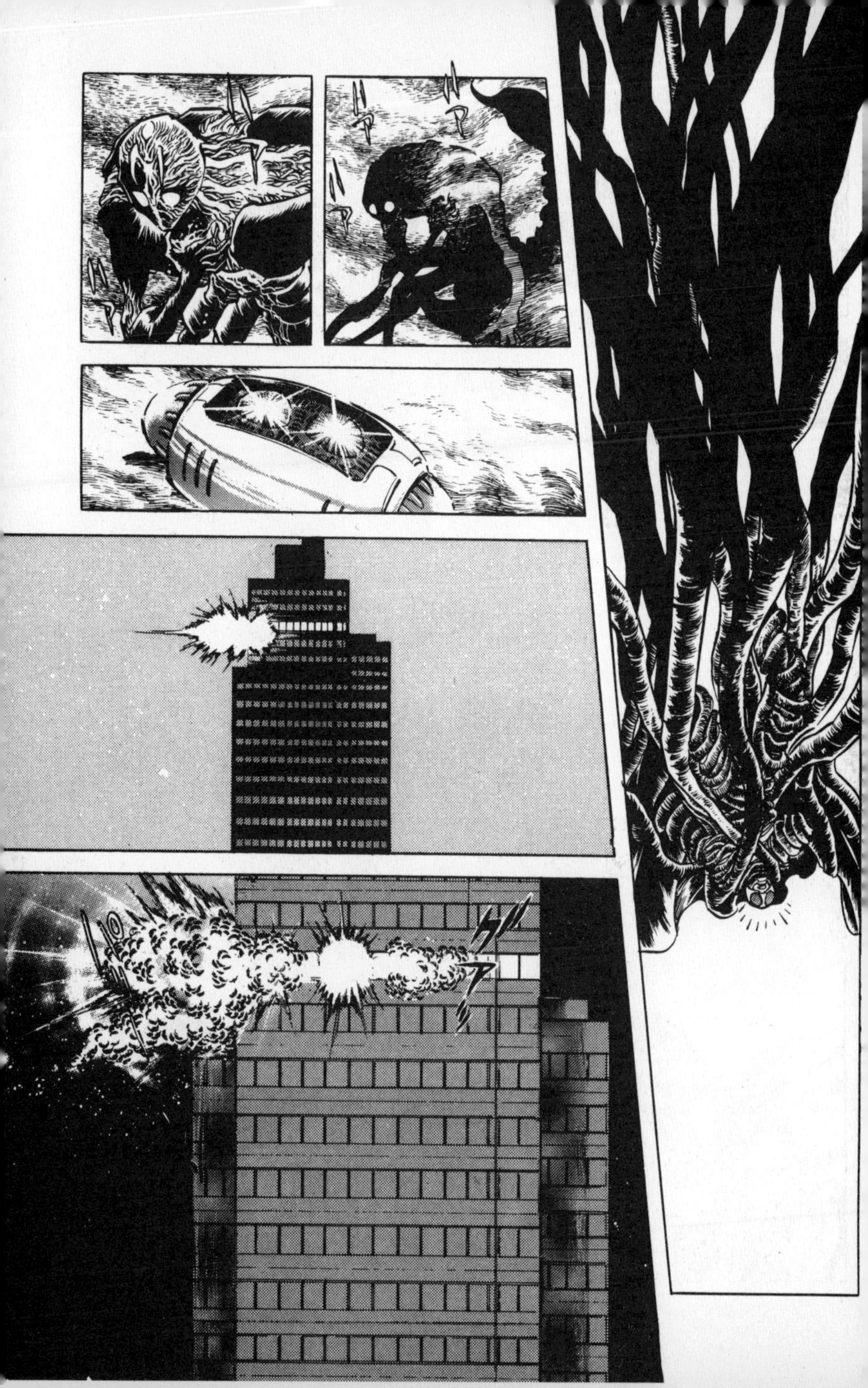
ハァ
ハァ
ハァ
ハァ
ハァ

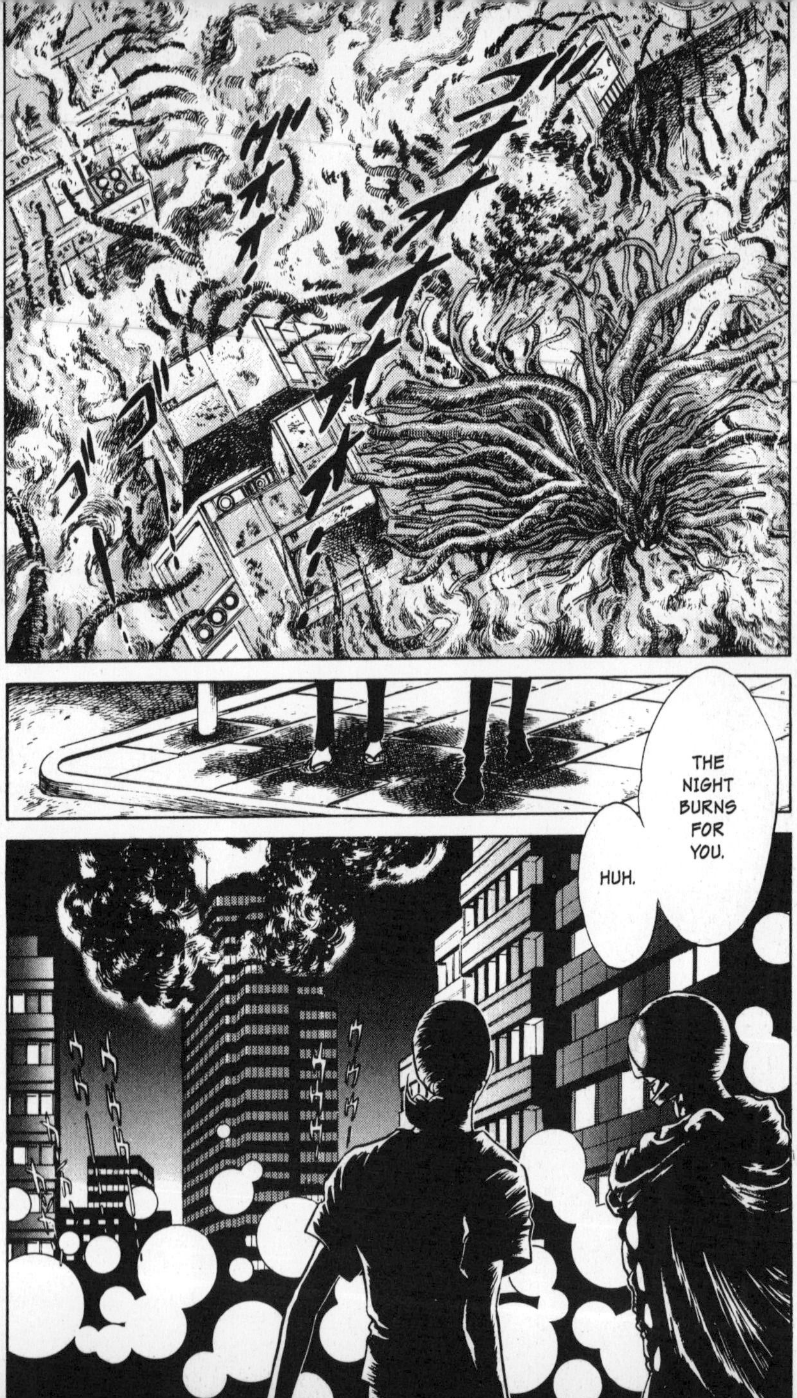
THE NIGHT BURNS FOR YOU.
HUH.

SO WHADDAYA THINK?
WILL YA WORK WITH US?
I KNOW YOU DON'T LIKE TO GIVE UP A VALUABLE SCOOP, BUT...
TO BE FRANK, YOUR LIFE'S IN DANGER.

14 シークレット・ファイル SECRET FILE

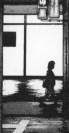

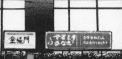

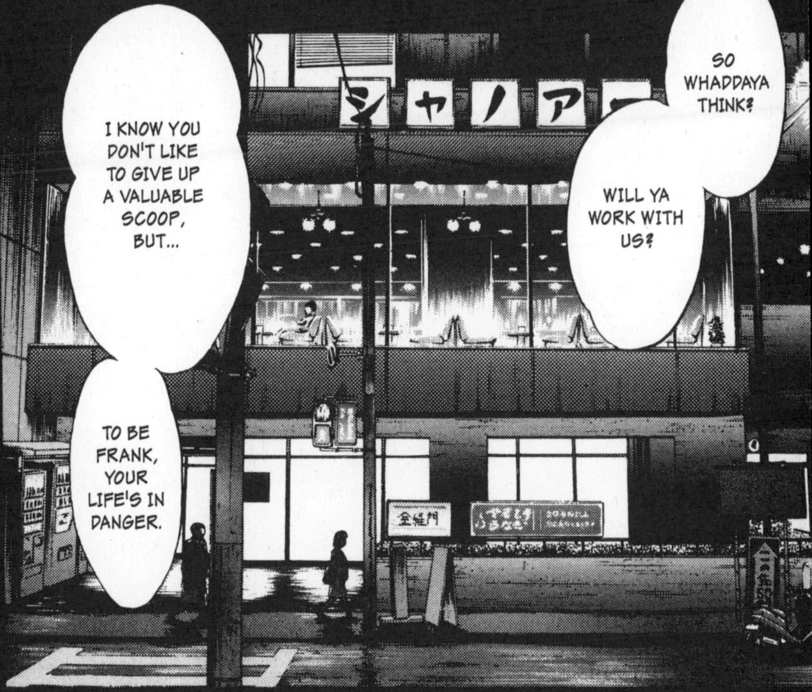

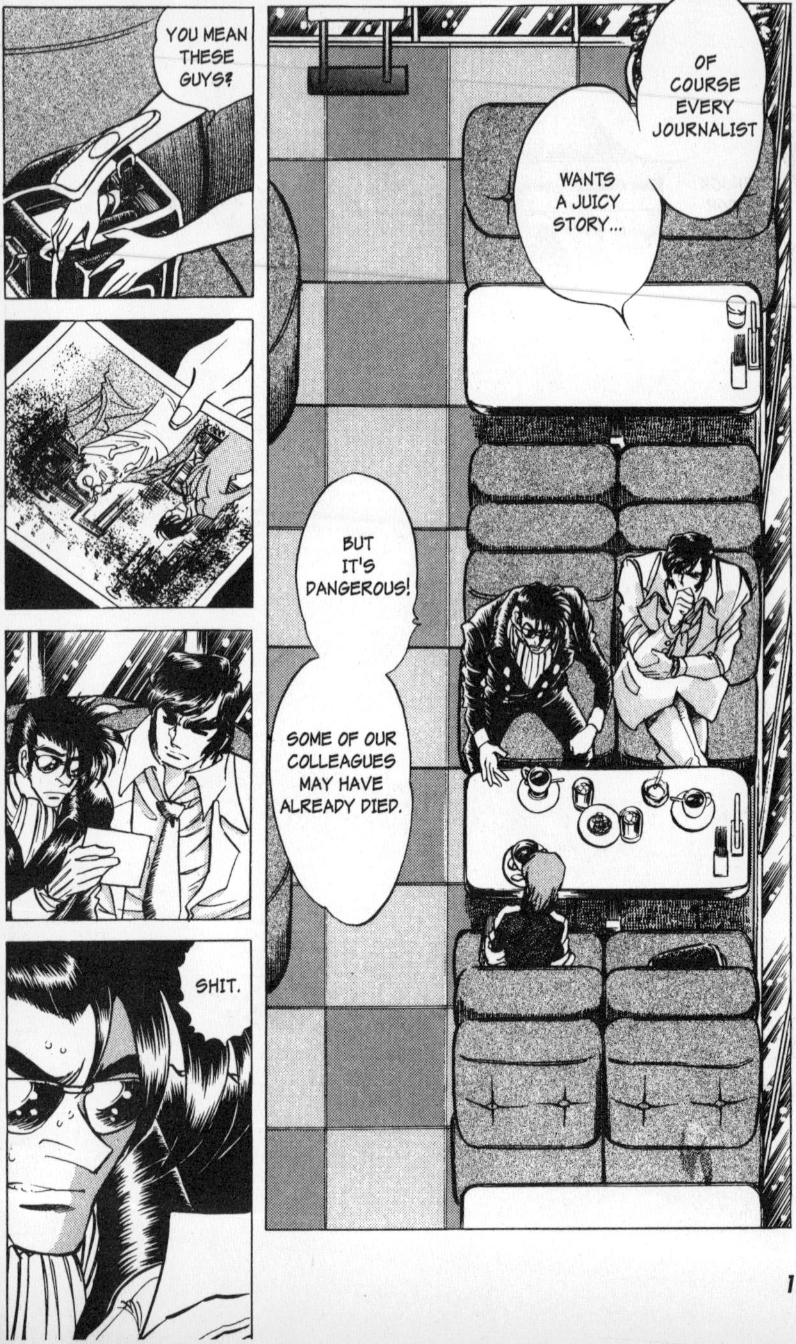
OF COURSE EVERY JOURNALIST
WANTS A JUICY STORY...
BUT IT'S DANGEROUS!
SOME OF OUR COLLEAGUES MAY HAVE ALREADY DIED.
YOU MEAN THESE GUYS?
SHIT.

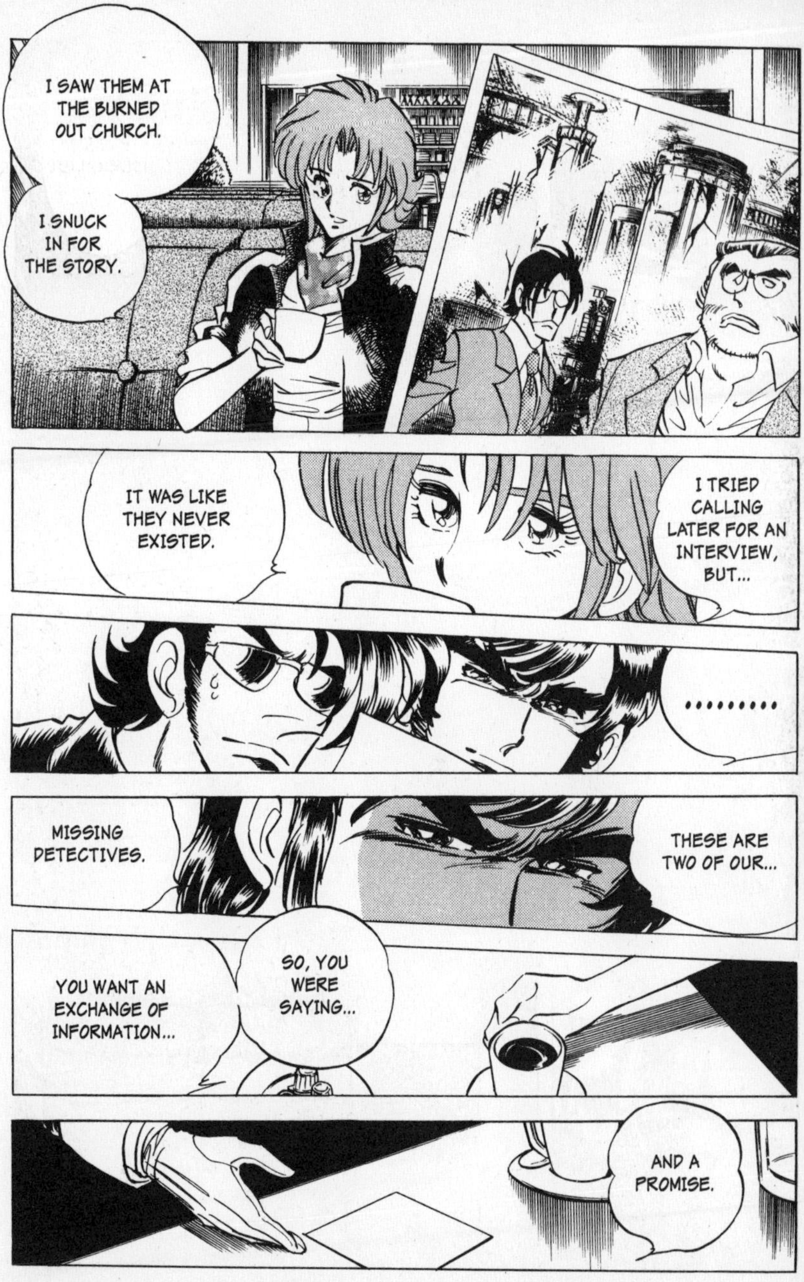
I SAW THEM AT THE BURNED OUT CHURCH.
I SNUCK IN FOR THE STORY.
I TRIED CALLING LATER FOR AN INTERVIEW, BUT...
IT WAS LIKE THEY NEVER EXISTED.
....
THESE ARE TWO OF OUR...
MISSING DETECTIVES.
SO, YOU WERE SAYING...
YOU WANT AN EXCHANGE OF INFORMATION...
AND A PROMISE.

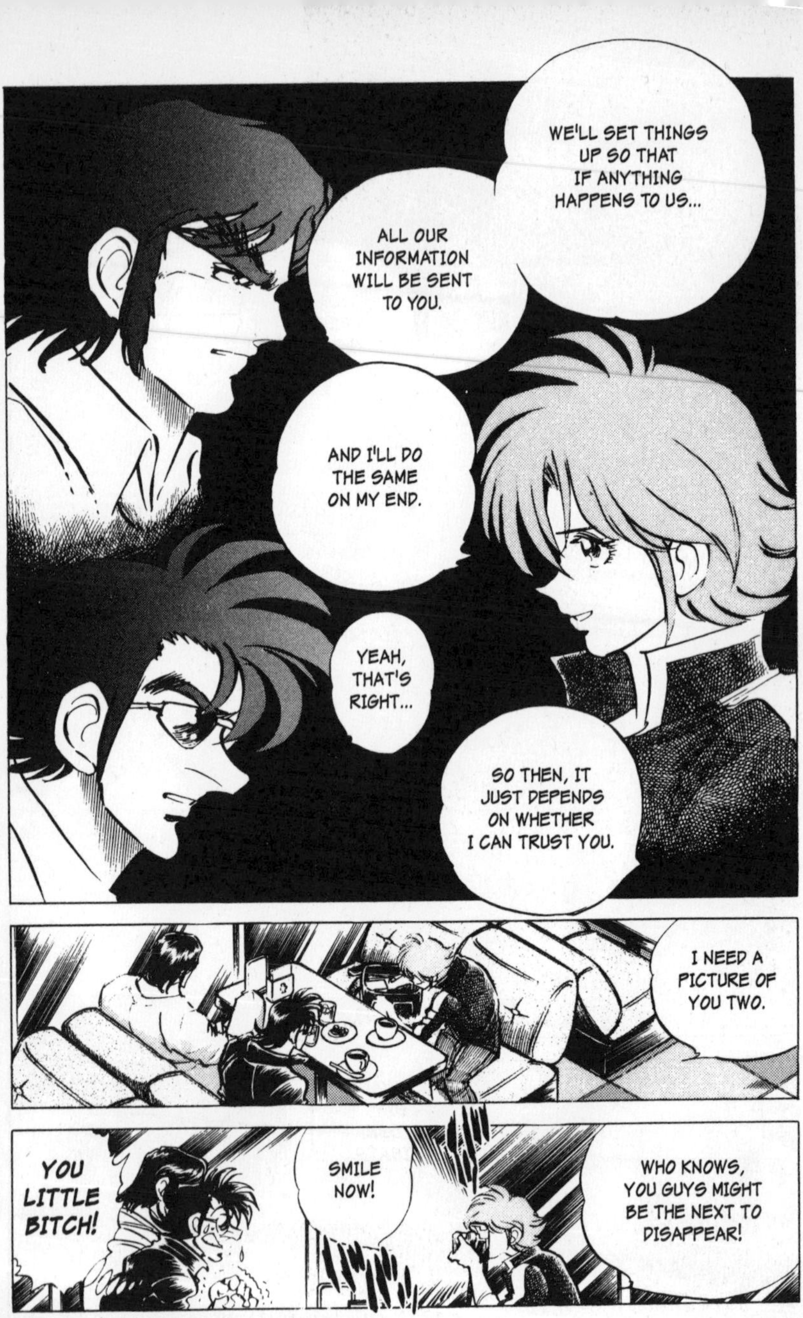
WE'LL SET THINGS UP SO THAT IF ANYTHING HAPPENS TO US...
ALL OUR INFORMATION WILL BE SENT TO YOU.
AND I'LL DO THE SAME ON MY END.
YEAH, THAT'S RIGHT...
SO THEN, IT JUST DEPENDS ON WHETHER I CAN TRUST YOU.
I NEED A PICTURE OF YOU TWO.
WHO KNOWS, YOU GUYS MIGHT BE THE NEXT TO DISAPPEAR!
SMILE NOW!
YOU LITTLE BITCH!

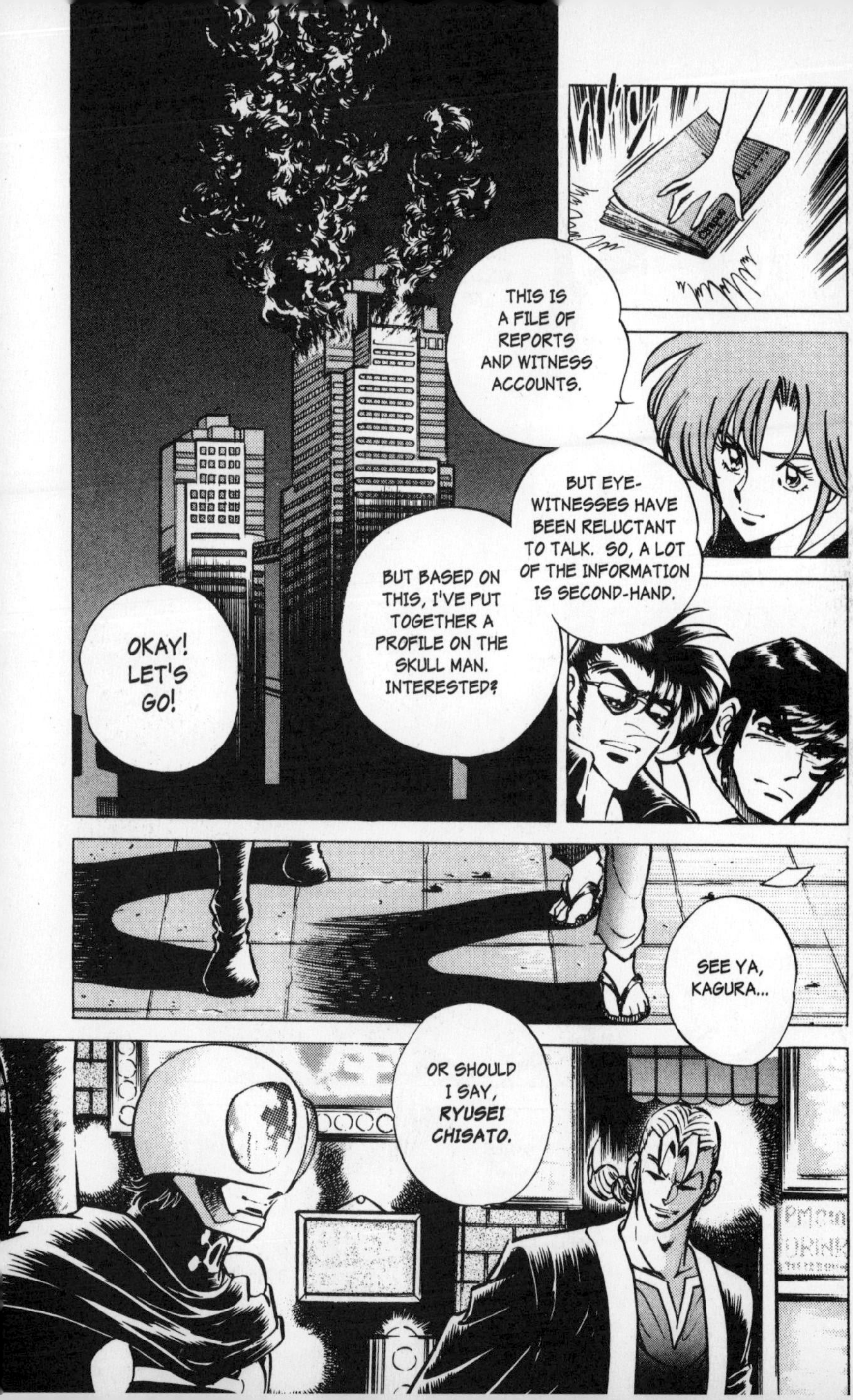
THIS IS A FILE OF REPORTS AND WITNESS ACCOUNTS.
BUT EYE-WITNESSES HAVE BEEN RELUCTANT TO TALK. SO, A LOT OF THE INFORMATION IS SECOND-HAND.
BUT BASED ON THIS, I'VE PUT TOGETHER A PROFILE ON THE SKULL MAN. INTERESTED?
OKAY! LET'S GO!
SEE YA, KAGURA...
OR SHOULD I SAY, RYUSEI CHISATO.

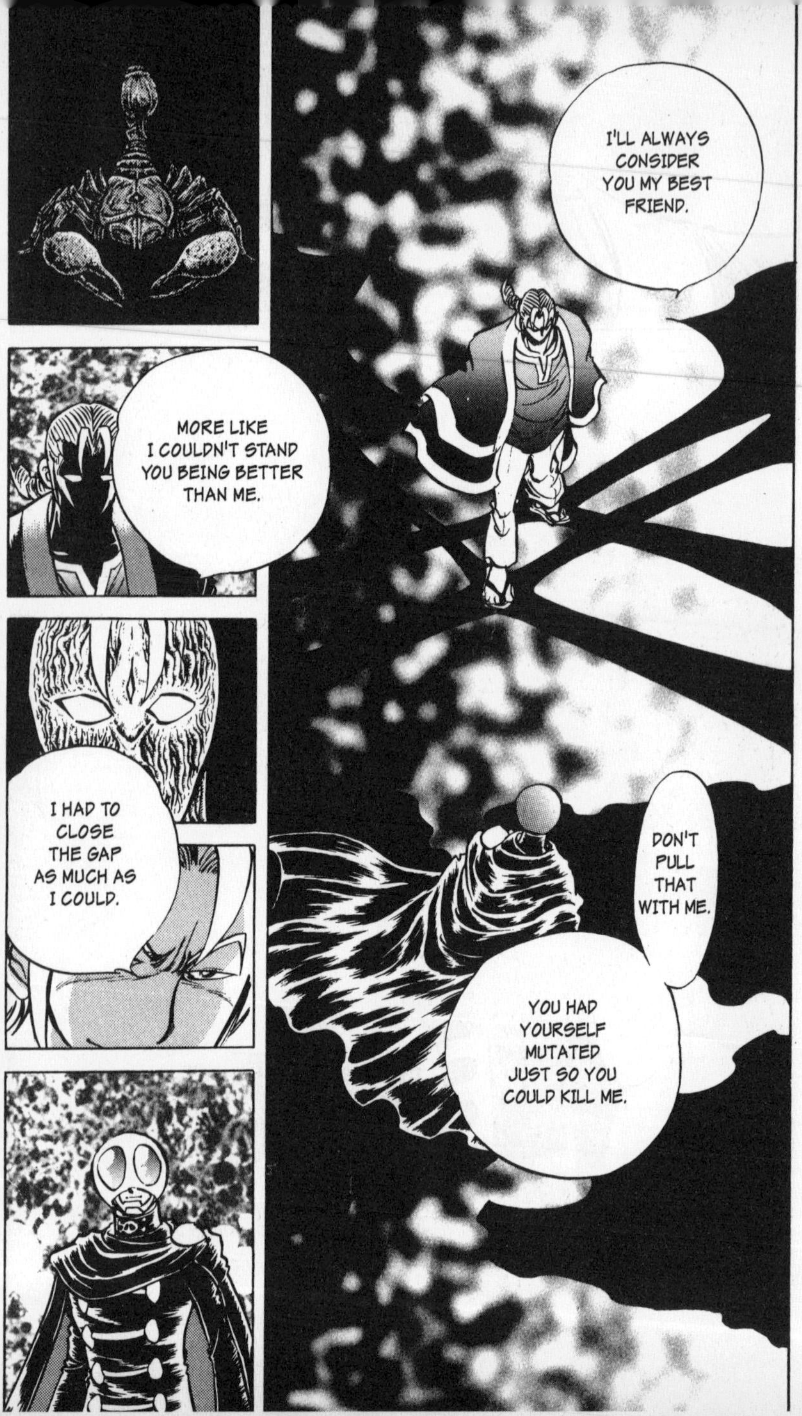
I'LL ALWAYS CONSIDER YOU MY BEST FRIEND.
DON'T PULL THAT WITH ME.
YOU HAD YOURSELF MUTATED JUST SO YOU COULD KILL ME.
MORE LIKE I COULDN'T STAND YOU BEING BETTER THAN ME.
I HAD TO CLOSE THE GAP AS MUCH AS I COULD.

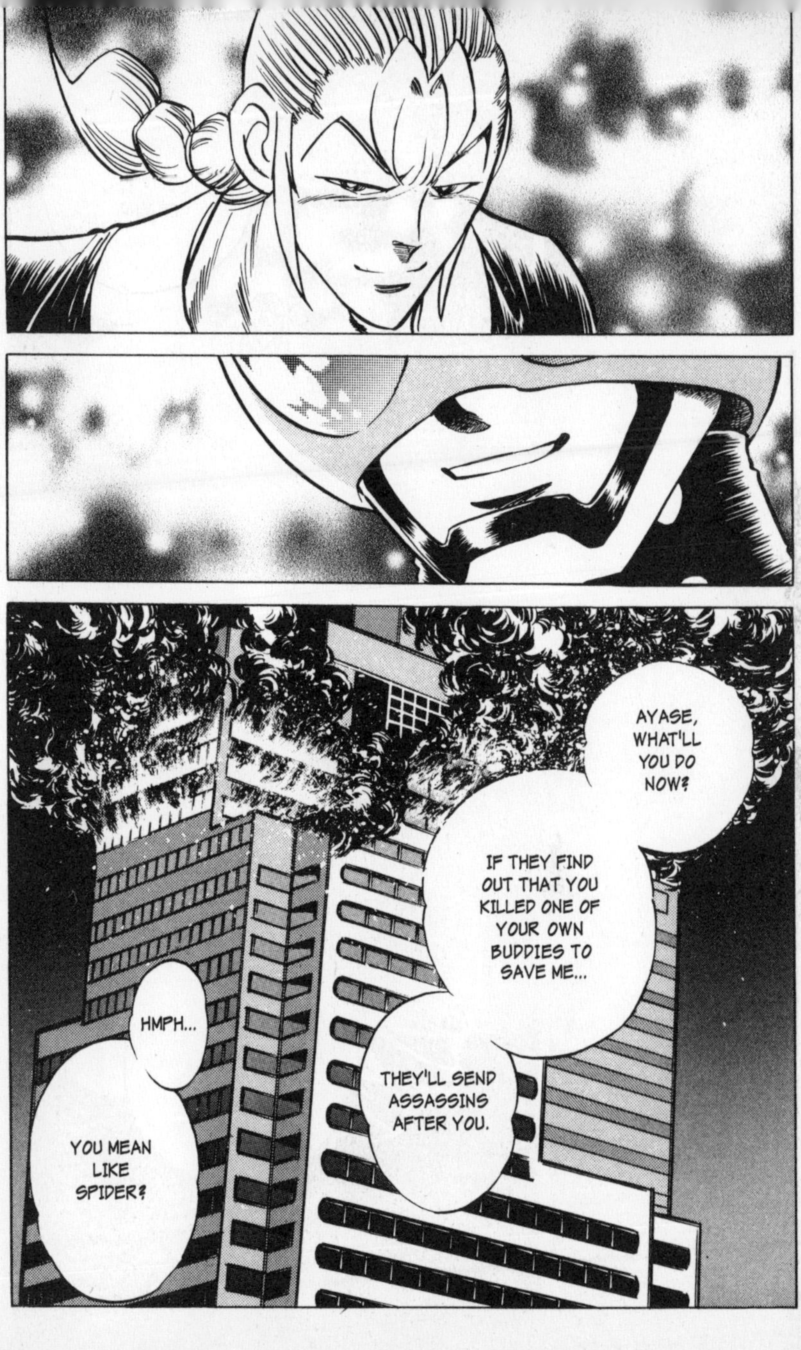
AYASE, WHAT'LL YOU DO NOW?
IF THEY FIND OUT THAT YOU KILLED ONE OF YOUR OWN BUDDIES TO SAVE ME...
THEY'LL SEND ASSASSINS AFTER YOU.
HMPH...
YOU MEAN LIKE SPIDER?

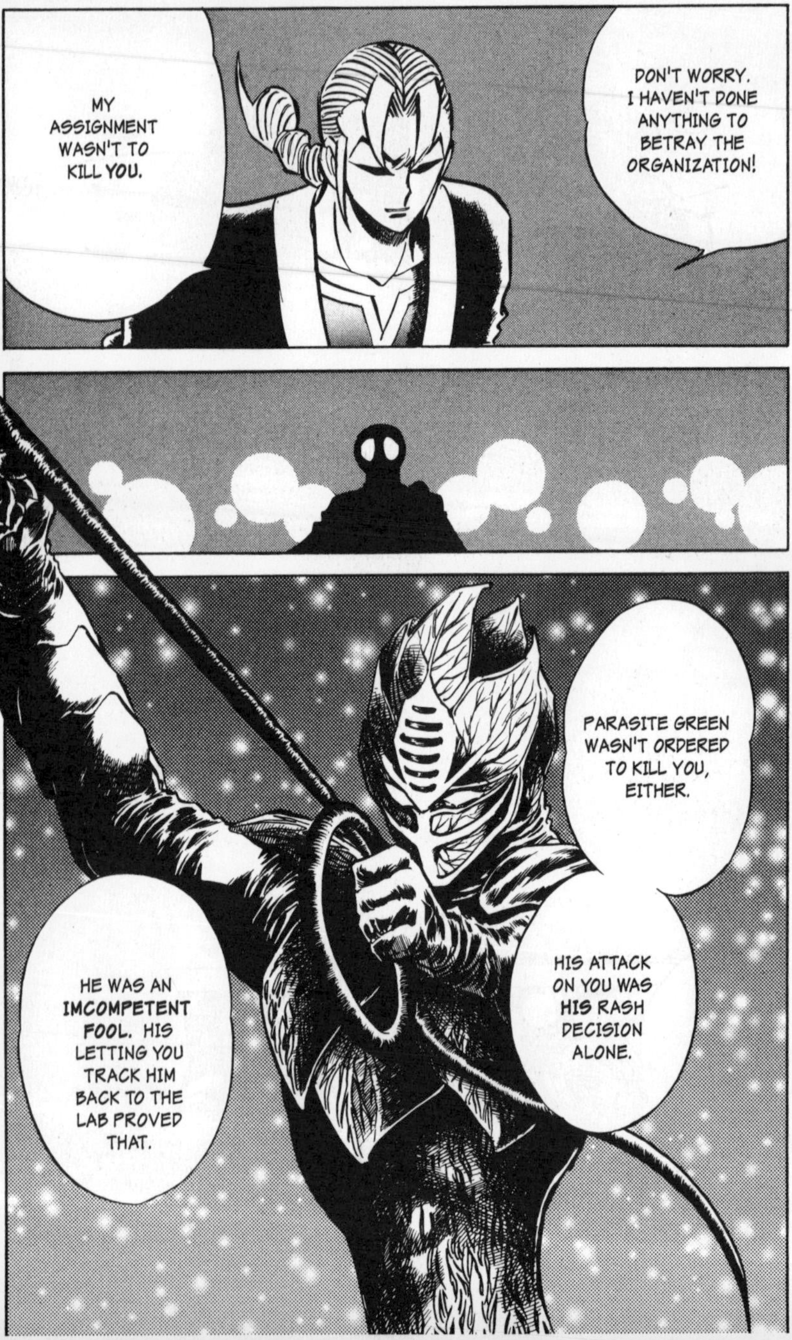
DON'T WORRY. I HAVEN'T DONE ANYTHING TO BETRAY THE ORGANIZATION!
MY ASSIGNMENT WASN'T TO KILL YOU.
PARASITE GREEN WASN'T ORDERED TO KILL YOU, EITHER.
HIS ATTACK ON YOU WAS HIS RASH DECISION ALONE.
HE WAS AN IMCOMPETENT FOOL. HIS LETTING YOU TRACK HIM BACK TO THE LAB PROVED THAT.

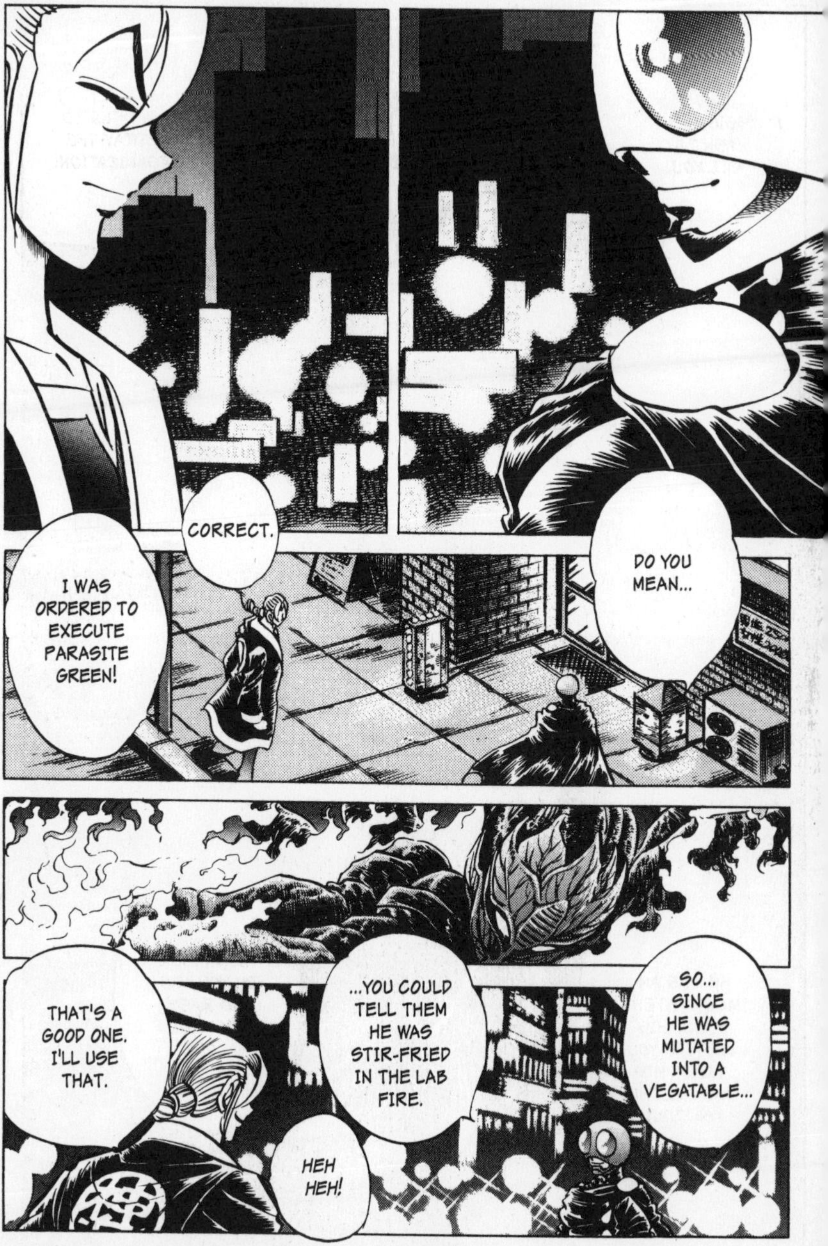
DO YOU MEAN...
CORRECT.
I WAS ORDERED TO EXECUTE PARASITE GREEN!
SO... SINCE HE WAS MUTATED INTO A VEGATABLE...
...YOU COULD TELL THEM HE WAS STIR-FRIED IN THE LAB FIRE.
HEH HEH!
THAT'S A GOOD ONE. I'LL USE THAT.

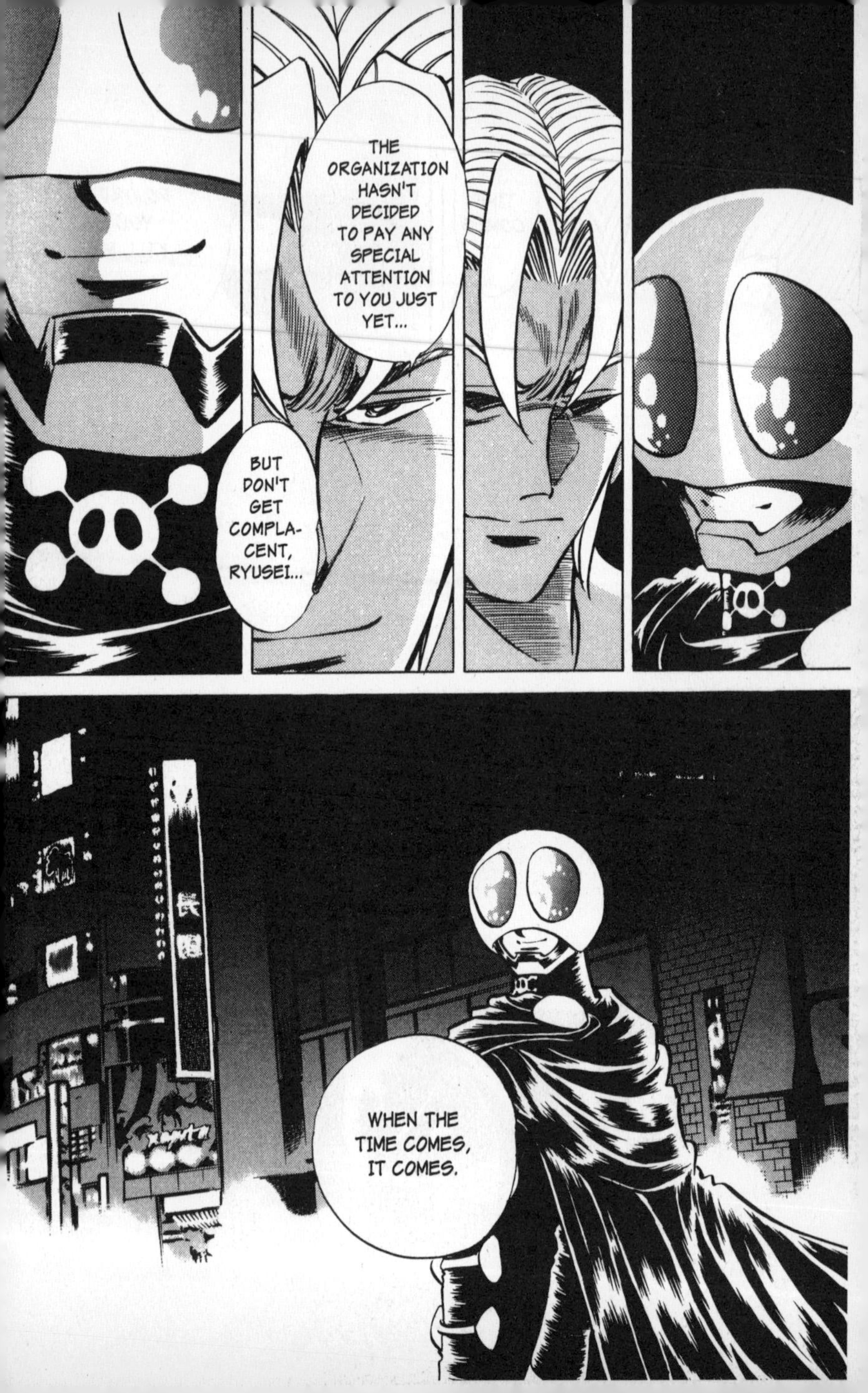
THE ORGANIZATION HASN'T DECIDED TO PAY ANY SPECIAL ATTENTION TO YOU JUST YET...
BUT DON'T GET COMPLA-CENT, RYUSEI...
WHEN THE TIME COMES, IT COMES.

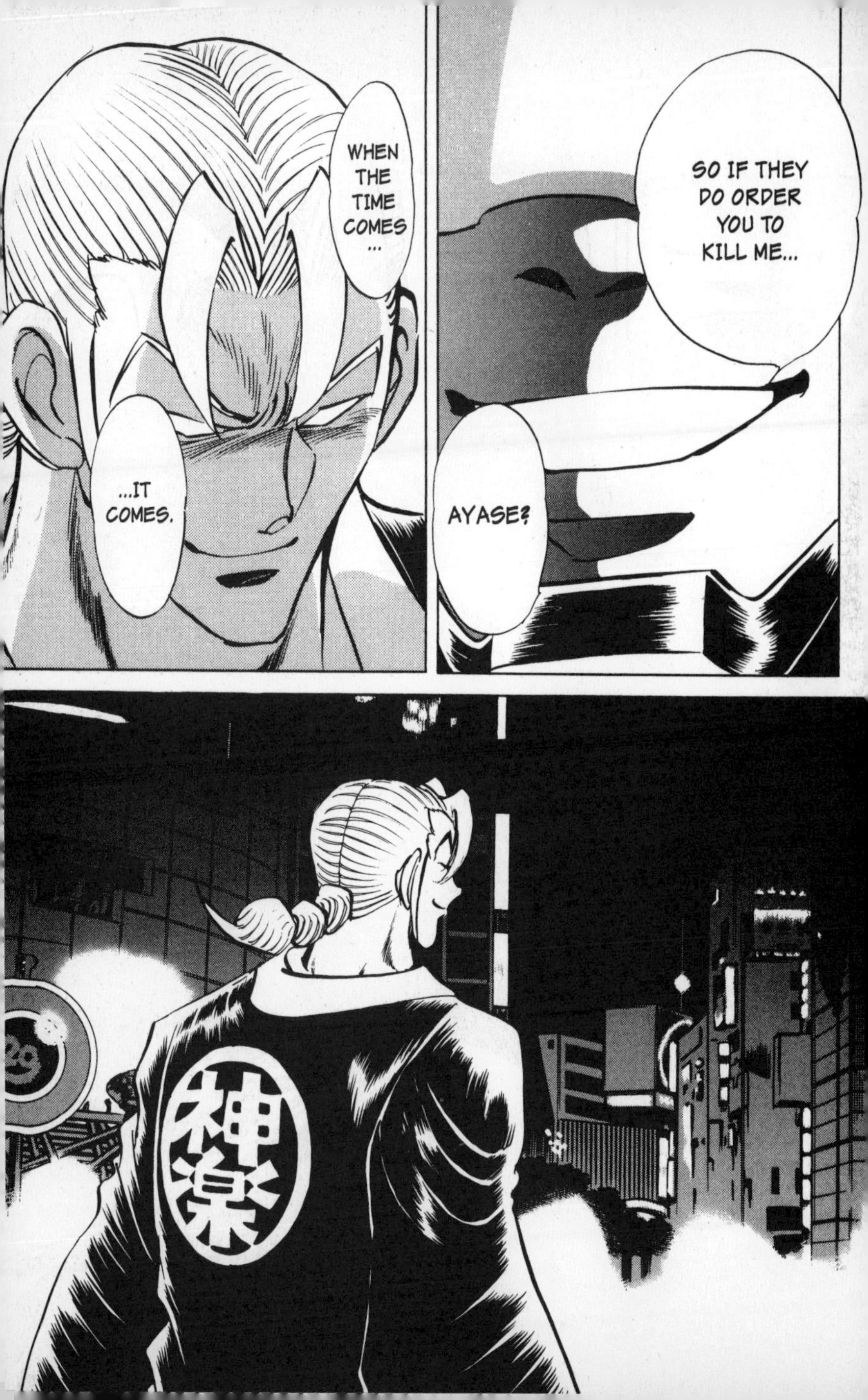
SO IF THEY DO ORDER YOU TO KILL ME...
AYASE?
WHEN THE TIME COMES...
...IT COMES.
神楽

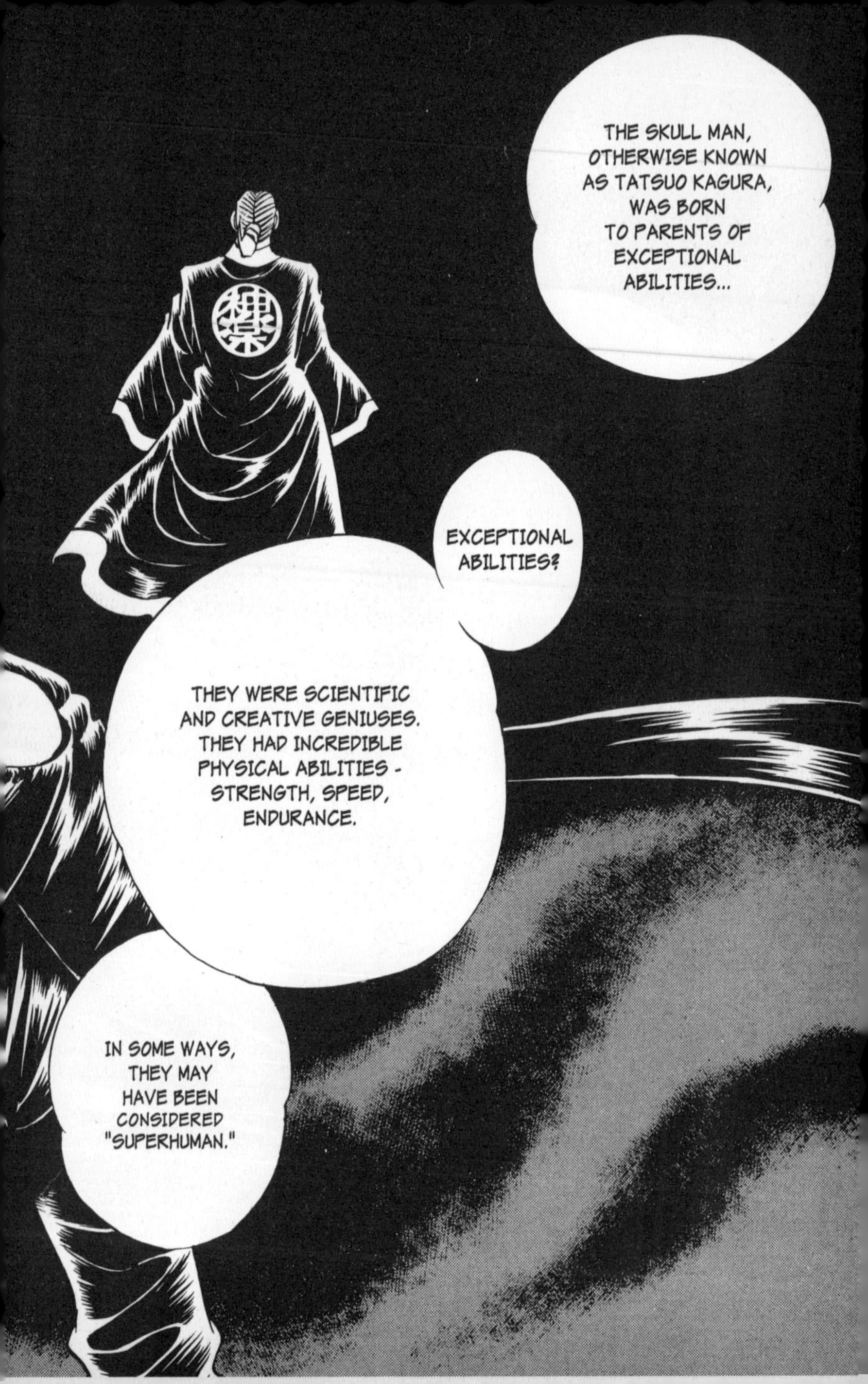
THE SKULL MAN, OTHERWISE KNOWN AS TATSUO KAGURA, WAS BORN TO PARENTS OF EXCEPTIONAL ABILITIES...
EXCEPTIONAL ABILITIES?
THEY WERE SCIENTIFIC AND CREATIVE GENIUSES. THEY HAD INCREDIBLE PHYSICAL ABILITIES - STRENGTH, SPEED, ENDURANCE.
IN SOME WAYS, THEY MAY HAVE BEEN CONSIDERED "SUPERHUMAN."

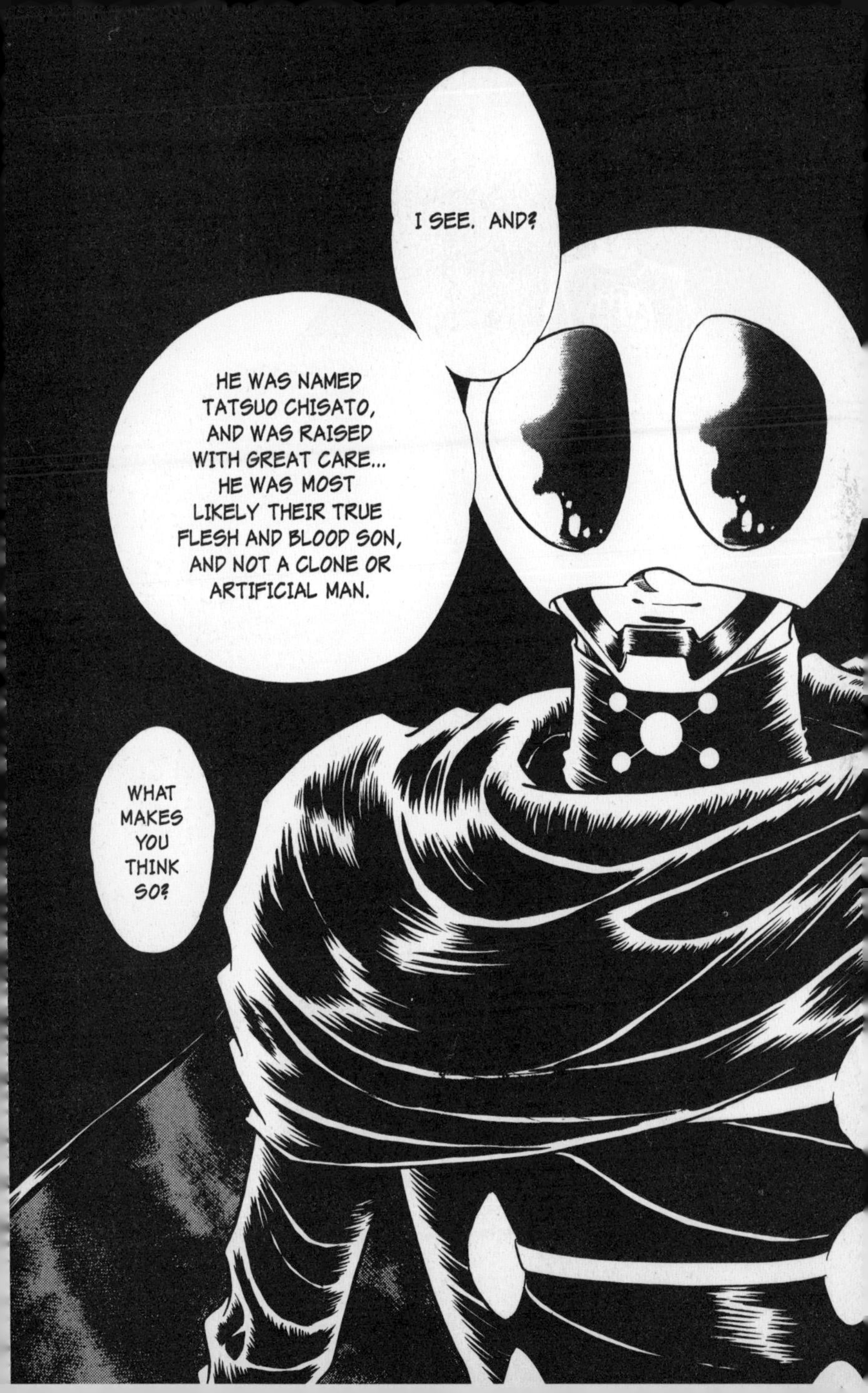
I SEE. AND?
HE WAS NAMED TATSUO CHISATO, AND WAS RAISED WITH GREAT CARE... HE WAS MOST LIKELY THEIR TRUE FLESH AND BLOOD SON, AND NOT A CLONE OR ARTIFICIAL MAN.
WHAT MAKES YOU THINK SO?

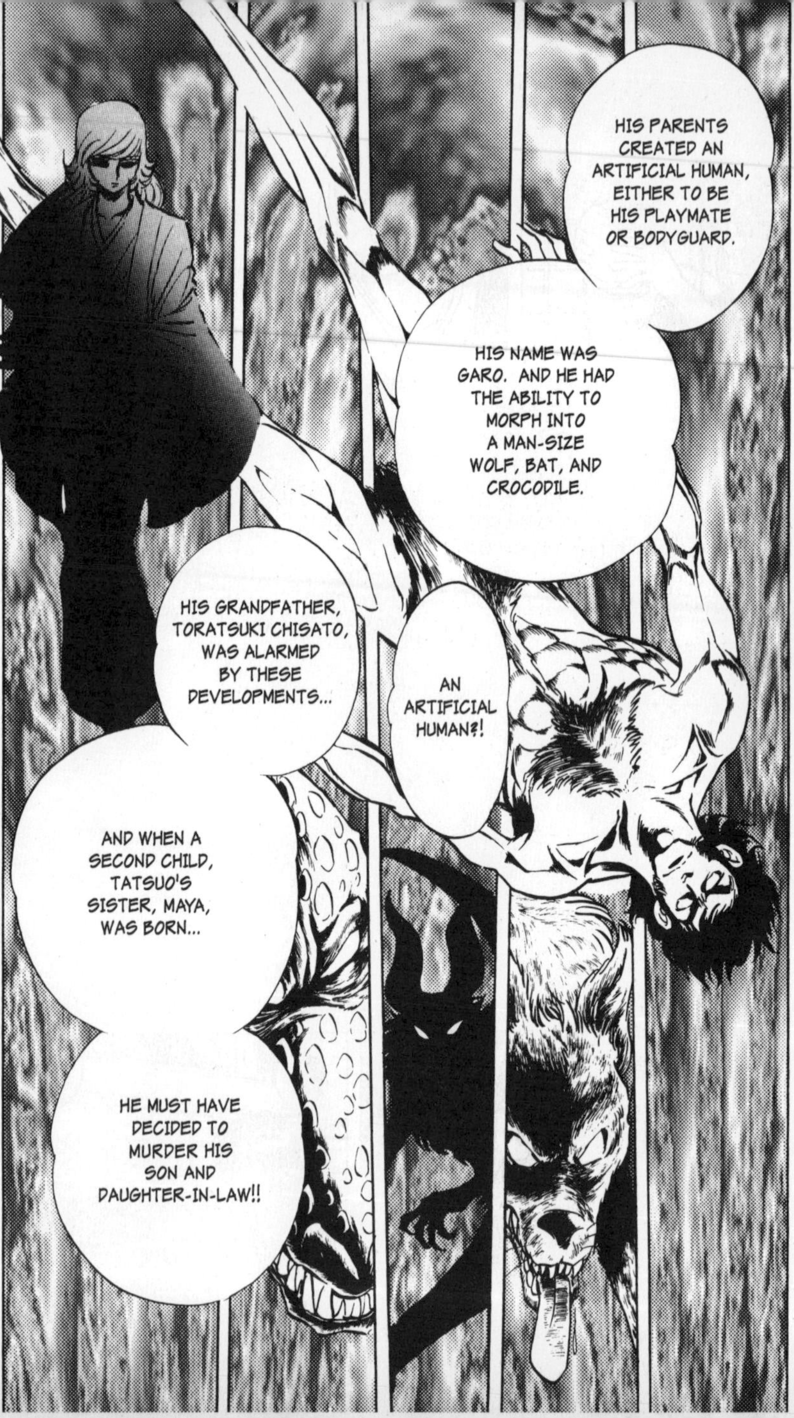
HIS PARENTS CREATED AN ARTIFICIAL HUMAN, EITHER TO BE HIS PLAYMATE OR BODYGUARD.
HIS NAME WAS GARO. AND HE HAD THE ABILITY TO MORPH INTO A MAN-SIZE WOLF, BAT, AND CROCODILE.
AN ARTIFICIAL HUMAN?!
HIS GRANDFATHER, TORATSUKI CHISATO, WAS ALARMED BY THESE DEVELOPMENTS...
AND WHEN A SECOND CHILD, TATSUO'S SISTER, MAYA, WAS BORN...
HE MUST HAVE DECIDED TO MURDER HIS SON AND DAUGHTER-IN-LAW!!

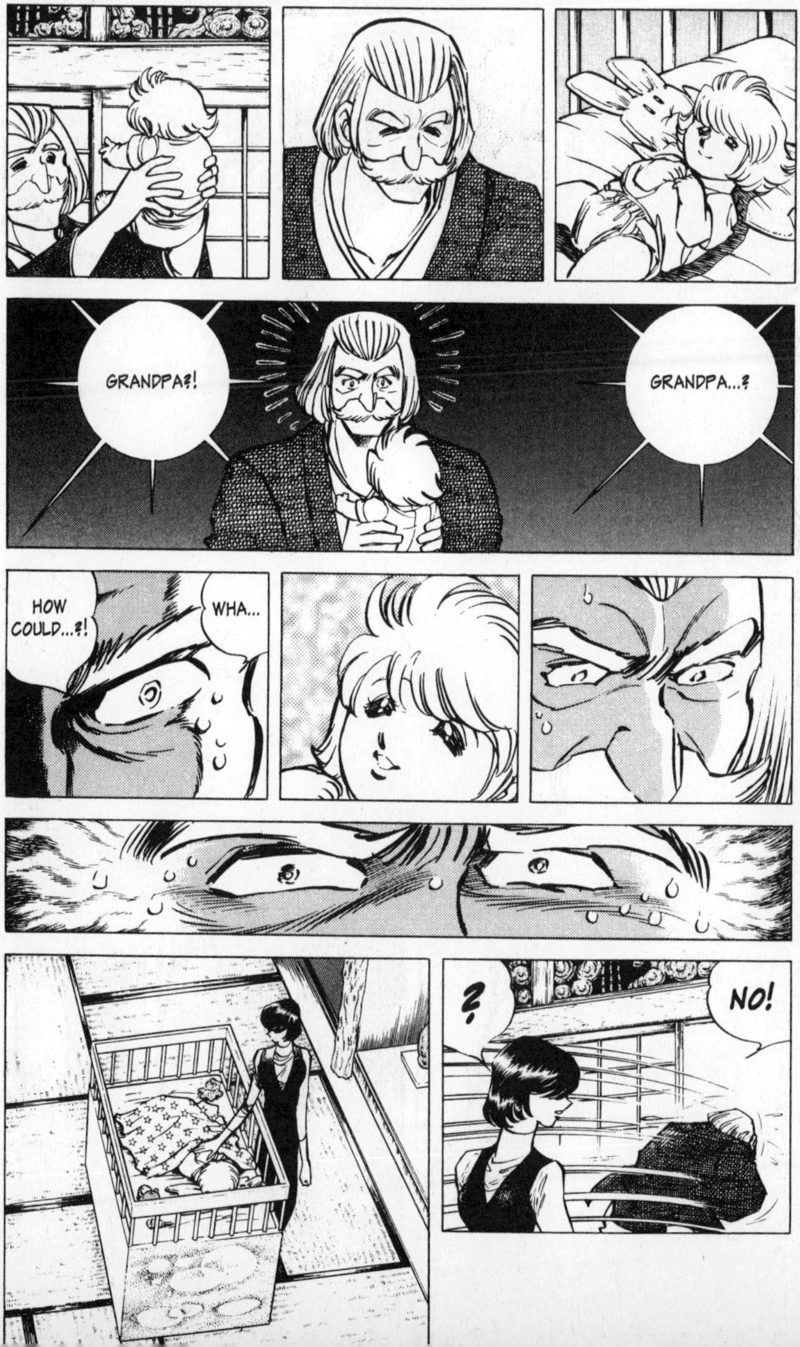
GRANDPA...?
GRANDPA?!
WHA...
HOW COULD...?!
NO!
?

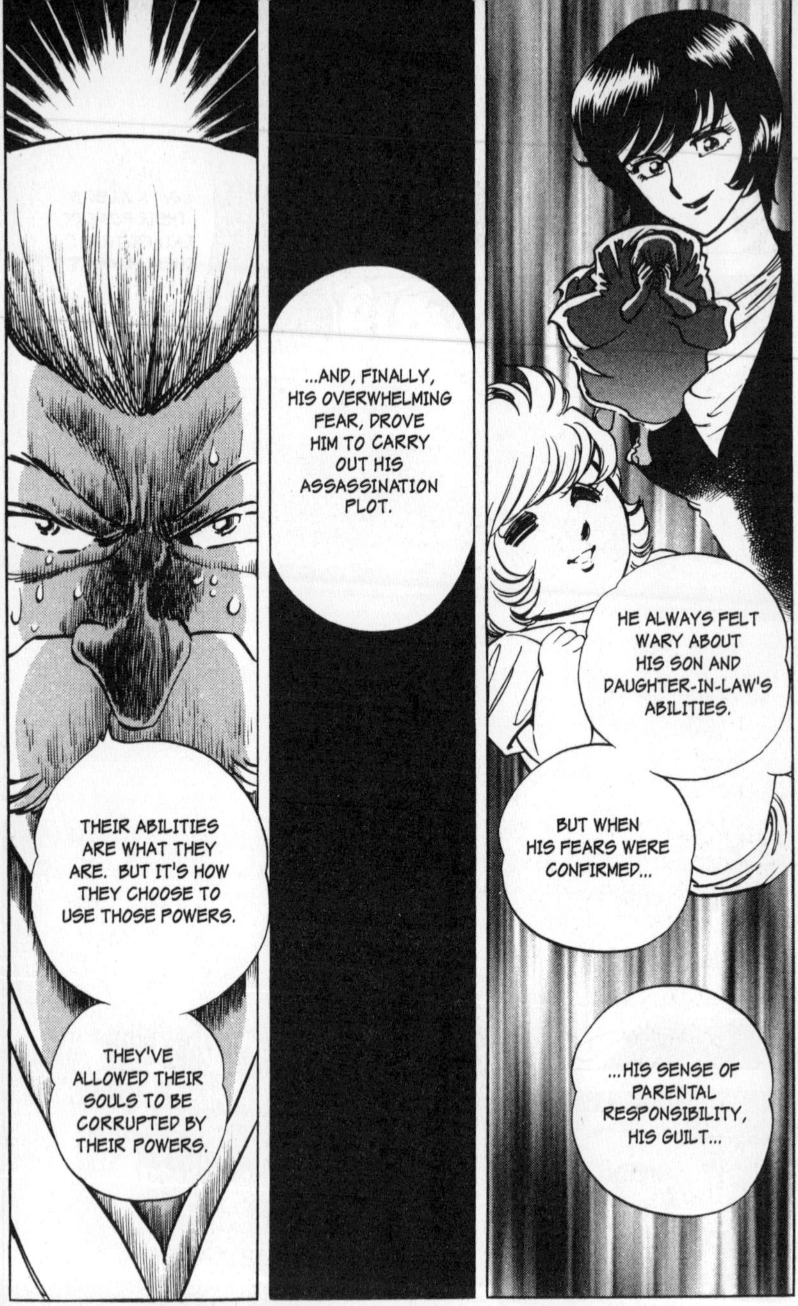
HE ALWAYS FELT WARY ABOUT HIS SON AND DAUGHTER-IN-LAW'S ABILITIES.
BUT WHEN HIS FEARS WERE CONFIRMED...
...HIS SENSE OF PARENTAL RESPONSIBILITY, HIS GUILT...
...AND, FINALLY, HIS OVERWHELMING FEAR, DROVE HIM TO CARRY OUT HIS ASSASSINATION PLOT.
THEIR ABILITIES ARE WHAT THEY ARE. BUT IT'S HOW THEY CHOOSE TO USE THOSE POWERS.
THEY'VE ALLOWED THEIR SOULS TO BE CORRUPTED BY THEIR POWERS.

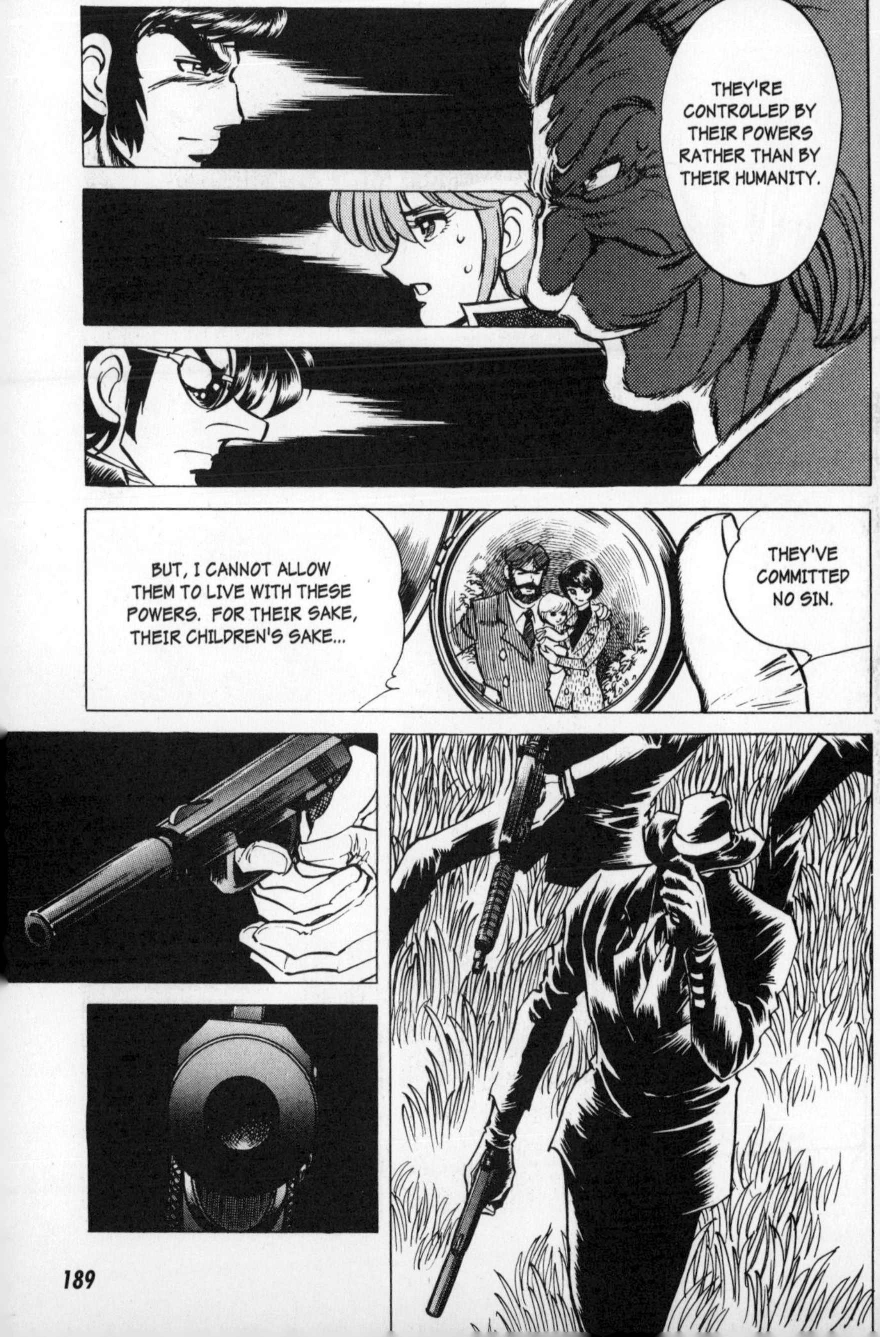
THEY'RE CONTROLLED BY THEIR POWERS RATHER THAN BY THEIR HUMANITY.
THEY'VE COMMITTED NO SIN.
BUT, I CANNOT ALLOW THEM TO LIVE WITH THESE POWERS. FOR THEIR SAKE, THEIR CHILDREN'S SAKE...

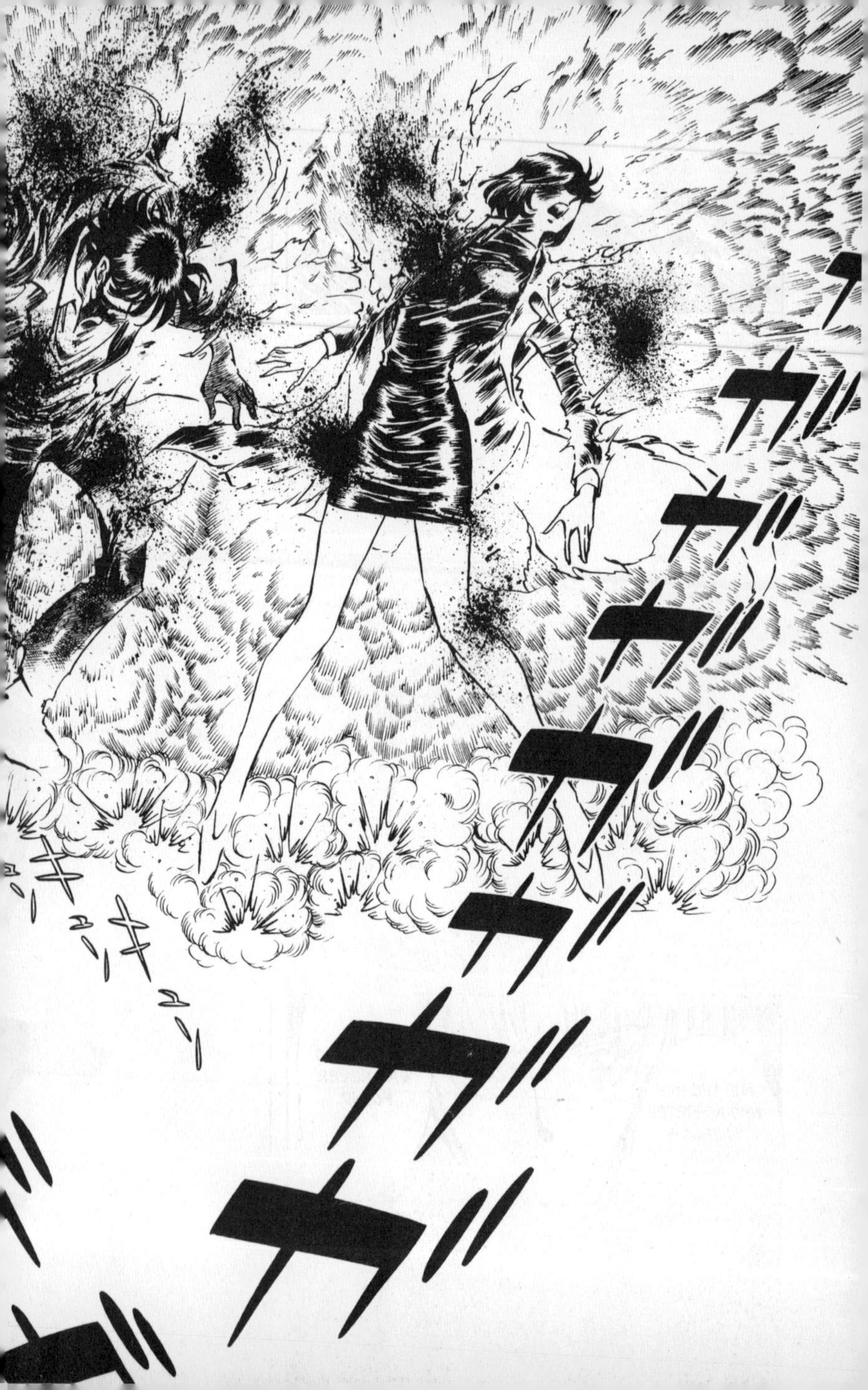
ガガガガガガガガ
キュンキュン

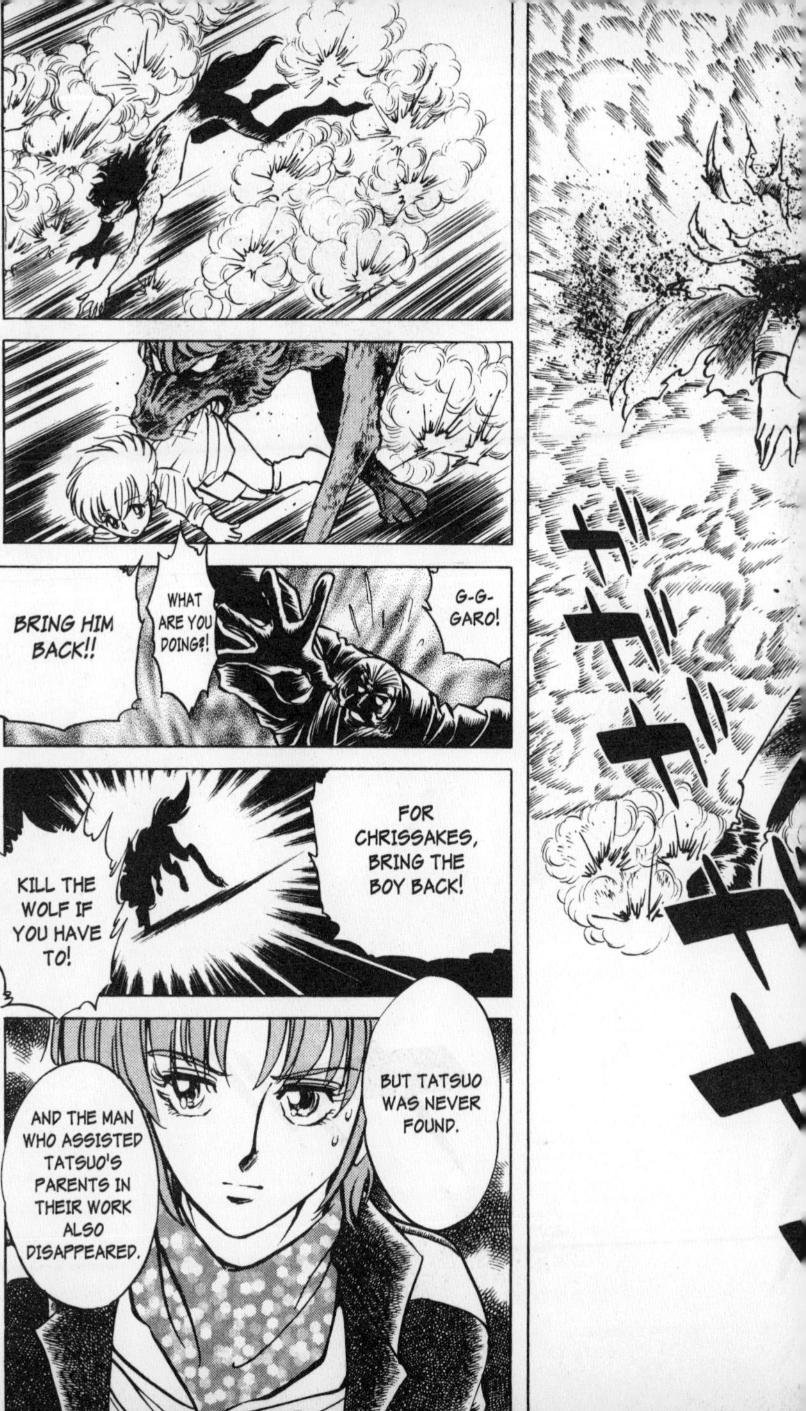
G-G-GARO!
WHAT ARE YOU DOING?!
BRING HIM BACK!!
FOR CHRISSAKES, BRING THE BOY BACK!
KILL THE WOLF IF YOU HAVE TO!
BUT TATSUO WAS NEVER FOUND.
AND THE MAN WHO ASSISTED TATSUO'S PARENTS IN THEIR WORK ALSO DISAPPEARED.

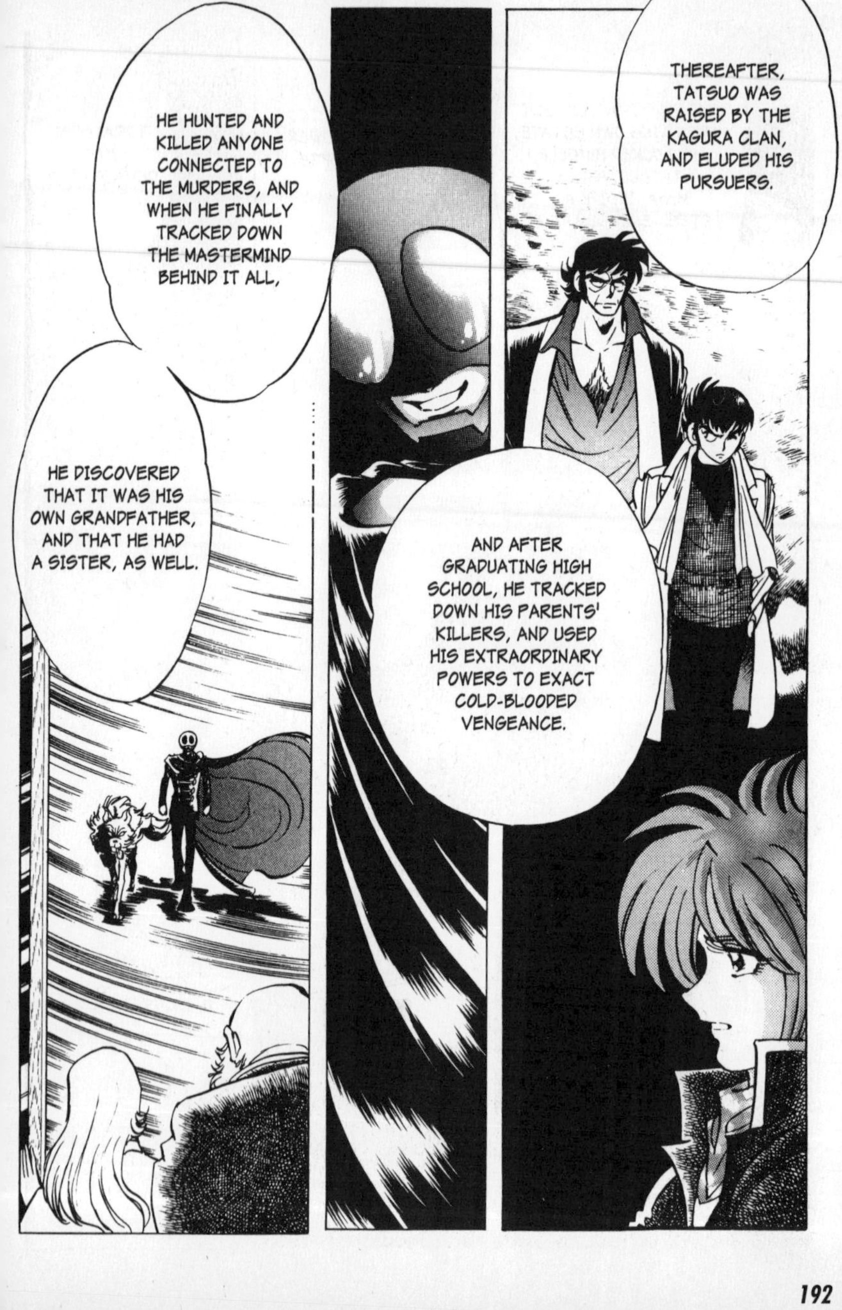
THEREAFTER, TATSUO WAS RAISED BY THE KAGURA CLAN, AND ELUDED HIS PURSUERS.
AND AFTER GRADUATING HIGH SCHOOL, HE TRACKED DOWN HIS PARENTS' KILLERS, AND USED HIS EXTRAORDINARY POWERS TO EXACT COLD-BLOODED VENGEANCE.
HE HUNTED AND KILLED ANYONE CONNECTED TO THE MURDERS, AND WHEN HE FINALLY TRACKED DOWN THE MASTERMIND BEHIND IT ALL,
HE DISCOVERED THAT IT WAS HIS OWN GRANDFATHER, AND THAT HE HAD A SISTER, AS WELL.

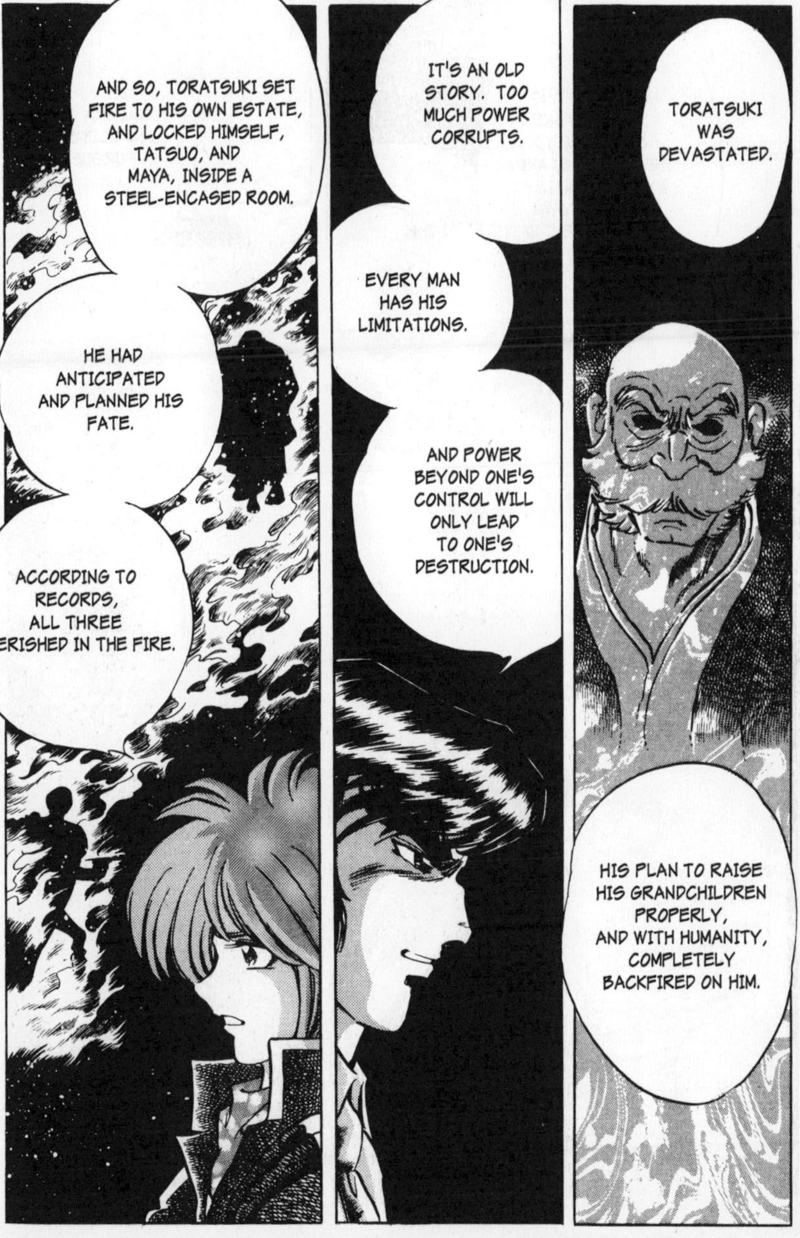
TORATSUKI WAS DEVASTATED.
HIS PLAN TO RAISE HIS GRANDCHILDREN PROPERLY, AND WITH HUMANITY, COMPLETELY BACKFIRED ON HIM.
IT'S AN OLD STORY. TOO MUCH POWER CORRUPTS.
EVERY MAN HAS HIS LIMITATIONS.
AND POWER BEYOND ONE'S CONTROL WILL ONLY LEAD TO ONE'S DESTRUCTION.
AND SO, TORATSUKI SET FIRE TO HIS OWN ESTATE, AND LOCKED HIMSELF, TATSUO, AND MAYA, INSIDE A STEEL-ENCASED ROOM.
HE HAD ANTICIPATED AND PLANNED HIS FATE.
ACCORDING TO RECORDS, ALL THREE PERISHED IN THE FIRE.

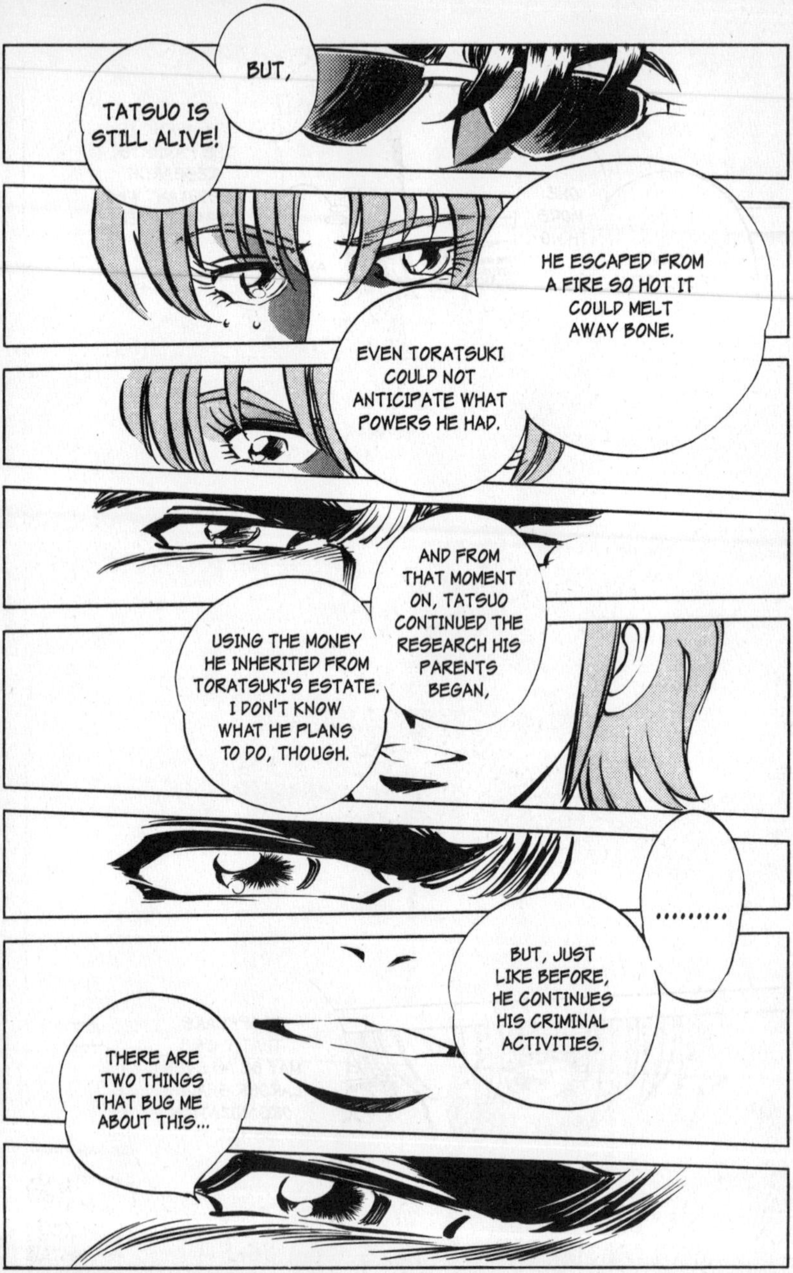
BUT,
TATSUO IS STILL ALIVE!
HE ESCAPED FROM A FIRE SO HOT IT COULD MELT AWAY BONE.
EVEN TORATSUKI COULD NOT ANTICIPATE WHAT POWERS HE HAD.
AND FROM THAT MOMENT ON, TATSUO CONTINUED THE RESEARCH HIS PARENTS BEGAN,
USING THE MONEY HE INHERITED FROM TORATSUKI'S ESTATE. I DON'T KNOW WHAT HE PLANS TO DO, THOUGH.
....
BUT, JUST LIKE BEFORE, HE CONTINUES HIS CRIMINAL ACTIVITIES.
THERE ARE TWO THINGS THAT BUG ME ABOUT THIS...

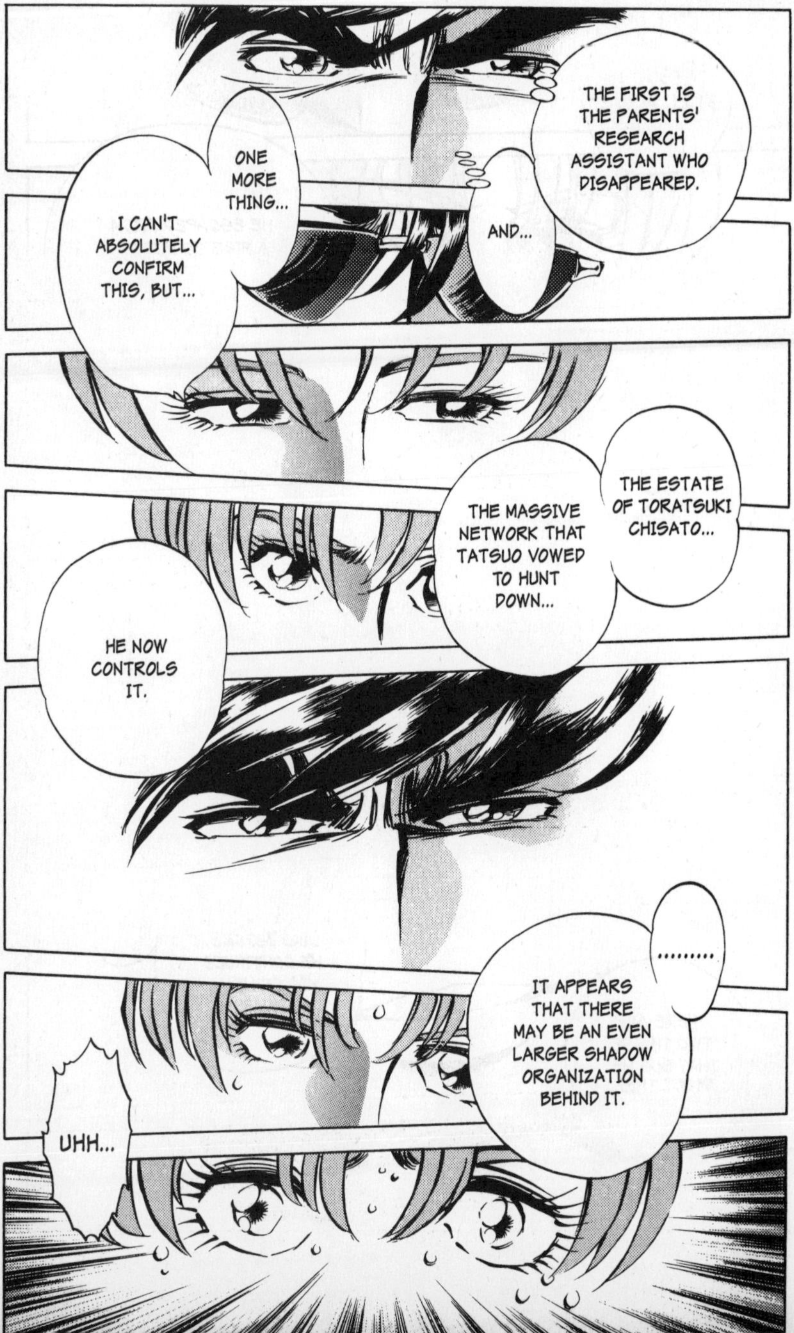
THE FIRST IS THE PARENTS' RESEARCH ASSISTANT WHO DISAPPEARED.
AND...
ONE MORE THING...
I CAN'T ABSOLUTELY CONFIRM THIS, BUT...
THE ESTATE OF TORATSUKI CHISATO...
THE MASSIVE NETWORK THAT TATSUO VOWED TO HUNT DOWN...
HE NOW CONTROLS IT.
....
IT APPEARS THAT THERE MAY BE AN EVEN LARGER SHADOW ORGANIZATION BEHIND IT.
UHH...

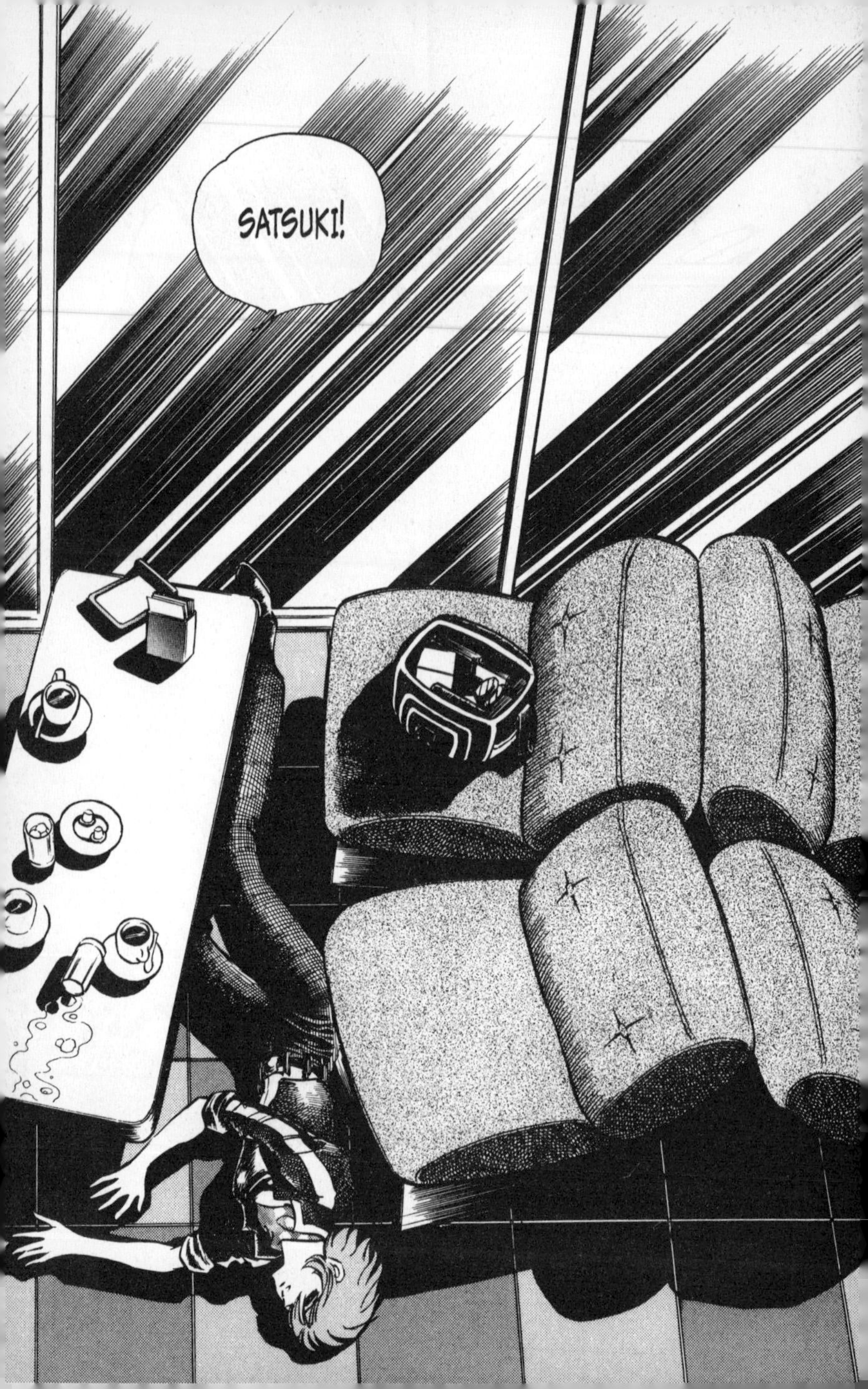
SATSUKI!

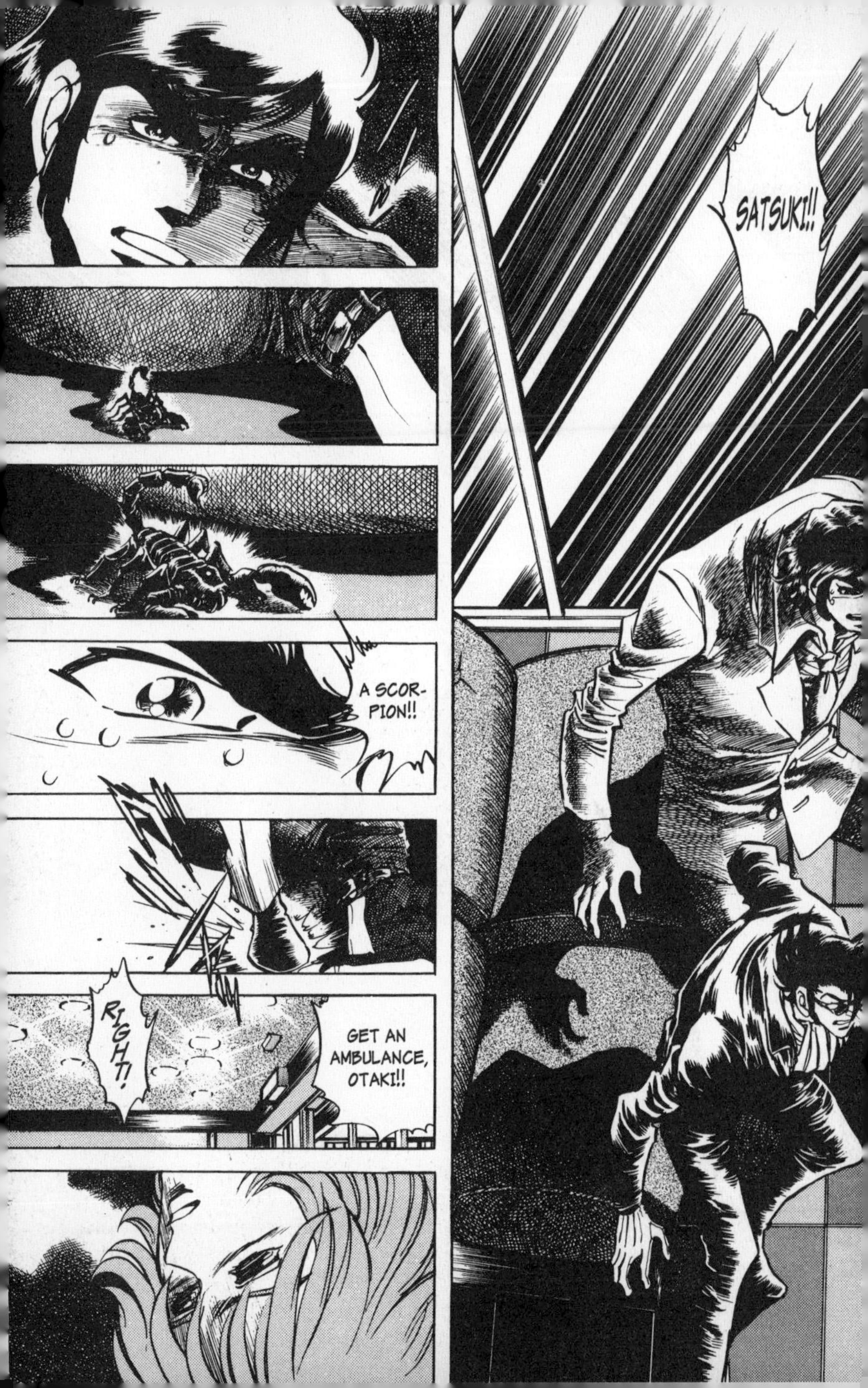
SATSUKI!!
A SCOR-PION!!
GET AN AMBULANCE, OTAKI!!
RIGHT!!

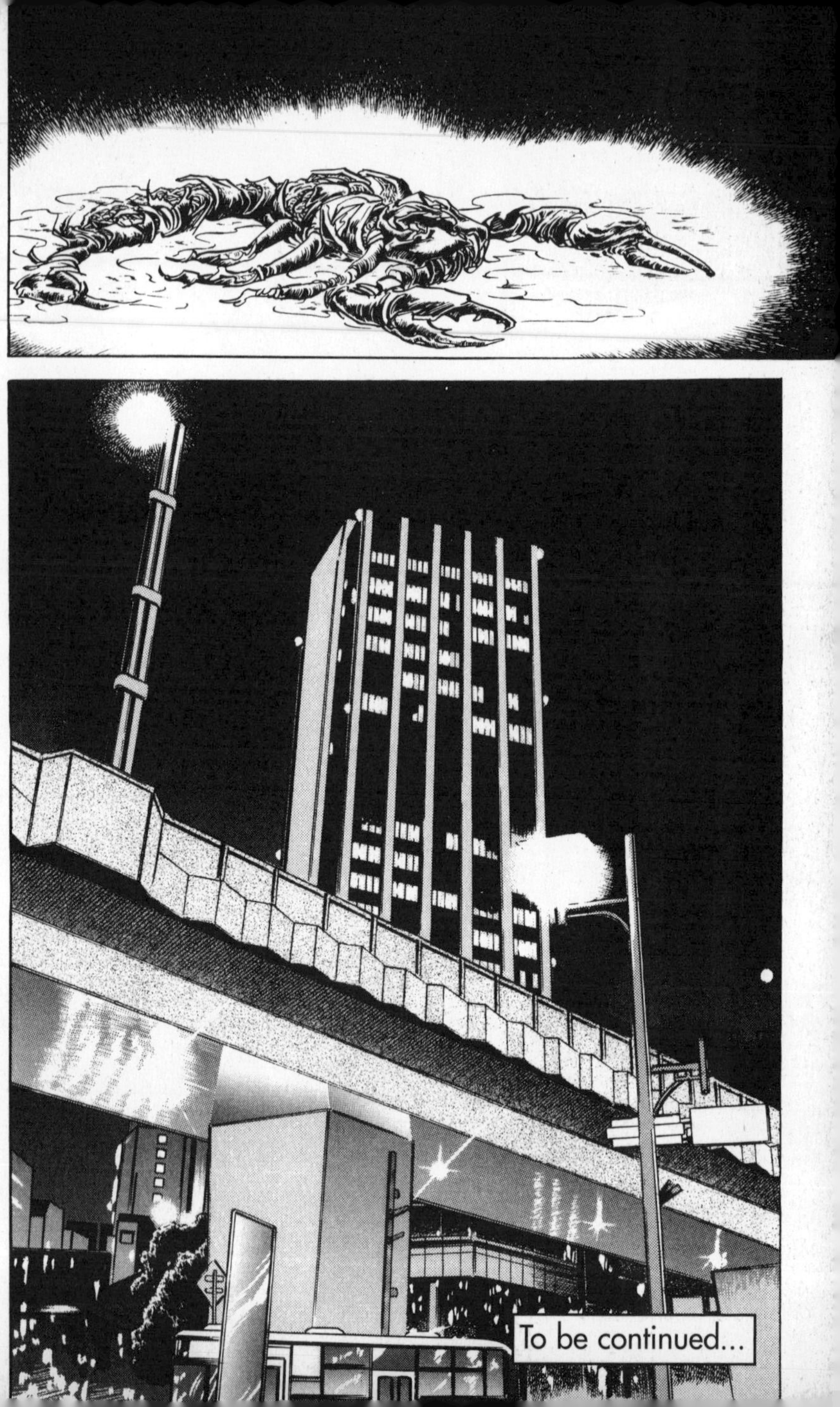
To be continued...

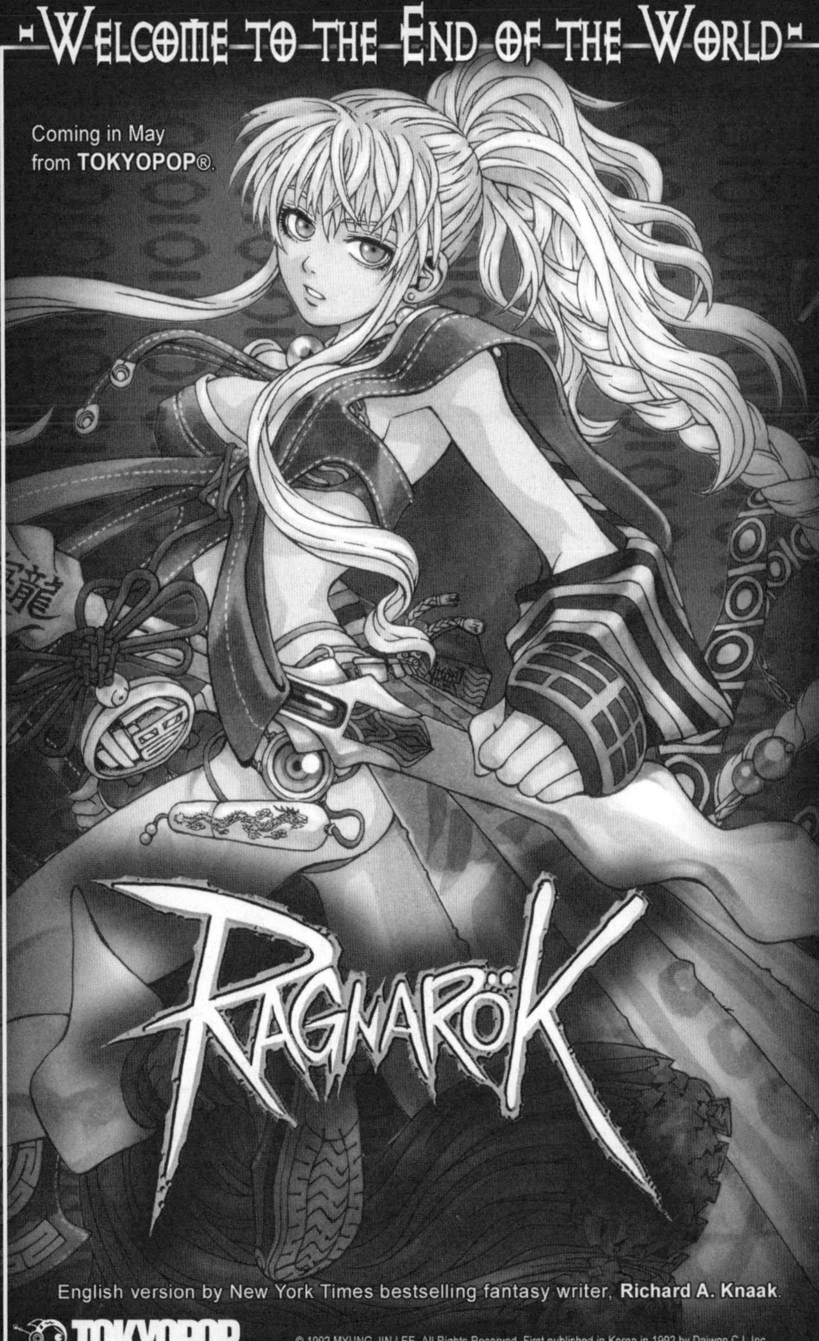
WELCOME TO THE END OF THE WORLD
Coming in May
from TOKYOPOP®.
RAGNARÖK
English version by New York Times bestselling fantasy writer, Richard A. Knaak.
TOKYOPOP®
© 1992 MYUNG-JIN LEE. All Rights Reserved. First published in Korea in 1992 by Daiwon C.I. Inc.
TOKYOPOP is a registered trademark and TOKYOPOP Manga is a trademark of Mixx Entertainment, Inc.

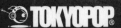

STOP!

This is the back of the comic.
You wouldn't want to spoil a great ending!

This comic is printed "manga-style," in the authentic Japanese right-to-left format. Since none of the artwork has been flipped or altered, readers get to experience the story just as the creator intended. You've been asking for it, so TOKYOPOP® delivered: authentic, hot-off-the-press, and far more fun!

DIRECTIONS

If this is your first time reading manga-style, here's a quick guide to help you understand how it works.

It's easy... just start in the top right panel and follow the numbers. Have fun, and look for more 100% authentic manga from TOKYOPOP®!